Social Work in the Era of Devolution

SOCIAL WORK
in the Era of Devolution

TOWARD A JUST PRACTICE

Edited by ROSA PEREZ-KOENIG, DSW,
and BARRY ROCK, DSW

FORDHAM UNIVERSITY PRESS
New York • 2001

Library of Congress Cataloging-in-Publication Data

Social work in the era of devolution : toward a just practice / edited by Rosa
Perez-Koenig and Barry Rock.— 1st ed.
     p.   cm.
   Includes bibliographical references and index.
   ISBN 0-8232-2080-X (hardcover) — ISBN 0-8232-2081-8 (pbk.)
       1. Social service—United States.   2. Human services—United States.
   3. Socially handicapped—United States.   4. Social justice—United States.
   5. United States—Social policy—1993-   I. Perez-Koenig, Rosa.
   II. Rock, Barry.
   HV95.S6194   2001
   361.973—dc21   00-052764

Printed in the United States of America
01 02   03 04 05 5 4 3 2 1
First Edition

CONTENTS

PREFACE

Mary Ann Quaranta, DSW

This book, under the capable editorship of Drs. Rosa Perez-Koenig and Barry Rock, is a good example of a town-gown relationship. The Fordham University Graduate School of Social Service and the Jewish Board of Family and Children Services collaborated on a conference focusing on the impact of the devolution of support for the delivery of social services to populations and persons in need.

Professions have a deep responsibility to attend to the changes that occur in society in order to ensure that their practices are responsive to the needs of the times in which they are offered. At the onset of this new millennium, we are inundated with magazines, journals, books, and broadcasts reminding us of the changes that have occurred during the past centuries, especially the changes of the last hundred years. There is also considerable forecasting of some of the changes we can expect to experience in the new century, particularly in its first decades. The main tenor of these reviews is the dramatic improvements that have occurred in our society as a result of technological and other changes that have been the result of innovations and experiments.

This book focuses on the changes that have occurred recently in the economic and political climate in this country. Regrettably, these changes do not represent growth or improvement, but rather are regressive and often oppressive. While deploring some of these changes, the social work profession is reacting in its usual responsible manner by pointing out how practitioners can respond to focus on the best interests of the clients. At the same time that we are examining ways in which our interventions can be accommodated and adjusted to new policies, we are

mindful of our role as advocates to restore the support required
to provide the services needed. There appear to be two main
streams that converge to make this situation as grim as the articles in this book depict. One is the dramatic shift from many
decades of belief in this country that the federal government is
the best agent for provision of basic support to people in need,
as opposed to that responsibility being carried by states and
communities, where there could be greater politicization of the
process and procedures. There is also greater unevenness in the
availability of help depending on how each state allocates the
funds provided by the federal government. While this has been
happening, the managed care approach to health and other
human services, including child welfare, emerged, with its emphasis on cost containment, often to the detriment of the children and families.

The chapters in this book represent an effort by experts in the
various affected areas of social work practice to examine the issues and to provide some guidance in new practice approaches.
I believe you will find, as I did, that the book is very comprehensive in its coverage; it provides a balance of critical analyses of
some of the developments and issues in the various fields, as
well as a practice-oriented approach to interventions that may
serve well at this time.

ACKNOWLEDGMENTS

For their unconditional support, the editors would like to acknowledge and thank Dean May Ann Quaranta of the Fordham University Graduate School of Social Service (FUGSSS), as well as our colleagues on the faculty. We wish to offer our special thanks to Dr. Alan Siskind, executive director of the Jewish Board of Family and Children Services, for promoting collaboration among practitioners of family and mental health agencies and academics. This collaboration has led so far to two very timely conferences and this book. We are also indebted to Elaine Congress, director of the FUGSSS doctoral program, FUGSSS Associate Dean John Cosgrove, and Drs. Pat Brownell, James Dumpson, and Meridith Hanson for their invaluable editorial assistance. Finally, our deepest appreciation goes to our spouses, Marjorie Rock and Eli Koenig, for their ongoing and sustaining encouragement.

INTRODUCTION

Rosa Perez-Koenig, DSW, and Barry Rock, DSW

> What shall we tell the American poor, once we have
> seen them? Shall we say to them that they are better
> off than the Indian poor, the Italian poor, the Russian
> poor? That is one answer, but it is heartless. I should
> put it another way. I want to tell every well-fed and
> optimistic American that it is intolerable that so many
> millions should be maimed in body and spirit when it
> is not necessary that they should be. My standard of
> comparison is not how much worse things used to be.
> It is how much better they could be if only we were
> stirred.
>
> Michael Harrington, *The Other America:*
> *Poverty in the United States* (1962)

INEQUALITY IN A BOOMING ECONOMY

On August 11, 1998, two articles on the same page of the *International Herald Tribune* dramatized the term "devolution." One headline read, "Plagued Health Care System: Now More Than 41 Million Americans Lack Insurance" (p. 3). The other, smaller article, "A Deeper Look at Poverty," reported that "Three in 10 Americans lived below the poverty line for at least two months during a three year period." And the lead headline of the *New York Times* on July 6, 1998, was: "Largest HMOs Cutting the Poor and the Elderly" (p. 1). The MSNBC website reported on October 15, 1998: "A new survey of emergency food programs in New York City showed that hunger is on the rise, and city soup kitchens and food programs are having a hard time keeping up with the demand. The survey showed that hunger rose most dramatically among children and the elderly" ("Hunger Increased in NYC").

This book includes chapters written by professional social workers who, as individuals and as representatives of their respective organizations, are committed to the promotion of social justice—especially among oppressed and vulnerable populations. Today, social workers and the social service delivery system face great challenges. While the profession places stricter demands for professional competencies and effective accountability, current social, political, and economic forces in the era of devolution have resulted in drastic changes in the social welfare system that we have known since 1935. This book addresses the implications of this dismantling of the safety net for the social work profession.

Regarding health care, the latest report from the U.S. Census Bureau indicates that 16% of the American population (43.4 million) lack any form of coverage (Pear, 1998) The reasons included welfare reform and the elimination of health benefits for employed people. Is this bad news surprising? The U.S. economy is said to be at a pinnacle. As we are writing in early January 1999, the New York, NASDAQ, and S&P 500 stock indices are at record highs.

It is no surprise to former secretary of labor Robert Reich, who said: "Most Americans don't have it so good. They have jobs, but most wages and benefits are stuck or continue to drop. Wealth has exploded at the top, but the wages of people in the bottom half are lower today in terms of purchasing power than they were in 1989, before the last recession. This is in sharp contrast to every previous recovery in the postwar period. . . . The reality is that Wall Street's advance hasn't been widely shared" (Reich, 1998, pp. 32–33).

Inequality has increased in spite of an unusually strong economy. The wealthiest 5% of families had 15.6% of the national income in 1969; by 1996 it had grown to 20.3%. However, in 1969 the poorest 20% of families had 5.6% of the income; by 1996 their share was reduced to 4.2% (Levinson, 1999, citing Levy, 1999; Thurow, 1999).

DEVOLUTION

The term "devolution" refers to several current social, political, and economic processes. One meaning is that social policy domains previously the responsibility of the federal government have "devolved," or been delegated, to the states. Another meaning is that devolution is the opposite of evolution—a form of social regression. It thus refers to the dismantling of the infrastructure of the welfare state and of the system of federally guaranteed entitlements. Facing these and other forms of cost cutting, cost containment, managed care, downsizing, and reengineering, social workers and their clients are feeling threatened by ominous social, political, and economic forces while the overall American economy seems to be thriving. These contradictions and factors are having a profound effect on how services are being provided and how practice is being conducted to very vulnerable, at-risk populations.

From a conservative (if not neo-populist) perspective, government has been perceived as too big, complex, intrusive, and generally greedy and incompetent. Devolution is thus welcomed by many because it is anti-dependency, communal, and empowering. A middle ground that might be embraced by social workers would criticize the destructive consequences of devolution and advocate for client services, entitlements, and rights—demanding a preservation of a federally institutionalized safety net—but also maximize opportunities for less bureaucratic intrusion by self-sufficiency, empowerment, and return to greater community control. In the chapters that follow, the reader will see these themes and this dual approach to devolution—critical of the dismantling of the safety net but supportive of individual and community empowerment—as both a negative and a potential.

SOCIAL INDICATORS

At the conference upon which this book is based, one of the keynote addresses focused on social indicators. Since Dr. Miringoff's remarks are not represented in a chapter, a brief summary of social indicators will now be presented, based on several of his previously published works as well as his keynote address.

Social indicators are the equivalent in the social realm of economic indicators in the financial realm: "The Index of Social Health is a method of monitoring the social well-being of American society. It is the only current measure that examines cumulatively so many social problems, affecting so many sectors of society, in a single assessment. While measures like the Index of Leading Economic Indicators routinely combine economic statistics to signal large-scale shifts in the economy, social data are almost never integrated in this way" (Miringoff, 1997, p. 4). The elements of Miringoff's index include infant mortality, child abuse, children in poverty, teenage suicide, drug abuse, high school dropouts, unemployment, average weekly earnings, health insurance coverage, poverty among those over 65, out-of-pocket health costs for those over 65, homicides, alcohol-related traffic fatalities, food stamp coverage, access to affordable housing, and the gap between rich and poor (Miringoff, 1997). The index measures the social health of a community, city, state, and/or the nation. It quantifies inequality, the gap between economic and social realities, and can be a means of assessing need or evaluating how well government programs and policies are progressing in problem solving.

Among some of the conclusions through 1997 are: "During the 1990's, the social health of the nation decreased by 6 percent. Thus far, the 1990's have recorded six of the eight lowest years since 1970"; and, "Health insurance coverage has worsened at a faster rate during the 1990's than any other problem" (Miringoff, 1997, p. 6). Those indicators which worsened through 1997 are health insurance coverage, drug abuse, average weekly earnings, high school dropouts, and food stamp coverage (Miringoff, 1997). A longer-term view is pessimistic as well: "Over the last several decades, while cumulative economic indicators portray an economy fluctuating between recession and recovery, but growing overall, most key social indicators show a long downward spiral and a severely declining quality of life" (Miringoff, Miringoff, & Opdycke, 1996, p. 17).

In his keynote address, Dr. Miringoff gave examples of community-based organizations utilizing social indicators in social action endeavors, and he encouraged the audience to engage in this kind of data-informed advocacy. In the final chapter of this book, Natalie Riccio makes use of social indicators in this way—at both the local level and the global level.

SOCIAL JUSTICE

Social justice is another important framework of this book. We are vulnerable to charges of being "naysayers" or "party poopers" by bringing attention to what is wrong in America while the economy seems to be in such superb condition. But as social workers we are primarily concerned with those whom the economy leaves behind. There is a danger that in the great enthusiasm that all is going well, the least advantaged citizens will be forgotten. After the boom of the postwar era into the 1960s, Michael Harrington was compelled to write his classic and influential book *The Other America* (1962) in order to help the country rediscover the considerable poverty that existed at that time.

An example of this attitude is found in a recent "Talk of the Town" in the *New Yorker* (Klein, 1999): "The President is on trial for high crimes and misdemeanors, and the State of the Union is, well, great. Almost every social and economic indicator is moving in the right direction" (p. 22). Then this after several columns of elaborating on this euphoria, as almost an afterthought: "Of course, one can point to imperfections in this glowing state of national affairs—the widening income gap between rich and poor" (p. 22).

The widening gap between rich and poor is of the utmost concern to social workers. It is a central issue of the principles of social justice. As we find in the writings of philosopher John Rawls (1971), but consistent with the profession's century-long traditions, conditions of inequality are justifiable only if the least advantaged benefit. If America is doing so very well but a minority of the population is falling further behind, there is a major breach in the mechanisms of redistribution of goods, services, and income.

Social work as a profession has a longstanding commitment

to social justice. This is clearly evident in the most recent version of the National Association of Social Workers' (NASW) Code of Ethics (1996), in which the mission of the profession is identified as rooted in six core values: service, social justice, dignity and worth of a person, importance of human relationships, integrity, and competence. The value of social justice is translated into the ethical principle that "Social workers challenge social injustice" (NASW, 1996, p. 5), which is further defined as follows:

> Social workers pursue social change, particularly with and on behalf of vulnerable and oppressed individuals and groups of people. Social workers' social change efforts are focused primarily on issues of poverty, unemployment, discrimination, and other forms of social injustice. These activities seek to promote sensitivity to and knowledge about oppression and cultural and ethnic diversity. Social workers strive to ensure access to needed information, services, and resources; equality of opportunity; and meaningful participation in decision making for all people. (NASW, 1996, p. 5)

These principles are further expanded into a section of ethical standards of social justice—"Social Workers' Ethical Responsibilities to the Broader Society"—which include social welfare, public participation, public emergencies, and social and political action (see NASW, 1996, pp. 26–27). The accrediting body for social work education in the United States, the Council on Social Work Education, also places social justice at the core of its mission and standards of accreditation. The Fordham University Graduate School of Social Service, whose faculty contributed many chapters to this book, has social justice as its core mission. Social justice's place at the heart of the American social work profession could not be clearer.

Social Policy as Context for Social Work Practice

The social work profession has always been committed to "contextual knowledge." Social workers have long subscribed to a contextual perspective, the "person-in-environment" being the best-known. This has been the bedrock of social work. The "person" stands for all client systems (individuals, families, groups, organizations, communities, and societies), and "environment" represents all levels of the external environment (the micro, mezzo, exo, and macro levels) and the internalized environment of the external world.

However, there are many contexts, since "context" refers to something that defines or influences that which occurs within. Contexts may include physical surroundings and conditions, social institutions, policies and laws, cultural values and practices, history, language, and people. People cannot be understood apart from contexts, nor can contexts be understood apart from the people to whom they refer (Witkin, 1999). In contextual knowledge, time and place are essential variables. The first section of the book focuses on policy as context, mainly in the United States (place) in current times, known as the era of devolution (time).

Tropman (1984, p. 268) defines "policy" as "an idea that is embodied in a written document which is ratified by legitimate authority and serves as a guide to action and is a result of policy process, a decision making process by the legislative, the courts and or executive directors." Policy is dynamic and as such involves a circular process: the development of the idea, its implementation, evaluation, and feedback that leads to the reformulation of the idea. Social welfare policy "can be approached by examining the character and functioning of . . . essential social functions—child-rearing; the production, consumption, and distribution of goods and services; social protection, and so forth" (Gilbert & Terrell, 1998, p. 2). Social welfare may be defined as the organization and "enduring patterns" of "these fundamental institutions" (Gilbert & Terrell, 1998, p. 2). Governmental policies usually reflect the climate and ideology of the dominant discourse.

The current era, known as the era of devolution, reflects the conservative climate that started in the late 1970s and culminated in conservative policies such as the social welfare policy known as the Personal Responsibility and Work Opportunity Reconciliation Act of 1996 (PRA). Although this policy claims to address the right to work, particularly of poor women with children, it really fails to capture the spirit of human rights. The spirit of human rights is clearly stated in the United Nations'

Universal Declaration of Human Rights, signed in 1948. In the United States, while civil and political rights have been generally accepted, economic human rights have been virtually ignored. Economic human rights, as expressed in Articles 23, 25, and 26, capture the true spirit of the right to work. Article 23 addresses the right to jobs at a living wage and just conditions; Article 25, the right to well-being of a person and his or her family, including food, clothing, housing, medical care, and necessary social services; and Article 26, the right to education. As we compare the U.S. federal social welfare policy with the UN Universal Declaration of Human Rights international policy, the PRA fails to capture the true spirit of human rights. The PRA is harsh and punitive in its mood. This policy has for the first time instituted a 5-year limit to public assistance for poor mothers and their children. This approach of threatening, punishing, and blaming the victim is evidence of disregard for poor and marginalized women and children, adding tremendous pressure to the already very stressful lives of poor people. The right to work must be implemented in ways that truly foster the well-being of people. Gil (1998) suggests reframing the concept of work in order to truly implement justice in this society.

It is through agency-based practice that social work can truly address the breadth and depth of the profession and the integration of all its essential areas, such as practice and its administration, research, and social policy. It is in the agency, the organization, that policy meets practice. It is through direct services to clients that policy is actualized, and from clients' feedback, policies are evaluated and then reformulated through social action.

STRUCTURE OF THE BOOK

This book will provide a framework for understanding the relationship between these macro-level forces and the micro-level delivery and practice of social services. It will provide knowledge, skills, and support for practicing social workers, human service workers, and health care practitioners to survive and to prevail in this environment. There are sections that cover macro and micro practice. The struggle for social justice is often thought of as being played out in the macro arenas of agency, community, local, state, and national social policy; however, this book also emphasizes that social justice issues are of major concern in direct practice.

From the early years of the 20th century through the early 1960s, there was a separation—if not at times a polarization—between those social workers who perceived their *function* as exclusively helping individuals and families, and social workers who perceived their *cause* as social action and the struggle for social equality. In the past several decades, a synthesis was established through the generalist practice model, based on ecological and systems perspectives. The strengths perspective is also very influential in contemporary social work (Saleeby, 1997). These themes are all evident in the chapters and reports that follow.

This book is based on a professional conference on this topic that took place at Fordham University's Lincoln Center Campus on January 12, 1998. The Fordham University Graduate School of Social Service and five community social service agencies in the greater New York City area sponsored the conference. The sponsoring community agencies were: Jewish Board of Family and Children Services, Agenda for Children Tomorrow, Steinway Child and Family Service, Harlem Dowling Westside Center, and Lakeside Family and Children Services. The volume is not intended to be the published proceedings of the conference, but rather a book based on and inspired by the conference. Many of the faculty of the conference have made contributions to the book based on their workshop materials and presentations.

This volume focuses on the effect of the dramatic changes taking place in the United States on the *practice* of social work and human and health services—specifically, welfare reform, child welfare reform, managed care, and cultural diversity. Although publications are available in these areas, no texts of this kind are directed *at practitioners*. The book will present a framework for understanding the impact of these macro-level changes on the practice of social work itself.

The structure of the book is a variation on a musical ABA

pattern: the A motif is macro, and the B is micro. Following prefaces by leadership of the several sponsoring organizations, this introduction by the editors sets the stage for the book and the frameworks to be advanced. Based on several of the keynote addresses from the conference plus other writings, the first section ("The Policy Context: Social and Economic Justice in the Era of Devolution") focuses on the social forces, processes, and policy changes and their implications. The first chapter, by volume co-editor Rosa Perez-Koenig, provides an in-depth explication of the concept of social justice. The next chapter, by Robert Hill, describes contemporary welfare reform and devolution in historical context, from the Social Security Act through the reforms of 1996. It is followed by a chapter based on one of the keynote addresses of the original conference, "The Ramifications of Welfare Reform on Vulnerable Populations," by Shirley Better. Dr. Better explores the long-term historical roots of today's devolution, but concentrates on the current impact of welfare reform on the inner city. In the fourth chapter, Patricia Brownell and Marilyn Moch examine policy changes directed at the aging population. Managed care is an important element in the process of devolution. In the fifth chapter, volume co-editor Barry Rock discusses diverse aspects of managed care and their implications for social work practice, organization, and education.

The next section ("Context Meets Practice: Public Issues/Private Troubles—Devolving Systems and Their Human and Practice Consequences") explores the consequences for practice of the policy context presented in the previous section. It covers practice issues in which devolution affects selected vulnerable populations: children and families, immigrants, persons with AIDS, and the elderly. This section has its own introduction. The concluding section ("Call to Action: Strengthening Communities"), which also has a separate introduction, contains chapters and reports from the field dealing with macro-level interventions at the grass roots—community planning and interagency collaboration, spirituality and ethics, and building community—including a discussion of community action and the use of social indicators at the global level. Thus this book attempts to integrate policy, practice, organizational, and community perspectives utilizing an ecological/system theory approach to social work practice and a strong value commitment to the strengths perspective and social justice.

REFERENCES

A deeper look at poverty. (1998, August 11). *International Herald Tribune*, p. 3.

Gil, D. (1998). *Confronting injustice and oppression*. New York: Columbia University Press.

Gilbert, N., & Terrell, P. (1998). *Dimensions of social welfare policy* (4th ed.). Needham Heights, MA: Allyn & Bacon.

Harrington, M. (1962; 1997 ed.). *The other America: Poverty in the United States*. New York: Simon & Schuster.

Hunger increased in NYC according to new survey 15 October 1998. Http://www.msnbc.com/local/WNBC/156214.asp.

Klein, J. (1999, 18 January). Giving Clinton the silent treatment ["Talk of the Town"]. *New Yorker*, pp. 21–22.

Largest HMOs cutting the poor and the elderly. (1998, 6 July). *New York Times*, p. 1.

Levinson, M. (1999, 10 January). Show me the money: A study of why Americans are wary of the future despite a bull economy [Review of Frank Levy's *The new dollars and dreams: American incomes and economic change*]. *New York Times Book Review*, p. 19.

Miringoff, M. (1997). *1997 Index of Social Health*. Fordham Institute for Innovation in Social Policy.

Miringoff, M.-L., Miringoff, M., & Opdycke, S. (1996). The growing gap between standard economic indicators and the nation's social health. *Challenge*, July–August, 17–22.

National Association of Social Workers. (1996). *Code of ethics*. Washington, DC: NASW Press.

Pear, R. (1998, September 26). Americans lacking health insurance put at 16 percent. *New York Times*, p. A1.

Plagued health care system: Now more than 41 million Americans lack insurance. (1998, August 11). *International Herald Tribune*, p. 3.

Rawls, J. (1971). *A theory of justice*. Cambridge: Harvard University Press.

Reich, R. (1998, 25 January). When naptime is over. *New York Times Magazine*, pp. 32–34.

Saleeby, D. (1997). *The strengths perspective in social work practice.* New York: Longman.

Thurow, L. (1999, 18 January). The boom that wasn't. *New York Times*, p. A17.

Tropman, J. E. (1984). Policy analysis: Methods and techniques. *Encyclopedia of social work* (18th ed.) (pp. 268–283). Washington, DC: NASW Press.

Witkin, S. L. (1999). Editorial: Identities and contexts. *Social Work, 44*(4), 293–297.

I
The Policy Context:
Social and Economic Justice
in the Era of Devolution

Actualizing Social Justice Within the Client/Social Worker Relationship

Rosa Perez-Koenig, DSW

A COMMITMENT to social justice has been a defining and unifying precept of the social work profession. From the time of social work's early pioneers, such as Mary Richmond and Jane Addams, and most particularly from the Progressive era forward, many social workers have dedicated themselves to the achievement of a truly just society, one in which the condition of its poorest members is the primary yardstick of the common good. The centrality of this commitment was recently underscored by the National Association of Social Workers in the latest edition of its Code of Ethics (1996), which explicitly identifies social justice as a core value of the profession (p. 1). The achievement of a fairer, more compassionate society through common social work practice is being reaffirmed, and the challenge of continuing socioeconomic injustice is being identified as a primary target of social work practice. At the same time, the Council on Social Work Education has identified the promotion of social and economic justice as a core competency in the professional education of social workers.

These restatements of the social justice precept have come at a time when government social policy and its legitimizing values have moved dramatically away from any real concern for the poor. The past two decades have witnessed a recrudescence of free-market, laissez-faire, and "liberal" ideology conspiring with a "devolutionary" right-wing vision for the dismantlement of desperately needed social welfare programs. The broad result of this self-serving capitalist crusade is that politically power-less, economically deprived, and socially marginalized people have been pushed further away from sharing in the prosperity of the commonwealth. With greater urgency than at any other time in its history, the social work profession must mobilize it-self and its client base to combat a powerfully pernicious assault that has taken place against the "have-nots" of our society.

The primary mechanism for this mobilization lies within the basic client/social worker relationship. Members of our profes-sion must realize that social justice is not merely an abstract principle, but a controlling guide to everyday practice. The on-going trend toward deeper socioeconomic divisions means that social workers must seek to actualize social justice in their rela-tions with those whom they serve. As it now stands, social work-ers are on the front line of the struggle for social justice, and their ability to meet the challenge ahead will hinge upon a fun-damental reorientation in the social work profession and its practice.

From its inception, the social work profession has at its base the client/worker relationship (see, among others, Richmond, 1917; Robinson, 1930; Reynolds, 1942; Biestek, 1957; Hollis, 1964; Rhodes, 1977; Perlman, 1979; Proctor, 1982; Petr, 1988; Coady, 1993), and different ideologies have influenced how this rela-tionship is actualized. Early direct practice approaches that fo-cused on the individual client were moralistic and/or deficit-oriented. Client/worker relationships were hierarchical ones in which the worker was considered an expert while the client was viewed as deficient or pathological.

Since the mid-1960s, social work theorists have increasingly argued that while the client/worker dyad is of fundamental im-portance for the attainment of valued results, restricting social work to a "single" client without regard to his or her socioeco-nomic environment was unrealistic and counterproductive. As Gutierrez and Ortega (1991) have written, the challenge to social work practitioners was to expand the focus from the individual client to include key support groups, community networks, and social systems that have an influence upon the client's "life space" (p. 334). As a result, social work practice recaptured the "social" in social work, owning again the bedrock "person-in-environment" concept in social work theory by broadening the scope of professional social work practice, placing emphasis on the environment, and including more than the "single" individual client.

New models of practice emerged, such as the systems approach, the ecological perspective, the interactional approach, and the empowerment and strengths perspectives (see, among others, Schwartz, 1976; Solomon, 1976; Germain & Gitterman, 1980; Lee, 1994; Saleeby, 1997). These models defined the client/worker relationship as mutual and reciprocal, as horizontal and democratic in nature. The client/worker relationship is viewed as one of true partnership in which the roles of teacher and learner were interchangeable between client and worker.

Also, the profession has identified generic elements in the client/worker relationship applicable to the various methods of social work practice. These elements are purpose, concern for others, commitment and obligation, acceptance and expectation, empathy, authority and power, genuineness, and congruence and its rational and irrational elements (Compton & Galaway, 1994). In addition, empirical studies cited by Gelso and Carter (1985) and Coady (1993) have found strong correlation between a positive alliance on the one hand and positive outcomes on the other. The strength of this bond is evident across the entire gamut of social work approaches and methods.

This fundamental reconception of the "subject" of social work poses a dilemma for practitioners. As the profession again discovers the need to alter the environmental circumstances of oppressed, disenfranchised, and vulnerable clients, a tension arises between satisfying the immediate needs of the client through the existing social welfare system and attaining the long-term goal of transforming that system—and in fact, society at large—into a force for greater social justice. This conflict expresses a profound division in approaches to social justice, and, in the final analysis, in paradigms of social justice. Fulfillment of clients' immediate needs requires social workers to operate within a "distributive" model of socioeconomic resource allocation, to increase the transfer of material assets to clients by working the existing system "harder and better." At the same time, the social worker must also strive to increase the political power of the economically disenfranchised as a prospective means for radically changing the social welfare system and the very structure of a deeply unjust society. This imperative is embodied in a distinctly different model of social justice, the "empowerment" paradigm that has been articulated by progressive social workers including Solomon (1976), Bricker-Jenkins and Hooyman (1986), Gutierrez and Ortega (1991), Gutierrez, Parsons, and Cox (1998), and Lee (1994). In effect, the commitment of the social work profession to the precept of social justice requires social workers to act as both "transactional" and "transformational" agents and, therefore, to simultaneously participate in "distributive" and "empowerment" constructs.

The governing model for social workers in the realization of "transactional" social justice appears in the theories of John Rawls. In *A Theory of Justice* (1971), Rawls investigated the fundamental moral premises upon which the social order rests, taking as his working example modern "liberal" societies with democratic forms of government and "free markets" (e.g., the United States). Rawls's baseline position is consistent with the "contractual" view of human society advanced by John Locke, and he shares with Locke the assumption that political order arises through voluntary agreements among rational human beings. That being so, Rawls can be characterized as a "liberal" philosopher. Indeed, his views are sharply critical of purely utilitarian theories of distributive justice, and might therefore appear hostile toward social justice as it has been construed by the social work profession, that is, in terms of meeting the greatest need. Yet at the same time, Rawls also takes sharp issue with meritocractic "free market" approaches to the allocation of social goods.

For the purposes of our discussion, we note that Rawls's theory has two basic principles of social justice: "(1) each person is to have an equal right to the most extensive basic liberty compatible with a similar liberty for others; and (2) social and economic inequalities are to be arranged so that they are both (a) reasonably expected to be to everyone's advantage, and (b) attached to positions and offices open to all" (1971, p. 60). It is portion (2)(a) of Rawls's formula to which our attention is drawn. Rawls argued that while a just distribution of goods may display an unequal pattern of distribution, this pattern must be to the advantage of all individuals, and most notably to those who are the "worst off" in a given society. According to what Rawls designates as the "difference principle," social and economic inequalities are to be upheld if, *and only if,* the resultant unequal distribution maximizes the benefits which the least advantaged members of society will receive. Thus, Rawls avers that while social and economic inequalities may be necessary and, to some extent, even desirable, *"their moral worth is to be judged by what they contribute to the welfare of the least advantaged"* (emphasis added, p. 100).

Looking carefully at Rawls's "difference principle," we find that it effectively transmutes individual "natural assets and abilities" into collective social assets. Of this result, Rawls writes: "The difference principle represents, in effect, an agreement to regard the distribution of natural talents as a *common asset* and to share the benefits of this distribution whatever it turns out to be. Those who have been favored by nature, whoever they are, may gain from their good fortune only on terms that improve the situation of those who have lost out" (1971, pp. 101–102). Thereafter, Rawls contends that any social order embodying the "difference principle" and the other principle of justice identified by his theory (i.e., the value of freedom) will ensure that all of its members have a baseline modicum of primary goods, and that this in turn will motivate them to lend support to the social system. As to the practical advantage of his social justice model, Rawls claims that "when society follows these principles, everyone's good is included in a scheme of mutual benefit and this public affirmation in institutions of each man's endeavors supports men's self-esteem" (p. 179).

Although Rawls's stress on "individual freedom" has often caused his critics to dismiss him as a "neo-liberal," the "difference principle" and its assertion of human agency as a common asset are plainly congruent with a "welfare" model of the socioeconomic system. In contrast to "neo-liberal," free-market constructions, the welfare model assumes that "markets" are inherently imperfect, but that their deficiencies can be overcome by systematic reallocation of resources (Dobb, 1969). Thus, welfare economics departs from the "self-interested" premises of the classical or neoclassical model; from a welfare perspective, the cardinal aim is allocative efficiency, that is, a fairer distribution of output according to the principle of the declining marginal utility of income. The welfare model aims at the realization of the "community's" interest in a reasonably fair distribution of economic resources. As its designation denotes, the welfare model leads to the advocacy of minimal household income policies for the purpose of attaining a fairer distribution of society's goods.

However, critics of the distributive approach to social justice have concentrated upon its failure to specifically address the underlying need for transforming the social structures and institutions that determine access to resources and to power (Wolff, 1977; Simpson, 1980; Young, 1990). From the standpoint of Iris Young (1990), for example, seeking greater "distributive justice" by working the existing system "harder" is entirely inadequate to the task at hand (p. 3). From Young's perspective, social justice cannot be attained by following fairer "procedural rules" as long as they are implemented within a social structure built upon relationships of domination and oppression. Decision making, division of labor, and culture are central categories in Young's "non-distributive" paradigm (1990). She argues that decision-making issues include not only questions of who by virtue of their positions have effective freedom and authority to make what sorts of decisions, but also the rules and procedures according to which decisions are made. Division of labor emphasizes exploitation of those who execute the tasks by those who define the tasks. Finally, Young argues that while culture is the most general of these three categories, it deserves distinct consideration in the discussion of social justice, as the injustice of cultural imperialism marks and stereotypes some groups at the same time it silences their self-expression. Hence the attainment of social justice requires a restructuring of the system altogether, rather than, as Rawls's theory would suggest, working the system harder.

Since the early 1980s, the validity of this critique of a distributional approach to social justice has been underscored by the growth of socioeconomic inequality in the United States. During the Reagan and Bush administrations, those at the apex of the socioeconomic pyramid enjoyed unfettered increases in their incomes, wealth, and power, while those on the lowest rung suffered contractions on all three of these crucial counts (Burt, 1992; Manning, 1998). From his extensive longitudinal analysis of social indicators, Marc Miringoff (1996) has concluded that the gap between rich and poor was wider in the "boom" times of the 1990s than during the pre-Reagan "stagflation" period of the 1970s. As Noam Chomsky stated in a 1995 interview with the *Harvard Educational Review,* the United States today is a society in which a major segment has been systematically marginalized, a rich society in which income and wealth disparities are nonetheless widening at an unprecedented pace, in which poor minority-group members are headed away from material betterment and political empowerment and toward destitution, incarceration, and despair. What emerged in the early 1980s, Philip Mattera has argued in his text *Prosperity Lost,* was an unprecedented alliance of business, the federal government, and the political Right, all dedicated to a restructuring of the U.S. political economy in favor of power and privilege (1990, p. 42). Wronka (1995), Gil (1998), and Witkin (1998), proponents of the use of the Universal Declaration of Human Rights of 1942 as a social work tool in assessments and interventions, indicate that an assessment of current conditions of working and nonworking poor people would find this country flagrantly guilty of committing tremendous injustices. As class divisions have become more pronounced, social conflict has undergone a correlative explosion. Conclusive evidence of mounting polarization and tension along the class lines that divide U.S. society has been presented by Karoly (1993) and by Houts, Brooks, and Manza (1993). As Andrew Howard (1995) concludes, "the weight of empirical evidence . . . suggests a sharpening of class antagonisms" (p. 379) within the United States—and, in fact, around the globe.

For the social work profession in the United States, the direct result of "neo-liberalism" in support of transnational capitalism is the attack on "big government" and the "solution" of welfare devolution. According to Robert Behn (1995), Ronald Reagan, at the very start of his first term as president, proposed a "devolutionary bargain" by offering the states freedom from the funding and administration of Medicaid if they would assume complete responsibility for the federal/state Aid to Families With Dependent Children (p. 38). In the view of Mimi Abramovitz (1995), since that time, "critics (have) blamed mounting poverty and rising welfare costs on the never fully implemented 'soft' social services and the behavior of poor people" (p. 190). Among others, Falcks (1995) has argued that welfare devolution has been orchestrated by powerful right-wing political and cultural strategies to ensure their dominance and has been advanced by exceedingly well funded organizational initiatives (p. 40). In effect, "devolution" is a code word for dismantlement of the social safety net to lower levels of government and, eventually, to the private sector (Brownell, personal communication, 1998).

What is truly striking about devolution is the extent of the support it has received from nominally progressive leaders and the immediacy of its impact upon the poor. In August 1996, President Bill Clinton signed the Personal Responsibility and Work Opportunity Act of 1996 (P.L. 104–193), making good on his pledge to "end welfare as we know it," and he joined with Republicans and conservative Democrats to do just that. There can be little doubt that the 1996 welfare reform has had a dramatic effect upon welfare in terms of caseload enrollments and expenditures. Between August 1996, when Clinton signed P.L. 104–193, and September 1997 the number of people on cash assistance in United States dropped by 1.7 million, "the biggest one-year decline in the history of welfare" (Glastris, 1997, p. 30).

It is by now evident that social workers will not be able to achieve justice for their clients by working exclusively under the premises of a distributive model. The Rawlsian construct retains value as a blueprint for how social justice could be achieved in a society committed to its attainment. The problem is that U.S. society no longer exhibits this commitment, and its political leadership has moved with alarming speed to disassemble the meager vestiges of past concern for the poor. Rather than "working" the system harder on behalf of their clients' immediate needs, social workers must now seek to work *against* a system that is intent upon denial of moral responsibility for responding to those same needs. Toward that end, social work practitioners are encouraged to embrace an "empowerment" approach to their relationship with clients, helping them to redress the tide of neo-liberal devolutionism. Several scholars, including Fay (1987), Gould (1987), and Gutierrez (1990), have argued that the theory undergirding empowerment-based social work practice is derived from a conflictual paradigm of society in which separate groups possessing differential power vie for control over societal resources. Plainly, that paradigm has become an increasingly accurate description of U.S. society. As such, the empowerment model is consistent with "radical," "neo-Marxist," and "liberation theology" conceptions of the social economy. These paradigms see the free market as inherently disposed toward allocative inefficiencies. Rather than simply seeking to redistribute output, they demand a complete restructuring of the economic system itself. Focusing upon the lopsided struggle between the economic elite and the downtrodden, radical economists seek to replace a laissez-faire system with one in which the fulfillment of basic human needs is an essential aim (Bernstein, 1989). In this construct, the transfer of resources from those most able to afford it to those most in need is a social justice entitlement.

Even before the need for "radical" steps targeted at the social system itself became evident, empowerment has been a guiding precept of contemporary social work theory and practice. As Solomon defined it more than 20 years ago, "empowerment refers to a process whereby persons who belong to a stigmatized social category throughout their lives can be assisted to develop and increase skills in the exercise of interpersonal influence and the performance of valued social roles" (1976, p. 6). More recently, Lee (1994) has proposed a "bifocal vision" to an empowerment approach that will enable the practitioner to envision the whole yet intervene in the particular configuration of needs each oppressed person may have (p. 22). Empowerment denotes the mobilization of clients' personal resources in concert with the provision of assistance in a manner that allows increasing reliance upon the former. Personal empowerment is crucial since it also involves clients' liberation from internalized oppressive forces. In keeping with the "person-in-environment" bedrock concept of social work, empowerment takes on a much broader and far more political dimension. Thus Gutierrez (1990) glosses the term "empowerment" as "a process of increasing personal, interpersonal, and political power so that individuals can take action to improve their life situations" (p. 149). Clearly, such action must be directed also toward altering the structural conditions of an unjust society in which the allocation of economic and political resources is stacked against social work clients (Pinderhughes, 1983). This conception directly challenges the assumption that social workers should merely assist disadvantaged clients in adapting their behaviors and beliefs to accommodate prevalent power structures. It argues, instead, that social workers must form offensive alliances with their clients to change the "system" itself. Thus the client/worker relationship becomes one of true partnership.

In addition to supporting the traditional "welfare" orientation of the social work profession toward a fairer and more effective distribution of economic resources, current circumstances demand that social workers simultaneously pursue the political empowerment of their clients and direct it toward the goal of structural reform. The implications for social work practice are manifold and profound. Consistent with a "narrow" view of client empowerment, social workers must continue to engage in activities that are geared toward the "content" of empowerment, for example, by facilitating in clients the development of specific skills, and activities through which they come to gain the power to respond to an unjust social system (Brown & Furstenberg, 1992). Clients' increasing cultural diversity requires that social workers become sensitive to the "cultural imperialism" inherent within and supportive of elite domination (Young, 1990, p. 23). Indeed, consistent with that imperative, social workers must recognize that social justice is not simply something to be imparted to the client; rather, it is what the client defines it to be from his or her particular cultural-historical viewpoint.

According to Swift (1983–1984), the empowerment model of human services is explicitly meant to replace the paternalistic assumptions that have predominated in our society and that have influenced the practice of social work. More recently, Gil (1998) has asserted that in the light of this legacy, client empowerment demands that social workers critically examine assumptions, policies, and practices that comprise their work, while reaffirming their commitment to comprehensive reform wherever manifestations of domination and oppression are found. To that end, social workers need to comprehend the dynamics of oppression and exploitation under the present system of transnational capitalism. As delineated by William Robinson (1996), transnational capitalism is the dominant force in the world today, and is characterized by the subordination of sovereign states to transnational capitalist interests, the hegemony of a transnational elite, and, most acutely, by the growth of socioeconomic inequality within and among national societies (p. 21). Social workers must be aware that the injustices they encounter in their clients' lives are not isolated or accidental, but systematic and all-encompassing.

As the corollary to thinking globally, social workers must activate social justice at the local level, that is, in their relations with their clients. As Compton and Galaway (1994) have put it, the ultimate, strategic mission of social work is to change the social system itself (p. 268). To accomplish that end, social workers must join forces with (and in many instances mobilize and lead) their clients in the ongoing political struggle to attain an authentically just society. In the end, social workers must engage in affirmative praxis to alter the macro conditions that generate and reinforce the problems their clients confront.

What is required, then, is not the mechanical replacement of the "distributional justice/welfare" orientation of the social work profession by a "radical/political empowerment" model of militant social work practice. Rather, what is needed is a commitment to struggle on two fronts at once: serving the client by laboring to increase resource transfers under the existing system, and serving the "person-in-environment" by fighting for systemic changes. It is, then, only by acting on both fronts that social workers can fulfill their profession's revitalized commitment to the precept of social justice.

REFERENCES

Abramovitz, M. (1995). Aid to families with dependent children. In R. L. Edwards (Ed.), *Encyclopedia of social work* (19th ed.) (pp. 183–194). Washington, DC: NASW Press.

Behn, Robert D. (1995). The management of reinvented federalism. In Thad L. Beyle (Ed.), *State government: Congressional Quarterly's guide to current issues and activities, 1995–1996* (pp. 138–139). Washington, DC: Congressional Quarterly.

Bernstein, M. (1989). *Comparative economic systems: Models and cases* (6th ed.). Homewood, IL: Richard D. Irwin.

Biestek, F. (1957). *The casework relationship.* Chicago: Loyola University Press.

Bricker-Jenkins, M., & Hooyman, N. (1986). *Not for women only: Social work practice for a feminist future.* Silver Spring, MD: NASW Press.

Brown, S. T., & Furstenberg, A. L. (1992). Restoring control: Empowering older patients and their families during health crisis. *Social Work in Health Care, 17*(4), 81–101.

Burt, M. R. (1992). *Over the edge: The growth of homelessness in the 1980s.* Washington, DC: Urban Institute Press.

Chomsky, N. (1995). Interview with Chomsky. *Harvard Educational Review, 65*(2), 127–134.

Coady, N. (1993). The worker-client relationship revisited. *Families in Society: The Journal of Contemporary Human Services,* May, 291–300.

Compton, B., & Galaway, B. (1994). *Social work processes.* Pacific Grove, CA: Brooks/Cole.

Dobb, M. (1969). *Welfare economics and the economics of socialism.* Cambridge: Cambridge University Press.

Falcks, D. (1995). Taking ideology seriously: A route to progressive power. *Social Policy, 26*(2), 34–50.

Fay, B. (1987). *Critical social science.* Ithaca, NY: Cornell University Press.

Gelso, C., & Carter, J. (1985). The relationship in counseling and psychotherapy: Components, consequences and theoretical antecedents. *The Counseling Psychologist, 13*(2), 155–243.

Germain, C., & Gitterman, A. (1980). *The life model of social work practice.* New York: Columbia University Press.

Gil, D. (1998). *Confronting injustice and oppression.* New York: Columbia University Press.

Glastris, P. (1997, October 20). Was Reagan right? *US News & World Report,* pp. 30–31.

Gould, K. (1987). Life model vs. conflict model: A feminist perspective. *Social Work, 32,* 346–351.

Gutierrez, L. M. (1990). Working with women of color: An empowerment perspective. *Social Work, 35,* 149–153.

Gutierrez, L. M., & Ortega, R. (1991). Developing methods to empower Latinos: The importance of groups. *Social Work With Groups, 14*(2), 28–43.

Gutierrez, L., Parsons, R., & Cox, E. (1998). *Empowerment in social work practice.* Pacific Grove, CA: Brooks/Cole.

Hollis, F. (1964). *Casework: A psychosocial therapy.* New York: Random House.

Houts, M., Brooks, C., & Manza, J. (1993). The persistence of class in post-industrial society. *International Sociology, 8,* 259–277.

Howard, A. (1995). Global capitalism and labor internationalism in comparative historical perspective. *Sociological Inquiry, 65,* 365–394.

Karoly, L. (1993). The trend in inequality among families, individuals and workers in the United States: A twenty-five-year perspective. In S. Danziger & P. Gottschalk (Eds.), *Uneven tides: Rising inequality in America* (pp. 19–97). New York: Russell Sage.

Lee, J. (1994). *The empowerment approach to social work practice.* New York: Columbia University Press.

Manning, S. (1998). The social worker as a moral citizen: Ethics in action. *Social Work, 42*(3), 223–230.

Mattera, P. (1990). *Prosperity lost.* Reading, MA: Addison-Wesley.

Miringoff, M. (1996). *Index of social health: Monitoring the social well-being of the nation.* Fordham Institute for Innovation of Social Policy. Graduate Center, Tarytown.

National Association of Social Workers. (1996). *Code of ethics.* Washington, DC: NASW Press.

Perlman, H. (1979). *Relationship: The heart of helping people.* Chicago: University of Chicago Press.

Petr, C. (1988). The worker client-worker relationship: A general systems perspective. *Social Casework, 69,* 620–626.

Pinderhughes, E. B. (1983). Empowerment for our clients and for ourselves. *Social Casework, 64,* 331–338.

Proctor, E. (1982). *Defining the worker-client relationship.* Chicago: Loyola University Press.

Rawls, J. (1971). *A theory of justice.* Cambridge: Belknap Press of Harvard University.

Reynolds, B. (1942). A changing psychology in social case work. *The Family, 13,* 107–111.

Rhodes, S. (1978). A developmental approach to the life cycle of a family. *Social Casework, 58,* 301–311.

Richmond, M. (1917). *What is social casework?* New York: Russell Sage.

Robinson, V. (1930). *A changing psychology in social casework.* Chapel Hill: University of North Carolina Press.

Robinson, W. (1996). Globalisation: Nine theses in our epoch. *Race and Class, 38*(2), 13–31.

Saleeby, D. (1990). Philosophical disputes in social work: Social justice denied. *Journal of Sociology and Social Welfare, 17*(2), 29–39.

Saleeby, D. (1997). *The strengths perspective in social work practice.* New York: Longman.

Schwartz, N. (1976). Between client and system: The mediating function. In R. W. Roberts & H. Northern (Eds.), *Theories of social work with groups* (pp. 44–66). New York: Columbia University Press.

Simpson, E. (1980). The subject of justice. *Ethics 90,* July, 490–501.

Solomon, B. (1976). *Black empowerment: Social work in oppressed communities.* New York: Columbia University Press.

Swift, C. (1983–1984). Empowerment: An antidote for folly. *Prevention in Human Services/Studies in Empowerment,* no. 3 (Winter–Spring), xi–xv.

Witkin, S. (1998). Human rights and social work. Editorial. *Social Work, 43*(3), 197.

Wolff, R. P. (1977). *Understanding Rawls: A reconstruction and critique of "A Theory of Justice."* Princeton: Princeton University Press.

Wronka, J. (1995). Human rights. In R. Edwards (Ed.), *Encyclopedia of social work* (19th ed., pp. 1405–1418). Washington, DC: NASW Press.

Young, I. (1990). *Justice and the politics of difference.* Princeton: Princeton University Press.

2

Welfare Reform: Skills Game or Shill Game?

Robert H. Hill, DSW

SINCE THE FOUNDING of the original American colonies, public assistance for the "able-bodied" needy has been a controversial social problem. The passage of the 1935 Social Security Act injected the federal government more into this controversy but failed to resolve the issue.

In essence, "welfare" has come to mean public assistance provided to individuals who do not have, nor have they earned, the means to meet their basic needs, according to a basic standard of living. Since its passage in 1935, the Social Security Act (and its subsequent amendments) has provided the basis for public social welfare policy in the United States and entitlement to this form of assistance. "Welfare reform" concerns the amendment of the 1935 Social Security Act by P.L. 104–193, the Personal Responsibility and Work Opportunity Reconciliation Act of 1996 (PRA), regarding means-tested public welfare entitlements, whereby recipients must demonstrate their need to a public authority to receive public assistance. As reflected in PRA, the term "welfare reform" has several meanings: (1) a completion of a major social policy paradigm shift regarding the roles of federal and state government; (2) a redefinition of the purpose of providing means-tested public assistance; and (3) a revision in the nature and extent of communal obligation. However, as discussions of welfare reveal significant historical differences about (1) the character of the target population, (2) the reasons for their neediness, (3) the objective of social welfare provisions, and (4) what these provisions accomplish, a sketch of the historical context of the Social Security Act, as well as the initial Act and subsequent key junctures up to PRA, is needed to provide an appropriate perspective for an understanding of "devolution" and for assessing what has changed and in what way.

Moreover, this overview will reflect the themes of "target population," "public perception," "welfare ideology," and "policy objective" as guideposts for this discussion to facilitate a policy practice orientation regarding this landmark legislation. PRA will then be similarly examined, and finally key issues will be highlighted with regard to substantive welfare reform.

HISTORICAL CONTEXT

The original American colonies adopted England's local public relief practices in which the work ethic emphasized individual and family self-sufficiency. Able-bodied unemployed males were the target population of this policy, and direct government support of welfare was not considered an appropriate role, other than in assigning local responsibility for this function. The prevailing ideology was that the family and the marketplace were the media by which individuals would meet their needs, except for those whose disabilities and lack of family members clearly indicated their neediness. Moreover, a breakdown of the ability of both the family and the marketplace would need to occur before an able-bodied person could seek temporary assistance from their community. Also, as it was believed that the able-bodied needy were morally wanting and lazy, the amount of aid would be less than adequate so as not to create dependency on public aid and to provide an incentive for self-sufficiency. Finally, "strangers" or transients were excluded from this local community support, as residency was a basic eligibility requirement. Prior to the 20th century, assisting the needy was essentially considered a role for private charity. In the 20th century a major change in this orientation occurred.

In 1911, after years of campaigning, state-funded mothers pensions began in Illinois. They had spread to most states by the time of the Great Depression in 1929 (Axinn & Levin, 1982). Mothers pensions were predominantly for white families whose fathers were absent due to death or desertion, with a minimal number of northern African-American families receiving assistance. However, reflective of the beliefs about the needy, cash assistance was only provided for the mother's children—mothers were always considered morally suspect. However, this marked a major break from the belief in a public assistance ideology in which government intervention was considered inappropriate. It marked the point at which communal values were publicly endorsed; specifically, that motherhood provided a needed function to the community, and father-absent families had become needy because of uncontrollable circumstances. Subsequently, the blind and the aged became categories of state support that followed a similar line of reasoning: the states had become the locus of residency, and public welfare departments were established to administer programs.

By 1933, after several years of worldwide economic depression, over 16 million Americans experienced economic dislocation, the most massive strike of agricultural workers ever held occurred, and state treasuries had been depleted. There was no longer a belief that the private economy could revive on its own and that the resources of the states were inadequate. Newly elected President Franklin Delano Roosevelt announced that the national economy had broken down and that emergency measures of federal intervention were required to jump-start the economy. However, in contrast to those "on the dole," the "new poor"—composed of the unemployed and working poor of this period—had "earned" public assistance in the form of federal cash assistance to state agencies for the unemployed, food, and work relief. However, as these initiatives were designed to stimulate the private sector and spur purchasing power, they were intentionally insufficient in scale in order to preclude their being viewed as an ongoing endeavor, even on an emergency basis.

As federally run programs encountered strong negative reaction from the private sector and the states (because of better wage scales than poorly paid segments of the private sector, such as agriculture, and preemption of states' rights), these federally funded programs came to be administered by the states and monitored by the federal government. Importantly, to underscore these programs as temporary and different from existing welfare programs, a separate state bureaucracy was established. Given both historical public policy regarding federal involvement in welfare and a continuing residual ideology regarding accepting public relief, this distinction was deemed necessary in order to obtain the approval and cooperation of a coalition of key conservative congressional leaders and the interests of business and industry, especially the agricultural sector.

However, it also marked the public acceptance of federal intervention based on communal values—that is, assistance for able-bodied individuals whose employment has been disrupted by the marketplace (Yankelovich, 1994), as well as acceptance of this intervention to restore the market economy, reflecting a continued belief in the American economy. States enacted a different policy: assistance was extended to those whose age (children and the elderly) and disability made them eligible. Mothers, however, continued to be excluded from assistance, as they were formerly excluded under the mothers pensions, now called widows pensions.

By 1935, however, public concern for income security was increasing, and President Roosevelt was awaiting a report from his Committee on Economic Security that addressed this need. By this point there were several very popular proposals being discussed publicly and recommended by U.S. congressmen. The proposals ranged from comprehensive, universal income support proposals to the consensus proposal—the "Townsend Plan" (Bruno, 1957)—which proposed a guaranteed pension for the elderly who had worked but who could no longer work, and a plan for assistance to those workers who had lost their jobs because of market contractions. Although the elderly became the core target group for policy, welfare activists within the president's cabinet were proposing not only a permanent federal welfare system but the inclusion of guaranteed income support for those families now receiving mothers pensions without a means or "morals" test, in addition to the other state-supported categorical programs financed by general revenues.

Roosevelt's Committee on Economic Security recommended two proposals for the aged: Old Age Assistance, for the elderly needy, and Old Age Insurance (pensions), which would be a mandatory system, funded by a payroll tax on the worker and the employer, providing temporary cash assistance for the unemployed, and centrally administered by the federal government. Collectively, these recommendations were incorporated into a federal proposal for a Social Security Act, which also included child health and welfare provisions and national health insurance. These proposals would establish not only a permanent welfare department within the federal government, but also a welfare ideology that addressed the forms of welfare assistance and the role of the federal government in providing welfare.

However, the target population of the Social Security Act was the aged who could no longer work, and public assistance considerations were considered transitional. Additionally, there would be policy trade-offs and revisions in developing support for passage of such far-reaching legislation that essentially deleted any substantial changes in past state practices of public relief, with the major exception that administrative discretion was now tempered by statutory fair hearings and accountability to a federal Social Security Board. Bauer and Gergen (1969) have called attention to the need to develop a "winning coalition" to realize a policy, and coalition support often means concessions. The Social Security Act entailed significant concessions to those seeking to retain inequitable wages in agricultural and domestic services; these sectors were excluded from coverage by the Social Security Act.

There were those who believed that providing cash aid for the mother, in addition to aid for her children, promoted immorality and undermined marriage; consequently, mothers were not covered under the Aid to Dependent Children (ADC) grants. These beliefs were so strong that although widows of wage earners would be covered a few years after enactment of the Social Security Act, it would take another two decades for "caretakers" to be included in ADC grants. The acknowledgment of this assistance for mothers would require close to another decade for the recognition of "family" assistance, and the change in the Social Security relief title from ADC to AFDC—Aid for Families With Dependent Children. What makes the initial omission of mothers from ADC all the more pernicious is that according to Yankelovich (1994), in 1939 the public endorsed mothers' remaining home to raise their children and maintain the household.

Given the exclusion of agriculture and domestic services (where significant number of African-American and Hispanic workers were employed) and the exclusion of support for women in social security and single-parent families, the marginality of these groups appears to be based as much upon racism and sexism as upon economic advantage. This continuing unequal treatment of minorities and women thus, tacitly, became federally endorsed. Moreover, as the able-bodied unemployed continued to be solely the responsibility of the states and their localities, not only did children of unemployed parents not receive any federal aid, but many localities instituted requirements for the able-bodied needy to perform public works jobs in exchange for relief. In essence, the distinction between unemployable adults and unemployed adults was reinforced; the former received federally matched state public assistance, while the latter receive cash for work relief.

THE SOCIAL SECURITY ACT

The major parts of the Social Security Act established social insurance programs—pensions and temporary unemployment assistance—financed by mandatory employer-employee payroll taxes and deposited in separate federal trust fund accounts. The Act provided assistance to the states for resumption of state public relief for their categorical poor groups—the aged, blind, and children of fatherless families (formerly called widows or mothers pensions, but now called ADC)—and maternal and child health and welfare services. The categorical public relief programs would be financed by formula-based federal-state matching funds for each state, which would set their respective eligibility and benefit levels and administer their programs. A federal Social Security Board was established, within which was a Bureau of Public Assistance to manage the "welfare," or categorical programs, for the poor.

The major impacts of this initial Act were numerous. First, the national ideology was expanded to include communal values in addition to market values, most notably reflected in federal assistance for fatherless families. Also established was federal intervention into the private economy to provide income support and redress the distribution of earned benefits from the standpoint of the worker; subsequently, in 1939, surviving family members were included. Those eligible for public assistance were now "entitled" to a fair hearing if they were denied aid, but means testing would remain, thus reinforcing the distinctions between social security, which had no such requirements, and public assistance. However, perhaps most significant was the grant of access to federal funds to provide federal assistance for welfare, which has been continually contested since its inception. This Act was also paradoxical, given that its intended policy objective was income security for the elderly and income insurance for workers experiencing temporary market disruption, yet the only federal funds in the Social Security Act were for welfare (i.e., the public relief recipient) and no federal funds would go for earned Old Age pensions (i.e., "social security") or temporary employment insurance. In essence, social security would continue to depend on the market economy, not public employment, and public relief, or "welfare," would resume as a state responsibility and federal entitlement funds would be tied to state assistance only for specified groups.

Welfare Reform Emerges

It was not until the early 1960s that welfare reform became a federal concern; however, this period also marked a change in the policy objective of welfare as income support, coinciding with emergent changes in the composition of welfare recipients from the aged (Old Age Assistance) to mostly single-parent families, when AFDC commenced. The 1960s marked the beginning of a 30-year period of welfare reform during which services and benefits were expanded, then contracted, then rationed. Welfare policy objectives shifted during this period from changing the behavior of recipients, to changing how the welfare system functions, to changing not only the welfare recipient and the system but also the federal role in welfare. During these decades, within the context of a changing economy, the public perception of welfare became negative, even among welfare recipients (Joint Center for Political Studies, 1993); the routes to welfare multiplied, as did the informal roles of welfare and the characteristics of recipients. Finally, public ideology changed regarding communal obligations and the definition of the problem, as reflected in the PRA.

WELFARE REFORM BEGINS

By the early 1960s, welfare was seen as part of a much greater, more complex problem—poverty. Welfare was part of a "culture of poverty" (Katz, 1986). Moreover, this culture of poverty was being transmitted from parent to child. A poverty standard, or annual income threshold, was developed to demarcate those whose incomes were below that level and therefore living in poverty. However, "poverty" was seen as resulting not only from a lack of income but also from a "lack of motivation, hope, and incentive" (Sundquist, 1969, p. 140); there was also acknowledgment of the failure of the public and private sectors of the economy, as well as a denial of opportunities for minority Americans and the poor to improve their standard of living.

The characteristics of ADC families had also changed from widowed families to female-headed, single-parent families resulting from desertion, divorce, and out-of-wedlock relationships, all of which supported a public perception of personal inadequacies. Welfare activists countered this view by pointing to welfare regulations requiring the absence of the male family head, and consequently promoting family breakup of families with unemployed fathers. ADC was reformulated as AFDC, which now also provided cash assistance for the parent, including families in which the father was unemployed. However, this unemployment factor did not explain those AFDC minority-group mothers who were never married, and especially teenage unwed mothers, who, contrary to public beliefs, accounted for only 15% of nonmarital births (U.S. Department Health and Human Services, 1995, p. 88). Counseling services and expanded benefits were proposed and accepted to reduce welfare rolls and to promote education, job skills, self-sufficiency, improved parenting, and citizenship.

REFORMING THE RECIPIENT

By the late 1960s, however, not only had a reduction in the number of welfare recipients not occurred, but there were several million more recipients of welfare. The cause of their neediness was divorce, desertion, and illegitimacy, with many recipients having additional children. Moreover, increasingly these recipients were African-American and Hispanic unwed mothers; however, white welfare recipients would continue to outnumber African-American and Hispanic recipients combined, and they reflected the same reasons for welfare eligibility. It is also important to note here that within the greater economy the role of mothers in two-parent families was changing. Married women, both African American and white, were now entering the labor force—whether by choice or circumstances—to augment the family income; 40% to 50% of the mothers in two-parent families worked outside the home. It should also be noted that from 1964 to 1974 there was a significant expansion of in-kind benefits available to welfare recipients, ranging from food stamps and health insurance to public housing and legal services. It should also be noted that by this time welfare was mostly for mothers with young children.

Against a backdrop of welfare recipients claiming their "right" to welfare, public perception was that welfare was now supporting unfavorable lifestyles. The federal government attributed this in part to "permissive" state welfare practices, as analysis of state records indicated a marked increase in acceptance rates for welfare cases (Axinn & Levin, 1982) as well as minimal decreases in the number of existing welfare recipients.

Welfare reform, as reflected in the 1967 Social Security Amendments, had the policy objective of promoting self-sufficiency through employment and training, but it also attempted to curtail permissive state practices. Work incentives were added, such as employment income disregards and day care. However, able-bodied adults and older children no longer in

school would be terminated from grants if they refused employment without good cause. A cap or freeze was placed on the
number of children supported by a family's welfare grant (this
was forestalled by two presidencies until it was repealed), but
this cap on a grant exempted recipients on welfare due to death
or unemployment of the male wage earner. These amendments
presage the emergence of "workfare" and requiring recipients
to demonstrate an interest in employment and job training activities. These amendments were then revised to include mothers
of children over 6 years old, with vocational rehabilitation replacing counseling and job placement the objective; weekly job
search evidence was required. The collective impact of these
amendments was minimal, in part due to state administrative
discretion, but also there was a lack of available support services
for mothers. Moreover, it was not possible to determine if those
mothers who found employment subsequently returned to welfare, as by 1970 it was believed that some welfare mothers re-
volved in and out of the labor market (Moynihan, 1973). In
addition to need resulting from death, desertion, or nonsupport
of the father, this revolving door suggested that welfare was
now being used as an income support while unemployed, suggesting that the strength of the economy affected welfare receipt.

ATTEMPTING TO REDEFINE THE PROBLEM

Subsequently, a very noteworthy, albeit aborted, welfare reform
of the 1970s was President Richard Nixon's Family Assistance
Plan (FAP), which, although promoted as a welfare reform, was
equally an attempt to raise the annual income of the working
poor. The FAP proposed a federal takeover of AFDC. Essentially, the plan would provide a guaranteed annual income that
could be augmented by earnings up to a given national income
standard. However, according to Steiner (1971, p. 314), 80% of
the welfare population, in 42 states, would not realize any gain
from the proposal. This was apparently a tactical policy strategy
and an intentional targeting of a subgroup of the welfare and
working poor populations. According to Moynihan (1973), 8 of
the 10 states with the highest percentage of welfare recipients

were southern states, which also provided the lowest cash grants in the country.

Additionally, the wages within these states were the lowest in the country and were so low that the proposed FAP annual income standard would have increased their annual income as well the income of those on welfare. Moreover, unemployment was a significant cause of welfare. For these states, FAP would replace welfare; for the much greater majority of states, FAP would subsidize their cash grants, but these additions would be at the state's discretion. This plan would have dismantled the ideological firewall between the working poor and the welfare recipient, but ideological differences, public distrust, welfare stereotypes, and the minimal guaranteed income standard were the main factors leading to aborting the FAP. However, the expansion of social services under Title XX of the Social Security Act, as well as the increased eligibility for food stamps, both of which were available to welfare recipients as well as the greater working class, increased unabated. Food stamps alone increased from $550 million in 1970 to $4.4 billion by 1975 (Axinn & Levin, 1982). The original social service goal of dependency reduction was now replaced by that of enhancing the quality of life (Katz, 1986). This was facilitated through the aggregation of formerly categorical federal-state government entitlements for specific services into federal block grants whose purposes were much broader. Thus was accomplished a dual purpose of reducing federal responsibility for specific social services while permitting flexibility in the use of federal funds.

This expansion of the purpose and type of social services, at state discretion, particularly day care, had added importance when, from the mid-1970s to 1980, the economy experienced a significant and prolonged downturn. The economy had shifted from a manufacturing, industrial base, with good wages, to a services economy, with much lower wages. Municipalities flirted with bankruptcy, significantly retarding public-sector job growth to sustain local economies; inflation eroded purchasing power. There was high unemployment, soaring among minorities, and Americans experienced downward mobility overall (Newman, 1988), a declining social and economic quality of life. Keyserling (1979, p. 349) has characterized the U.S. economy from 1953 to 1979 as "a roller-coaster economic performance—six periods of inadequate upturn, stagnation, and recession, with a chronic rise in unemployment because each upturn at its peak has tended to leave us with more unemployment than the previous one." Further, he pointed out that the economic recovery from each cycle left greater and greater numbers of minorities behind.

In the early 1980s, among the poor, an inchoate subgroup called the "underclass" was discovered (Auletta, 1982). The underclass were characterized as socially and economically exploitative, abandoning their families, involved with drugs and illegal activities, and impervious to law and orderliness and traditional employment. Welfare recipients were considered part of this membership, and African-American and Hispanic minorities, particularly unwed mothers and high school dropouts. were considered prime candidates for such a lifestyle.

THE REAGAN REFORMS

The election of Ronald Reagan as president in the 1980s marked the renascence of conservative welfare ideology that sought to return welfare solely to the states, dismantle federal welfare programs, and, in the name of weeding out welfare fraud and abuse, restore discipline among the needy. Income subsidies for working welfare recipients were terminated and food stamp allocations were reduced, as were housing assistance and welfare grant formulas. Categorical social services were bundled into block grants with reduced funding. There was public support for the policy of reducing the federal government's role in welfare and reducing welfare dependency. Early in his administration, President Reagan encouraged dependency reduction through state welfare reform experiments promoting private-sector employment (Katz, 1989).

STATE WELFARE-TO-WORK EXPERIMENTS

States used different approaches, involving voluntary or mandatory participation, with welfare recipients, including unemployed male spouses and parents with children over age 6. Basic education, job search, skills development, unpaid work experience (workfare), and job placement were used in some combined form, with or without work-related social services supports. Although the average cost of these programs was modest, the more expensive per capita experiments yielded more notable positive results, with recipients making encouraging wage and income increases, such as in the work experiments in Massachusetts and California.

The Massachusetts Employment and Training Program required all welfare recipients to sign up for the program, but initially the program selected recipients who volunteered in response to social service incentives. This approach yielded a participation rate of nearly 50% of those eligible. About half of those who participated found jobs above the minimum wage, and half of those who found jobs stayed off welfare. Approximately 12% of the overall eligible population experienced positive gains (Burtless, 1995). This program was implemented in a state with a healthy economy, low general unemployment, and a tight labor market. However, the welfare rolls increased as the economy declined, budget deficits increased, and the state resorted to expedient, much less costly, and less effective work requirements.

The California Greater Avenue for Independence (GAIN) Program was enacted when the state was experiencing financial difficulties. Reflective of the then-current profile of welfare recipients, a significant number of California welfare recipients had a limited education and lacked basic job-finding skills; many of them were African-American and Hispanic persons with limited employment experience. However, greater wage and income gains were realized in one county, where a charismatic executive emphasized job finding, than were realized in another county emphasizing basic education and job training skills to increase their employability. But these impressive earnings gains, of up to 49% income increases, were short-lived: nearly two-thirds of the experimental group had become unemployed by the end of the third-year assessment of this initiative, and a sizable number of recipients had not worked for the entire 3-year period (Handler, 1995, p. 71). Overall, these welfare-to-work experiments were important for demonstrating that local governments could directly move a segment of the welfare population off the rolls, but these experiments were also notable for suggesting that welfare recipients need different service/resource combinations, as well as a healthy local economy and a tight labor market. These experiments also demonstrated the vulnerability of welfare recipients to economic downturns. Nonetheless, the positive results of welfare-to-work experiments in moving recipients off welfare provided support and program design experience in the development of the Family Support Act of 1988.

THE FAMILY SUPPORT ACT OF 1988:
REFORMING THE SYSTEM AND THE RECIPIENT

The Family Support Act was passed in the last months of the Reagan presidency. However, its implementation was not required until 1990, and it would take 8 years to be fully phased in. Each year had AFDC enrollment percentage goals for specific segments of recipients, and there were mandated periodic state program performance reviews in order to receive continued funding. The Family Support Act sought to reform both the recipient and the state government welfare bureaucracy, and its policy objectives were to promote self-sufficiency of welfare recipients, family responsibility, and mandatory state government activities. Divorced and never-married long-term welfare recipients, high school dropouts, unemployed fathers, and nonsupportive fathers were the targets.

According to Wilson (1985), this target population was significantly composed of minority welfare recipients. The centerpiece of this legislation was JOBS—the Job Opportunity and Basic Skills program (*1992 Green Book,* pp. 610–615). JOBS mandated the participation of AFDC mothers of children over 3 years old. There was state discretion to require participation of mothers of children over 1 year old. Also, the Act's emphasis on the goal of restoring family responsibility meant that divorced and never-married welfare mothers were required to identify the fathers of their children and to pursue child support petitions in the family court. These awards would go to the state to offset welfare grants. The states were now required to provide employment-related costs for basic skills training, job search skills, transportation and job expenses, and day care; those who became employed would be allowed to continue Medicaid coverage for 1 year. JOBS program participants were required to perform verifiable job search activities for a specified number of weeks each year.

If no job was found, individuals were required to participate in a "community work experience program" in a public-sector job, performing workfare, working for a specified number of hours depending on the grant amount, for 6 to 9 months; this would also provide the basis to assess their vocational ability. Subsequently, these recipients were to be involved in a program of employment-related activities for up to 20 hours per week until they found a job requiring at least 30 hours of work per week. The states were expected to tailor their JOBS program to the needs of their welfare population. Lack of adequate child care significantly hampered recipient participation. Although the impact of the JOBS welfare reform was minimal in moving welfare recipients into regular employment, this naturally varied according to the state or regional economy. Overall, however, the wages of these jobs moved recipients off the welfare rolls but not out of poverty (Handler, 1995, pp. 76–95 passim). Moreover, the loss of in-kind benefits—particularly health coverage—kept these families one step from returning to welfare if a child took ill, not to mention a job loss resulting from a downturn in the economy.

Ellwood (1988) documented a pattern of recurring need for welfare due to unemployment in the same year the Family Support Act was enacted. This pattern of recurring unemployment and divorce contributed to the growth of AFDC in the 1990s. Making even more provocative contributions to increased AFDC rolls, however, were AFDC mothers who had never married—they represented close to half of all AFDC cases (1996 Green Book, p. 516). According to the author of a frequently cited study of welfare recipients (Pavetti, 1995), when including total periods of previous welfare use, more than 40% had received welfare for 5 or more years, and teenage African-American mothers made up a large percentage of long-term users (Mead, 1994). Welfare dependency by African-American, never-married mothers who dropped out of school, went on welfare, and received assistance for as long as 10 years became the public stereotype of the average welfare recipient. In actuality, this was a small but politically notorious group of recipients who were part of a much larger population.

What was understated was that a significant segment of this population consisted of recipients who worked but who could not, for a variety of reasons, maintain a job, and who intermittently returned to welfare until the next job. According to Mc-Fate (1995), this group of AFDC users made up almost half of this long-term population, in addition to another 20% whose employment earnings still needed to be supplemented by AFDC. Finally, there was yet another group of this long-term population who were functionally disabled. According to McLaughlin (1997), 8% of AFDC recipients are on welfare for 8 or more years. Given the picture of young, never-married single mothers raising the next generation of minority welfare recipients, as well as the alarm of finding noncitizens who were greater users of Supplemental Security Income than U.S. citizens (*1996 Green Book,* p. 1308), before the JOBS program was fully implemented it was replaced by P.L. 104–193, the Personal Responsibility and Work Opportunity Reconciliation Act of 1996 (*1996 Green Book*).

The Personal Responsibility and Work Opportunity Reconciliation Act (PRA)

PRA made significant changes in the welfare system, inclusive of the roles of federal and state government as well as the welfare recipient. The main policy objectives of this act were to (1) terminate AFDC entitlement to federal cash benefits; (2) limit the total and per capita welfare expenditures and regulate state welfare activities; (3) revise the nature and extent of welfare assistance; (4) restore parental responsibility for family formation and child support; and (5) promote employment and other behavioral changes. The policy targets were never-married, long-term users of welfare, teenage mothers, nonsupportive fathers, unemployed parents in two-parent households, and noncitizens, who, with exceptions, are now ineligible for any welfare assistance (but Act revisions were introduced immediately after enactment).

Federal entitlement to AFDC cash assistance was repealed and replaced by capped annual block grant funding to the states for Temporary Assistance for Needy Families (TANF). States alone now determine who is eligible for this assistance and the total cash they will receive (Medicaid remained a federal means-tested individual entitlement, as did food stamps, but additional limitations and restrictions were introduced for food stamps).

Under TANF, after 2 years of assistance, except for exempt mothers of young children, able-bodied adults must be actively involved in a number of federally stipulated work activities, as specified by their state; also, there are specified, graduated weekly work activity hours, or workfare, for those who do not find jobs. TANF cash assistance has a 5-year lifetime limit. States have annual work activity enrollment targets, and there are penalties and incentives for goal achievements, particularly in welfare enrollment decreases from the state's baseline year and for decreases in state nonmarital childbearing, especially among teenagers. To receive assistance, teen parents are required to live in a parent's home or in another adult-supervised setting, as well as to attend school. States are required to pursue child support collections, and unwed welfare mothers are required to cooperate in establishing paternity or they will be sanctioned by the state. Federal child care entitlements were also repealed and replaced by block grant child care funding, requiring states to target at least 70% of these funds to TANF recipients. Finally, the eligibility process for certifying childhood disability under Supplemental Security Income is substantially revised, excluding certified professional judgment of developmental disability, to rely on the standard objective measures formerly employed by the Social Security Administration.

In essence, PRA completed the federal goal of devolution initiated under the Reagan administration and, in the process, transformed assistance to needy children into short-term, transitional assistance with the goal of employment in the private sector. It provides a one-time 5-year period of assistance for this transition from welfare to work to occur. PRA permits states to exempt 20% of its welfare population from the 5-year federal welfare assistance limit. It has a national state enrollment goal into this program of 50% by 2002, and after this 5-year period states may use their own funds to provide assistance to whomever they choose. Major concerns are: Will recipients be able to enhance their skills and to find and maintain employment? Will recipients have access to needed social supports?

WELFARE RECIPIENTS AND THE ECONOMY

Single-parent families, essentially female-headed, are a target population of TANF, and this group has been estimated to be 2 to 3 million adults. However, it is important to note that this population is not homogeneous. According to McFate (1995), 60% to 80% of these recipients use welfare temporarily, ranging from a single spell to multiple spells over a period of years. The TANF exemption of 20% of the welfare population from the 5-year lifetime use provides an ostensibly reasonable but conservative estimate of those who are unemployable for a variety of reasons. These are the long-term users of welfare, mostly high school dropouts with no work experience or job skills.

Another important negative impact of the TANF 5-year lifetime limit affects those who have worked off and on over a number of years, whose spells of emergencies or unemployment have spanned as much as 7 years (McFate, 1995). The jobs these recipients find do not have health coverage and pay low wages, making purchasing of health care impossible, and do not provide leave time for caring for ill children. These are characteristic features of jobs in the "secondary" or "casual" labor sector, where there is also high job turnover. Moreover, there is increased competition from foreign labor for jobs in this low end of the labor market (Kuttner, 1997). There are already signs that welfare recipients are merely displacing the working poor (Uchitelle, 1997). In some areas, there is also serious concern that the rate of entry-level low-skill job growth may take decades to absorb the current welfare recipients requiring work in several metropolitan areas (Finder, 1996). This glut in the supply of low-skilled labor also results in keeping wages low. As suggested here, the traditional economic belief of a "tight" labor market (i.e., a low unemployment rate, favoring low-skilled labor) is superfluous for this sector of the marketplace. Additionally, the dynamics of low job skills and increased labor supply, resulting in lower wages, points to the key issue of recipients exiting welfare with jobs whose wages do not move them out of poverty (Burtless, 1995), which reflects the outcomes of the previously mentioned welfare-to-work experiments (Gueron, 1987).

This indicates a two-tiered problem that welfare recipients will encounter. First, as discussed by Blank (1995), the work skills of welfare recipients will limit their job prospects to the low end of the services sector, where, according to Bureau of Labor employment projections, jobs in cleaning services, as home health aides and nursing aides, as well as in retail, mostly in grocery stores, will occur (U.S. Department of Labor, 1995). Not only will these jobs require social support subsidies for health and child care, but cash assistance may also be required for periods of involuntary unemployment. For example, according to a U.S. Bureau of Labor Statistics study, 30% to 40% of African-American workers remained unemployed 3 years after being laid off from firms that were downsizing (Walker, 1996). Second, in order to compete for jobs that pay a family wage, recipients will require assistance to markedly improve their job skills. Some think such skills upgrading will be a long-term project, and the welfare-to-work experiments noted earlier indicate that the government is not effective in enhancing the skills of welfare recipients. Moreover, this "skills game" refers not only to basic math, reading, and writing, but also to work habits, language, dress, and the ability to interact with clients and customers (Pouncy & Mincy, 1995).

As some studies indicate, however, emphasis on the "skills game" implies it is the worker who is the problem, whereas the realities of the economy point to the supply of jobs, the changing relationship between employer and employee, and earnings trends in the low-skills sector of the economy. For example, according to Newman (1995), in Harlem, New York, an inner-city community, there were 14 persons applying for every fast-food job opening. Moreover, working up the career ladder in these situations was markedly limited and next to useless in using the job skills in securing better-paying jobs in other private industry. Some analysts of the economy see a trend toward less investment in workers and fewer opportunities for advancement by employers.

"Outsourcing" has become a catchword for loss of permanent jobs, a powerless labor force, and fewer fringe benefits, all in the name of becoming "more competitive." There has been a significant expansion of the use of temporary or contract workers (Kuttner, 1997), in some instances by the very same companies that are downsizing. Increasingly, a wage-only contract is replacing the former social contract between employer and employee. While this new labor relationship has ostensibly rewarded the high end of the labor market, such as high-technology industries, there has been concomitant increasing wage inequality at the low end of this very same services sector; those with little skill are getting less. It should also be noted that the globalization of the economy relieves American industry of its dependence on American labor, hence economic opportunities are much more geographically dispersed and much less costly to purchase in developing countries. Capital no longer needs as close a connection to labor, even in high-technology sectors (Wolman & Colomosca, 1997). Consequently, a net result of this new services economy will be the need to subsidize not just labor, but also industry in order to retain a mix of jobs in all regions of the country. Moreover, even in these instances where employers are subsidized to remain in a locality, it does not necessarily result in employment opportunities but more so in tax revenues, as is the case with Wall Street in New York City, where, according to a *New York Times* article, "the fortunes of industry and the fortunes of New York diverged" (Johnson, 1997).

A key issue for welfare reform is having accessible jobs in order to promote skills. In terms of jobs in a given local economy, it may not be a skills game but a jobs shell game being played on a global table that occurs. This has significant implications for the low end of the services economy, and for welfare reform's being more than a shill game for the federal government's jettisoning of responsibility for the needy.

REFERENCES

Auletta, K. (1982). *The underclass.* New York: Random House.

Axinn, J., & Levin, H. (1982). *Social welfare: A history of the American response to social need* (4th ed.). New York: Longman.

Bauer, R. A., & Gergen, K. J. (1969). *The study of policy formation.* New York: Free Press.

Blank, R. (1995). Outlook for the U.S. labor market and prospects for low-wage entry jobs. In D. S. Nightingale & R. Haveman (Eds.), *The work alternative* (pp. 33–70). Washington, DC: Urban Institute Press.

Bruno, F. (1957). Social insurance. *Trends in social work* (pp. 257–269). New York: Columbia University Press.

Burtless, G. (1995). Employment prospects for welfare recipients. In D. S. Nightingale & R. Haveman (Eds.), *The work alternative* (pp. 71–106). Washington, DC: Urban Institute Press.

Ellwood, K. (1988). *Poor support.* New York: Basic Books.

Finder, A. (1996, August 25). Welfare clients outnumber jobs they might fill. *New York Times,* pp. A1, A46.

Gueron, J. (1987). Welfare to work programs. *Policy Studies Review, 6*(4), 733–743.

Handler, J. F. (1995). *The poverty of welfare reform.* New Haven, CN: Yale University Press.

Johnson, K. (1997, March 7). Wall Street leads, but New York economy doesn't follow. *New York Times,* pp. B1, B6.

Joint Center for Political and Economic Studies. (1993). *Neglected voices: What low-income Americans think of welfare reform. Advanced summary.* Washington, DC: Joint Center for Political and Economic Studies.

Katz, M. (1986). *In the shadow of the poorhouse.* New York: Basic Books.

Katz, M. (1989). *The undeserving poor.* New York: Pantheon Books.

Keyserling, L. (1979). The problem of high unemployment. *Policy Studies Journal, 8*(6), 349–358.

Kuttner, R. (1997). *Everything for sale.* New York: Knopf.

McFate, K. (1994). *African American views of the welfare system and welfare reform.* Washington, DC: Joint Center for Political and Economic Studies.

McFate, K. (1995). *Making welfare work.* Washington, DC: Joint Center for Political and Economic Studies.

McLaughlin, M. (1997). Toward real welfare reform. In A. J. Carten & J. R. Dumpson (Eds.), *Removing risks from children* (pp. 83–112). Silver Spring, MD: Beckham House Publishers.

Mead, L. (1994). Poverty: How little we know. *Social Service Review, 68*(3), 222–250.

Moynihan, P. (1973). *The politics of a guaranteed income: The Nixon administration and the Family Assistance Plan.* New York: Random House.

Newman, K. (1988). *Falling from grace.* New York: Free Press.

Newman, K. (1995). Dead end jobs. *The Brookings Review, 13*(4), 24–27.

1992 Green book. U.S. House of Representatives: Committee on Ways and Means. Washington, DC: Government Printing Office.

1996 Green book. U.S. House of Representatives: Committee on Ways and Means. Washington, DC: Government Printing Office.

Pavetti, L. (1995) *Questions and answers on welfare dynamics.* Washington, DC: Urban Institute.

Pouncy, H., & Mincy, R. B. (1995). Off-welfare strategies for welfare bound youth. In D. S. Nightingale & R. Haveman (Eds.), *The welfare alternative* (pp. 157–183). Washington, DC: Urban Institute.

Steiner, G. (1971). *The state of welfare.* Washington, DC: Brookings Institute.

Sundquist, J. L. (1969). For the poor, opportunity. *Politics and policy* (pp. 111–154). Washington, DC: Brookings Institute.

Uchitelle, L. (1997, April 1). Welfare recipients taking jobs often held by the working poor. *New York Times,* pp. A1, A16.

U.S. Department of Health and Human Services. (September 1995). *Report to the Congress on out-of-wedlock childbearing* (DHHS Publication No. (PHS)95-1257). Washington, DC: Government Printing Office.

U.S. Department of Labor: Bureau of Labor Statistics. (December 1995). *Employment outlook: 1994–2005.* Bulletin 2472. Washington, DC: Government Printing Office.

Walker, B. S. (1996, September). Pink slips downsizing African Americans. *Emerge, 7,* 50–57.

Wilson, W. J. (1985). Cycles of deprivation and the underclass. *Social Service Review, 59*(4), 541–559.

Wolman, W., & Colomosca, A. (1997). *The Judas economy.* New York: Addison-Wesley.

Yankelovich, D. (1994). How changes in the economy are reshaping American values. In H. J. Aaron, T. E. Mann, & T. Taylor, (Eds.), *Values and public policy* (pp. 16–53). Washington, DC: Brookings Institute.

3

The Ramifications of Welfare Reform on Vulnerable Populations

Shirley Better, DSW

No OTHER RECENT SOCIAL WELFARE POLICY ENACTMENT has so closely linked the human service professional and the public welfare recipient than the 1996 Welfare Reform Act. In no other time in the recent past have the fates of both been so intricately tied. Both groups, who have been allies and estranged partners, are now joined at the hip as they muddle through an uncharted journey toward economic self-sufficiency for the poor. Public welfare workers, welfare recipients, and others must now reassess their roles and status in this market economy. This chapter reviews the particulars of this social legislation and suggests a proactive role for human service workers.

While the title chosen for this chapter is academically correct, I considered others, for example, "The War on Poverty Has Resumed: Human Service Workers Rescue the Truly Disadvantaged!" I was immediately prepared to see every aspect of the new welfare policy as an unmitigated disaster for the poor; however, all is not lost. Liberals and conservatives alike want to reduce the concomitant shortcomings and evils of governmental dependency: a permanent underclass, lowered self-esteem, social stigmatization. Some conservatives suggest that the increase in single parenthood can be laid at the feet of welfare, as it encourages undesirable behavior in women. Further, it is suggested that there has been a disappearance of the work ethic among the poor because of governmental dependency. I will suggest later that institutional racism and structural poverty are also responsible for some of the above social ills.

The central goal of assisting the poor into jobs is a worthy one, even if legislated paths to get there are often relentlessly unfair. It is suggested that social workers and others must cull from this radical shift in social legislation those aspects that can be modified to meet the needs of the poor.

THE CREATION OF PRA

Let us begin with a brief overview of the forces that spurred the creation of HR 3734, the Personal Responsibility and Work Opportunity Reconciliation Act of 1996 (PRA).

Political Ramifications

The country has shifted from a liberal ideology that the government should maintain a benevolent role to the unfortunate, that tax dollars should be used to provide an economic floor for the disadvantaged—the Social Security Act of 1935. With the advent of the Reagan-Bush administration in 1981, the federal government moved to a conservative stance which held the view that too many resources were being transferred from the taxpayers to a nonproductive group, welfare recipients. Put another way, the economy was being hurt by too much of our resources leaving the GNP to support a dependent class.

Over the next 25 years, billions were cut from the public welfare portion—AFDC, food stamps, and Medicaid—of the Social Security Act. AFDC, school lunch programs, food stamps, housing subsidies, and employment and training programs were reduced by 40% during 1981 and 1982, and by another 19% in 1983. A harsher view of the poor themselves and of programs created to assist them was adopted by some in Congress and other governmental arenas. In many ways, the nation has moved from treatment of poverty to punishment of indigence. The election of the Reagan-Bush administration was only the most recent manifestation of this shift. Vernon Van Dyke states:

> The shift toward mandatory "workfare" and "learnfare" began before Reagan entered the White House and culminated in the Family Support Act of 1988, which he signed and which imposes obligations on those receiving aid and thus attempts to put disci-

pline and a sense of responsibility into their lives. The act involves the paradox that an administration hostile to big government and dedicated to liberty called for the use of government in a paternalistic and authoritarian effort to enforce social mores on the poor. (1995, p. 179)

Economic Changes

Technological and economic changes represented by the global marketplace have had a tremendous effect on how Americans view themselves in relation to the rest of the world. We do not feel as confident as we did even 10 years ago about our ability to compete with other countries. We worry about whether we will lose our jobs to global forces. White-collar workers and some professionals have been stunned by the rapidity of losing their jobs to the downsizing of the 1990s, another economic force influenced by the global marketplace. And 1997 turned out to be an economic bonanza for American businesses, but not for the American worker.

The effects of a global marketplace may also be felt in the American stock market and by the American investor. As I write, the stock market has dropped more than 500 points in one day, and economic pundits are suggesting that the country is in for a major correction. Certainly there is now uncertainty for many small investors and the upper middle class, who have entered the market in large numbers in the last 4 years. The volatility of the stock market is increasing the incertitude of American citizens.

There is a growing gap in personal income between the social classes. This is not a new phenomenon; this growing gap has been noted since the 1980s. Finally, the ranks of the poor are still unacceptably high; the overall poverty level in the United States in 1995 was 14.7%. A 1998 United Nations report documents that the United States, with the highest per capita income in buying capability among the 17 ranked countries, also has the highest level of poverty (United Nations Development Program, 1998).

Social Ramifications

Do the growing gap in personal income and the chaotic economic climate contribute to a change in the nature of the social contract among American citizens? The answer is a resounding yes. The growing physical and emotional separation between the socioeconomic classes is contributing to changing attitudes. America is becoming more segregated into separate worlds. While there has always been some separation in living spaces, this is becoming more pronounced as the middle and upper classes flee to gated communities within the cities. This has accompanied the flight since the 1960s of the more affluent to the suburbs. Even the racial minorities are increasingly separated in their living spaces according to socioeconomic status. This separation is reducing the feeling of sympathy or empathy for the disadvantaged. The term "empathy fatigue" is appropriate—it was coined by international relief workers to denote the state of emotional numbness and disregard that seemed to descend on countries and their citizens after repeated famines throughout the world.

This same sense of empathy fatigue seems to be at play in our country today. And because personal contact is so limited, it is easier for the middle class to accept that the poor are responsible for their poverty. Further, the middle class is so concerned about its own economic security that there is little psychic energy left over to identify with the poor.

A brief review of the general provisions of the 1996 Welfare Reform Act follows (concentrating on several of the provisions that have the most serious impact on the most vulnerable among the poor):

1. Temporary Assistance for Needy Families (TANF)—Replaces AFDC with one block grant to states that combines AFDC, administration, AFDC–Emergency Assistance, and JOBS.
2. Five-year limit—Families are limited to 5 years on assistance in a lifetime, but 20% of caseload may be exempted.
3. Teen parents—Teen parents must live in an "adult supervised setting" and stay in school to receive payments.
4. Child care—Title IV-A Child Care folded into Child Care Development Block Grant. Child care funding has been increased nationally, but there are no guarantees of sufficient child care for mandatory work/training participants.
5. Drug felons—Those who have been convicted of a drug felony are prohibited from receiving aid.

6. Work requirements—Parents *must* work after 24 months on aid; may be required to work sooner. Able-bodied adults must be involved in seeking or training for jobs.
7. Legal immigrants—Current recipients are ineligible for SSI and food stamps. Exceptions include refugees and aliens in first 5 years in United States, persons with FICA earnings in 40 quarters, and veterans.
8. Child support—States must eliminate assistance to a caretaker who refuses to cooperate in obtaining child support.
9. Loss of benefits—The head of the family must find work within 2 years, or the family will lose cash benefits.

Current State of Poverty in America

The ramifications of the goal of economic self-sufficiency will be first examined through some current statistics of the welfare rolls. There are two areas to examine: (1) the number of persons who have left the rolls, and (2) the lack of hard data on what has happened to those individuals.

The White House reported that the welfare rolls dropped nationally by 1.4 million people between August 1996 and May 1997, a decrease of nearly 12% (Rosin & Harris, 1999). An August 1998 report by the Manpower Research Development Corp. stated that the welfare rolls had dropped by 27% nationwide since the enactment of welfare reform 2 years earlier (Rivera & Healy, 1998). Some have called this decline totally unprecedented in the history of welfare. All of which leads us to ask: Where did those 2 million people go? The only national study to date, a statistical analysis by the President's Council of Economic Advisers in the fall of 1997, estimated that 44% of the decline was due to improved economic conditions and 31% to welfare reforms, primarily tougher work requirements (75%) (New York Times News Service, 1998). As for the other 25%, the Council of Economic Advisers admitted that it did not have a clue. No one else has done a thorough analysis either. Public Welfare Departments across the country plead lack of funds to do such an analysis. However, local welfare agency officials know that negative statistics could be used against them. Thus we find that most states have not studied what has happened to those who have lost aid.

The Manpower Research Development Corp. concluded, after a 6-month study, that there had been a significant drop in the welfare rolls in Los Angeles County. With a 725,000-person welfare caseload, Los Angeles County is larger than any state except California and New York. The study found that 43% of welfare recipients who participated in Greater Avenues for Independence (GAIN), a workfare program, found jobs, compared to 32% of those not involved in workfare. However, it has been harder to move minority females off welfare; nationally, there has been a slower decrease in metropolitan areas.

Further, while personal income is higher for those working, few welfare recipients earn enough to rise above poverty levels. Thus they continue to be eligible for food stamps, Medicaid, and other welfare programs. Experts were concerned that this report would be received cautiously because the gains were mostly due to the surging economy and low unemployment rates. One can only wonder what the experts would say now that the stock market and the economy are showing signs of volatility.

Those who are declaring the welfare reform a success based on these early statistics are betraying a startling amnesia regarding what the welfare reform proponents hoped to accomplish by the dramatic change in "welfare as we know it." The law would do much more than just withdraw aid from the poor and force them into any available job. Its goal was economic self-sufficiency: moving welfare recipients into living-wage jobs. All the new welfare legislation can really guarantee is that if a recipient does not work (at whatever job he or she is assigned to), the recipient will not get benefits. There is a 5-year lifetime limit on receiving aid for able-bodied adults.

We can extrapolate some of the ramifications for the poor who have no safety net. A December 1997 survey of the Los Angeles Coalition to End Hunger and Homelessness offers a sign of the possibilities. Of nearly 300 people who visited local food pantries from September through November of that year, 42% reported that it was their first time in 6 months (Los Angeles Times Staff Writers, 1998). Nationally, 86% of cities surveyed by the U.S. Conference of Mayors in 1997 reported an increase in demand for emergency food assistance: "On average, requests for food at soup kitchens and food pantries had risen by 16%, and

38% of those seeking emergency food aid were employed, according to the Conference of Mayors, up from 23% in 1994" (Healy & Pasternak, 1997). The soup line is a known indicator of the direst economic circumstances for the poor. This is at a time when unemployment in America has hit a 20-year low! Some of those opposed to the new welfare policy may want to claim that this rise in food requests is due to the new law. However, the new welfare law is not yet fully implemented and cannot by itself cause this increase. If we are enjoying the lowest unemployment rate in 20 years, and former welfare recipients can only account for a portion of those seeking emergency food now, what will happen when the welfare recipient attempts to enter the job market? What will be the chances for new workers when present workers at the lowest rungs of the work ladder are unable to make ends meet in the best economic climate we have had in 20 years? And there are dark clouds on the horizon as world markets are experiencing downturns.

Some economists expect that the downside of an expanding supply of new workers will be a depression of wages and an early return to the welfare rolls (Mink, 1998). Another problem is that too few employers offer on-the-job training programs to help entry-level workers rise into more highly skilled positions. The first job may be as good as it gets. Continued poverty is likely to be the fate of most welfare recipients who will find work in relatively low-paying jobs.

RAMIFICATIONS OF WELFARE REFORM

I want to provide a two-pronged approach to looking at the inherent roadblocks that accompany welfare reform: institutional racism and the barriers to economic self-sufficiency.

Institutional Racism

American minority groups are disproportionately represented in the ranks of the poor. This group will be heavily affected by welfare reform; they are the "truly disadvantaged," as Wilson (1987) calls them, for they are not only poor, but isolated and stigmatized as well. In a book I am completing, entitled *Institutional Racism: A Primer on Theory and Strategies for Social Change,* one chapter discusses my theory that there is a mutual interchange among the major social institutions that reinforces inequality for racial/ethnic minority groups. The theory avers that racism acts like an invisible web that interconnects the major social institutions—housing, education, employment, and politics.

Through institutions' policies, practices, and procedures, racial/ethnic minorities are inextricably caught in a system that routinely metes out lesser portions of the rewards that each of these institutions offers. For example, poor minority members are trapped in de facto apartheid as it relates to housing in America. They find themselves living in areas that are labeled ghettos, barrios, and reservations. These living areas have an overabundance of underemployment and crime, and inadequate housing stock and open space. The areas spawn despair. The communities maintain children in close contact with a myriad of unhealthy elements in the community—gangs, drug dealing, and so forth. Since America uses as its medium for public education the neighborhood school, poor minority children are mandated to these schools, which have been documented as below par. An inferior education reduces the chances of qualifying for a living-wage job. The above scenario is an example of the interconnection between three major social institutions—housing, education, and employment.

This same interchange of negative policies and procedures within social institutions influences the life chances of the poor, who are disproportionally minorities. However, we must often be reminded that the majority of poor in America continue to be white. The new welfare reform, if shaped only by the market economy and/or structural racism, will not bode well for any of our citizens.

BARRIERS TO ECONOMIC SELF-SUFFICIENCY

Let us examine in detail the apparent barriers that welfare recipients will have to overcome along with institutional racism and structural poverty.

Job Creation

It is possible that a sizable number of former AFDC recipients will be able to find jobs. For a crucial number, though, this will not be the case. What needs to be considered is what is meant by a "job." Public Welfare Departments across the country freely admit that their mandate is to get recipients employed at any job, even if at minimum wage.

First, where are these jobs to come from for poorly educated and untrained individuals? In California, recent immigrants from Mexico, Central America, and parts of Asia have occupied the low-wage jobs at the bottom of the economic ladder; often they are paid below the minimum wage. Any day of the week, we see in California and other parts of the country Latino males (many are legal residents) standing on the street corners soliciting a day's work. Many individuals are unable to find steady employment at even below the minimum wage.

Second, there is the inherent danger that no one seems to be focusing on: the temptation of exploitation. There will be some unscrupulous employers who will recognize that they can make a profit hiring individuals who are desperate for a job at well below the minimum wage. Who is to ensure the quality of working conditions? We have read of the group of Asians in El Monte, California, who were held as virtual slaves working in a sweatshop making garments piecemeal. We read the story of the deafmutes from Mexico who were also virtual slaves selling trinkets on the streets of New York City. Are we prepared to see more of this? Another major issue that has barely surfaced is the competition with established unions that will be created by the welfare-to-work program.

Third, we need to examine the quality of the job. When we speak of jobs available for women forced off welfare, often we are speaking of jobs in which they may work less than 20 hours in any given week. When we speak of a job, consideration must be given to how many hours they will work a week, at what wages, and under what sorts of working conditions. In the California's welfare-to-work program, GAIN, politicians in the early 1990s emphasized the number of mothers who were "working" as a result of going through the program. However, officials did not acknowledge that recipients were employed primarily at minimum-wage jobs, and often for no more than 20 hours per week. During this time, recipients maintained their Medicaid card, food stamps, and cash benefits. That experience, if repeated in the new welfare-to-work programs, will hardly qualify as economic self-sufficiency.

Fourth, a great concern of Public Welfare staff I have talked with is what is called in some states "post-employment services." This program's mandate is assisting recipients in staying on the job and moving up to a better job with a living wage. Many states are developing collaborations with private industries to determine how jobs for this population can be located or created and then maintained. The concern expressed regards the competency of the welfare staff to accomplish their mission. Under the most optimum conditions, there are some high hurdles the recipients will need to leap over, such as poor health, lack of marketable skills, poor job preparedness, and illiteracy.

Transportation

Many of the skilled and low-skilled jobs have moved to the suburbs, reducing the number of jobs available to persons living in urban areas. A large percentage of welfare recipients dwell in the inner city. Further, some cities (e.g., Los Angeles) have poor mass transit systems, adding to the difficulty of the working public. However, we are seeing more and more community organizations tackling this problem across the country, many successfully. For example, Job Express, located in Chicago, is a plan of Suburban Job-Link Corporation. It "works by removing two of the main obstacles to steady employment: lack of reliable transportation and lack of information about job openings" (Bardoe, 1996, p. 19).

Wage Levels

This is the highest risk for many recipients: Can they make a living for their family? Many are very frightened of this. Being forced to go to work is often accepted well—the fear is, what will happen to me and my children if I don't make enough money? There is a new reality for poor people. They are finding out a hard truth about the new American economy: it has become dangerously reliant on workers whose labor does not command a living wage. Capitalism chases cheap labor. I calculate that for a single female with two children under the age of 5 years, it would take an annual income of $17,000 to adequately meet basic living expenses and to be slightly above the poverty level. That would mean a job earning approximately $8.85 per hour. To get this level of wages, a female would need to have some technical skills and possibly be computer literate. Thus, bringing this mythical welfare recipient out of poverty is going to require training—training that is being discouraged in some states, notably California.

Child Care

There is good news and bad news in this area. The good news is that the federal government and most states have increased the funds available for child care. Many states are paying child care costs to the recipient or directly to the provider based on the regional market rate. This functions positively in two ways for women. First, younger women can go to school or to a job and be provided with funds to hire whomever they want to care for their kids. Second, some recipients (e.g., older females) may opt to become child care providers, thus gaining full-time employment. Already at least 29 states have welfare-to-day-care training programs. If each state ensures that all child care providers are required to receive some training in early childhood development, this may work well. It should be emphasized that we must seek a policy change that mandates some training in early childhood development as a requirement to participate in home-based child care. California is gearing up to meet a projected shortfall of 150,00 day care slots by encouraging all segments of the community to become involved, including churches and neighborhood organizations. A 1998 article in the *Los Angeles Times* states: "As an enticement, the first 1,700 new providers will receive up to $250 worth of toys, smoke alarms and other start-up equipment in exchange for attending about eight hours of county-sponsored classes. State licensing, which allows providers legally to care for as many as eight young children on their own, requires an additional 15 hours of health and safety training" (Dickerson, 1998, p. A14). The bad news is that many local welfare departments are having difficulty setting the process in motion. A recent study, one of the first to examine the child care practices of southern California's Latino community, stated that many Latinas would use licensed child care centers if they were available; however, they are not. In fact, more than 60% of the Latina mothers surveyed said they had either lost a job or were unable to work because they could not find suitable child care (Tomas Rivera Policy Institute, 1998). Further, the job of child care provider has been notorious for its low wages and high turnover rate. It will be interesting to discover how many women are satisfied to maintain a permanent job as a child care provider.

Recommendations

Stated earlier was an alternative title for this chapter, "The War on Poverty Has Resumed: Human Service Workers Rescue the Truly Disadvantaged!" The negative side of welfare reform is the inadequate preparation (and some would say cynicism) on the part of government as it tackles the task of moving welfare recipients off the welfare rolls. The lack of well-considered practices, polices, and procedures is reminiscent of the web of institutional racism. Persons are and will continue to be caught in these policies, policies that work in tandem in social institutions. These current policies are overwhelming the poor in what we can call a web of urban poverty. This can be forestalled if we in the human services sound the clarion call to establish a system that unravels this web.

The devastating effect of welfare reform may be the lack of collaboration between social institutions and social service agencies that are focusing on the poor—the web of urban poverty.

What Must Be Done?

Unless there are local collaboratives, the legacy of welfare reform will be that persons fall through the cracks in the system.

Local collaboratives would bring all human service agencies to-gether to plan systematically around the needs of the poor (see Figure 3.1).

The goal of the collaboratives must be more than a focus on minimum-wage jobs, but one which ensures that policy deci-sions across social service agencies operate in ways to enhance the ability of the vulnerable to move to self-sufficiency. Unfortu-nately, this cannot be done inexpensively. The human service practitioners must spearhead the development of these collabo-ratives. Not all collaboratives will be shaped the same, but they should reflect the uniqueness of the needs in the local commu-nity. We will need to increase our skill in bridging the many disciplines that focus on the poor in some fashion; however, so-cial workers are well skilled for this task.

Along with the local collaboratives, we must ensure a safety net within the public assistance framework. Some professionals in the field of public assistance suggest that the state develop a single integrated safety net that pools federal, state, and county resources as an alternative to the current system under which local governments, by default, must aid any indigent resident

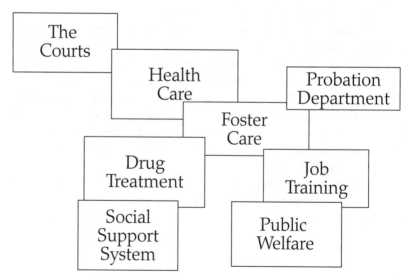

FIGURE 3.1. LOCAL COLLABORATIVES TO COMBAT STRUCTURAL POVERTY

who loses eligibility for federal/state benefits. In California this is called "General Relief"; it provides $212 per month. The state-wide safety net should include the following provisions:

1. It should cover hardship cases, such as families with abused or neglected children, the disabled, emancipated foster youth at risk of homelessness, children of parents who are not readily employable, and those beyond the 5-year limit.
2. The state must provide for those families who may be disqualified from receiving aid and food stamps due to drug-related convictions.
3. The state must provide localities with a level playing field by establishing work requirements that take into account unemployment rates, job availability, and the availability of job training, child care, and other services with which to assist recipients to work.
4. The state must develop tax incentives and economic benefits targeted to both large and small employers who hire welfare recipients.
5. The state must ensure the adequacy and availability of child care funds to support recipient needs as determined by work participation rates.

These are only a few examples of in-depth policy practices we must create if this new social welfare policy is not to create the sort of havoc that was created, for example, by the deinstitutionalization of the mentally ill and the failure of the development of community-based mental health care services.

CONCLUSION

Human service workers will need to use this opportunity of revolutionary change in the role of government to renew the profession. This renewal can be done by showing our ability to meet the challenge of the 1996 Welfare Reform Act. We will need to put the needs of the poor first and use our professional training to restitch the safety net.

REFERENCES

Bardoe, C. (1996). *Employment strategies for urban communities.* Chicago: Neighborhood Works.

Dickerson, M. (1998, August 12). A new army of child-care workers. *Los Angeles Times*, p. A14.

Healy, M., & Pasternak, J. (1997, December 27). New face in line at soup kitchen: Working poor. *Los Angeles Times*, p. 10.

Los Angeles Times Staff Writers. (1998, August 22). Official business/courts and government: Welfare-to-work study flawed, group says. *Los Angeles Times*, Metro, p. 2.

Mink, G. (1998). *Welfare's end.* Ithaca, NY: Cornell University Press.

New York Times News Service. (1998, January 21). Welfare rolls are smallest in 25 years. *Chicago Tribune*, p. 6.

Rivera, C., & Healy, M. (1998, August 20). L.A. County succeeding in bid to get poor off aid. *Los Angeles Times*, p. 1.

Rosin, H. & Harris, J. (1999, August 3). Welfare reform is on a roll: Working poor still struggle, study says. *Los Angeles Times*, p. 5.

Tomas Rivera Policy Institute. (1998). *Child-care needs of Latina mothers.* Clairmont: California Wellness Foundation.

United Nations Development Program. (1998). *Human development report.* New York: Oxford University Press.

Van Dyke, V. (1995). *Ideology and political choice.* Chatham, NJ: Chatham House Publishers.

Wilson, J. W. (1987). *The truly disadvantaged.* Chicago: University of Chicago Press.

4

A Society for All Ages: Older Adults and the Social Contract

*Patricia Brownell, PhD, and
Marilynn Moch, PhD*

Introduction

THE AGING OF SOCIETY is a global phenomenon. In developing as well as post-industrial nations, the population is aging at a historically unprecedented rate. The increase in the overall number of older adults as well as the ratio of the aging population to other segments of society has raised concerns about drains on limited resources and—in the United States—the sustainability of social welfare institutions like Social Security into the 21st century (Binstock, 1998).

This chapter will discuss the implications of an aging global society within the context of the Code of Ethics of the National Association of Social Workers (1996), the International Declaration of Human Rights (1948), and the conceptual framework of the 1999 International Year of Older Persons. We believe that older people are a resource in all societies and that they are yet to be fully tapped. Older people have the knowledge, skills, cultural heritage, and life experience that can and should be used to help all societies accommodate the unprecedented aging of the world population (Sidorenko, 1998).

At the same time, old age is correlated with chronic disabilities that may require reciprocity of caregiving and support from the younger generation to the old. This is the social contract that has been observed informally generation after generation, and which was legislated in the United States as part of the Social

Security Act in 1935 and again in 1965 with the establishment of Medicare (Axinn & Levin, 1997).

In a Senate debate over the Personal Responsibility and Work Opportunity Reconciliation Act of 1996 (PRA), Senator Daniel Patrick Moynihan stated that if we can abandon our children by changing Aid to Families With Dependent Children from an entitlement to a block grant, our elderly will be next. The PRA represents the beginning of devolution as family policy (M. Waterman, personal communication, November 30, 1998).

DEMOGRAPHICS OF AGING

As a worldwide phenomenon, aging is more evident in post-industrial countries but occurring more rapidly in developing countries. In 1994 there were nearly 500 million people aged 60 and above, and by 2025 the number is expected to reach 1.2 billion, 14% of the global population. Of these, 137 million will be those known as the "old-old," 80 years of age and above (Motsinger & Smith, 1991).

While the total world population is expected to increase by a factor of three between 1950 and 2025, the number of those over 60 is expected to increase by a factor of ten. In the United States, the fastest-growing age group is those 85 and older. This is the age at which most people will experience one or more debilitating health problems. The most pressing and treatable health problems of older persons throughout the world, including the United States, are "related to heart functions, hearing, teeth, diabetes, visual impairment and osteoporosis" (United Nations, 1994, p. 1). To these may be added the mental problems caused by social isolation and depression, and Alzheimer's disease and related neurological disorders. Not only are the health costs increasing with larger numbers of older persons, but the social costs of caring for the disabled and old-old fall heavily on families, especially women (World Health Organization, 1991).

Although there is a trend toward more years of potentially productive life, forced retirement, scattered families, and social norms that exclude the elderly rob society of their contributions and too often lead to increases in physical and mental illnesses that increase the costs of elder care. The World Health Organization (WHO) concluded that it is not at all clear whether sickness and disability have declined parallel with mortality rates. According to WHO (1991), increased longevity has been accompanied by disability, reducing the quality of life and increasing the need for health and social services.

In the United States, the voting power of older adults (with the support of their adult children who, until the 1960s, were required to contribute to their support if these older adults were unable to manage on their own) has expanded institutionalized social welfare programs for older persons. This has resulted in a financial support system of Social Security and Medicare that has reduced the over-65 poverty rate to 10.8% (U.S. House of Representatives, 1998).

Although this rate is low compared to that of the population at large—especially children, who have a poverty rate of 20.5% (U.S. House of Representatives, 1998)—race, ethnicity, gender, and marital status define subgroups of elders whose poverty rate far exceeds that of the general population. Older single women of African descent, for example, have a poverty rate of almost 60% (U.S. House of Representatives, 1994). In a study of older persons in New York City in the 1990s, the average income of African-American subjects exceeded that of their Latino counterparts, suggesting that elder deprivation among that ethnic group is even more severe (Cantor & Brennan, 1993).

DEVOLUTION AND OLDER PERSONS IN THE UNITED STATES

"Devolution in the most general terms refers to pushing more power out to state and local governments from the federal government" (P.A. Times, 1997, p. 1). Since 1994, with the publication of the Contract With America, devolution has been debated as shaping the future of government on the national, state, and local levels (P.A. Times, 1997).

The more affluent elderly were not directly affected by federal legislation emanating from the Contract With America agenda. In fact, through the Contract With America Advancement Act of 1996, working older Social Security recipients were advantaged through tax easements, at the expense of disentitling end-stage alcoholics and substance abusers from Supplemental Security Income. However, the immigrant elderly became prime targets for cuts in social welfare benefits through the immigrant provisions of the PRA, apparently because they were considered a nonvoting and therefore expendable population from whom considerable savings could be wrested.

As a result of the PRA, Supplemental Security Income (SSI), Medicaid, and food stamps would be denied for most legal immigrants until they became U.S. citizens. The Congressional Budget Office (1996) has estimated that by 2002 approximately 260,000 elderly legal noncitizen immigrants, including those receiving SSI, would be denied Medicaid under the new law. Through pressure from the voting adult children of many of these elderly, as well as state and local officials fearful of having to pay for their care, some of the most egregious aspects of this legislation were suspended for the immigrant elderly already in the United States through the passage of the Balanced Budget Act of 1997. However, the PRA remains in place for immigrants arriving after August 27, 1996, and subsequent legislation raised the income limits to sponsor new immigrants, making it more difficult for families to sponsor aging parents (U.S. House of Representatives, 1998).

A current pressing legislative agenda item for Congress is the Social Security Trust Fund. The first of the post–World War II babies are now beginning to enter their fifties. Based on projections of the aging of baby boomers, the Social Security Trust Fund as currently formulated will begin to run a serious shortfall between 2013 (Concord Coalition, 1998) and 2035 (American Association of Retired Persons, 1998). According to many policy analysts, the Social Security Trust Fund will continue to be viable throughout the next millennium with some adjustments related to contribution formulas, immigrant patterns, and benefits adjustments, as well as minor changes in age and salary cap for taxation purposes (Fierst, 1997).

Those seeking to benefit from more radical changes in the Social Security program are attempting to influence public opinion about its viability in the years ahead. Most notably, proponents of individualism and personal responsibility are suggesting that wage earners should be able to choose to invest their Social Security or FICA taxes in individual accounts that can be invested in high-interest-earning stocks (Shipman, 1997). This would effectively break the intergenerational social contract, established during the New Deal, that each working generation would pay into the Social Security Trust Fund for the generation preceding them, and subsequent generations will do the same for them. If this proposal were to become policy, it would have the effect of bringing devolution down to the individual level. The volatility of the marketplace and the sporadic attachment to the labor market for many low-wage earners, particularly women and minorities, make the privatizing of the Social Security program a serious threat to the well-being of this generation of older adults and of generations to come (Fierst, 1997).

A related proposal involves moving to a voucher system for Medicare. The cost of health care is increasing faster than inflation, and the Medicare Trust Fund is expected to begin running a deficit soon after the year 2000. Proponents of this approach to ensuring health care coverage into old age argue that establishing vouchers would "decentralize authority over Medicare; individuals, rather than government, would make decisions about the type of health coverage [that] was best for them" (Oberlander, 1999, p. 203). Critics of this approach argue that vouchers would undermine the universal nature of the Medicare social insurance program. The resulting fragmentation would weaken the support of maintaining and improving program benefits for the public insurance program if the wealthy opt out of Medicare for private insurance. This could leave the public Medicare program with a sicker insurance pool, fewer revenues, and more inequality of care (Oberlander, 1999).

INTERNATIONAL PERSPECTIVES ON AGING

Throughout the world, people are not only living longer, but are living "more successfully" as well (Rowe & Kahn, 1998). As a result, older persons are an important resource for intergenerational families, as community volunteers, and as a productive, experienced, and stable workforce. However, the continued perception of older persons as a drain on productive resources lies behind attitudes and policies toward older persons similar to the anti-immigrant legislation in the United States—and worse. In Germany, legislation was introduced to remove voting privileges from older people, the argument being that since there were so many of them, they would force elected officials to support their needs at the expense of the rest of society. In Nigeria, when food was scarce, allowing the old to die from starvation was seen as acceptable because it made more food available for others. In the United States, cutting publicly funded health benefits for the elderly who cannot afford to pay for all of their own care is nearly universally accepted as a necessary cost-cutting measure. We need to step back and take a new look. We need to find another way.

THE NATIONAL ASSOCIATION OF SOCIAL WORKERS (NASW) CODE OF ETHICS

Section Six of the NASW Code of Ethics charges social workers with the responsibility for working toward the general welfare of society. This includes working for social policies that benefit vulnerable populations not only in the United States, but in the global community as well. A new section of the Code of Ethics, revised effective January 1997, charges social workers for the first time with becoming involved politically to change or support social welfare policies that ensure the well-being of all people, not just those who are advantaged (NASW, 1996).

INTERNATIONAL DECLARATION OF HUMAN RIGHTS

The International Declaration of Human Rights, signed in 1948, is an important statement of principles that all governments and people throughout the world should observe (United Nations, 1948). The principles of the Declaration affirm the rights of all people to live in dignity and free of oppression. The article of the Declaration that is most pertinent to a discussion of the responsibility of government and communities to ensure the well-being of all people is Article 25: "Everybody has a right to a standard of living adequate for the health and well-being of himself and his family, including food, clothing, housing and medical care and necessary social services, and the right to security in the event of unemployment, sickness, disability, widowhood, old age or other lack of livelihood in circumstances beyond his control."

This important document, signed by representatives of the international community—including the United States—in the wake of atrocities committed during World War II, defined universal human rights as including rights to housing, food, and medical care (Witkin, 1998). These are rights that social workers have fought for since the profession's beginning in the Progressive era, and they are yet to be realized (Witkin, 1998). The debate about human rights, the long-term viability of social welfare programs that sustain people into productive old age, and the individual cost of sustaining these programs that are intended to benefit a community of people, not just a privileged few, is not just specific to the United States. It is really an international one.

Although the United States has signed the Declaration, Congress has yet to ratify any of the Conventions that provide the specific implementation guidelines and allow compliance to be monitored. These include the Convention on the Rights of the Child and the Women's Convention, which would provide more accurate international monitoring on the status of older women. The debate about devolution in the United States involves not only the question of the extent to which it is the responsibility of government to provide for such economic and social rights (as opposed to civil rights often incorporated into foreign aid and political decisions), but also the extent to which such issues come under the purview of the states, not the federal government.

INTERNATIONAL YEAR OF OLDER PERSONS (IYOP) 1999

In 1992, the United Nations General Assembly decided "to observe the year 1999 as the International Year of Older Persons

(IYOP) . . . in recognition of humanity's demographic coming of age and the promise it holds for maturing attitudes and capacities in social, economic, cultural and spiritual undertakings, not least for global peace and development into the next century" (United Nations General Assembly, 1992). The theme selected for the year, "Towards a Society for All Ages," is one that enables the generations to invest in one another and share in the fruits of that investment, guided by the twin principles of reciprocity and equity (United Nations, 1998). IYOP plans and activities conceptualized older persons as integral members of society and as integrated with those in other stages of the life cycle. According to Julia Alvarez, UN delegate from the Dominican Republic, it is essential to integrate older people into society and not segregate them; otherwise everyone in society will lose and no one will win.

Two criteria for realizing this integration were given by UN Secretary-General Kofi Annan during the International Day of Older Persons in October 1997 at the United Nations. First, the promotion of lifelong individual development is essential to ensure that people reach old age with life skills, good health, family supports, and vocational experience. Second, nations must create a policy environment in which people of all ages can actively participate in society, receiving care and support when necessary (United Nations, 1997).

In the same forum, Dick von Stanwitz pointed out that the highest incidence of depression in the United States for men is between ages 65 and 70, when they are expected to retire. He stated that the time of retirement should be the launching into a new period when older people can continue to grow. We need to balance the financial preparation that is thought to be so important as we enter the last third of life with the challenge to the young-old to continue to develop and contribute. We need to create the support systems for such a launching.

Jeanne Smith, chair of the United Nations Nongovernmental Committee on Aging for 1996 and 1997, believes that older persons' participation in planning and development activities will contribute greatly to their country's future, but in order to do this they need to be part of the process. According to Smith, planning for older populations frequently takes place somewhere else, without the direct participation of older persons themselves. Participation as a human right is a fundamental value of the Nongovernmental Committee on Aging. To be able to work toward solving one's own problems and to contribute toward one's society's future is not only a privilege, it is a right. Helen Hamlin, retired social worker and chair of the Nongovernmental Committee on Aging effective 1998, further states that the Nongovernmental Committee on Aging wants to be sure that members understand the roles, responsibilities, and needs of older persons as they exist in the community, with full exercise of human rights (United Nations, 1997).

RESEARCH ON SUCCESSFUL AGING

People's capacity to age "successfully" has been demonstrated through research, most recently funded through the McArthur Foundation. Rowe and Kahn (1998) state that lifestyle choices can significantly increase people's health and productivity into old age. This further challenges the notion that old age is synonymous with dependency and need for care. It also emphasizes, however, that the social contract between generations must be maintained to ensure a fair and equitable distribution of resources across the life span to achieve the goal of productive and healthy aging. To quote Robert Browning: "Grow old along with me! / The best is yet to be, the last of life / For which the first was made" (Palgrave, 1953, p. 367).

IMPLICATIONS FOR SOCIAL WORK PRACTICE

The growth of the old-old suggests a continued need for services and resources to support and assist the frail elderly and their families. In addition, immigrant elders and older people from communities of color, which continue to bear disproportionate burdens of poverty and harsh working conditions, require social welfare policies that are sensitive to the differential needs of older people. As noted above, Section Six of the revised NASW Code of Ethics charges social work practitioners with the ethical responsibility to work toward the social welfare of all people (NASW, 1996).

The ecological framework within which social workers practice, along with the NASW Code of Ethics, suggests a multiplicity of practice responses to ensure the optimal well-being of older people and the continuation of the intergenerational social contract forged by the Social Security Act of 1935. These include individual and family interventions to support those families caring for frail elderly members; group and community interventions to ensure that older people continue to play a vital role in their communities; policy advocacy to ensure that intergenerational programs like Social Security remain viable through the 21st century; and participation in the international human rights movement to strive for the full realization of Article 25 of the Universal Declaration of Human Rights (Moch, Motsinger, & Smith, 1996).

Historically, social workers have had a special mission within society to serve the poor and vulnerable (Axinn & Levin, 1997). However, the vitality and health of older people today provide exciting opportunities to utilize the strengths perspective in working with older adults (Saleeby, 1996). In the following section, we review briefly a selection of programs utilizing and building on the skills, knowledge, and wisdom of older adults, programs that reflect the principles of the IYOP and the strengths perspective in social work practice.

EXEMPLARY PROGRAM MODELS

Examples of exemplary program models that utilize and celebrate the unique skills, wisdom, and talents of older adults to benefit their communities and societies are the Retired and Senior Volunteer program (RSVP) and the Retired and Senior Volunteer Program International (RSVPI). These programs are at the cutting edge of the aging revolution. According to RSVPI's executive director, Ann O'Sullivan: "the IYOP helps focus attention on the phenomenon of worldwide population aging [and] the unprecedented social challenges these dramatic demographic changes create. The essential principle upon which RSVP initiatives are built—i.e., that senior volunteers benefit both from their communities and themselves by their contributions—suggests that senior volunteering is a very powerful way to respond to the social challenges creating by the Aging revolution" (O'Sullivan, 1998, p. 1).

Both RSVP and RSVPI support the development of programs nationally and internationally to utilize older adults' ability to contribute to their communities after retirement. The principles upon which RSVP programs are based reflect the four dimensions of the conceptual framework for the IYOP identified by the United Nations (O'Sullivan, 1998). First, RSVP projects represent practical actions supporting the independence, participation, care, and self-fulfillment of older persons. Second, RSVP provides an enabling environment fostering lifelong education, skills upgrading, and healthy lifestyles. Third, RSVP fosters multigenerational relationships. And fourth, RSVP ensures that older persons have opportunities to participate and contribute as well as receive care when needed, establishing a society that fosters reciprocity and equity.

While RSVP programs are based in the United States, RSVPI programs have expanded in the international arena. Programs have been launched in the United Kingdom, Australia, Italy, India, Spain, Africa, Northern Ireland, Hong Kong, Malaysia, and Singapore. Currently a new program is under development in Columbia, South America, with support from the Kellogg Foundation (A. O'Sullivan, personal communication, October 31, 1998). These programs provide opportunities for older people to contribute their talents and knowledge to their communities in ways that are culturally congruent and unique to the countries and cultures in which they live.

Another program that should be highlighted is that of the Third Age Center at Fordham University in New York City. The Third Age Center has begun a successful educational program for older adults that provides opportunities for intellectual stimulation and educational achievement. This innovative program exemplifies the approach to serving the elderly from a strengths perspective, building on what is known about the continuation of learning throughout the lifespan as promoting successful aging (MacQueen, 1996).

Elders Share the Arts, an intergenerational arts program, pairs older adults—often from senior centers—with schoolchildren. The older adults are usually identified from a different ethnic background than the children: the purpose is to begin to break down ageist and ethnic/racial stereotypes on the part of both generations through forging relationships between them using art forms as vehicles.

As an example of one project, older people (whose origins were in the Caribbean) from a senior center were paired with a grade school class of primarily African-American children. The project they chose was for the children to write biographies of the older adults. The children interviewed the senior center members and wrote vignettes about their life histories, focusing on an event or achievement about which the older adult felt proud. These were compiled in a booklet that was distributed to all participants. The project culminated in a party given by the schoolchildren for the older adults at which both brought their favorite records or tapes and taught each other dances from their respective eras (the electric slide and the boogie-woogie) (S. C. Jaffe, personal communication, 1998). This exemplifies the joyous culmination of mutual learning and the gift of sharing between generations.

Conclusion

The initiatives and programs discussed in this chapter are examples of social work practice that celebrate aging and strengthen intergenerational relationships. They are built on the assumption that old age is a phase of life where growth and the ability to contribute to social well-being remain strong and vital. They also serve to remind us how essential it is to continue maintaining and strengthening the social contract across generations. The young of today are the old of tomorrow. Social welfare policies and social work practice based on the vision—grounded in reality—of the healthy and productive older adult can ensure continued progress in achieving the world vision of a society for all ages.

References

American Association of Retired Persons. (1998). *Boomers approaching midlife: How to secure a future?* Washington, DC: AARP Public Policy Institute.

Axinn, J., & Levin, H. (1997). *Social welfare: A history of the American response to need.* New York: Longman.

Binstock, R. H. (1998). Personal responsibility and privatization in public policies in aging. *Public Policy and Aging Report, 9*(2), 6–9.

Cantor, M. H., & Brennan, M. (1993). *Growing older in New York City in the 1990's: A study of changing lifestyles, quality of life and the quality of care* (Vol. 2). New York: New York Center for Policy on Aging of the New York Community Trust.

Concord Coalition. (1998). *Saving social security: A framework for reform.* Vol. 1: *Defining the problem.* Washington, DC: Author:

Congressional Budget Office. (1996). *Budget report.* Washington, DC: Government Printing Office.

Fierst, E. U. (1997). Social security is a safety net. *Critical Issues in Aging, 1,* 8–9.

MacQueen, K. (1996). Third age rising. *Inside Fordham, 30*(2), 31–37.

Moch, M., Motsinger, C., & Smith, J. (1996). *Challenges to older people's economic security around the world. Final report on the sixth annual commemoration of the United Nations International Day of Older Persons: A preparatory event for 1999 International Year of Older Persons, October 3, 1996.* New York: United Nations.

Motsinger, C., & Smith, J. (1991). *Humanity comes of age: Promise or peril? Proceedings of the NGO Committee on Aging Symposium.* New York: United Nations.

National Association of Social Workers. (1996). *Code of Ethics.* Washington, DC: NASW Press.

Oberlander, J. (1999). Vouchers for Medicare: A critical reappraisal. In M. Minkler & C. L. Estes (Eds.), *Critical gerontology: Perspectives from political and moral economy* (pp. 203–220). Amityville, NY: Baywood Publishing Company.

O'Sullivan, A. (1998). 1999: The International Year of Older Persons. *International Exchange, 1*(1), 1–4.

Palgrave, F. T. (Ed.). (1953). *The golden treasury of the best songs and lyrical poems*. New York: New American Library.

P.A. Times. (1997). Devolution: Making it work. *American Society for Public Administration, 20*(4), 1–10.

Rowe, J. W., & Kahn, R. L. (1998). *Successful aging*. New York: Pantheon Books.

Saleeby, D. (1996). The strengths perspective in social work practice: Extensions and cautions. *Social Work, 41*(3), 241–336.

Shipman, W. G. (1997). Retiring with dignity: Social security versus the private markets. *Critical Issues in Aging, 1*, 7–8.

Sidorenko, A. (1998). *Towards a society for all ages: International Year of Older Persons, 1999*. New York: United Nations Department of Economic and Social Affairs.

United Nations. (1948). *International Declaration of Human Rights*. New York: Author.

United Nations. (1994). *Aging, health and disability*. New York: Author.

United Nations. (1997). *UN proceedings*. New York: Author.

United Nations. (1998). *UN focal point for the International Year of the Older Person 1999*. New York: Department for Policy Coordination and Sustainable Development (http://www.un.org/DPCSD).

United Nations General Assembly. (1992). *Proceedings*. New York: United Nations.

U.S. House of Representatives. (1994). *Green book: Briefing book for the House Ways and Means Committee*. Washington, DC: Government Printing Office.

U.S. House of Representatives. (1998). *Green book: Briefing book for the House Ways and Means Committee*. Washington, DC: Government Printing Office.

Witkin, S. (1998). Greetings. *Social Work, 43*, 101–103.

World Health Organization. (1991). *Report on the world health situation*. New York: United Nations.

5

Social Work Under Managed Care: Will We Survive, or Can We Prevail?

Barry Rock, DSW

> I believe that man will not merely survive: he will prevail.
>
> William Faulkner, Nobel Prize Speech, Stockholm,
> December 10, 1950

INTRODUCTION

MANAGED CARE IS TRANSFORMING the financing and delivery of health, mental health, and child welfare throughout the United States. Social work services are being greatly affected as well. Although there is some enthusiasm for innovations brought about by managed care, there is also much criticism—often expressed through a consumer backlash, with consequent government actions to contain certain managed care practices. Social workers are understandably concerned that the profession's traditional constituencies—such as the poor, chronically ill, the frail elderly—are not receiving the services they need under managed care. A form of rationing to high-risk and vulnerable populations may be taking place.

Managed care is a market-driven economic arrangement for the delivery of health services that is very popular today in the business world. It may not be a lasting phenomenon in its contemporary form. However, there are underlying principles and concepts attached to managed care, some of which predate managed care, that may outlast the current economic mechanisms and are potentially supportive of many social work endeavors. Examples are brief, goal-directed treatment; outcome measures; primary and preventative care; and case and care management. There are real ethical concerns that must be examined, and social workers—both micro and macro practitioners, as well as researchers—must focus on the most vulnerable populations and how they will be treated under managed care.

The dilemmas to be worked on in the managed care arena are not different from dilemmas and ambiguities in other settings and institutions within which social workers have traditionally functioned. There have always been concerns about confidentiality, autonomous practice and accountability, and the various limitations and distortions of funding mechanisms on the provision of services. The social work profession has a history of successfully working within host systems while simultaneously changing those systems and advocating for clients. It is, however, necessary for social workers to become creditable players making value-added contributions in order to influence the system for the better.

This chapter will express a proactive attitude toward the opportunities and potentials that managed care has for social work. At the same time, it will maintain a critical stance toward the real dangers that managed care may have for our client populations as well as for the general community of consumers. An ability to tolerate ambiguity is a historic strength of the profession; we have often been able to work within a system and challenge and change it at the same time. The chapter asks: Will the social work profession merely survive, or can it prevail under managed care? A series of survival, transitional, and prevailing activities are offered, which can also be understood as short-term, intermediate, and long-term goals. A vision of where social work may go in this "brave new world" is presented.

Survival? Yes!

Survival of the social work profession is very likely. The outlook for employment is excellent. Organizations providing mental health/behavioral health often favor the social work therapist because of the lower costs of our services compared to those of psychiatrists and psychologists. A recent report not only documents the high rate of success of social work students seeking postgraduate employment but points to an interesting pattern in the job tasks of mixing clinical and case management skills, a development that is understandable given the evolving managed care environment. Social work can survive in the immediate future through behavioral health/mental health; short-term treatment/brief therapy; network memberships and social work independent practitioners' associations (IPAs); case management; and discharge planning/length-of-stay reduction. Social workers seem to be in demand by managed behavioral health care organizations because social workers are less expensive than other mental health providers, and also because of their versatility: social workers can provide traditional psychotherapeutic treatments, but also family therapy, case management, advocacy, and other services. In order to take market advantage of this, social workers would be wise to join IPAs so as to enhance their bargaining positions by the power of large-group membership. One of the keys to survival under managed care is that risk is shifted from insurance companies to providers— providers must thus join together to spread the risk over a large group of practitioners.

Other keys to professional survival are case management and discharge planning/length-of-stay reduction. In the pre–managed care, but post–PPS/DRG era (Prospective Payment System based on Diagnosis-Related Groups), social workers in hospitals made substantial value-added contributions to length-of-stay reduction through aggressive but highly professional discharge planning services (Rock et al., 1996; Rock et al., 1995; Rock & Auerbach, 1994). In the managed care era, the profession of nursing has usurped social work in this function through utilization review, which has often subsumed discharge planning under the rubric of case management. Concerning this issue, Sophia Dziegielewski (1998) has said:

> In today's health care environment, many other disciplines are doing the tasks that have traditionally been considered the role of social workers. In turn, social workers are also doing some of the

tasks that have traditionally belonged to other disciplines. . . . In this era of behavioral managed health care, nurses and physicians who are referred to as critical providers of medical services have a great deal of power in establishing a firm place in the delivery of health care services. Social workers, as are many other allied health professionals, are not considered essential. Therefore, nurses in particular can and often do compete for jobs or direct services that were usually done by social work professionals. (pp. 26–27)

There is no easy and clear path for the social work profession to regain its role in this area. There is some anecdotal evidence from mature managed care environments in which nurses perform social work case management and discharge planning functions: hospital administrators at acute medical facilities have expressed dissatisfaction over time with the nurses' inability to do psychosocial assessments. The resultant negative outcomes are increased readmissions (discharge plans not grounded in sound psychosocial assessment collapse, necessitating rehospitalization) and increased patient/family complaints. It may be a matter of strategic patience until core social work skills are again recognized as essential to the health care enterprise. More likely, the ambulatory care/primary care arena presents an excellent opportunity for the profession to expand its role while keeping alive the case management and assessment skills developed over the course of the 20th century, but also to demonstrate the link between high-level biopsychosocial assessment and positive health outcomes.

TRANSITIONAL STAGE

For most social workers, survival alone is a necessary but not sufficient end point. In order to begin movement to a more prevalent, leadership role in health care, there are some transitional steps:

1. Cross-training beyond traditional professional education and credentialing
2. Skill mix and use of social work assistants
3. Reengineering: delayering; decentralization

(Note that a new vocabulary is emerging which social workers must learn. These terms are migrating from the world of corporate and health finance consultants; they will be defined below.)

Many social worker leaders in health care have greatly resisted all of the above. Cross-training is an interprofessional process in which selected skill repertoires of one profession are taught to another, and vice versa. An example of this is nursing/ social work case management, discharge planning, and home care assessment. This is done either in the interest of replacing one profession with another (the highly threatening worst case which many social workers rightfully fear) or creating a more flexible, efficient delivery system that gets more productivity across a greater range of problem solving from both disciplines. Recent practice experience discourages a rigid cross-training scenario and encourages informal cross-training—for example, a social worker and a utilization management nurse working together, and both evolving their own division of labor, areas of common skills, and learning from each other.

If cross-training represents a type of horizontal integration of personnel across professions, skill mix looks at vertical integration, usually within a professional group. The social work profession long ago determined that there were levels of education and competencies appropriate for different skills and task accomplishment. In the managed care environment, examining differential skill mix is seen as a measure to enhance both efficiency and quality, the latter because the higher-level professional is free to practice at the highest levels, delegating other tasks to staff with less professional preparation. It appears that this way of thinking may have gone too far in the nursing profession, but perhaps not far enough in social work. It is particularly controversial in social work because of the debate of many decades concerning clinical versus concrete services, which we hope is now better synthesized as the profession has adopted a generalist, ecosystem framework.

Both cross-training and skill mix are forms of reengineering, which can result in downsizing. Reengineering has been defined as "the fundamental redesign of the work process involving producing a product or a service, rapid and large scale performance improvements in the process being redesigned, and often, the aggressive use of information technology" (Mechling, 1994, qtd. in Edwards, Cooke, & Reid, 1996, p. 476). Organizational beliefs, behaviors, and structures often must change, as well as job definitions (Edwards et al., 1996).

Among the more popular corporate reengineering strategies that are dramatically affecting social work departments are delayering and decentralization. Delayering involves the elimination of supervisory and middle management positions in an effort to flatten the organizational structure, based on the notion that bureaucratic layers are inefficient and expensive, that supervision is not necessary for highly trained health care professionals, and that much of middle management fails to make value-added contributions to the organizational effort. This is particularly painful for the social work profession, which invented supervision as it is known today and is highly invested in the educational, administrative, and supportive functions of supervision (Kadushin, 1976) as fundamentally value-added. This approach to reorganization ignores the need, especially in health settings, of dedicated personnel to organize the delivery system, to interface the delivery system with community, social service, and social welfare systems, and to create seamless networks of continuous care. Although such a vision is essential in high-quality managed care, there is a naïveté that it will just happen, even while removing from organizations staff who could in fact bring this about. Decentralization in its most radical form entirely eliminates professional departments such as social work, and assigns practitioners to semi-autonomous interdisciplinary teams who are empowered to deliver a "product line."

In spite of the many (and not unjustified) reservations that social workers have, it is imperative that the profession be open to and participate in all of these activities in positive and proactive ways, while maintaining appropriately critical thinking and good judgment, in order to provide a transition toward an ascension of the profession to new leadership roles. Unfortunately, there is a tendency toward extreme positions among social workers—either a total rejection of managed care or a mindless promotion of it. "Managed care is neither a disaster nor a panacea" (Kane, 1996, p. 9). Critical thinking is often missing. In addition to the necessity to do outcome evaluation in the managed care context, there is a major opportunity for social work researchers to inform policy.

Although there is an emerging consumer and health care professional backlash around the negative consequences of managed care (Mitchell, 1998), a comprehensive critical analysis is lacking. This is an ideal role for schools of social work. Without a critical analysis of policy, program, and evaluation data, only incremental change can occur. A very significant article on medical outcome research regarding HMOs was published in the *Journal of the American Medical Association* and widely reported in the media: "Differences in 4-Year Health Outcomes for Elderly and Poor, Chronically Ill Patients Treated in HMO and Fee-for-Service Systems: Results From the Medical Outcomes Study" (Ware, Baylliss, Rogers, Kosinski, & Tarlov, 1996). The article concluded: "During the study period, elderly and poor chronically ill patients had worse physical health outcomes in HMO's than in FFS systems; mental health outcomes varied by study site and patient characteristics. Current health plans should carefully monitor the health outcomes of these vulnerable subgroups" (p. 1047). The study suggests that HMOs are rationing care for the primary constituents of social workers—the poor, the chronically ill, and the elderly. The lead headline of the *New York Times* (Kilborn, 1998, p. A1) was: "Largest H.M.O.'s Cutting the Poor and the Elderly." Social workers can do similar research stressing the psychosocial aspects of health care—this would be especially timely now that many states have waivers to transfer all Medicaid recipients to managed Medicaid. It is being suggested that such research be motivated by the positive intent to improve the delivery system and to advance the social work profession as a serious player in managed care.

Can Social Work Prevail? An Agenda for Change for the Profession

New patterns of social work service delivery must evolve. In the context of policy analysis, program development must take place for innovative systems of delivery of social work services in health care, followed by program evaluation to demonstrate outcome. Among the emerging patterns are:

1. *Locus of care.* The locus of care is shifting from in-patient acute, tertiary, and specialty/subspecialty care to ambulatory and community-based care and to physician offices, group practices, and HMOs.

2. *Modalities.* The social work modalities that are expected to be in high demand are short-term treatment, case and care management, and prevention. Short-term treatment is relatively well defined in social work; case management is less so, although some form of it has been practiced by most social workers as a part of their practice since the inception of the profession at the beginning of the 20th century. For acute care problems/populations, case management will be the modality of choice and will undoubtedly involve close collaboration between nurse case managers and social workers; there is a major opportunity for social work leadership in this area. For chronic populations, a new "disease management model" needs to be developed in which social workers will exercise leadership in the comprehensive long-term management of frail, at-risk populations such as the chronic mentally ill, the homeless, HIV patients, and so forth.

3. *Reimbursement.* A radical transformation in health care reimbursement is taking place by the replacement of the fee-for-service and indemnity insurance system by partial- or full-risk capitation. Capitation has been described as "a prospective payment to a provider paid on a per capita basis" (Al-Assaf, 1998, p. 3). Corcoran and Vandiver (1996) state: "Under a capitation model, the managed care organization has a single administrative structure that assumes fiscal and clinical responsibility for the client in his or her community. Capitated managed care operates with a cap to the entire costs. In other words, funding for all of a person's care is internal to the managed care organization, and that [*sic*] funding for all the enrolled members is capped" (pp. 43–44).

There are considerable unrealized opportunities for social workers under capitation. Because risk has shifted from insurance companies to providers, providers must manage costs under the limits of the capitated arrangements and at the same time assure quality. With high-risk populations, social work treatment, case management, and prevention become essential to this enterprise.

In a more far-ranging model, social work services can be organized in the community and services contracted to hospitals, doctors, and HMOs. This can be government supported, private not-for-profit, or proprietary.

4. *Research, evaluation, outcome data.* As never before, social workers will be responsible for proving their worth on both a case-specific and aggregate level.

5. *Supervision and administration.* The current "politically correct" fad in health care is to delayer, and to devalue supervision and administration. This represents a crisis for a profession that has always prided itself on its supervisory/administrative skills. Two issues of immediate concern are:

a. Where is the evidence of the value-added contribution of the organizational hierarchy in social work? Conceptually, we see social work not as individual and independent practice, but rather as a systematic delivery of care. We have not proven this, however, and hospital administrators and downsizing consultants are not buying this argument.

b. What new patterns of education and socialization are necessary to bring about not only more independent practitioners, but ones who can assume coordinating and administrative roles previously performed by social work supervisors/administrators?

SOCIAL WORK EDUCATION

There are considerable implications for schools of social work and both class and field curricula in the above—both for health care social work and other fields of practice in which similar social change is taking place. The challenge for the world of professional education is to overcome the traditional conservatism and long duration involved in curricula development and codification. There are also changes in the practice/agency domain that can greatly affect the social work educational experience. In those geographical areas in which schools of social work place many students in health and mental health settings, especially if there is high penetration of managed care, there seems to be an emerging paucity of field instructors along with a weakening of agency and hospital commitment to education, including medical education.

Among the reasons for this are downsizing of staff, making it difficult to carve out time for field instruction responsibilities; changes in reimbursement, which limit funds to support medical education in hospitals settings (social work education in hospitals traditionally benefited from the overall mission of education of teaching hospitals—this is now eroding); and, most importantly, managed care credentialing most often excludes social work students in internships, resulting in student cases not being eligible for reimbursement (Raskin & Blome, 1998). Also, a continuously changing and chaotic organizational context makes traditional education difficult. An approach to helping students cope with the constant flux of the situation is to get them to focus on client/patient *need* as universal and constant, even though the delivery system may be highly variable at the moment.

There is a need for greater participation of the schools in field education, more timely updating of the curriculum, and new models of education/field education for social work in health care:

1. *Curriculum.* Among the areas for curriculum development are practice emphasizing short-term, goal-directed treatment with measurable outcomes; courses in administration covering reengineering, downsizing, delayering, and contracting, as well as strategies for coping with these phenomena; policy classes incorporating extensive material on health reform and managed care, as well as advocacy in these areas; more consideration throughout the curriculum to interdisciplinary collaboration and more independent, self-directed practice with the expectation of less available supervision and administration because of downsizing and delayering. Skills in the uses of technologies are also critical.

2. *Field work.* Although it has been an issue for decades, the notion of greater synergy between field and class is more urgent then ever. In the era of devolution and managed care, the pressures on practice settings and their staffs are unprecedented.

The consequences of these social processes on staff and administration are high turnover, burnout, and low morale. "Contemporary social work . . . must function in an atmosphere of increasing ambiguity and paradox. . . . Addressing loss of security has become a primary . . . focus" (Edwards et al., 1996, p. 473). It is difficult to provide field instruction in such an atmosphere. In addition, as indicated above, managed care credentialing is disenfranchising students from following managed care cases. Conditions in the field are changing at a very fast pace. Social work education curriculum is not keeping pace, and the gap is widening (Raskin & Blome, 1998; Witkin, 1998).

In order to bring about change, schools and field agencies need to become proactive in better integrating field and class. Among mechanisms to achieve this are greater faculty presence in agencies and practitioner presence at schools; funded student units; focus groups between faculty and field instructors; and collaboration in grant development and research. Since outcome research is so central in managed care, this is a natural arena for collaboration. Courses need to be modified quickly to incorporate cutting-edge knowledge and skills.

3. *Research.* Social work research has been historically polarized between, on the one hand, random assignment and controlled experimental designs, and on the other hand, practice research, single-subject design, qualitative research, and grounded theory (Gantt, Pinsky, Rock, & Rosenberg, 1990). The various approaches to quality assurance (QA), quality management (QM), total quality management (TQM), and continuous quality improvement (CQI) may point to a potential common ground (Al-Assaf, 1998; Edmunds et al., 1997). Social workers are ethically obliged to participate in the systematic collection of data to evaluate the effectiveness of practice in order to demonstrate accountability, primarily to clients, and also to agencies and funding and regulatory bodies. The systematic collection of data to evaluate the effectiveness of practice may be viewed on a continuum: from chart recording, single-subject designs, program evaluation, quality assurance reviews, and computerized statistical systems to advanced experimental research. At each step along the continuum, adherence to scientific principles should be maximized.

Managed care demands outcome measures. The requirements vary greatly from company to company and from plan to plan, but the demand for measurable outcomes is universal. A major agenda for the social work profession for the new millennium is to integrate practice and research.

The following is an actual example of the administration and faculty of Fordham University Graduate School of Social Service mobilizing for the managed care era:

Since the beginning of the 1996 academic year, the school has engaged in numerous activities and initiatives to advance social work goals in the managed care arena. These activities and initiatives include:

1. A study of interrelationships of graduate education for social work and public health led to the establishment of a joint degree program between the School of Social Work and the Public Health Division of a Medical School, including a specialization in managed care in the social work program.

2. An innovative continuing education program was jointly sponsored by the School of Social Work and the Medical School for persons with an MPH or MSW degree.

3. A grant funded a demonstration project for a fieldwork student unit in a not-for-profit group health practice in a lower-income community to demonstrate the effectiveness of social work services in primary care settings. A second such project is anticipated using a similar concept in which social work student interns will be placed in the offices of primary-care physicians at a hospital.

4. Technical assistance in managed care readiness has been conducted to several human service organizations in the community.

5. A managed care advisory committee consisting of members of the faculty and representative leaders from the field was established in October 1996. The committee sponsors five active and productive subcommittees:

   a. Technical Assistance—one completed and several active, contractual projects providing managed care–related technical assistance to social service agencies; developed a conceptual model of skills/knowledge that social workers can use as consultants to various managed care players/ stakeholders.

    b. Research—outlined a beginning agenda for social work managed care research; is advisory to the funded research project named above.

    c. Curriculum—organized two student surveys, provided faculty development workshops, is advisory to two faculty members who have developed two courses on managed care and social work, currently being offered.

    d. Continuing Education—with the underwriting support of a major insurance company, three interdisciplinary courses are being offered: introduction to managed care; Medicaid managed care; and contracting. This is co-sponsored by the School of Social Work, the Public Health Division of the Medical School, and the School of Business.

    e. Child Welfare—to establish the School of Social Work leadership in advising the local child welfare community on criteria, standards, and best practices in the evolving policy shifts as the city and state apply managed care concepts to child welfare.

All of the above activities have resulted in the establishment (July 1998) of an Institute on Managed Care and Social Work under the sponsorship of the Fordham University Graduate School of Social Service. The overall purpose of the institute is to integrate the many activities of the school regarding managed care and social work into a structured, centralized, cohesive whole so that the school and university can provide leadership to the community in social work and managed care curriculum, service delivery, technical assistance, and research.

DIRECTIONS IN U.S. HEALTH POLICY

The agenda for the social work profession in the era of managed care will be greatly affected by the direction (or lack of direction) of national health policy. Since the failure of the Clinton Health Security Act of 1993, the de facto national health policy in the United States in the late 1990s may be characterized as free-market dominated, in the absence of federal guidelines, protections, or codification of patient rights. In the fall of 1998, White House and congressional momentum to pass a patient's bill of rights under managed care failed because of the persistence of the

president's personal scandals and the initiation of an impeach-
ment process (Pear, 1998b).

Even the national programs of Medicare and Medicaid are devolving to the states and to the for-profit sector through managed Medicare and managed Medicaid, although there is a
recent trend of commercial managed care companies retreating
from contracts for the public programs (Allen, 1998; Steinhauer,
1998). The gross cost of health care in the United States reached
the trillion-dollar level in 1996 although the growth rate had
been flat for the previous 5 years—an outcome that many attributed to the impact of managed care. In late 1998 there was news
of considerable rate increases in managed care, and health care
costs in general may inflate again. These developments coexist
with appalling statistics that the number of uninsured has
reached 43.3 million, or 16% of the population (Pear, 1998a).
There is thus profound inefficiency in the system as it exists.

Commercial managed care may in fact fail to ultimately deliver on its promise of lower costs, greater efficiency, and higher
quality. There are compelling arguments that for-profit, market-
driven health care, in the absence of a national health policy
guiding and regulating it, cannot work (Wilkerson, Devers, &
Given, 1997). Certainly from a social work perspective there are
serious concerns regarding managed Medicaid and Medicare
and its effects on primary social work constituencies—the poor,
the frail, the disabled.

Wilkerson, Devers, and Given state:

> The appeal of free-market competition relies on two very impor-
> tant assumptions. The first is that increasing economic efficiency
> is necessarily more desirable than other social objectives. The sec-
> ond is that the relevant market is, in fact, perfectly competitive.
> When either of these assumptions is not true for a particular mar-
> ket, economic theory suggests that other, non-market mecha-
> nisms, including various forms of government intervention, may
> lead to either more efficient outcomes or outcomes that are better
> in other ways. (1997, p. 11)

Although it has been argued here that many of the underlying
mechanisms of managed care—capitation, primary care, prevention, care management—have positive potential for social work

and social work's traditional constituencies, it is equally clear that a for-profit, market-driven system will be problematic at the least, and more likely disastrous for the most vulnerable, at-risk populations. A national health policy is crucial to set the rules, the boundaries, and the limits; to establish minimum standards of quality and access; and to regulate the public benefits in a manner consistent with social justice and equity.

CONCLUSION

New models of practice and service delivery, as well as educational strategies to support them, must evolve for the social work profession to be a major and dynamic force in shaping the health/mental health/social welfare system that is to come, and to become a leader of biopsychosocial health care. This includes critical analysis and advocacy in support of national health care reform. We can prevail.

REFERENCES

Al-Assaf, A. F. (1998). *Managed care quality: A practical guide*. Boca Raton: CRC Press.

Allen, M. (1998, October 5). Fear greets cut in H.M.O. for the elderly. *New York Times*, p. B1.

Corcoran, K., & Vandiver, V. (1996). *Maneuvering the maze of managed care: Skills for mental health practitioners*. New York: Free Press.

Dziegielewski, S. (1998). *The changing face of health care social work: Professional practice in the era of managed care*. New York: Springer.

Edmunds, M., Frank, R., Hogan, M., McCarty, D., Robinson-Beale, R., & Weisner, C. (Eds.). (1997). *Managing managed care: Quality improvement in behavioral health*. Washington, DC: National Academy Press.

Edwards, R. L., Cooke, P. W., & Reid, P. N. (1996). Social work management in an era of diminishing federal responsibility. *Social Work, 41*(5), 468–479.

Gantt, A., Pinsky, S., Rock, B., & Rosenberg, E. (1990). Practice and research: An integrative approach. *Journal of Teaching in Social Work, 4*(1), 129–143.

Kadushin, A. (1976). *Supervision in social work.* New York: Columbia University Press.

Kane, R. (1996, July/August). Assessing managed care: Is it healthy for the elderly? Striking a balance. *Aging Today,* pp. 9, 12. Quoted in Krell, G. (1997). Impact of the elderly on the health care system and its implications for the delivery of social services. In F. Safford & G. Krell (Eds.), *Gerontology for health professionals: A practice guide* (pp. 236–255). Washington, DC: NASW Press.

Kilborn, P. T. (1998, July 6). Largest H.M.O.'s cutting the poor and the elderly. *New York Times,* p. A1.

Mitchell, C. G. (1998). Perceptions of empathy and client satisfaction with managed behavioral care. *Social Work, 43*(5), 404–411.

Pear, R. (1998a, September 26). Americans lacking health insurance put at 16 percent. *New York Times,* p. A1.

Pear, R. (1998b, October 10). Senators reject bill to regulate H.M.O.'s. *New York Times,* p. A1.

Raskin, M. S., & Blome, W. W. (1998). The impact of managed care on field instruction. *Journal of Social Work Education, 34*(3), 365–374.

Rock, B. D., & Auerbach, C. (1994). A study of hospitalized elderly patients no longer acutely ill. *Journal of Social Service Research, 20*(1/2), 41–54.

Rock, B. D., Auerbach, C., Goldstein, M., Harris, M., Kaminsky, P., Quitkin, E., & Beckerman, N. (1996). Research changes a health care delivery system: A biopsychosocial approach to predicting resource utilization in hospital care of the frail elderly. *Social Work in Health Care, 22*(3), 21–37.

Rock, B. D., Cohen, C., Goldstein, M., Quitkin, E., Beckerman, A., & Auerbach, C. (1995, May). The management of alternate level of care patients utilizing a computerized data base. *Health and Social Work, 20*(2), 133–139.

Steinhauer, J. (1998, October 7). New York bracing for Medicaid managed care. *New York Times,* p. A1.

Ware, J., Baylliss, M., Rogers, W., Kosinski, M., & Tarlov, A.

(1996). Differences in 4-year health outcomes for elderly and poor, chronically ill patients treated in HMO and fee-for-service systems: Results from the medical outcome study. *Journal of the American Medical Association, 276,* 1039–1047.

Wilkerson, J. D., Devers, K. J., & Given, R. S. (Eds.). (1997). *Competitive managed care: The emerging health care system.* San Francisco: Jossey-Bass.

Witkin, S. L. (1998). Mirror, mirror on the wall: Creative tensions, the academy, and the field. *Social Work, 43*(5), 389–391.

II

Context Meets Practice: Public Issues/Private Troubles—Devolving Systems and Their Human and Practice Consequences

INTRODUCTION

Rosa Perez-Koenig, DSW, and Barry Rock, DSW

THE RETRENCHMENT from social justice that has taken place in the federal and state welfare policies during the past two decades has intensified client needs. It has also generated an equally compelling need for the social work profession to redefine its mission in terms of social justice. Part I of this book addressed public issues, providing a macro scope as it relates to social and economic justice in the era of devolution.

The question naturally arises: Can politically relevant social justice values be used as a guide in clinical social work practice with clients? Wakefield (1988a, 1988b) responded to that question by arguing that clinical work can and should be governed by precepts of justice. Following a Rawlsian model of justice, Wakefield found that "the psychological property of self-respect is perhaps the most important social primary good with which justice is concerned" (1988b, p. 355). Wakefield took the development of self-respect as the cardinal means through which clinical social workers could actualize the precept of justice. Building upon Wakefield, Swenson (1998) asserts that social justice as the organizing value of social work does apply to clinical work. Swenson alludes to models of social justice other than the Rawlsian one. Her thinking seems congruent with Young's (1990) conception of social justice. Young identifies oppression and domination as central concepts rather than distribution. She argues that these social injustices—oppression and domination—constrain self-development and self-determination among marginalized groups in U.S. society. Young's social justice paradigm strengthens the argument for the unique contribution of clinical social work to social justice.

Furthermore, the chapters in Part II attest to the interconnectedness between public issues and private troubles. These contributions address the private troubles of individuals, families, and/or small groups who are members of oppressed and vulnerable populations. As Schwartz (1969) stated, "private trouble is simply a specific example of a public issue . . . a public issue is made of private troubles" (p. 25).

In the chapters that comprise this part of the book, the authors collectively demonstrate that social and economic justice can inform and direct clinical social work practice with clients' specialized problems and issues. Part II consists of five chapters successively devoted to three of the most vulnerable populations among those at risk: poor children, particularly those who have been sexually abused or whose parents have died of AIDS; immigrants; and the terminally ill elderly. Each of these populations has been affected by ongoing "welfare reform," and several of the authors express their forthright opposition to the course that welfare policy has taken during the reign of the "neo-liberal," devolutionist ideology. Nevertheless, these authors are specifically concerned with micro- or case-level issues and the particular needs of distinct client groups.

The violence of sexual abuse to a child's self-development and the work required for the child's liberation from oppressive internalization continues to be a formidable challenge to the helping professions. Chapter 6, "Testing a Therapeutic Model for Empowering Child Victims of Sexual Abuse," by Ellen Brickman, Mary Boncher, Mel Scheideman, and Sonya Dickerson, deals with the evaluation of an innovative group work method that seeks to empower children who have undergone the victimization of sexual abuse. Social work with groups has proven particularly effective in working with oppressed, marginalized populations (Brenton, 1989; Gutierrez & Ortega, 1991; Gitterman & Shulman, 1994). Death rates from AIDS in the United States and infection with HIV, the AIDS virus, are no longer declining. The incidence of new infections with HIV is dangerously high among minority women, particularly African Americans and Latinas. In Chapter 7, Felix Lorenzo addresses the complex issues entailed in helping Latino children whose parents have died of AIDS. The new policies of the era of devolution have caused a wave of terror among the "legal" aliens.

These legal immigrants have experienced a regressive, exclusionary approach almost as terrible as those felt by "illegal" immigrants. Carol Kaplan and Roni Berger furnish us with Chapters 8 and 9, respectively, which describe particularized needs of immigrant clients. Kaplan's chapter deals with social work interventions geared to assisting the reintegration of immigrant families who leave children in their homelands and are able to send for them only after a substantial time lapse. Berger provides an overview of the traumatic experience of immigrants and of principles needed by clinicians in their therapeutic interventions with this population. Gerontology social work is the subject of the final chapter of this section. The downsizing that is taking place in hospital systems is evident in the dismantling of clinical services to the terminally ill elderly, a most needed service as evidenced in the chapter "Palliative Care: Facilitating Decision Making About Death and Dying," by Margaret Souza and Eugenia Siegler. The authors particularly highlight the importance of advocacy work in clinical practice with the terminally ill elderly.

Because the chapters in Part II address a range of subjects, it is difficult to generalize about their content. Nevertheless, the common theme that runs throughout this section is that of meeting the needs of clients through practice models in which social justice precepts are in place. In aggregate these chapters are in keeping with what Saleeby (1990) calls the "four cornerstones" of the profession's symbolic and existential infrastructure: (1) an ethic of indignation; (2) humane inquiry and understanding; (3) focused compassion and caring; and (4) the quest for social justice (pp. 34–38). As these chapters demonstrate, it is possible to apply precepts of social justice in clinical work, and it is essential to do so at this historical juncture, in which social injustices abound and even masquerade as "welfare reform."

References

Brenton, M. (1989). Liberation theology, group work, and the right of the poor and oppressed to participate in the life of the community. *Social Work With Groups, 12*(3), 5–18.

Gitterman, A., & Shulman, L. (Eds.). (1994). *Mutual aid groups, vulnerable populations, and the life cycle* (2nd ed.). Itasca, IL: F. E. Peacock.

Gutierrez, L., & Ortega, R. (1991). Developing methods to empower Latinos: The importance of groups. *Social Work With Groups, 14*(2), 23–43.

Saleeby, D. (1990). Philosophical disputes in social work: Social justice denied. *Journal of Sociology and Social Welfare, 17*(2), 29–40.

Schwartz, W. (1969). Private troubles and public issues: One social work job or two? In *Social welfare forum* (pp. 22–43). New York: Columbia University Press.

Swenson, C. (1998). Clinical social work's contribution to a social justice perspective. *Social Work, 43*(6), 527–537.

Wakefield, J. C. (1988a). Psychotherapy, distributive justice, and clinical social work, Part 1: Distributive justice as a conceptual framework for social work. *Social Service Review, 62*(2), 187–210.

Wakefield, J. C. (1988b). Psychotherapy, distributive justice, and social work, Part 2: Psychotherapy and the pursuit of justice. *Social Service Review, 62*(3), 353–381.

Young, I. (1990). *Justice and the politics of difference.* Princeton: Princeton University Press.

6

Testing a Therapeutic Model for Empowering Child Victims of Sexual Abuse

Ellen Brickman, PhD, Mary Boncher, MS,
Mel Schneiderman, PhD, and
Sonya Dickerson, MSW

INTRODUCTION

THE ISSUE OF EMPOWERMENT is central to any work with sexually abused children, particularly with minority children and families also struggling with issues of poverty, racism, inner-city survival, and involvement in the child welfare system. This chapter addresses the question of whether and how abuse-specific services to these children can effectively ameliorate the children's sense of powerlessness and increase their sense of agency. To this end, we describe a treatment program for sexually abused children, within the framework of a large child welfare agency, and discuss the findings of an exploratory study assessing the effectiveness of this treatment.

We begin the chapter with an overview of the impact of child sexual abuse, which drives the need for services to this population. We follow with a description of the Child Sexual Abuse Treatment Service's treatment orientation and some key aspects of the program, with an emphasis on how treatment is used to help abused children regain an age-appropriate sense of empowerment and control in their lives and to recover from the trauma of their abuse. The chapter will go on to discuss an exploratory study of the effectiveness of the Child Sexual Abuse Treatment Service, again with special emphasis on change in children's sense of power and control as it relates to trauma. We conclude by considering the implications of the research for clinical work, as well as with suggestions for further research and evaluation in this field.

THE IMPACT OF CHILD SEXUAL ABUSE: NEED FOR TREATMENT

There is extensive evidence from both child victims and adult survivors of sexual abuse that such abuse can have a profound short- and long-term negative impact on the victims. Kendall-Tackett, Williams, and Finkelhor's (1993) review of research on the effects of child sexual abuse revealed a relatively common set of symptoms frequently manifested by child victims of sexual abuse, including promiscuity, low self-esteem, fear, post-traumatic stress disorder, neurosis, anxiety, inappropriate sexual behavior, and depression. Moreover, the effects of child sexual abuse extend well into adulthood. Abuse survivors manifest a broad range of psychiatric disorders, with especially high incidence of post-traumatic stress disorder and other fear- and anxiety-related problems (Beichtman, Zuker, Hood, & DaCosta-Granville, 1992; Saunders, Villeponteaux, Lipovsky, Kilpatrick, & Veronen, 1992; Briere & Runtz, 1993).

Both child victims and adult survivors of child sexual abuse have also been found to have a more external *locus of control* than do their non-abused counterparts; that is, they are more likely to attribute what happens to them to forces outside of themselves and outside their control (Bolstad & Zinbarg, 1997; Moyer, DiPietro, Berkowitz, & Stunkard, 1997; Rhodes, Ebert, & Meyers, 1993). Generally, research suggests that a more *internal* locus of control is associated with better adjustment (see Nowicki, 1986, for review). The constructs of control, power/powerlessness, and helplessness are key elements in several theoretical models of trauma (Carlson, Furby, Armstrong, & Shlaes, 1997; Herman, 1992; van der Kolk, 1987). However, variables related to one's sense of control have been included in only a handful of studies of adult survivors and, to our knowledge, have not been studied in child victims of sexual abuse.

The range, severity, and duration of problems experienced by victims of child sexual abuse have been the impetus for the development of treatment programs to address and/or prevent the psychological sequelae of abuse. In 1987 the New York Foundling, a large child welfare agency in New York City, developed the Child Sexual Abuse Treatment Service (CSATS), an in-house therapy program for sexually abused children and their families. The children and families served by CSATS are poor, usually from racial or ethnic minority groups, and generally live in disenfranchised and disintegrating communities. Many of their lives have been affected by homelessness, drug addiction, AIDS, and violence. Thus, the sexual abuse is often only one of many issues for families who are already disempowered (Boncher, 1994).

The frustration and sense of powerlessness often experienced by poor minority families is compounded when they enter the child welfare system. For example, in a policy study of New York City's institutional responses to child sexual abuse, nonoffending mothers talked about feeling blamed by child welfare caseworkers, frustrated at not being able to obtain information, and helpless as they watched their child go through repeated interviews and examinations and as court cases dragged on for years (Brickman, 1993).

This sense of powerlessness can be even greater for the children who are the subjects of these investigations. They often receive even less information than the adults in their lives about what decisions are being made and why. They may be removed from their homes with little warning and against their will, and generally have no input into decisions regarding their placement. This can reinforce the sense of helplessness they experienced during the sexual abuse, which we discuss in more detail later in this chapter. This is consistent with trauma theory, which suggests that prior experiences with powerlessness and anxiety set the conditions to experience difficult events traumatically (Carlson et al., 1997).

TREATMENT ORIENTATION OF THE CHILD SEXUAL ABUSE TREATMENT SERVICE

The CSATS uses Sgroi's (1982) definition of child sexual abuse as any sexual act, contact or noncontact, which is imposed on a child by a person in a position of either power or authority and trust. This definition emphasizes the power dynamics usually endemic in child sexual abuse situations and underscores the violation of trust often entailed in the perpetrator's access to the child, as well as the ability to perform the abuse and command secrecy. The abuse may be intra- or extra-familial. It may be a onetime incident or occur over a number of years in the child's life. It may involve the viewing or production of pornography, being forced to watch the sexual abuse of a sibling, sexualized exposure of the child's or adult's body, fondling, or a form of penetration.

The purpose of the CSATS is to (1) ensure the protection and safety of the child and help prevent further abuse; (2) facilitate the child and family's healing from the effects of the abuse; and (3) work with the family to restructure itself in such a way as to promote non-exploitative relationships and developmentally appropriate role functioning. At the CSATS, treatment is approached from a stance of respect for the child and family's own healing process, as well as from multi-systems, abuse-specific, and traumagenic perspectives.

Multi-Systems Perspective

Because so many of the families are simultaneously struggling with abuse and issues of poverty, racism, substance abuse, and other larger social problems, the CSATS provides comprehensive, multidisciplinary case planning and clinical services within a child welfare agency. Case planners assist the family in negotiating the complex set of systems with which they may be involved. One aim is increasing the child's and family's active participation in decisions being made about them, thereby increasing their sense of control and commitment to fulfilling their goals. Case planners also provide outreach as well as advocacy around such issues as income maintenance, housing, education, medical services, and other concrete services. The family, case planner, and clinicians work closely together and make collective decisions regarding treatment planning.

Abuse-Specific Perspective

An abuse-specific perspective is used within the clinical component of the CSATS. Research has consistently suggested that abuse-specific therapy is more effective at reducing symptoms in sexually abused children than is general supportive therapy (Finkelhor & Berliner, 1995). While the treatments in different programs vary in emphasis or treatment orientation, there are common aspects to abuse-specific treatment (Berliner & Saunders, 1996; Beutler, Williams, & Zetzer, 1994). These include providing opportunities for the child to express issues and feelings about the abuse experience, the offender, the non-perpetrating parent(s), and the self; corrective information about sexual abuse and sexuality; teaching the child to think and feel differently about the event; teaching the child to manage behaviors; prevention information; and abuse response skills.

Traumagenic Perspective

In keeping with current theory and research (see, e.g., Carlson et al., 1997; Finkelhor & Browne, 1985; Friedrich, 1990; Gil, 1991; Herman, 1992; James, 1989; Rowan & Foy, 1993), the CSATS conceptualizes the symptom constellation of sexually abused children as a potential manifestation of psychological trauma and treats symptomatic children from a trauma perspective. The literature on psychological trauma has grown tremendously since the formal recognition of post-traumatic stress disorder (PTSD) as a diagnostic entity in the *DSM-III* in 1980 (Blake, Albano, & Keane, 1992; Wilson, 1995), and there is now a common understanding of factors that contribute to trauma. The usual human response to perceived danger is a complex system of physical and psychological reactions that serve to mobilize the threatened individual for action (Herman, 1992). When such action has no effect and there is a real or perceived lack of control over the situation, both animals and people become distressed (Carlson et al., 1997). This lack of control and sense of powerlessness, together with the person's perception of the event as extremely negative, are seen as critical elements that make an event traumatic. For individuals who are traumatized, the overwhelming negative nature of the traumatic event is thought to inhibit psychological and physiological integration of the experience and related feelings, resulting in persistent symptoms (Carlson et al., 1997; Greene, 1993; Herman, 1992; van der Kolk, 1987; Wilson, 1995).

Understanding each child's unique experience of his or her abuse, including the family situation, previous experiences of helplessness, whether the child felt overwhelmed and powerless during the abuse, and what happened to the child after disclosure, is crucial to assessing the impact of the abuse and conceptualizing and providing treatment. The child's symptoms offer insight into his or her experience. Finkelhor and Browne (1985) pose a model of four traumagenic dynamics to characterize the responses of traumatized child victims of sexual abuse. The four dynamics that often converge in the experience of child sexual abuse are:

1. *Traumatic sexualization* resulting from the child's experience of being used as a sexual object, being taught to behave in provocative ways, and/or feeling intense excitement during the abuse, even if fear or coercion were involved.
2. *Betrayal* stemming from the child's realization of being harmed by someone he or she trusted, or from nonsupportive or blaming responses of family members or the abuser after disclosure.
3. *Powerlessness* caused by the invasion of the child's territory and body space and the child's potentially frustrated attempts to stop the abuse.
4. *Stigmatization* related to shame about the behaviors involved in the sexual abuse, pressure about secrecy, and reactions to disclosure.

While CSATS uses the entire traumagenic dynamics model in the conceptualization of treatment issues, the dynamic of powerlessness is emphasized here, consistent with the theme of this chapter. According to Finkelhor and Browne (1985), "disempowerment, the dynamic of rendering the victim powerless, refers to the process in which the child's will, desires, and sense of efficacy are continually contravened" (p. 532). The powerlessness may expand to become central to the child's self-image (James, 1989). This is especially likely if the abuse interferes with the developmental tasks of autonomy or individuation, when definition of self and issues of self-control are critical (Friedrich, 1990). If the child's caretaker is either overprotective or overly passive, the child's sense of control and efficacy may be further eroded or distorted.

Disempowerment is manifested through fear or anxiety, an impaired sense of self-efficacy and coping skills, the loss of impulse control, and/or an extreme need to control or dominate. James (1989) notes that the child may exhibit maladaptive attempts to gain mastery over the abuse; to re-create a sense of power, excitement, or fear; to seek revenge; to be punished or hurt; and to meet other emotional needs that are related to the overwhelming experience of helplessness. Consequently, imbuing a child who has been traumatized with an age-appropriate sense of power and control is a constant activity, "like a heartbeat, that must be present throughout treatment" (James, 1989, p. 73). Accordingly, corrective experiences that promote the child's appropriate expression of agency are needed in the clinical setting and in the child's home, school, and recreational environments.

Treatment Program and Modalities

The Child Sexual Abuse Treatment Service blends the multi-systems, abuse-specific, and traumagenic dynamics perspectives to assess and treat children who have been sexually abused. Even those abused children who are not traumatized, and who may not be displaying any symptoms, are given an opportunity to talk about their experience in a supportive environment.

Throughout intake and treatment, children/adolescents and their families work with the clinician and case planner to determine the appropriate course of treatment. This process sets the stage for the clients to gain a sense of control over their recovery from victimization. Art, psychodrama, sand play, movement, and writing therapy techniques as well as talk therapy are used in both individual and group treatment of children and adolescents. While groups tend to be more structured than individual therapy, the CSATS's general treatment orientation in both modalities is similar. The following description of treatment focuses predominantly on the group modality for children/adolescents, which counters the isolation and stigmatization prevalent in families of abuse victims.[1]

The groups, with 6–7 members each, are time limited (12 to 14 weeks), closed membership, and, except for the children's and non-perpetrating parent's groups, gender-defined. Groups are offered two times a year, one cycle in the fall and one in the winter/spring; many members return to participate in a number of cycles as they work through various issues or deepen their work around a particular issue.

The groups are theme-oriented and structured. The theme orientation is designed to facilitate disclosure and the identification, expression, and resolution of issues and feelings related to the abuse. A directive group treatment approach also helps members to experience relief from secrecy and to understand their behavior in the context of their experiences. The structure provides safety and predictability. It creates boundaries, helps facilitate trust, and minimizes anxiety and resultant acting-out behaviors. Children are taught to become aware of how their behaviors are influenced by their thoughts and feelings, as well as to self-monitor and control their behaviors. Reflection, relaxation techniques, cognitive restructuring, and self-directed time-outs are used to accomplish these goals. Group rules emphasize respect, mutual cooperation, and individual choice in level of participation to reinforce a sense of personal control and facilitate the reconstructive work. Attention is paid to group dynamics in order to give members an opportunity to reflect on their interactions and develop more appropriate peer relations.

The treatment process generally follows a sequential format allowing for the development of enough trust, feelings of safety, and ability to contain one's emotions to undertake the work of reconstructing and resolving the trauma. Initially, safety is developed by collectively establishing and then following through with rules, forging the therapeutic contract, and setting individual and group goals. Once trust and cohesion are adequately established, members begin to share their sexual abuse and other traumatic experiences. Through various activities, they explore the impact of the abuse, express their thoughts and feelings, reexamine misconceptions about the abuse, and reframe how they think and feel. Ways of taking care of and protecting the self and having healthy relationships with others are discussed and experienced. Members actively prepare for and engage in group termination activities, culminating in a program-wide celebration of the work.

A few examples of work produced during different stages of the group process reflect the changes children undergo around issues of power and control. During his second cycle of group, a 6-year-old boy who had been sexually abused by his father expressed his experience of what had happened to him. When asked to create an image of himself and his perpetrator, he sculpted and then painted a fragile-looking figure of himself seated, arms outstretched, legs incapable of holding up the body (see Figure 6.1). He then created a solid, dark, menacing figure of the perpetrator (see Figure 6.2). He was able to reconstruct aspects of his experience and express feelings of powerlessness and fear, as well as to begin resolving his anger at his perpetrator, by acting out his abuse using the sculptures (see Figure 6.3).

FIGURE 6.1: SIX-YEAR-OLD BOY'S SCULPTURE OF SELF.

FIGURE 6.2: SIX-YEAR-OLD BOY'S SCULPTURE OF PERPETRATOR.

Later in the same group cycle, he began to assert his developing sense of power through another project in which group members collectively created a life-size perpetrator (see Figure 6.4). During the project, the children talked about the perpetrator's having many faces—happy, mad, sad, and scary. They also described how big the perpetrators' legs were and collectively decided to include a depiction of the penis. Each child then chose what he or she wanted to say to his or her perpetrator and individually performed a psychodrama. This involved standing on a chair (to be at eye level with the perpetrator figure) and expressing feelings toward and asking questions of the perpetrator. Other children gave support and feedback to the performing child. This 6-year-old boy told the perpetrator figure how frightened he had been, but that he would never let anyone hurt him again. Initially he spoke very quietly, but with encouragement from the group he raised his voice. At the suggestion of another child, he agreed to have the entire group join him in yelling at his perpetrator.

FIGURE 6.3: SCULPTURES USED IN ROLE-PLAYING.

In our second example, an 11-year-old girl who had been sexually abused by her custodial uncle for 7 years used obsessive-compulsive tendencies to defend against her feelings of powerlessness and anxiety. Over the course of 3 years of individual and group treatment, her changing artwork showed growing relaxation and her decreasing need for rigid control of her environment (see Figures 6.5, 6.6, and 6.7). Her early work consisted primarily of paintings with highly constricted use of line and color. Over time, as she appeared to develop a more internal locus of control and become less anxious, she gained the ability to mix colors, "draw outside the lines," and explore more freeform and dynamic compositions.

EFFECTIVENESS OF THE CHILD SEXUAL ABUSE TREATMENT SERVICE

These case illustrations, as well as other anecdotal data and staff observations, strongly suggest that the treatment program is ef-

FIGURE 6.4: CHILDREN'S GROUP COLLAGE.

fective at helping children begin to overcome their sense of powerlessness, develop an age-appropriate sense of control, and
experience lower levels of psychological and behavioral prob-
lems/symptoms. While this anecdotal and observational evidence is compelling, New York Foundling was also interested in
whether these changes could be documented in a more empirical fashion. Moreover, while other child sexual abuse treatment
programs have demonstrated their effectiveness in program
evaluations, there have, to our knowledge, been few evaluations
of programs specifically developed in the context of a child welfare agency. Because of the unique issues facing this population,
we were uncertain how well study findings from most other programs would translate to the CSATS. As noted earlier, the children at the CSATS are dealing not only with the experience of
having been sexually abused, but also with a myriad of other
family and social problems, sometimes including the trauma of
separation from their biological families and communities and,
perhaps, disrupted placements resulting in constant upheaval in

FIGURE 6.5: ARTWORK DONE AT BEGINNING OF TREATMENT.

their lives. A study focused on the CSATS, which deals exclusively with a child welfare population, permitted the opportunity to explore whether treatment could be effective at addressing the psychological sequelae of sexual abuse, even in the context of the multiplicity of stressors in these children's lives.

To set a context for interpreting the findings of the present study, we review briefly the findings of other evaluations of child sexual abuse treatment programs and then discuss the findings of the CSATS evaluation.

Research on the Evaluation of Child Sexual Abuse Treatment Programs

Only recently has there been a trend toward systematic evaluation of the effectiveness of programs to treat sexually abused children. These evaluations have generally used pre-post designs exploring symptomatology as a function of a specific treat-

FIGURE 6.6: ARTWORK DONE IN MIDDLE OF TREATMENT.

ment. Finkelhor and Berliner (1995) located and reviewed 29 treatment outcome studies of sexually abused children. All but one of the reviewed pre-post studies, as well as several more recent studies, found significant improvement for the treated children as a group on at least one of the outcome measures over time periods ranging from 9 weeks to 12 months. While results of most individual studies were equivocal, a number of studies showed improvement in child-reported anxiety, post-traumatic stress,[2] depression, and self-esteem (Berliner & Saunders, 1996; Clendenon-Wallen, 1991; Cohen & Mannarino, 1992; De Luca, Hazen, & Cutler, 1993; Deblinger, Lippman & Steer, 1996; Deblinger, McLeer, & Henry, 1990; Hoier & Inderbitzenn-Pisaruk, 1987; Kitchur & Bell, 1989; Lanktree & Briere, 1995; Rust & Troupe, 1991; Sinclair, Larzelere, Paine, & Jones, 1995). Looking at all of these studies together, the results suggest certain patterns: While anxiety, depression, and other post-traumatic symptoms appear to be relatively amenable to treatment, sexual problems and externalizing problems such as aggressiveness

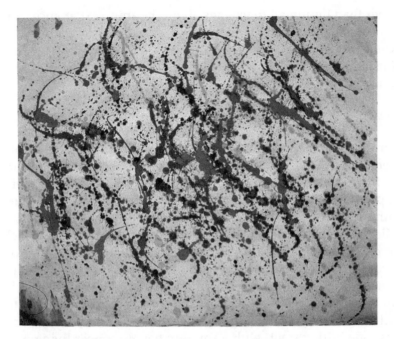

FIGURE 6.7: ARTWORK DONE AT END OF TREATMENT.

and acting out stand out as the most resistant to change. Moreover, different symptoms appear to change at different points in treatment, suggesting a multi-stage process of symptom reduction (see, e.g., Lanktree & Briere, 1995).

Two aspects of the research on child sexual abuse treatment programs were striking in the context of our evaluation of New York Foundling's program. First, as noted earlier, few if any of the programs discussed in the evaluation literature had been housed in the context of a child welfare agency and dealt exclusively with a child welfare population. Second, we were unable to find any studies that specifically explored children's sense of power over their own lives. As discussed earlier, this construct, and the importance of helping sexually victimized children regain a sense of age-appropriate control over their lives, is one of the key elements of the CSATS treatment philosophy. Moreover, because of our interest in the social conditions in children's lives that set the stage for feelings of powerlessness, we were interested in exploring a generalized sense of control and power, rather than limiting it to feelings about the abuse experience. For this reason, as indicated below, generalized *locus of control* (the extent to which children make internal versus external attributions about why things happen) was identified as a central construct for this evaluation.

Evaluation Study Methodology

Our discussion here will focus on a sample of 30 of the 46 children in the Child Sexual Abuse Treatment Service during the study's intake period. While 44 children/families agreed to participate in the study, complete baseline data (obtained at the beginning of the fall treatment cycle) were only obtained on 30 children, and final data (collected at the end of the spring cycle) were available on 15 of them. As indicated in Table 6.1, two-thirds of the sample were female. Most were either Hispanic (primarily Puerto Rican or Dominican) or black (primarily African American or West Indian). Their ages ranged from 8 to 16, with a mean age of 12. Slightly under half were living with at least one birth parent, with a roughly equal number living in a residential treatment program run by the child welfare agency. The rest of the children were in foster boarding homes or kinship foster care. It should be noted that most (23) of the children were already in treatment prior to the beginning of this study; for them, the study captures a "slice of time" in ongoing treatment.

For this chapter, our discussion of findings centers on issues of power and feelings of control. While our evaluation study included measures of several other constructs (e.g., child's behavior, social skills, etc.), we focus here on a locus of control measure as well as two other measures, assessing anxiety and trauma symptomatology, which are related to locus of control both conceptually and, in this study, statistically. The three standardized instruments used to capture these constructs have all displayed high reliability and validity in standardization samples and other research studies. Instruments used in the assessment included:

- The *Nowicki-Strickland Locus of Control—Children's Scale* (LOC-C) (Nowicki & Strickland, 1973), a scale with 40 Yes-No ques-

TABLE 6.1. DESCRIPTION OF SAMPLE

Characteristic	n	%
Gender		
Female	20	67
Male	10	33
Ethnicity		
Latino	15	50
Black	13	43
Caucasian	2	6
Child's Living Arrangement		
Birth Family	13	43
Residential Program	12	40
Foster Home	4	13
Kinship Foster Home	1	3
Prior Treatment at CSA		
Have received prior treatment	23	77
New in fall cycle	7	23
Relationship of Perpetrator		
Non father-figure	14	47
Father-figure	11	37
Unknown	5	17
Nature of Abuse		
No penetration	17	57
Anal or vaginal penetration	13	43

tions that classifies children along a continuum ranging from highly internal to highly external locus of control.

- The *Revised Children's Manifest Anxiety Scale* (RCMAS) (Reynolds & Richmond, 1978), a 37-item self-report instrument for children in grades 1 through 12 that assesses a variety of anxiety symptoms in children. These symptoms are grouped into three subscales: worry and oversensitivity, physiological anxiety, and fear/concentration anxiety.
- The *Trauma Symptom Checklist for Children* (TSCC) (Briere, 1996), a 54-item self-report measure developed for the evaluation of children who experienced traumatic events, including physical

and sexual abuse. The TSCC consists of six subscales: anxiety, depression, post-traumatic stress, sexual concerns, dissociation, and anger.

All children over age 8 were recruited for this study, with consent obtained first from their caregivers and then from the children. Data were collected from both children and parents/caregivers at the beginning of the fall cycle and the end of the spring cycle, with an average of 9 months between the two interviews. Measures were orally administered to the child in individual interviews, typically by a member of the research team.[3] Most interviews were conducted in a single session, though some of the youngest children took two or even three sessions to complete the assessment because of limited concentration abilities.

Study Findings

At the baseline point (n = 30), locus of control was explored in relation to demographic variables, abuse factors, and other mental health/behavioral variables assessed in this study. There were no differences in locus of control based on gender, age, or ethnicity. Similarly, there were no differences between children who were abused by parent figures and those who were abused by others, nor between children who experienced penetration as part of their abuse and those who did not. These abuse factors were selected for inclusion in the study because other research has demonstrated that they have an impact on the severity of children's symptomatology, with those abused by parent figures and those experiencing penetration often being more symptomatic. While the present study did find that children who were penetrated scored higher on the anger and sexual concerns subscales of the TSCC, this finding did not extend to locus of control.

Locus of control at the baseline point was then examined in relation to the other measures used in this study. While it was not related to self-esteem, social skills, or caregiver ratings of problem behaviors, locus of control was significantly related to both level of anxiety as measured by the MAS and trauma symptomatology as measured by the TSCC.[4] For both of these measures, a more external orientation on the LOC-C was associated with greater symptomatology. This finding is consistent with a large body of research suggesting that an internal locus of control is associated with better adjustment in children (see Nowicki, 1986, for review).

Change in Outcome Measures Over Time

Follow-up data were available on 15 of the 30 children assessed at baseline. While children showed no change in self-esteem or social skills, and few changes in behavior as rated by caregivers, they showed highly significant changes in locus of control, and significant changes in the anxiety and trauma constructs which were associated with locus of control at the baseline point. Paired t-tests were used to compare children's scores on these three measures at the two data-collection points. As indicated in Table 6.2, the children in treatment became significantly more

TABLE 6.2. MEAN OUTCOME MEASURE SCORES AT BASELINE AND FOLLOW-UP ASSESSMENTS

Measure	Mean-Baseline (SD)	Mean-Followup (SD)	t (df)
RCMAS Overall	1.18 (.59)	.83 (.45)	2.14 (11)
PSMAS Physiological	1.19 (.72)	.68 (.32)	2.47 (11)*
PCMAS Worry	1.29 (.71)	.95 (.55)	1.60 (11)
RCMAS Fear	1.05 (.55)	.83 (.54)	1.73 (11)
LOC-C Externality	19.13 (5.84)	11.67 (4.63)	− 4.77 (14)***
TSCC Overall	.94 (.57)	.61 (.51)	− 2.07 (9)
TSCC Anxiety	1.05 (.72)	.51 (.59)	− 3.01 (8)*
TSCC PTS	1.09 (.47)	.59 (.57)	− 2.94 (8)*
TSCC Depression	.97 (.72)	.67 (.84)	− 1.50 (9)
TSCC Anger	1.04 (.84)	.82 (.69)	− .82 (9)
TSCC Sex Conc.	.57 (.35)	.29 (.25)	− 1.68 (7)
TSCC Dissoc.	.84 (.74)	.50 (.32)	− 1.72

Key: *p ≤ .05; **p ≤ .01; ***p ≤ .001

internal in their orientations over the 9-month study period. On a 40-point scale, with 1 indicating the most internal orientation and 40 the most external, mean scores on the LOC-C dropped from 19.1 to 11.7; this finding was highly statistically significant (p < .001). The children also displayed significant improvements in overall anxiety (RCMAS), physiological symptoms of anxiety (RCMAS-Phys.), trauma-related anxiety (TSCC-Anxiety), and post-traumatic stress symptoms (TSCC-PTS). All of these changes were statistically significant at the .05 level.

Discussion

The findings of this study were relatively consistent with prior research on treatment outcome for sexually abused children. Specifically, the patterns of improvement in some of the anxiety and post-traumatic stress measures, but no improvement in dissociation, anger, or sexual concerns, is one that has been seen in several other studies of this nature (see Finkelhor & Berliner, 1995). With regard to abuse-related variables, the findings of the present study are consistent with research showing that children who have experienced penetration as part of the abuse are more symptomatic than those who did not. However, this study did not find a relationship between abuser being a parent figure and symptom levels that has been demonstrated in other studies. This may be a function of the fact that all of the children in the present sample were in a child welfare population, and thus *all* of them—including those whose sexual abuse was not perpetrated by a parental figure—had experienced some form of parental abuse, neglect, or, at best, highly inadequate parenting. Consequently, our analyses were not necessarily comparing children who had been sexually abused by parents to those whose parents were non-abusive. Rather, we may be comparing parental sexual abuse to other forms of parental abuse or neglect, which have also been consistently demonstrated to result in psychological and behavioral problems (see, e.g., Malinosky-Rummell & Hansen, 1993). The emotional upheaval resulting from the disruptions of trust and the traumatic betrayal experienced by children sexually abused by parental figures were likely to be present in the other children in this sample as well. The evaluation of the CSATS demonstrated particularly interesting patterns with regard to locus of control. First, the lack of correlation between age and locus of control at the baseline point ran counter to consistent findings that, in the course of normal development, children become more internal in their orientations as they get older (Nowicki & Strickland, 1973). The absence of this pattern in the present sample suggests that the experience of being sexually abused, especially in the context of other risk factors in children's lives, may interrupt the normal course of development and the normal changes that occur in how children view the world and their place in it.

The second important finding related to locus of control was that this variable, more than any of the others measured, showed a highly significant change over the study period, with children becoming more internal over the course of treatment. This finding offers strong support for the trauma theory model used by the program, with its emphasis on addressing the sense of helplessness and powerlessness engendered by the experience of sexual abuse. While only an experimental design could demonstrate conclusively that the shift in locus of control was a direct result of treatment, and not a function of maturation or some other artifact, the current finding certainly highlights the importance of using locus of control as an assessment tool and of including it in further research in this field.

It is especially noteworthy that the change in locus of control was more dramatic than the other changes in symptomatology displayed by the children. One hypothesis, based largely on anecdotal evidence and clinical observations of program staff, is that changes in children's sense of power and control are necessary precursors to changes in other symptom domains. In fact, perhaps a growing sense of internal control over one's environment is needed before children can begin to do the psychological work required to address other problems such as fear, dissociation, or traumatic sexualization. There is some evidence (e.g., Lanktree & Briere, 1995) for a stage process of symptom reduction, in which different symptoms get addressed and resolved at different stages of treatment, in a clear sequential process. It may be that one of the first domains to respond to effective treatment is the sense of oneself as an active being, with some degree of control over one's immediate world. This would be consistent with trauma theory, which views the experience of being helpless and out of control as setting the stage for the abuse to be traumatic. It is therefore not unreasonable to assume that that damage to one's sense of power and control must be "undone" before the trauma itself can be resolved.

This possibility raises interesting clinical and programmatic questions. If symptom reduction occurs in a stage process, and locus of control is a necessary precursor for other changes, should treatment involve using different interventions at different stages? Are there indicators at each stage that the symptoms addressed in that stage have changed "enough" for the next stage of treatment to begin? Do all children progress through the stages in the same sequence, and what determines the rate of change at each stage? These are questions that could be explored through systematic and longitudinal research and program evaluation, with multiple assessments of child clients at different stages of the therapeutic intervention process. Particularly, incorporating assessments of the child's locus of control into evaluation studies would be valuable in identifying the role which this construct may play in facilitating the resolution of traumatic experiences.

An additional area worthy of further exploration is the role of prior stressors—particularly those associated with the experience of powerlessness—in the lives of sexually abused children. Specifically, to what extent do these stressors increase the likelihood that the abuse will be experienced as traumatic, and what role do they play in the effort to resolve the trauma? Because of the relatively homogeneous sample in the New York Foundling program (i.e., all were poor, members of minority groups, and involved in the child welfare system), our research offered little opportunity to examine these questions, but they are important ones to consider in further research.

CONCLUSION

Both the clinical evidence derived from the progress of children in the Child Sexual Abuse Treatment Service and the research findings from an evaluation of that treatment program highlight the importance of children's sense of control in the healing from sexual victimization. We conclude with a poem written by an adolescent girls' group in the CSATS which reminds us of the power that children derive from their own participation in the healing process:

GROUP POEM #10A

a color symbolizes a feeling
a feeling symbolizes a color
and both things together
mean many things . . .

today we went behind the closed doors
and found the colors
some mixed, some segmented, some layered
all telling stories . . .

a tapestry
for all to see
we celebrate the vibrancy of light
of hope . . .

like a piece of broken glass
that will someday be put together
our work requires great strength . . .

NOTES

1. Caregivers are also encouraged to be in treatment and/or to participate in collateral work with the child's therapist, whenever possible.

2. Post-traumatic stress is conceptualized in the review as one subset of trauma symptoms, consistent with Briere's (1996) factor analysis of his Trauma Symptom Checklist for Children, used in much of the research cited above.

3. While most of the children were interviewed by a member of the research team, a small number were interviewed by their own therapist when it was deemed too distressing for them to be interviewed by a stranger.

4. The correlation between locus of control and anxiety yielded an r of .38, p < .05; locus of control and TSCC scores were correlated at 50, p < .01.

References

Beichtman, J. H., Zuker, K. L., Hood, J. E., & DaCosta-Granville, A. (1992). A review of the long-term effects of child sexual abuse. *Child Abuse and Neglect, 16*(1), 101–118.

Berliner, L., & Saunders, B. (1996). Treating fear and anxiety in sexually abused children: Results of a controlled 2-year follow-up study. *Child Maltreatment, 1*(4), 294–310.

Beutler, L. E., Williams, R. E., & Zetzer, H. A. (1994). Efficacy of treatment for victims of child sexual abuse. *The Future of Children, 4*(2), 156–176.

Blake, D., Albano, A. M., & Keane, T. (1992). Twenty years of trauma: Psychological abstract 1970 through 1989. *Journal of Traumatic Stress, 5*(3), 277–284.

Bolstad, B. R., & Zinbarg, R. E. (1997). Sexual victimization, generalized perception of control, and posttraumatic stress disorder symptom severity. *Journal of Anxiety Disorders, 11*(5), 523–540.

Boncher, M. (1994). Services for families in which a child has been sexually abused. In E. Holzer (Ed.), *Future directions in serving the most troubled children and families: A collection of papers presented at the 1993 annual meeting of the Council of Family and Child Caring Agencies* (pp. 2–5) (Available from COFCCA).

Brickman, E. (1993). *Public policy responses to child sexual abuse: Final report.* New York: Victim Services.

Briere, J. (1996). *Trauma Symptom Checklist for Children.* Odessa, FL: Psychological Assessment Resources.

Briere, J., & Runtz, M. (1993). Child sexual abuse: Long-term sequelae and implications for assessment. *Journal of Interpersonal Violence, 8,* 312–330.

Carlson, E., Furby, L., Armstrong, J., & Shlaes, J. (1997). A conceptual framework for the long-term psychological effects of traumatic childhood abuse. *Child Maltreatment, 2*(3), 272–295.

Clendenon-Wallen, J. (1991). The use of music therapy to influence the self-confidence and self-esteem of adolescents who are sexually abused. *Music Therapy Perspective, 9,* 73–91.

Cohen, J. A., & Mannarino, A. P. (1992). *The effectiveness of short-term structured group psychotherapy for sexually abused girls: A pilot study.* Paper presented at a lecture series on therapy for sexually abused children. University of Pittsburgh School of Medicine.

Deblinger, E., Lippman, J., & Steer, R. (1996). Sexually abused children suffering posttraumatic stress symptoms: Initial treatment outcome findings. *Child Maltreatment, 1,* 310–322.

Deblinger, E., McLeer, S. V., & Henry, D. (1990). Cognitive behavioral treatment for sexually abused children suffering post-traumatic stress: Preliminary findings. *Journal of American Academy of Child and Adolescent Psychiatry, 29,* 747–752.

De Luca, R., Hazen, A., & Cutler, J. (1993). Evaluation of a group counseling program for preadolescent female victims of incest. *Elementary School Guidance Counseling, 28,* 104–114.

Finkelhor, D., & Berliner, L. (1995). Research on the treatment of sexually abused children: A review and recommendations. *Journal of the American Academy of Child and Adolescent Psychiatry, 34*(11), 1408–1423.

Finkelhor, D., & Browne, A. (1985). The traumatic impact of sexual abuse: A conceptualization. *American Journal of Orthopsychiatry, 55,* 530–541.

Friedrich, W. N. (1990). *Psychotherapy of sexually abused children and their families.* New York: Norton.

Gil, E. (1991). *The healing power of play: Working with abused children.* New York: Guilford Press.

Greene, A. H. (1993). Child sexual abuse: Immediate and long-term effects and interventions. *Journal of the American Academy of Child and Adolescent Psychiatry, 32*(5), 890–902.

Herman, J. L. (1992). *Trauma and recovery.* New York: Basic Books.

Hoier, T., & Inderbitzenn-Pisaruk, H. (1987). *Brief treatment of sexually abused children.* Presented at the West Virginia Psychological Association Meeting, Pipestem, WV (October).

James, B. (1989). *Treating traumatized children: New insights and creative interventions.* Lexington, MA: Lexington Books.

Kendall-Tackett, K. A., Williams, L. M., & Finkelhor, D. (1993).

Impact of sexual abuse on children: A review and synthesis of recent empirical studies. *Psychological Bulletin, 113,* 161–180.

Kitchur, M., & Bell, R. (1989), Group psychotherapy with preadolescent sex abuse victims: Literature review and description of an inner-city group. *International Journal of Group Psychotherapy, 39,* 285–310.

Lanktree, C., & Briere, J. (1995). Outcome therapy for sexually abused children: A repeated measures study. *Child Abuse and Neglect, 19,* 1145–1155.

Malinosky-Rummell, R., & Hansen, D. J. (1993). Long-term consequences of childhood physical abuse. *Psychological Bulletin, 114*(1), 68–79.

Moyer, D. M., DiPietro, L., Berkowitz, R. I., & Stunkard, A. J. (1997). Childhood sexual abuse and precursors of binge eating disorders in an adolescent female population. *International Journal of Eating Disorders, 21*(1), 23–30.

Nowicki, S. (1986). *Children's Nowicki-Strickland Internal-External Locus of Control.* Unpublished manual, Emory University.

Nowicki, S., & Strickland, B. (1973). A locus of control scale for children. *Journal of Consulting and Clinical Psychology, 40,* 148–154.

Reynolds, C. R., & Richmond, B. O. (1978). What I think and feel: A revised measure of children's manifest anxiety. *Journal of Abnormal Child Psychology, 6,* 271–280.

Rhodes, J. E., Ebert, L., & Meyers, A. B. (1993). Sexual victimization in young, pregnant and parenting African-American women: Psychological and social outcomes. *Violence and Victims, 8*(2), 153–163.

Rowan, A. B., & Foy, D. W. (1993). Post traumatic stress disorder in child sexual abuse survivors: A literature review. *Journal of Traumatic Stress, 6*(1), 3–20.

Rust, J. O., & Troupe, P. A. (1991). Relationship of treatment of child sexual abuse with school achievement. *Journal of Early Adolescence, 11,* 420–429.

Saunders, B. E., Villeponteaux, L. A., Lipovsky, J. A., Kilpatrick, D. G., & Veronen, L. J. (1992). Child sexual assault as a risk factor for mental disorders among women. *Journal of Interpersonal Violence, 7,* 189–204.

Sgroi, S. M. (1982). *Handbook of clinical interventions in child sexual abuse.* Lexington, MA: Lexington Books.

Sinclair, J. J., Larzelere, R. E., Paine, M., & Jones, P. (1995). Outcome effects of group treatment for sexually abused adolescent females living in a group home setting: Preliminary findings. *Journal of Interpersonal Violence, 10*(4), 533–542.

van der Kolk, B. (1987). *Psychological trauma.* Washington, DC: American Psychiatric Press.

Wilson, J. P. (1995). The historical evolution of PTSD diagnostic criteria. In G. S. Everlym & J. M. Lating (Eds.), *Psychotraumatology* (pp. 9–26). New York: Plenum.

7

Bereavement Issues to Consider for Latino Children Whose Parents Die of AIDS

Felix Lorenzo, CSW

SEVEN TO TEN THOUSAND AMERICAN CHILDREN are orphaned each year when their mothers die from AIDS (Gardner & Preator, 1996). A significant number of families affected by AIDS are minority families. According to a Centers for Disease Control (CDC) report in 1995, the majority of infected women in the United States are women of color. This report cites that 77% of AIDS cases among women have occurred among African Americans and Latinos, and 90% of these have dependent children (CDC, 1995). As a consequence of this daunting reality, the number of orphans has increased in direct proportion to the increased number of women infected with HIV.

The AIDS epidemic was reportedly overwhelmingly represented among gay men in its initial phases. AIDS as a threat to women was underestimated, and to this date, epidemiological studies capturing the levels of infection among women are still not conclusive in their estimates. Some projects, such as The Orphan Project in New York City, have attempted to obtain a more accurate figure on the number of infected women (Michaels & Levine, 1992). The study cited that by the end of 1995, it was estimated that maternal deaths would have orphaned approximately 24,000 children in the United States, and projections estimate more than 7,000 children orphaned per year (Michaels & Levine, 1992). Caldwell, Fleming, and Oxtoby (1992) used a similar method to estimate that 10,000 children are orphaned annually. However, these estimates are probably low since the HIV infection is spreading rapidly throughout the population of childbearing women. While the use of new forms of therapy to fight the HIV infection has increased the life expectancy of many infected individuals, such treatments do need to be taken under strictly regimented schedules. Many of our clients find it difficult to follow such regimens and often drop out of treatment. A significant number of these women will not benefit from these treatments, and consequently the number of children orphaned will continue to rise.

The literature beginning to address the needs of these children reports the slow pace at which these needs have been acknowledged in the social service arena (Dane & Levine, 1994). However, those of us in the area of mental health, working or supervising work with children, have experienced a rapid increase of the number of orphan children due to AIDS in our facilities. Many of these children are not referred to us until after their parents have died, and after they begin to present difficulties in the adjustment to the new living environments or in their schools. The children often appear confused, overwhelmed, and depressed. Their caretakers may be equally confused, often experiencing their own bereavement process, in spite of which they are trying to carry out their responsibilities for attending to these children with limited support.

There are some special circumstances surrounding the lives of these poor, inner-city children that need to be taken into consideration in understanding their bereavement process. Death is not a single, separate episode in the midst of a stable life. Multiple losses are often the case in their lives. In some instances, the death of a parent comes after these children have been exposed to deaths of siblings, uncles, aunts, and friends. The AIDS epidemic has forced many children to face the consecutive disintegration of their fragile support system, and of what they have known as a family. Under such circumstances, reactions of pain and anxiety to the loss and separation tend to become exacerbated, rendering the child chronically exposed to a pervasive feeling of hopelessness and helplessness. Others appear to become numb to the losses and instead act out in school and at home the turmoil going on inside of them.

The bereavement process is complicated by the other kinds of adjustments these children are called upon to endure, including relocation to a new residence, legal problems concerning permanency and custody, and a host of other practical realities (Dane, 1994). The long journey of stress that often accompanies the illness of a parent and the witnessing of their physical deterioration is not over with the parent's death. These children continue to be exposed to changes and adjustments while they are expected to simultaneously fight for physical and emotional survival. They need to learn to live with a chronic sense of vulnerability, without emotional security, and with a lack of permanency in their lives. All these factors can have an impact on their ability to mourn their losses, come to some resolution of their bereavement problems, and regain hope in a future.

Among Latino children there are certain patterns related to the role of the family, as prescribed by the culture, that may delay or derail the bereavement process. Family members experience the pressure of taking care of their children and grandchildren, as well as other extended members in the family if someone dies. Grandparents, in particular, are seen as the ones responsible to carry on with the responsibilities left behind by the deceased. These individuals often cannot access the much-needed support services due to language barriers and the often entrenched belief that the family matrix is the place where problems are to be solved. Going outside the family to receive support may be experienced as a source of shame for the individual, or as an admission that one is not capable of taking care of the family. There is also fear of being perceived as failing to carry out one's responsibilities to the family, which can be a major source of shame and embarrassment in Latino culture.

BEREAVEMENT AMONG CHILDREN: CONCEPTUAL AND EMPIRICAL LITERATURE

Initial understanding of childhood bereavement stemmed from the understanding of adult grief reactions proposed by Freud (Freud, 1917/1957). These views emphasized the need to decathect from the loved object. Early theorists questioned the ability of a child to endure this process due to a lack of ego development needed in the process of using more advanced defenses. The view of the time was that individuals were not capable of experiencing a true bereavement process until late adolescence (Wolfenstein, 1966). Practitioners relied for their observations on adults who were in treatment and reported on the loss of a loved one in childhood; therefore, the clinical understanding of the time was to see the reaction to the death of the parent as a pathological one in the context of treatment. It was emphasized that children relied on pathological defenses such as denial, splitting of the ego, or idealization of the lost object. The mobilization of these primitive defenses was believed to distort the course of development (Shapiro, 1994). More recent perspectives have acknowledged other factors affecting the bereavement process. The emphasis has now shifted so that bereavement is seen as an appropriate reaction to the loss of a loved object. More weight has also been placed on the environmental resources available to assist the child in negotiating the loss (Furman, 1974). This view emphasizes the fact that with appropriate response from surviving parents and other adults, grieving children can be helped to complete their mourning in ways that do not compromise their ongoing development.

The work of John Bowlby (1969, 1980) on attachment theory and on the impact of loss and separation in children has emphasized the primary importance of the environment in the facilitation or distortion of the bereavement process. Bowlby (1980) emphasized the role of the conscious or unconscious needs of the adults and caretakers in this process. His work confirms the view that children are capable of grieving in developmentally appropriate ways when the distortions and defenses of adults do not interfere. The process of bereavement is seen as a combination of intrapsychic and social experiences.

Shapiro (1994) reports that different studies point in the direction of emphasizing the family's participation in the bereavement process. The family's roles include the need for the caretaker to provide the child with an accurate version of reality, appropriate to his or her age and stage of cognitive functioning; freedom for the child to be able to express feelings about illness and death; inclusion in some kind of family ritual; and stable caretaking in a consistent and caring way. The conclusion in this study is that depending on the child's age and stage of development, he or she may be extremely confused and fearful about the circumstances and implications of the death, and will need a great deal of support and clarification.

Of particular relevance in the bereavement process is the negative impact resulting when children are prevented from experiencing and discussing their feelings in relation to the loss. This attitude tends to complicate natural bereavement. Ellis (1989) has labeled this process as "disenfranchising children from their grieving." Parents who feel they are protecting their children by not talking about the death actually leave the child unprotected from potentially negative consequences of delayed, restrained, or unresolved grief. Some adult psychopathologies are associated with the truncation of the bereavement process at the appropriate age.

A growing body of literature is attempting to explain the factors affecting on the bereavement process for children whose parents have died of AIDS. Unfortunately, this work is appearing slowly and is more conceptual and anecdotal than experimental in nature. This literature describes complicating factors deriving from the stressful circumstances surrounding those dying of AIDS. Such factors interrupt or delay the bereavement process, in detriment of development, and cause conflicts in the long-term process of adaptation needed by these children.

In addition, these children may also experience a change in their self-concept following the death of a parent. Separation anxiety and fear of abandonment tend to increase. The death of a parent from AIDS may additionally increase children's sense of isolation, as they are aware of the stigma associated with the disease (Seigel & Freund, 1994). Children who undergo these changes will inevitably feel diminished by the experience. The exchange of information needed by children to deal with the cause of death and to gain a better grasp of the implications of the illness is often missing from families where AIDS is the cause of death. This is in order to avoid dealing publicly with the cause of death and its possible implications (Dane, 1994). Lack of information about parental death from AIDS supports the denial mechanism, which, when operative for longer than the typical period of shock, impedes bereavement.

Experimental Studies Around Bereavement

Some experimental studies are reported with children undergoing the bereavement process. These studies focus on reactions a few months after the death of a parent; the construction of the image of the parent a year after the death; the role that adults may play in the creation of such an image; and the severity of bereavement reactions in relation to other preexisting factors.

A study by Silverman and Worden (1992) reports on a nonclinical group of 125 dependent children aged 6–7 years who were examined within 4 months of the death of a parent. The analysis focused on normative behavior in the domains of the children's reactions to the death itself, their affective experience, their efforts at remaining connected to the deceased, their social network and support system, and changes in their families resulting from the death reaction of the children in specific domains. Important conclusions of this study were that the event was stressful and affected many aspects of their lives. There was, however, little indication of serious dysfunctional behavior in the long term. These children were dealing not only with the death of a parent, but with the death of a way of life. The youngsters in this study were trying to make the loss real and to find out what really happened to their parents. The analysis of the data points to the importance of understanding the children's context in the social and family system. It also points to an inner resiliency that needs to be taken into consideration.

Nickman, Silverman, and Normand (1998) found that during the year following a parent's death, children in a community-based sample were found to have developed an inner construction of the dead parent. The altered relationship appeared to facilitate their coping with the loss and with accompanying changes in their lives. The deceased parents were present in the children's waking thoughts. The study concludes that the inner representation of the parent allows the child to remain in a relationship with the departed, and this relationship changes as the child matures and as the intensity of the grief lessens. An important aspect of the study is the suggestion that bereavement should not be viewed as a psychological state that terminates or from which one recovers. The intensity may lessen and the child may become oriented more to the future, but a point of closure signifying the end of the bereavement process does not seem to be compatible with this study.

Elizur and Kaffman (1983) describe the severity of childhood bereavement reactions. Their study is drawn from a longitudinal study of 25 adolescent kibbutz children who lost their fathers during the October War of 1973. The effects of child, family, and circumstantial variables were examined in an effort to assess their relative contribution to the intense emotional disturbance exhibited by half of the group. The findings suggest that pre-traumatic family and environmental factors are significant determinants of the duration and severity of bereavement. The study concluded that those children who experienced a more severe reaction represented those who had a combination of factors stemming from the child and the family. More important, the study suggests that reactions taking place during the early months of bereavement were largely determined by pre-traumatic antecedent variables (e.g., the child's emotional condition before the loss and the presence or absence of family conflict), while post-traumatic factors (e.g., the quality of the mother-child relationship and the mother's ability to cope with the stress of loss) were more influential during the years following bereavement.

Psychosocial Aspects of AIDS

Children coming from multi-problem families often encounter AIDS as one among many other tragedies in their lives. The long sequence of inconsistent, abusive, and confusing relationships between parents and children affects their psychological development and is compounded by the specific stressors related to AIDS. In a long sequence of disappointments, the death of a parent becomes the ultimate form of separation and loss.

Tony was an attractive, friendly 9-year-old Puerto Rican boy referred to the clinic because of behavioral problems experienced both at school and with his grandmother at home. Because of his mother's chronic substance abuse and neglect of his needs, Tony had been removed from her care. His grandmother asked to take him and was granted legal guardianship. Tony was well related and quite verbal. He was seen in biweekly sessions in individual treatment. I attempted to engage his grandmother in doing some family work as often as she was able and willing to come to sessions. Tony consistently expressed his desire to return to his mother. He was constantly concerned about her drug use and the possibility of her becoming incarcerated. Both Tony and his grandmother were very attached to Tony's mother in spite of their complaints about her behavior, and both showed concern for her safety. They shared the expectation that she was going to "kick the habit" and return to a normal life. During the first year in treatment, Tony had great difficulty in letting go of the idealized image of the mother who was going to leave the drugs to return for his custody. Tony's mother was diagnosed with AIDS after he had been in treatment for over a year. The mother shared this information with him without any preparation. She told him that now that she knew she had AIDS and she had decided to enter a program to "get her life together and take him to live with her to a new home." Tony was extremely excited about the prospect of being returned to his mother, and he totally ignored the fact that his mother was deteriorating rapidly. The grandmother was immersed in her hopes for a miracle cure, because as she stated, "It wasn't fair that her daughter wouldn't have a second chance." Trying to work around the reality of the disease and the preparation for the impending death proved to be most difficult, as I often encountered strong denial and anger from Tony and his grandmother when I attempted to help them to accept her illness and make preparations for the future. Tony was devastated when his mother died. Since he kept hoping she would take control of her life and regain custody, her passing was the ultimate form of disappointment, coming from a mother who never kept her word to him. I vividly remember him saying session after session after her death, "She never did what she promised."

THE LATINO FAMILY STRUCTURE

The Latino family's adaptability to multiple roles in caretaking often cushions extremely painful experiences for these children.

In the Latino culture, the concept of family encompasses not only the nuclear family but also an extended network of relatives. The family is seen as the unit that holds all its members together, providing protection and caretaking for life (Papajohn & Spiegel, 1975). Transferring child care responsibilities from one member of the family to another is not seen as a sign of neglect (Garcia Preto, 1982); in fact, it is a common practice in many situations, and particularly in times of crisis. There is a social expectation that family members will become responsible for other family members, and their children, when there are problems, particularly health-related problems (Soriano, 1991).

The role of the grandmother in these families is of particular relevance (Garcia Preto, 1982). The grandparents serve as a stabilizing force in the family during these crises. They bring together different people within the family and bridge the time between when the parent's illness intensifies and when the parent dies (Chachkes & Jennings, 1994). Other relatives may play an equally important role in securing a place for these children. However, often these grandparents are old and not emotionally prepared for this task, including the long-term caring required by the children. In spite of this reality, their perceived sense of obligation toward the family, as well as the expectations emanating from the culture and family for them to fulfill this function, leaves them with little space to renounce this responsibility. In addition, their conscious or unconscious hope that they can undo, through their grandchildren, the mistakes they believe they made with their children often prevents them from contemplating the idea that others may assume responsibility for the children. In such cases, their guilt and sense of obligation supersede the needs of the child. Thus, instead of exploring more appropriate long-term permanent arrangements, the grandparents see themselves locked into the caretaker role. Should these plans fail to materialize because the grandparents become ill or the grandchildren are too difficult for them to handle, the children have to face a new separation with its concomitant feelings of loss and abandonment when they are removed from the grandparents. This situation interferes with the kind of appropriate environment where the mourning related to the bereavement process is possible.

Some of these children are not able to use additional resources, such as support groups, to carry out the necessary tasks for bereavement. The culturally entrenched belief that the family is the only safe place to deal with and speak about their problems often cuts these children off from additional resources needed in this time of transition. Since these are the values of the family, any perceived acknowledgment of the inability to take care of their own is a grave injury to the sense of pride that is so highly valued by Latinos. The HIV diagnosis adds to the sense of secrecy for fear of rejection by other family members and members of the community. This situation leaves the child and the family particularly vulnerable and at risk of not receiving the appropriate support services available in the community (Zayas & Romano, 1997). When it comes to obtaining support from other sources where children can go and talk about their feelings, the family may try to derail the process for the sake of protecting itself from having to expose potentially shameful information. The predominant fear is that exposing a problem of one of its members may make the whole family liable for a bad reputation. Secrecy becomes an end in itself. Such an attitude conspires against the needs of the children to find others undergoing the same problems. Under these circumstances, children are left without a place to do their mourning outside their families. This situation becomes even more detrimental in families with multiple losses, where the adults may resist open discussions on these matters in order to protect themselves from the pain resulting from other deaths in the family.

Tony's family provides a good example. During the course of Tony's mother's illness, my attempts at getting the grandmother to evaluate possible alternatives for Tony's long-term care were met with resistance. The grandmother felt that she, as the closest relative, had total obligation for his caring, regardless of the fact that she was old, had chronic health conditions, and was also dealing with her other son's diagnosis of being HIV positive. She felt that something in her child rearing had gone terribly awry to have her two children dying of AIDS. This time she hoped to "do the right thing" with Tony, who would also be the only permanent reminder of her daughter. While I also agreed that she truly cared for Tony, and was willing to provide him with the very best she could afford materially and psychologically, it seemed to me that it was very important that she consider and make use of other alternatives available, such as the support in the community, including support groups, the use of a home attendant to assist her, and so forth. The grandmother truly felt she should and would be able to do it all by herself, and was terrified at the prospect of other service providers finding out that her daughter had AIDS.

When Tony's mother died, his uncle's health was also deteriorating. Tony needed to talk about his pain, but his grandmother insisted that prayer was the answer to the problem. She insisted that he should be happy for his mother because she was now in heaven. It was only during the individual sessions, twice a week, that he was more comfortable and able to open up and reveal his pain and anger, his sense of disappointment, and his uncertainty about the future. His grandmother always rejected my suggestion that he attend a support group with other children in the same situation. Fortunately, she had a good enough relationship with me and continued to attend the family sessions where Tony could address some issues with her. Since I was so close to them, and being Latino myself, I had become "a part of the family," as the grandmother often stated. This meant I was part of the inner circle where she could allow herself and also allow Tony to open up and speak about the many pent-up feelings associated with the loss. The grandmother's insistence that Tony's mother was in heaven was her way of precluding the expression of sadness. Knowing the strong influence that the Catholic faith had in this family, I introduced the concept that even Jesus cried when he came to see his friend who had died. The grandmother could work with this concept and became more open to expressing her pain.

IMPLICATIONS FOR PRACTICE

There are important considerations in working with Latino children who have parents with AIDS, or whose parents have died of AIDS. Of particular relevance are the following:

1. *Offer respect and consideration for the family's perspective and*

plans. The therapist needs to understand the particular beliefs of the family and of the culture in order to intervene and advocate for the child. It is of high importance for the Latino families to feel respected. Exploring their plans prematurely or questioning them about their arrangements may be perceived by the family as intrusive and culturally insensitive. It is only when a therapist becomes a real part of the family's "inner circle" that his or her recommendations begin to have a real effect on future planning. The work with the family should focus on understanding the particular meaning this death has for the rest of the family and the particular ways the family understands the distribution of future responsibilities. The worker must be aware that the family may try many different arrangements within its structure, including sending the child to the country of origin with other relatives, before they are ready to explore alternatives outside the family. Since these relatives mean well for the child, a psychoeducational approach may be helpful in describing the child's need to mourn the death of the parent and the need for a stable environment in order to secure this process.

The therapist who has secured a strong working alliance with the family may then provide recommendations as to how the family may be able to provide such an environment, given their particular circumstances. As the family feels ready to explore other alternatives, the therapist may be in a position to make further recommendations.

2. *Create the emotional climate where the child is able to speak about the loss.* It is equally important to assess the family's ability to let the child speak about the deceased parent. If such an environment does not already exist within the family, the individual therapy session should become the means by which some of this work may take place, where the child can experience the freedom to disclose painful and confusing feelings related to the death and separation. The family tradition of memorializing the death may be explored, and sometimes the therapist can help plan such rituals if he or she feels comfortable in such tasks. The focus should be on opening up spaces for the child to acknowledge the death of the parent and to begin to construct an internal image of the parent that comes as close as possible to the reality of the deceased. Therefore, the family's religious beliefs can be

of assistance in creating the appropriate climate for the expression of sadness. Once a context that embraces family members' shared perspective is established, appropriate mourning is possible and expressions of sadness and loss can be normalized. It is a good opportunity to use the family's religious beliefs in a therapeutic context, as long as it is done sensitively and respectfully.

3. *Educate service providers about cultural values affecting bereavement decisions.* Many agencies deal with these children and their families in bureaucratic ways as they attempt to deal with the legal aspects of custody. As important as such legal aspects are in the child's future, these services must be sensitized to the psychological journeys these children must traverse in life. The conceptual and empirical literature cited throughout this chapter confirm the fact that bereavement is both an inner psychic process and a social process. The need to provide a consistent, safe, and caring therapeutic environment for the individual child client in this process is as important as the need to foster or create a family environment that allows for the expression, processing, and working through of these feelings. Being sensitive to and understanding of the cultural and familial patterns is of a great assistance in this endeavor, particularly in the clinical work with Latino families affected by AIDS.

REFERENCES

Bowlby, J. (1969). *Attachment and loss.* Vol. 1, *Attachment.* New York: Basic Books

Bowlby, J. (1980). *Attachment and loss.* Vol. 3, *Loss: Sadness and depression.* New York: Basic Books.

Caldwell, M. B., Fleming, P. L., & Oxtoby, M. J. (1992). Estimated number of AIDS orphans in the United States. *Pediatrics, 90,* 482.

Centers for Disease Control. (1995). AIDS among women—United States, 1994. *Morbidity and Mortality Weekly Report, 44,* 81–84.

Chachkes, E., & Jennings, R. (1994). Latino communities: Coping with death. In B. O. Dane & C. Levine (Eds.), *AIDS and the new orphans: Coping with death* (pp. 77–100). Westport, CT: Auburn House.

Dane, B. O. (1994). Death and bereavement. In B. O. Dane & C. Levine (Eds.), *AIDS and the new orphans: Coping with death* (pp. 13–31). Westport, CT, : Auburn House.

Dane, B. O., & Levine, C. (1994). *AIDS and the new orphans: Coping with death.* Westport, CT: Auburn House.

Elizur, E., & Kaffman, M. (1983). Factors influencing the severity of childhood bereavement reactions. *American Journal of Orthopsychiatry, 53,* 668–676.

Ellis, R. (1989). Young children: Disenfranchised grievers. In K. J. Doka (Ed.), *Disenfranchised grief: Recognizing hidden sorrow* (pp. 201–211). Lexington, MA: Lexington Books.

Freud, S. (1917/1957). Mourning and melancholia. In J. Rickman (Ed.), *A general selection from the works of Sigmund Freud* (pp. 124–140). Garden City, NY: Doubleday.

Furman, E. (1974). *A child's parent dies: Studies in childhood bereavement.* New Haven: Yale University Press.

Garcia Preto, N. (1982). Puerto Rican families. In M. McGoldrick, J. Pearce, & J. Giordano (Eds.), *Ethnicity and family therapy* (pp. 164–185). New York: Guilford.

Gardner, W., & Preator, K. (1996). Children of seropositive mothers in the U.S. AIDS epidemic. *Journal of Social Issues, 52,* 177–195.

Michaels, D., & Levine, C. (1992). Estimates of the number of motherless youth orphaned by AIDS in the United States. *Journal of the American Medical Association, 268,* 3456–3461.

Nickman, S. L., Silverman, P. R., & Normand, C. (1998). Children's construction of a deceased parent: The surviving parent's contribution. *American Journal of Orthopsychiatry, 68,* 126–134.

Papajohn, J., & Spiegel, J. (1975). *Transaction in families.* San Francisco: Jossey-Bass.

Seigel, K., & Freund B. (1994). Parental loss and latency age children. In B. O. Dane & C. Levine (Eds.), *AIDS and the new orphans: Coping with death* (pp. 43–58). Westport, CT: Auburn House.

Shapiro, E. R. (1994). *Grief as a family process: A developmental approach to clinical practice.* New York: Guilford.

Silverman, P., & Worden, W. (1992). Children's reactions to the death of a parent in the early months after the death. *American Journal of Orthopsychiatry, 62,* 93–104.

Soriano, F. (1991). AIDS a challenge to Hispanics and their families. In M. Sotomayer (Ed.), *Empowering Hispanic families: A critical issue for the 90's* (pp. 59–74). Milwaukee: Family Services of America.

Wolfenstein, M. (1966). How is mourning possible? *Psychoanalytic Study of the Child, 21,* 93–123.

Zayas, L. H., & Romano, K. (1997). Motherless children: Family interventions with AIDS orphans. In E. Congress (Ed.), *Multicultural perspectives in working with families* (pp. 109–124). New York: Springer.

8

When Children Arrive Later: Helping the Separated and Reunited Immigrant Child

Carol P. Kaplan, PhD

INTRODUCTION

First- and second-generation immigrant children, according to a recent estimate, constitute the fastest-growing segment of the U.S. population under the age of 18 (Board on Children and Families, 1995). While many of these children and adolescents immigrate together with their families, this chapter will address those who have had disrupted immigration experiences—in particular, separations and subsequent reunions with a biological parent or parents who may have immigrated to the United States at an earlier point. At present, scant research exists concerning this group of youngsters, and exact figures are not known. However, a small number of studies, as well as the impressions of clinicians, indicate that substantial numbers of young people fall into this category. It is noteworthy that the phenomenon of separation and reunion of children with their parents has been recognized in other countries as well, since immigration has become a global phenomenon (Prince, 1968; Kosar, 1988; Christiansen, 1980; Da Costa, 1976; Glasgow & Gouse-Sheese, 1995).

Fanshel, Finch, and Gundy (1992), in their study of 129 poor clients on the Lower East Side of New York, identified certain exogenous variables that indicated families at risk. One of these variables was separation due to immigration. The authors found that while most parent-child separations in their sample resulted from children's placement in foster care, 18 clients were having problems with their children as a consequence of separations and subsequent reunions imposed by the exigencies of immigration. They recommended preventive interventions to help clients deal with immigration-related separations.

Zayas (1993) has described finding severe separation anxiety and reactive attachment disorders among young Hispanic children, problems which he believes to originate in a situation common among Latin American immigrants. That is, the youngsters have remained in the home country in the care of extended family or friends while the parents have immigrated to the United States to work; or, even when the children were born in the United States, the parents have sent them back to their native countries for economic reasons. Ginsburg and Silverman (1996) found a higher incidence of separation anxiety and fearfulness among Hispanic children and adolescents from low-income families than among Caucasian youth. Their study may buttress Zayas's clinical impression, although this bears further investigation.

Despite the relative paucity of data about separated and reunited immigrant children, the information that does exist suggests that while certain dimensions remain constant, many different scenarios may play themselves out. Furthermore, each one of these variations will have its own impact on the experiences of separation and reunion, and therefore on the child's development. To begin with, the parents of the youngsters under discussion have probably immigrated to the United States (or another developed country) because of economic hardship and lack of opportunity in their native land, and they may well struggle economically for many years after they arrive. In addition, they may or may not be documented. Second, the children's separation from the parents may begin in infancy or at a later age, and it may last one or two years or many years. Third, the children's ages may range from toddler through latency to adolescence when they are reunited. Fourth, prior to the reunion, the nature of the relationship with the biological parents will have varied widely. The children may have lived on and off with them or they may have had only relatively brief contacts; these contacts may have occurred often or only occasionally. There may have been visits, or only letters and phone calls. Finally, the children's living situations in the home country will have varied from stable and nurturing arrangements with close relatives, to frequently changing, neglectful, or even abusive conditions.

The ecological perspective (Germain, 1991), which views individuals as constantly interacting with influences from the personal, social, and environmental domains, informs this chapter. Clearly, the impact of separation and the presence of attachment-related problems among reunited children will depend on a variety of factors. These include the age of the child at original separation and at the point of reunion, the length of time and the number of times separated, the quality as well as the number of changes in caretaking arrangements in the home country, the degree of attachment to surrogate parents in the native land, and the quality of the connection maintained by the biological parents during the period of separation. In addition, at the point of reunification the attitudes and behaviors of parents, children, and others in the social support system will all play significant roles. Finally, the environments in which children and their families live, both in the homeland and in the United States, will influence their adaptation. For example, many immigrant families are poor, and poverty constitutes a significant stressor both directly and indirectly (Larner & Collins, 1996; Duncan, Brooks-Gunn, & Klebanov, 1994; Sherman, 1994; Kaplan & Munoz, 1997).

This chapter will address some clinical issues for children, adolescents, and families that may arise in the process of separation and reunion due to immigration. First a review of the literature will be presented, with a focus on the nature of the stresses that have been identified as appearing in this group. Second, several case examples will be offered. Third, suggestions for both clinical work and future research will be made, especially with regard to protective factors that may mitigate risk and promote resilience and adaptation.

LITERATURE REVIEW

The critical importance for children's healthy development of secure attachment to a primary nurturing figure, as well as the impact of separation in creating psychosocial difficulties, has long been established in the clinical literature (Bowlby, 1969, 1973, 1980; Ainsworth, 1980). Current research too continues to link children's insecure attachment to their parents with various forms of emotional distress, including separation anxiety, depression, and behavior problems (Armsden, McCauley, Greenberg, & Burke, 1990; Wright, Binney, & Smith, 1995). When separation is prolonged and feelings of loss persist, children may become permanently detached, chronically depressed, and subject to persistent and diffuse rage (Garmezy & Masten, 1994).

Many commonly occurring situations involving separation of children from their parents are well known to produce negative emotions, including anxiety and depression. Divorce is one such experience (Wallerstein & Kelly, 1980; Beck & Blank, 1997). In another example, the child welfare literature suggests certain parallels between children in the foster care system and children who reunite with their parents after having experienced a separation due to immigration. There is, of course, a caveat in that the emotional and behavioral problems of children who enter foster care may also be attributable to prior maltreatment, while immigrant children may or may not have been maltreated. Notwithstanding this possible distinction, children who have been separated from their parents—whether because of placement in foster care or because of parental emigration—not infrequently exist in a state of what Wilkes (1992) has called "limbo." Referring to children in the child welfare system, Wilkes uses this term to describe a prolonged period of separation from a nurturing family, with persistent confusion, conflict, or uncertainty about future plans, parental authority, and family relationships. Wilkes maintains that such a period of limbo has a negative influence on children's emotional development, leading to difficulties with attachment, self-esteem, and appropriate behaviors. Similarly, authors such as Littner (1976) have written about foster children's feelings of rejection and loss. Barth (1990) studied 55 former foster children at the age of 21 and found in all a significant level of depression.

As noted above, immigration is a global phenomenon, and children who have been separated from and reunited with immigrant parents have been studied in a number of countries, not only the United States. Kosar (1988) studied a group of Turkish children of migrant workers living in Germany and discovered that a large number of these children had experienced separations from and reunions with both mothers and fathers, a fact detrimental to their development. In a 1968 article, Prince described his work with children from the English-speaking Caribbean who were being seen in London at a child guidance clinic. These children had been left behind by their parents, who took advantage of their British Commonwealth status and immigrated to London, subsequently reuniting with their children of various ages. The children's most frequent problem was depression, resulting from sources including original loss of the biological mother, loss of the surrogate mother when they immigrated, and problems that developed in the process of reunion. For example, when the child failed to respond gratefully to the reunion (as the parents expected), the parents felt hurt and offended, and mutual resentment developed. Not surprisingly, Prince found that the longer the parent-child separation, the greater the reunion difficulties. When children had been left at a very young age they never bonded to the biological parents at all. When they were left at an older age and were attached to the parents, they reacted strongly to the separation with feelings of rejection. Those youngsters who had experienced a number of separations from caregivers during the years of the parents' absence had a diminished ability to establish trusting relationships with adults.

In Canada, as in England, the pattern of family immigration has tended to be uneven, with parents leaving children in their homeland and then bringing them over at a later time. Christiansen (1980) studied children from the English-speaking Caribbean who had been reunited with their parents and subsequently referred to a social agency in Toronto. These children were acting out, but initially had presented as depressed and withdrawn. Their behavior seemed to be influenced by such factors as their perception of the separation from the parents, their situation after the parents left, the length of the separation, and their developmental stage at the time of reunion. Da Costa (1976), also in Toronto, found that 67% of reunited schoolchildren were depressed, even when they were considered by their teachers to have adjusted well to their new Canadian lifestyle. The author noted a number of issues that children arriving in Canada must deal with, including children's confusion about family relationships, their fear of stepfathers, the parents' disappointment or even shame when they and the child fail to establish an early rapport, and feelings of mutual rejection between child and parent.

In the United States, Thrasher and Anderson (1988) investigated 30 West Indian families receiving services in a Brooklyn agency. Similar to the situations described above in England and Canada, these authors found that indeed many adults initially arrive in the United States alone, leaving children to be cared for by relatives in the homeland. Then, many years may elapse before the entire family is reunited. These authors describe the family household as multigenerational, including extended kin because of the pattern of sponsorship of relatives in the United States. They maintain that conflict frequently occurs between parents and children in the reconstituted family. The adults quite often hold more than one job in addition to educational training, leaving children unsupervised or with a variety of caretakers. Physical punishment is culturally sanctioned and even valued as a child-rearing practice, which may place these families in conflict with the dominant culture. Even though people from the Caribbean do not generally believe in taking problems outside the family, they will be more likely to seek professional help if children are having problems in school since they value education very highly.

In a 1995 article describing group work with adolescents who had reunited with their immigrant parents in Canada, Glasgow and Gouse-Sheese stated that it is important to examine a number of issues in order to fully understand the youngsters' feelings of abandonment and rejection. These include the adolescents' attitude toward the immigration of parents, the relationship with caregivers while parents are abroad, expectations about life in Canada, and experiences after arrival. These authors found that teenagers who described feeling abandoned had felt this way from the moment of the parental departure. Despite being told that the parents (usually mothers) were away working to make a better life for them in Canada, the children would have preferred to have their parents stay with them regardless of economic hardship. Receipt of money was nonetheless regarded as a sign of caring, while a parent's failure to send money was seen as proof of rejection.

Many of the teens whom Glasgow and Gouse-Sheese worked with were more strongly bonded to surrogate parents in the Caribbean than to their biological parents. Thus they felt a sense of loss and alienation upon leaving those relationships behind, especially since the leave- taking was often hurried and did not allow for a proper good-bye. Yet upon arriving in Canada they were discouraged from discussing their caretakers in the West Indies. As a result of both the rapidity of departure and their parents' unwillingness to accept their other attachments, the children were not allowed to grieve. The authors found that two conditions were helpful in facilitating the child's reunion with the biological parents: first, the caretakers in the Caribbean endorsed the emigration, and second, the biological parents were able to allow some discussion of the child's earlier feelings of abandonment.

The authors found that Caribbean youngsters gladly joined their parents in Canada despite their doubts about leaving loved caretakers behind. This occurred primarily because of the expectations of wealth and opportunity created both by the media and by the parents when they visited the children prior to the reunion. Thus, when the youngsters did emigrate their illusions were quickly shattered by the harsher reality they faced daily. For one thing, the parents, who may have seemed relaxed, attentive, and generous when visiting, were often stressed, critical, and unavailable both physically and emotionally. Second, the youngsters were shocked to discover the financial reality of their parents' lives. Having come to regard the parents' financial provision to them and their Caribbean caretakers as acts of love and as atonement for years of abandonment, the teens were keenly disappointed as well as angry at the parents. They tended to become generally suspicious of their parents' motives, as well as more sensitive to anything that seemed to signify further rejection.

Already vulnerable in a strange land, these Caribbean youngsters tended to withdraw and ignored their parents' attempts to draw them out, precipitating a cycle of rejection and counterrejection. Parents, feeling hurt and disappointed, accused their children of being ungrateful. In their own minds, their struggles to bring their children to Canada represented the ultimate act of parental love, but the boys and girls did not share this view. However, the sharp feelings of mutual hurt and rejection were suppressed. Often the result was abuse in various forms. Some parents, in an effort to affect the children's behavior in positive ways, told their children that they never should have been born, or threatened to send them back. This threat, in turn, reinforced the youngsters' feeling of having been abandoned in the first place, as well as the sense of isolation and helplessness in a new country. Also, their dream of reunion with parents was now destroyed.

This issue of narcissistic injury was the most common of all the themes discussed in the groups conducted by Glasgow and Gouse-Sheese. They write that the sharing and universalizing of such feelings by the adolescents was an essential therapeutic factor, which also facilitated further group cohesion and lessened the isolation and pain of the youngsters. The group also provided opportunities to educate and normalize for the teens their own as well as their parents' feelings.

Other themes that arose in the groups included those of cultural degradation (i.e., the parents denigrated the home country and its culture, and by extension their children who had recently arrived), material and emotional exploitation (i.e., the boys and girls felt that their parents had brought them to Canada either to help the parents improve their financial position or to provide themselves with emotional closeness and support), and physical abuse. Interestingly, the teens frequently claimed that the parents' physical abuse represented nothing more than their way of caring and teaching correct behavior. However, their angry complaints about teachers and other adult authorities, as well as their feelings of disillusionment with their new life, belied these protests. In fact, the authors maintain that the ongoing abuse, whether physical or psychological, had a devastating impact on the youngsters' well-being. Some became severely depressed and even suicidal, others expressed paranoid thoughts that the parents were trying to kill them, and still others admitted to thoughts of killing their parents.

Despite all the problems of reunion, however, the reunited youngsters found a wide variety of ways of coping. Some developed a semblance of a parent-child relationship, others became either indifferent to their parents or totally dominated by them, and in some instances role reversals occurred between children and parents. Other young people returned to the Caribbean, were taken into foster care, moved out on their own, or moved in with relatives.

CASE EXAMPLES

In this section we discuss three cases in which clinical interventions were offered to children with a range of problems. The first, the case of Sandra, describes a 10-year-old girl from the English-speaking Caribbean adjusting to a recent reunion with her mother. The second, the case of Maria, involves a 13-year-old girl from Guatemala with multiple problems. The third, drawn from the clinical literature, highlights severe separation anxiety in Hector, a 9-year-old boy from the Dominican Republic.

The Case of Sandra

Sandra, a 10-year-old girl, had recently come to live in Brooklyn with her unmarried working mother, Mary. Sandra had lived with her maternal grandmother in the English-speaking Caribbean from the age of 6 months. Three years prior to Sandra's arrival in New York, the maternal grandmother contracted breast cancer and Mary returned to the Caribbean for a year to live with her mother and Sandra. Two years later she brought Sandra to New York to join her because her mother had become terminally ill. However, their relationship did not go well. Mary felt that Sandra did not appreciate the sacrifices she had made for her, and in frustration she took her daughter to a community agency. When Sandra first came to see the social worker, she presented as a depressed, constricted girl with flattened affect and a low energy level. It soon became apparent that she mourned the loss of her grandmother and her culture and that she found adjusting to living with her mother and attending a new school difficult. Interestingly, Sandra's arrival had reawakened feelings in Mary about a remarkably similar experience in her own childhood: at 9 years of age, Mary herself had been reunited with her own parents after having been raised by her grandmother in a different part of the Caribbean. The social worker felt that this parallel separation and reunion may have been the precipitating factor in Mary's decision to seek help for Sandra.

Sandra was seen weekly for about 6 months, and Mary was seen weekly by the same clinician. Sandra began actively participating in an after-school program and reported having friends. She went to the top of her class academically. In the treatment situation she began to explore her feelings about moving to New York and about leaving her grandmother, and became less constricted. However, when asked directly about her feelings she became defended and formal, saying things like "Now I am accustomed to being in New York," or "I am doing well in all my academic areas." On the other hand, she was much more expressive using the medium of play. For example, she created scenes of vehicles going back and forth over bridges, oceans, and mountains (i.e., between the Caribbean and New York). The following is an excerpt from one of these sessions:

WORKER: I see you are building a bridge.
SANDRA: This end is the Islands, with palm trees. And here is Brooklyn. These are tall buildings.
WORKER: Now the car is going over the bridge.
SANDRA: She (the driver) is wearing sunglasses. Sometimes people wear sunglasses so no one can see that they have been crying.
WORKER: Is that why this lady is wearing sunglasses?
SANDRA: She doesn't want people to see her eyes. I'm going to draw a picture of her.
WORKER: She seems to looks like Barbie.
SANDRA: Yes, it is Barbie—Barbie wearing sunglasses.

WORKER: Wow, I think Barbie is somebody who really knows how to say how she feels.

While the worker helped Sandra to express her feelings using play, she also worked with Mary. She empathized with the losses and sadness that Mary had sustained in childhood, as well as in her adult life, which in turn helped Mary to be more empathetic with Sandra. The therapist was also able to provide guidance to Mary in setting limits with Sandra, who constantly tested her mother. Limit setting was difficult for Mary to do because of her guilt. Eventually, totally frustrated, she would either hit Sandra or threaten to send her away, thereby increasing her daughter's anxiety and depression. As their work progressed, Mary began to describe to the social worker her efforts to refrain from such behaviors. The worker also encouraged her to talk with Sandra about their new life together rather than simply berating her for being unappreciative. In order to encourage this discussion, the therapist held a joint session with Mary and Sandra in which they showed her photographs of people in both places. This helped Sandra construct a narrative of her life experience and fostered a sense of continuity between her life in the Caribbean and her life in Brooklyn and helped to reduce her feelings of fragmentation. Mary and Sandra both tended toward stoicism, perhaps as a result of cultural conditioning. Now, using the photographs, they were able to begin a dialogue about the separation and reunion experiences each had had. As Mary became more able to understand and express her own feelings of abandonment and loss in her childhood, she was able to allow Sandra to express similar feelings and to comfort her daughter. They even began to verbalize their sadness over the imminent death of Sandra's grandmother.

The Case of Maria

Maria, a 13-year-old girl from Guatemala, had been raised by her grandmother in a small village from the age of 2, when her parents left to work in the United States. When Maria was 8 years old her parents, both of whom were working in low-paying factory jobs, brought her to the United States to join them and her two older brothers. Maria had a heart condition, and within 2 weeks of her arrival in the United States she was hospitalized and underwent open-heart surgery.

Maria came to the attention of a social agency when she was referred for outpatient treatment following 2 weeks of inpatient psychiatric hospitalization. The sequence of events leading up to this hospitalization were as follows: Maria truanted from school and spent the day with her 21-year-old boyfriend, Eduardo, with whom she had been sexually active since age 12. When her mother, Ana, found out she beat Maria with a belt, leaving marks on her arms. Maria told her school counselor, who then called Child Protective Services (CPS). That evening Maria attempted to take a bottle of pills but was stopped by her brother. Later she told the CPS worker that she would kill herself if she were not allowed to live with her aunt, and the CPS worker initiated the hospitalization.

Maria acknowledged that her depression preceded the relationship with her boyfriend. She attributed this depression to the conflictual relationship she felt she had had with her mother as long as she could remember, as well as to her parents' fighting all the time. She believed Ana was trying to control her. Maria was doing poorly in school, was obsessed with Eduardo, and was in constant conflict with her mother. Ana followed her around all the time in order to keep her away from the boyfriend. Maria admitted to occasional thoughts of suicide as well as thoughts of hurting her mother (e.g., by using a pair of scissors).

Ana several months earlier had pressed charges of statutory rape against Eduardo because she felt strongly that her daughter was too young for such an intense relationship. Eduardo had pleaded guilty, and a sentencing date had been scheduled. After spending 2 months in jail, he was released on 5 years' probation, with an Order of Protection mandating that he stay away from Maria. As soon as he was released, however, Maria's mood improved. She admitted to her therapist her dream of eloping with Eduardo and going back to Guatemala. She said that most of her extended family, especially her maternal aunts, disagreed with her mother's stance regarding Eduardo, and that their current age difference would not be regarded as unusual in her village in Guatemala. In fact, she maintained, were they to return to Guatemala they would be welcomed as a married couple and could settle close to her grandmother—whom she greatly missed. Maria was unwilling to explore her feelings of abandonment by her parents at age 2, or to talk about her arrival in this country and immediate hospitalization for open-heart surgery. She persisted in her opinion that her mother was controlling and that they had never gotten along, and she was more concerned about her relationship with Eduardo. The worker felt concerned that Maria might be planning to get pregnant as a way of forcing her mother to accept the relationship with Eduardo.

Ana, for her part, insisted that her daughter's relationship with her boyfriend was inappropriate and intolerable, although she admitted that not everyone in the family agreed with her. Ana expressed frustration at her daughter's attitude toward her. She believed that she had always tried hard to be a good mother and longed for a loving mother-daughter relationship, but she recognized that nothing had been the same once she left Maria at age 2. Moreover, their relationship had just gotten worse after Maria's arrival in the United States and her immediate surgery. In her frustration, Ana remained adamant that her daughter must live with her and not with any other family members.

This case can undoubtedly be viewed from many different angles, some of which may relate to Maria's painful and frightening hospitalization in a new country with a strange language when she was only 8 years old. Other perspectives, however, illustrate some of the many potential complications that enter the picture when children are separated from and then reunited with parents who have emigrated. Certainly the loss of her parents at age 2, then the loss of her beloved grandmother at age 8, followed by the traumatic hospitalization and surgery, predisposed Maria to depression and a fierce attachment hunger. Also, it appeared that the parents had many conflicts and fought a great deal. Maria found her father emotionally unavailable, and she felt too angry at her mother to turn to her for comfort and support, which might help to explain her precocious sexual involvement. The cultural reinforcement for Maria's behavior cannot be minimized, however. Her relationship with Eduardo not only met with the approval of other relatives, but also held out for her (at least in her fantasy) the possibility of reunion with her grandmother and the home culture.

The Case of Hector

Zayas (1995) reports the case of Hector, a 9-year-old boy from the Dominican Republic living with his single mother. He had been left with extended family in a rural town in his country of origin when he was 18 months old. When he was 4 years old his parents brought him to the United States, where his father disciplined him harshly. His parents separated when he was 6, and he was once again sent to the Dominican Republic, where he remained until the age of 8.

Upon his return to the United States, Hector was distractible, complained of frequent stomachaches, and suffered from enuresis. He had violent outbursts during which he hit classmates. Hector had trouble making friends, and described hearing strange sounds in his closet and bed as well as voices whispering to him. He feared death constantly, and each day he would walk several blocks to wait for his mother at her bus stop after work. As soon as she arrived he would show great relief, saying he was glad she had not been hurt or killed. When seen for evaluation Hector appeared anxious, and he dejectedly put his hands on his head or face. He admitted that he felt sad, and reported that while living in the Dominican Republic he worried that his mother might be hit by a train and run over. He also described a recurrent dream in which a man killed his mother.

Zayas points out that the kinds of separations and reunions experienced by Hector and his parents constitute adaptive strategies that enable immigrant families to survive and create opportunities for themselves and their children. Nevertheless, these practices may exact a price. In addition to the potentially negative consequences of the separations themselves for the children's development, the quality of care the children receive in the homeland varies considerably. Then, when children and parents are reunited, they may be virtual strangers to one another. The result can be extreme separation anxiety and disorders of attachment of the kind evident in Hector's case.

In Hector's situation, as in Maria's, a number of factors complicate the picture. In the first place, Hector actually experienced multiple separations and reunions, including the separations from his parents at ages 18 months and 6 years and reunions at ages 4 and 8. In addition, his parents' marriage broke up, which resulted in an additional loss, that of his father. Then, too, it is possible that the father's harsh discipline may have been traumatic and may have left lasting impressions of violence. However, the quality of care that Hector received during his sojourns in the Dominican Republic is unknown. Therefore, it is unclear whether or not he ever felt securely attached to these caretakers. If he were, then separations from them would have been highly stressful. On the other hand, he may never have attached to caregivers in his homeland, and may even have been maltreated by them.

Here emerges the inevitable paradox that the process of separation and reunion presents to immigrant children. On the one hand, insecure attachments, whether to their parents or to their caretakers, produce developmental problems that have the potential to impair the capacity to form relationships and to trust. On the other hand, if the children form strong bonds with their parents, or with the caretaker or caretakers in the homeland (as in the cases of Sandra and Maria), they will very likely experience feelings of loss and abandonment. In either case, upon reunion the child's relationship with the parent may be complicated by anxiety, depression, or—especially for adolescents like Maria—anger. Clearly, too, as indicated by the cases of Sandra and Maria, adaptation to a new culture will pose additional challenges. Yet at the same time that the child is struggling with difficult emotions, the parent or parents may well be expecting that their boy or girl will show appreciation, and that the reunion will constitute a joyful vindication of all their sacrifices.

DIRECTIONS FOR FUTURE RESEARCH AND INTERVENTIONS

As noted above, little research has been conducted on immigrant children and families who have experienced separation and reunion. A clear need exists for more precise information regarding this group. In the first place, it is vital that we learn more about the actual numbers of individual youngsters and their families who fit the category under discussion. Second, the clinical literature cited above suggests directions for research that can amplify our knowledge about what problems actually appear, as well as about their dimensions. Third, systematic investigation may point to strengths in separated and reunited children and adolescents that protect them from developing serious difficulties, and this phenomenon too bears further study. For despite grave stressors, many youngsters evidence resilience, which means that they manage to cope in the face of adversity, even if they may be subject to varying degrees of emotional distress (Rutter, 1989; Norman, Turner, & Zunz, 1994; Fraser, 1997).

At present many clinicians and researchers have begun to explore the relationship between risk factors and resilience. This chapter has attempted to illustrate some of the ways in which uneven immigration of families produces what Kirby and Fraser (1997) have termed "cumulative stress," leading to heightened vulnerability and chains of risk. In other words, both immigration and separation in themselves constitute stressful events for children, but when combined with personal vulnerabilities—as well as with the wide variety of stresses that can occur when immigrant families separate and reunite, such as those discussed above—it becomes more likely that negative consequences will result.

Maria's and Hector's situations illustrate the type of risk chain that produces a major impact because it occurs early in the child's life. Maria experienced separation from her parents at age 2, then separation from her beloved grandmother at age 8, followed by a traumatic hospitalization and surgery and finally the continuing strain of family conflict. In a similar fashion, Hector had multiple experiences of separation and loss, as well as trauma. Sandra's case appears to have involved a less dramatic risk chain. Nonetheless, Sandra, in addition to separations from both her mother and grandmother, had to cope with the imminent death of her grandmother due to breast cancer.

Along with exploring the concepts of cumulative stress and risk chains, researchers are beginning to examine what are termed "keystone" risks, which are defined as those "which make a child most vulnerable to problems and that, if left unattended, will cause problems to remain or worsen. . . . [They] are markers for intervention" (Fraser & Galinsky, 1997, p. 269). In other words, research might help to pinpoint particular keystone risks in separated and reunited immigrant children and adolescents, which in turn could guide both preventive and interventive strategies.

The cases presented above, as well as the situations described in the literature review, illustrate some of the many variables that might usefully be investigated as possible keystone risks. The case of Sandra, for example, suggests that multigenerational experiences of separation and loss could amplify those involved in the process of immigration. Furthermore, Sandra's case, as well as Maria's, points to the problematic nature of certain cultural values that may have been adaptive in the homeland but become maladaptive when youngsters must adjust to a reunion with their parents in a new country. For one thing, immigrant parents, as described in the literature as well as in the cases cited above, may utilize corporal punishment of children and adolescents, considering it a culturally approved mode of discipline. Yet this kind of authoritarian parenting style seems to adversely affect the parent-child relationship, creating depression and anger in the youngsters, and may bring parents into conflict with child welfare authorities. Another example is the stoicism—apparently culturally conditioned—shown by Sandra and her mother, which had the potential to prevent open expression of feelings in the absence of therapeutic intervention. In a third example, Maria's premature sexual involvement, which was considered culturally appropriate by some family members and might have appeared normative in a small village in Guatemala, carried the potential for early pregnancy and therefore a further risk for a young teenager in the United States.

Just as problems develop ecologically through multisystem chains that involve individual, family, and environmental conditions, often with roots in very early childhood, recent studies show that the influence of risk factors may be mitigated by multisystem protective factors that both focus and draw upon the strengths of individuals, families, and communities to produce resilience in the face of risk (Garmezy, 1994; Norman et al.,

1994; Fraser & Galinsky, 1997). At the present time far more is known about risk factors than about protective factors. However, resilient children appear to have benefited from one or more protective conditions, even though the relative weight and exact combination of such conditions remain unclear.

Norman et al. (1994) summarized individual attributes that have been associated with resilience in young people, as well as protective characteristics of the family, school, peers, and community. They divided the individual attributes into genetic and biological factors and personality factors. The former were easy temperament or disposition as well as intellectual capacity, while the latter consisted of self-efficacy, realistic appraisal of the environment, social problem-solving skills, a sense of direction or mission, empathy, humor, and adaptive distancing. Family protective factors were high-quality prenatal care for mothers, a warm, positive relationship between the child and a caring adult, positive family environment and bonding, high parental expectations, family responsibilities for the children, positive parental modeling, good parenting skills and supervision, family traditions and rituals, family support for the youth's competency and life goals, and extended family support. School and peer protective factors included opportunities for involvement, high expectations for performance, and a caring, supportive school climate. Communities that provided a sense of caring, commitment, and mutual protection were found to be effective.

Kirby and Fraser (1997, p. 20) divide protective factors for children into three categories, which essentially overlap with those posited by Norman et al. (1994). The first, which they call "broad environmental conditions," includes opportunities for education, employment, growth, and achievement. The second, "family, school and neighborhood conditions," consists of social support, the presence of a caring and supportive adult, a positive parent-child relationship, and effective parenting. The third, "individual, psychological and biological characteristics," subsumes easy temperament in infancy, self-esteem and self-efficacy, competence in normative roles, and high intelligence.

What preventive and interventive strategies might be designed to enhance protective factors and foster resilience in separated and reunited immigrant children? A growing body of evidence supports the ecological and multisystem perspectives, demonstrating that resilience is promoted by factors that resonate from individuals and families through neighborhoods, schools, and the larger society (Fraser & Galinsky, 1997). In other words, any intervention that successfully empowers individuals and families has the potential to also have a favorable impact on larger systems, and vice versa.

For example, Congress and Lynn (1994) described a social group work program that was developed in an urban public elementary school to meet the needs of immigrant children. These children were struggling with feelings of loss, depression, and alienation as they attempted to adjust to new communities, new social customs, and a different kind of school. The authors did not investigate whether any of the children had experienced separation and reunion; their purpose was rather to highlight ethical questions and dilemmas that confront the practitioner as well as to improve culturally sensitive social work practice. However, the multilayered benefits of this kind of group intervention in schools are undeniable. By offering group support to children and various kinds of services to families, social workers can provide early intervention that may serve to prevent further problems by potentiating a series of protective qualities in a variety of areas. These include improving the self-esteem and competence of the children, enhancing the parenting skills of the parents, and creating a caring school environment.

Sandra's presenting symptoms were similar to those of the children described by Congress and Lynn—that is, depression and problems of adjustment to a new school and a new environment. The interventions with Sandra and her mother—individual and family therapy—were conducted in a community agency rather than a school, but they appear to have created a feedback loop that had a positive impact on Sandra and Mary on multiple levels. As Sandra worked through her feelings of loss, her innate intellectual ability blossomed. Her success in school inevitably enhanced her sense of competence and self-esteem, and she made friends. Then, as she felt less depressed and became more successful, her mother in turn no longer experienced her as unappreciative. Accordingly, Mary became more open to suggestions regarding effective parenting and less likely to use corporal punishment. As her parenting skills were enhanced the mother-child relationship improved, which further enabled Sandra to mourn her losses and move on, adapting to her new community.

The group described above by Glasgow and Gouse-Sheese (1995), for adolescent immigrants to Canada, was also conducted in a school setting. These youngsters, who had been separated from their parents for periods ranging from 4 to 15 years, were having difficulties adjusting to their new conditions. The teens appeared to benefit from the group, using it for sharing, universalizing, and participating in exercises designed to help them empathize with their parents' situations as immigrants. These exercises undoubtedly promoted the capacity for adaptive distancing, which has been linked with resilience. No intervention was provided for the parents themselves, although it might have proven beneficial since a positive parent-child relationship is considered a protective factor. Yet the resilience literature indicates that even in the absence of a positive relationship with parents, other factors may also be protective and may serve as mediating or moderating influences in situations of risk. Thus, one might reasonably conclude that—in addition to the support of the group—the young people benefited not only from their relationship with caring adults (the group leaders) but from the experience of the school as a committed, supportive environment.

The cases of Maria and Hector would appear to illustrate more risk than resilience. This, as noted above, probably reflects the fact that for both youngsters a chain of risk exists, beginning in very early childhood, that renders them both very vulnerable. Yet even in these cases, conditions related to resilience can be seen. For Maria, social support did exist in her environment in the form of relatives who supported her choices, despite the dissonance between these choices and predominant values in the United States. And although one might question how realistically Maria appraised her environment, she certainly did not lack self-efficacy, defined as the belief in one's ability to influence one's environment. Hector, for his part, had a committed and caring mother who brought him for treatment. Whether additional protective factors emerged in these cases to moderate the considerable degree of risk for both Maria and Hector remains unknown.

Conclusion

The purpose of this chapter has been to focus on a group of children and adolescents that has been little studied. A small but growing body of evidence indicates that immigrant children who have been separated from and reunited with parents who had previously immigrated to the United States constitute a significant population at risk, albeit one that is rarely recognized. As such, it merits attention from both clinicians and researchers. Clinical work with immigrant children who have lived through separation and reunion will benefit from continued research, as well as evaluation of the effectiveness of both preventive and therapeutic interventions. In addition, the body of knowledge on intervention must continue to build upon the wisdom and knowledge of practitioners who work with these young people and their families.

On the basis of those clinical experiences cited in the literature and in this chapter, certain directions appear promising. Young people need to be encouraged to express themselves in an accepting environment, with younger children using the medium of play. Parents and families can benefit from support as well as education in order to improve parenting skills, promote an intergenerational dialogue, and reduce the incidence of verbal and physical abuse. In particular, parents and children alike may need help to relinquish unrealistic expectations of the reunion. Social supports outside the immediate family—for example, in extended family networks and schools—should receive attention because of their potential to provide children with caring relationships. Schools are logical places to reach youngsters preventively in order to assist their adjustment to a new situation; and school personnel are also gatekeepers because they are in a position to identify children who may require therapeutic services.

The strengths perspective (Saleeby, 1996) promises to be most effective in the design of clinical interventions. The poor minority family—whether or not they have been subject to separations and reunions due to immigration—can benefit from an approach that respects multiple versions of reality, uses descriptive language rather than labels, reminds them of all that they are doing right rather than merely emphasizing problems and deficits, and focuses on solutions (Kaplan & Munoz, 1997).

Indeed, in both research and direct practice it will be most useful to emphasize resilience and protective factors instead of focusing exclusively on risk and pathology. Furthermore, the wider community must be included in efforts to support the children and families who have been described in this chapter. Such an effort implies large-scale policies and programs, informed by research and practice experience, that will be directed not only toward amelioration of pain but toward prevention, empowerment, and genuine opportunities. In this way, reunited immigrant children can join the next generation of American children in achieving their potential and contributing fully to society.

REFERENCES

Ainsworth, M. (1980). Attachments beyond infancy. *American Psychologist, 44,* 709–716.

Armsden, G., McCauley, E., Greenberg, M., & Burke, P. (1990). Parent and peer attachment in early adolescent depression. *Journal of Abnormal Child Psychology, 18*(6), 683–697.

Barth, R. (1990). On their own: Experiences of youth after foster care. *Child and Adolescent Social Work Journal, 7*(5), 419–439.

Beck, P., & Blank, N. (1997). Enhancing therapeutic interventions during divorce. *Journal of Analytic Social Work, 4*(3), 63–81.

Board on Children and Families, Commission on Behavioral and Social Sciences and Education, National Research Council, Institute of Medicine. (1995). Immigrant children and their families: Issues for research and policy. *The Future of Children, 5*(2), 72–89.

Bowlby, J. (1969). *Attachment* (2nd ed.). New York: Basic Books.

Bowlby, J. (1973). *Separation: Anxiety and anger.* New York: Basic Books.

Bowlby, J. (1980). *A secure base.* New York: Basic Books.

Christiansen, J. (1980). *West Indians in Toronto: Implications for helping professionals.* Toronto: Family Service Association of Metropolitan Toronto.

Congress, E., & Lynn, M. (1994). Group work programs in public schools: Ethical dilemmas and cultural diversity. *Social Work in Education, 16*(2), 107–114.

Da Costa, G. (1976). Counseling and the black child. In V. D'Oyley (Ed.), *Black students in urban Canada.* Toronto: Ontario Ministry of Culture and Recreation.

Duncan, G., Brooks-Gunn, J., & Klebanov, P. (1994). Economic deprivation and early childhood development. *Child Development, 65,* 296–318.

Fanshel, D., Finch, S., & Gundy, J. (1992). *Serving the urban poor.* Westport, CT: Praeger.

Fraser, M. (1997). The ecology of childhood: A multisystems perspective. In M. Fraser (Ed.), *Risk and resilience in childhood: An ecological perspective* (pp. 1–9). Washington, DC: NASW Press.

Fraser, M., & Galinsky, M. (1997). Toward a resilience-based model of practice. In M. Fraser (Ed.), *Risk and resilience in childhood: An ecological perspective* (pp. 265–275). Washington, DC: NASW Press.

Garmezy, N. (1994). Reflections and commentary on risk, resilience, and development. In R. Haggerty, L. Sherrod, N. Garmezy, & M. Rutter (Eds.), *Stress, risk and resilience in children and adolescents: Processes, mechanisms and interventions* (pp. 1–18). New York: Cambridge University Press.

Garmezy, N., & Masten, A. (1994). Chronic adversities. In M. Rutter, E. Taylor, & L. Hersov (Eds.), *Child and adolescent psychiatry.* London: Blackwell Scientific Publications.

Germain, C. (1991). *Human behavior in the social environment: An ecological view.* New York: Columbia University Press.

Ginsburg, G., & Silverman, W. (1996). Phobic and anxiety disorders in Hispanic and Caucasian youth. *Journal of Anxiety Disorders, 10*(6), 517–528.

Glasgow, G., & Gouse-Sheese, J. (1995). Themes of rejection and abandonment in group work with Caribbean adolescents. *Social Work With Groups, 17*(4), 3–27.

Kaplan, C., & Munoz, M. (1997). Working with poor minority adolescents and their families: An ecosystemic approach. In E. Congress (Ed.), *Multicultural issues in working with families* (pp. 61–75). New York: Springer.

Kirby, L., & Fraser, M. (1997). Risk and resilience in childhood.

In M. Fraser (Ed.), *Risk and resilience in childhood: An ecological perspective* (pp. 10–33). Washington, DC: NASW Press.

Kosar, N. (1988). A psychosocial study of a group of young Turks living in the Federal Republic of Germany. *International Social Work, 31*(4), 263–272.

Larner, M., & Collins, A. (1996). Poverty in the lives of young children. In E. Erwin (Ed.), *Putting children first* (pp. 55–75). Baltimore: Paul H. Brookes.

Littner, N. (1976). *Some traumatic effects of separation and placement.* New York: Child Welfare League of America.

Norman, E., Turner, S., & Zunz, S. (1994). *Substance abuse prevention: A review of the literature.* New York: New York State Office of Alcohol and Substance Abuse Services.

Prince, G. (1968). Emotional problems of children reunited with their migrant families in Britain. *Maternal and Child Care, 4,* 239–241.

Rutter, M. (1989). Psychosocial resilience and protective mechanisms. *American Journal of Orthopsychiatry, 57*(3), 316–331.

Saleeby, D. (1996). The strengths perspective in social work practice: Extensions and cautions. *Social Work, 41,* 296–305.

Sherman, A. (1994). *Wasting America's future: The Children's Defense Fund report on the costs of child poverty.* Washington, DC: Children's Defense Fund.

Thrasher, S., & Anderson, G. (1988). The West Indian family: Treatment challenges. *Social Casework, 69*(3), 171–176.

Wallerstein, J., & Kelly, J. (1980). *Surviving the breakup: How children and parents cope with divorce.* New York: Basic Books.

Wilkes, J. (1992). Children in limbo: Working for the best outcome when children are taken into care. *Canada's Mental Health, 40*(2), 2–5.

Wright, J., Binney, V., & Smith, P. (1995). Security of attachment in 8–22 year olds: A revised version of the Separation Anxiety Test, its psychometric properties and clinical interpretation. *Journal of Child Psychology and Psychiatry and Allied Disciplines, 36*(5), 757–774.

Zayas, L. (1995). Family functioning and child rearing in an urban environment. *Developmental and Behavioral Pediatrics, 16*(3), 521–524.

9

Immigration and Mental Health: Principles for Successful Social Work Practice

Roni Berger, PhD, CSW

INTRODUCTION

The United States has always been a country of immigrants. Almost 1.5 million new immigrants enter the country each year, of which about 15% are undocumented (Fix & Passel, 1994; Cox & Ephross, 1998). The composition of immigrants has constantly changed. In the 19th century immigration from Africa and western Europe peaked, followed by immigration from eastern and southern Europe in the late 19th and early 20th century. During the second half of the 20th century, immigrants have increasingly come from South and Central America, the Caribbean, and Asia, joined in recent years by an influx of immigrants from the former Soviet Union (Cox & Ephross, 1998).

The reasons for immigration are numerous and varied. Some come to the United States in search of a better economic and social situation (e.g., immigrants from South and Central America and from some parts of Asia). Others come to unite with family members. Still others flee political, religious, and social persecution (e.g., Jews who emigrated from the former Soviet Union, refugees from some Asian countries, and Cubans). Some immigrants can maintain dual citizenship and keep their original citizenship during and after immigration. This leaves them free to "undo" the change and go back to their country of origin if they are unhappy with the relocation. For many immigrants, however, the move is irreversible; their previous citizenship is denied, and they "burn all the bridges" by deciding to immigrate.

Immigration has been recognized as a macro crisis that creates emotional distress and affects diverse aspects of individual and family functioning and well-being (Harper & Lantz, 1996). Specifically, it has short- and long-term emotional and psychological effects that create unique mental health issues, requiring intervention of helping professionals (Garza-Guerrero, 1974). Consequently, social workers, psychologists, psychiatrists, educators, and related professionals need to be familiar with the typical needs and unique mental health issues of immigrants, and should be trained in useful and effective strategies to address these needs (Christensen, 1992).

The purpose of this chapter is to review typical mental health issues related to immigration and to suggest guidelines for addressing them. It includes four parts. The first part reviews the process of immigration and its related stresses. The second part discusses the effects of immigration on mental health. The third part suggests guidelines for the development and delivery of mental health services for immigrants. And the final part of the chapter presents a case example.

THE PROCESS AND STRESSES OF IMMIGRATION: EFFECTS ON INDIVIDUALS AND FAMILIES

Immigration is a long and complicated process that causes multiple stresses. Drachman and Shen-Ryan (1991) identified three phases in this process: departure, transit, and resettlement. The departure phase includes the decision to immigrate and preparations for leaving. This is the phase of dilemmas and debates. It is the period of "culture loss," that is, experiencing diverse objective losses involved in leaving one's culture of origin. The major decisions that need to be made produce intense tensions that create emotional conflicts and increased familial discord. Preparations involve separation from people, places, and possessions, with the prospect, in some countries, of never seeing them again. In some countries, the finality of the separation is symbolized by the act of giving up one's citizenship and returning one's passport. This often leaves the immigrant without any citizenship and with no formal documents. The lack of identifying papers is an embodiment of the feeling of "being nobody" and the loss of affiliation that characterizes this phase of immigration. The second phase of the immigration process is the transit, the actual move from the country of origin to the new country. This phase is characterized by temporality and uncertainty ("living in suitcases") and sometimes involves long waits in a refugee camp or a detention center while bureaucratic procedures are carried out. Leaving their country of origin, immigrants experience multiple losses. These include loss of a familiar physical, social, and cultural environment, destruction of significant relationships with family, friends, and neighbors, and loss of a language, a belief system, and socioeconomic status. It also means loss of familiarity with cultural clues, acceptable patterns, the ability to adequately perceive reality, and the context for meaning making.

The third phase is resettlement: the relocation and adjustment to the rules and norms of the new culture (Garza-Guerrero, 1974; Stewart, 1986). The initial period in the new country requires addressing basic needs such as getting a job, finding a place to live, and learning a new language and elementary rules and norms.

Immigration often means having to change a career, and frequently involves taking a step down the professional ladder. Physicians become health care providers, engineers become technicians, and teachers become child care workers. Immigrants who were seniors in the profession are required to pass a certification test again with novices who just graduated. Many have to step down to nonprofessional jobs, and others remain unemployed. Previous achievements and credentials go unrecognized, and the immigrant is required to gain them afresh. For example, experienced drivers need to pass a driving test, credit history is not recognized, and becoming eligible for a credit card is a difficult and unpleasant process.

The immigrant needs to get used to a different language, a different climate, different smells, different currency, and a different way of measuring weights, distances, and temperatures. Each minute aspect of everyday life is different: the norms in interpersonal interaction and the hidden codes of social behavior, the laws of acceptable and unacceptable behaviors, merchandise on the shelves of the supermarket. While all these experiences are familiar to anyone who travels abroad, the traveler's self-confidence is protected by the knowledge that the situation of lack of orientation is temporary and the security of a familiar world continues to exist back at home. Immigrants live for many years—sometimes for the rest of their lives—with a constant feeling of foreignness. The intensity of this feeling varies for different immigrants, but it is always there as an inevitable component of the immigrant's life.

Being absorbed in the struggle to survive often deprives immigrants of the opportunity to be in touch with the emotional meaning of their move and to mourn their losses. As immigrants become more familiar with the new society, they become more aware of the permanence of some of the losses, such as reduced social and professional status. In addition, new losses emerge, mostly the bitter loss of a dream because of discrepancies between pre-immigration expectations and the reality of life in the new country. This realization of the multiple losses cause pain and frustration (Coles, 1968; Harper & Lantz, 1996). Concurrent with the aforementioned reactions, this phase is also characterized by the immigrants' efforts to rehabilitate their sense of worth and their feeling mastery over their own lives that were lost to immigration and to develop ways of functioning that are appropriate for the new reality.

Mental Health Issues Related to Immigration

Three types of immigration-related mental health problems can be identified.

1. *Problems directly created by the immigration process.* Given that the immigration process involves multiple losses, uprooting, and social, economic, and cultural insecurity, and requires major adjustment, it creates an "existential vacuum" and a sense of emptiness and meaninglessness in the life of the immigrant. Such an existential vacuum generally occurs in reaction to a major disruption in a person's life, cultural confusion, or rapid

change (Harper & Lantz, 1996). It often leads to an identity crisis, a shaken sense of self, lowered self-esteem, confusion, disorientation, frustration, and anger (Berger, 1996a), and may cause anomic depression (Lantz & Harper, 1990).

For refugees who leave their homeland involuntarily, feelings of helplessness and anger further deepen the emotional wound caused by immigration and may contribute to getting obsessively "stuck" in the experience of being rejected. This "unfinished business" may limit the immigrant's ability to adjust to and cope with the new reality.

Immigration directly affects especially vulnerable populations such as adolescents, the elderly, and stepfamilies. These populations are caught in a combined developmental and cultural transition and therefore experience a unique pileup of stresses (Baptiste, 1990; Berger, 1996c, 1997b). At the same time, immigration has cut them off from their support system of friends and relatives. Those relatives and comrades who immigrated with them are busy in their own struggle to acculturate and are not available to offer the necessary guidance and support. Consequently, such special populations experience a multidimensional crisis. In addition to accumulating developmental and situational stresses, they also experience scarcity of resources to deal with those stresses.

The extent of the problems experienced by immigrants depends on several factors. The first is the degree of difference between their original culture and the new culture. While all relocation produces considerable stresses, cross-cultural immigration creates an "earthquake" in the way people think, conceptualize, and make meaning. The greater the difference between the culture of origin and the absorbing culture, the higher the probability that the person experiences a culture shock in addition to culture loss. "Culture shock" refers to the subjective internal experience of anxiety experienced by immigrants as a result of their relocation (Stewart, 1986). A second factor is the availability of family and friends who have lived longer in the new culture. Since they are more familiar with the language and norms of the absorbing country, these others can serve as mediators and interpreters. Lastly, the extent and nature of problems depends on the history of coping with stresses (Baptiste, 1993).

2. *Preexisting problems magnified by the immigration.* Because immigration is an extremely stressful situation, it adds burdens to previously stressed individuals and relationships, turning problems that were negligible or manageable prior to immigration into insurmountable obstacles. Internal tensions in the marital and parental subsystems are exacerbated because the pace of acculturation to the new sociocultural environment is different for all family members. Children move at a very different developmental pace and rhythm through the immigration cycle (Landau-Stanton, 1985). Impressionistic data suggest also that woman adjust faster than men. Consequently, individuals may be at different places of the continuum of acculturation at different times, thus further broadening inter-generational and inter-gender gaps (Landau, 1983; Gold, 1989).

3. *Traditional mental health problems carried over from the country of origin.* Immigrants who suffered from a variety of mental health problems, such as mood disorders, cognitive disorders, psychotic disorders, somatoform disorders, and chemical dependency, bring these problems with them. In some cases during immigration, drugs used in the country of origin are not available and treatments are discontinued. These changes, coupled with cross-cultural differences in diagnosing and treating mental health, as well as the stresses involved in immigration, intensify preexisting problems.

CHALLENGES AND OBSTACLES TO PROVIDING MENTAL HEALTH SERVICES TO IMMIGRANTS

The aforementioned cultural characteristics and typical issues of immigrants set some cultural barriers to providing mental health services to immigrants. One obstacle stems from the fact that the perception of need is culture-specific (Cox & Ephross, 1998). Some behaviors that would be the grounds for seeking professional help in American culture are accepted as normal in other cultures. In some cultures, such as the Irish, excessive drinking is normative, while in American culture the same behavior would be considered a drinking problem; acceptable physical disciplinary methods in the Russian culture would be perceived as child abuse; and so forth. These differences in need definition create a discrepancy in identifying situations that require professional intervention. While the Western-oriented mental health provider may think there is a problem, the immigrant may define the situation as perfectly normal and acceptable and therefore be reluctant to seek help or cooperate when a third party (e.g., school or medical staff) is referred for help.

The perception of having a problem that a service can help solve also depends on expectations and values that are shaped by culture (Cox & Ephross, 1998). Immigrants who have been persecuted and discriminated against may not acknowledge their situation as solvable by services.

Attitudes toward acceptable sources for help also vary among cultures. In many Asian cultures mental health problems are perceived as bringing shame on the family (Harper & Lantz, 1996). Therefore, immigrants from those countries will prefer informal help from relatives, pastors and priests, and compatriots, and will refuse to seek mental health services for fear of embarrassing their family.

Perception of what counts as "help" is also culture-specific. Many Asian and Eastern European cultures are not as open as Westerners to the idea of therapy, and "just talking" is not valued for problem solving. They often fail to understand possible benefits from support groups because expressing feelings in public, self-disclosure, and sharing one's troubles "with strangers" are culturally discouraged.

Previous experiences with services in their culture of origin often affect immigrants' attitudes toward mental health services (Cox & Ephross, 1998). In some countries of origin mental health services have been abused for political control. For example, in the former Soviet Union a "psychiatric history" may impede promotion in work, getting a driver's license, or gaining other privileges, causing fear and distrust toward mental health providers. Thus Russian immigrants are often reluctant to use mental health help, especially public services that are perceived as a surveillance mechanism of the government (Handelman, 1983, Berger, 1996c).

Self-perceptions of immigrants influence their patterns of seeking and using help. Diverse patterns of coping with identity issues have been identified in immigrant populations (Berger, 1997a). Immigrants who tend to cling to their culture of origin and distance themselves from the new culture may seek traditional modes of getting help, such as healers and botanica. Immigrants who seek to acculturate to the new culture or who developed self-hatred and internalized the stereotypical view of their culture by others may be more amenable to services provided by Americans according to Western standards.

Language can also present a barrier to providing mental health services. Lack of fluency with the English language is a major stressor for immigrants (Zapf, 1991). Topics addressed in mental health are often sensitive and hard to talk about. Having to do so in a language in which one is not fluent intensifies the difficulties and limits immigrants' ability to express delicate nuances of their feelings.

GUIDELINES FOR SOCIAL WORK PRACTICE WITH IMMIGRANTS

The challenges and "traps" in addressing immigrants' mental health needs call for developing new models and strategies for adjusting traditional mental health service delivery and therapeutic principles. This section reviews the following principles that proved helpful in providing mental health services to immigrants: (1) developing professionals' awareness and knowledge of cultural aspects of mental health issues and use of therapy; (2) tapping a variety of services; (3) avoiding unnecessary stigmatization; (4) using case management and group work; (5) using direct, solution-focused, and active methods of treatment; (6) using workers from the same culture as the clients; and (7) providing services in the immigrant's original language.

1. *Developing professionals' awareness and knowledge of cultural aspects of mental health issues and use of therapy.* Services need to address the unique cultural heritage of each group of immigrants (Nah, in press). To do so effectively, professionals need to educate themselves to become culture-sensitive and commit to train for working with culturally diverse populations (LaFrom-

boise, Foster, & James, 1996). This does not necessarily mean that they should know the norms of all the diverse cultures of their clients, but it does mean that they have to be aware that different cultures approach mental health issues and services in various ways. They should use the help of their clients, professionals, and religious and community leaders from the clients' culture to guide their work.

2. *Tapping a variety of services.* It is crucial to develop a variety of services to respond to the diversity of immigrants' needs and attitudes toward seeking and using mental health services. A diverse "basket of services" allows the worker to tailor differential interventions to address the unique needs of different groups of immigrants while taking into consideration their sensitivities and special circumstances. For example, immigrants from certain cultures are suspicious of the establishment and withdraw from any unnecessary contact with governmental services. Immigrants from other cultures are more familiar with official and public services and refrain from using nonprofit, voluntary, and private services (Cox & Ephross, 1998). Some immigrants prefer to receive services from professionals of their own culture because they feel that such professionals understand their experience and are more trustworthy. Other immigrants perceive services provided by professionals from their own culture to be less worthy and prefer to be served by American professionals. The diversity of services also enables immigrants to make their own decisions about which services they wish to use. Encouraging such self-determination is of the utmost importance in working with immigrants because it helps them to regain control of their own lives, something that has been often lost to immigration.

3. *Avoiding unnecessary stigmatization.* The DSM-IV suggests a diagnosis of adjustment disorder "when an identifiable stressor leads to impaired relationships in the patient's work or social life" (Morrison, 1995, p. 454). This seems to include most, if not all, immigrants. However, applying a psychiatric diagnosis to a normative emotional reaction is not helpful and may present additional risks, rather than support, to the immigrant's mental health. Whenever possible, the mental health professional must refrain from pathologizing normal reactions to the stress of im-

migration. Normalizing immigrants' experience reduces their anxiety, promotes more effective functioning, and frees them to concentrate on problem solving (Berger, 1997b).

Avoiding stigmatization has organizational and clinical aspects. Organizationally, offering services in neutral settings such as schools and community centers is highly effective given the sensitivity of immigrants from certain cultures to the stigma of receiving mental health services. This makes services accessible and attractive to a larger target population (Berger, 1996c). Clinically, focusing on normative acculturation issues and validation is critical in servicing immigrants. It is important to help immigrants recognize that their problems are caused by objective circumstances rather than by their own failure (Leader, 1991; Berger, 1996c). The anxiety and confusion caused by immigration decrease immigrants' self-confidence and sense of mastery over their own lives. Interventions that are informed by a strengths perspective validate the feeling of disorientation as a normal part of the immigration process rather than a personal weakness of the immigrant. Such interventions are useful in helping immigrants regain trust in themselves and their abilities and rehabilitate their self-perception.

Even in cases that call for more than a short-term preventive or crisis intervention, it is advisable to start with normative acculturation issues and, once a certain level of trust is achieved, to use it as a "jumping board" for further clinical interventions. A very effective model of service is that the same workers split their time between community-based preventive short-term services and clinical therapeutic services (Berger, 1996c). This facilitates the transfer of immigrants who need long-term therapeutic services to clinical settings because they are accompanied by a familiar worker toward whom they have developed initial trust.

4. *Using case management and group work.* Specifically, two modalities prove to be helpful in servicing immigrants: case management and group work. Case management offers the versatility, multiple perspectives, and flexibility necessary to address the many diverse economic, social, and psychological needs of immigrants. Group work is very useful because it provides immigrants with a support system to substitute the natural supports lost to immigration. Sharing the experience validates

their feelings, enables them to mourn losses, alleviates their loneliness, and allows them to gain a more realistic perception of their difficulties. In the group, participants also acquire a better understanding of American norms and rehearse social skills essential for living in the new culture. Mastery of social knowledge and skills helps group members gain a sense of control over their lives, raises their self-confidence, improves their acclimatization to the new culture, and empowers them (Glassman & Skolnik, 1984; Furnham & Bochner, 1986; Berger, 1996b). Groups also empower their members by exposing them to more experienced immigrants who can serve as powerful role models and instill hope: "Here is somebody who knows from personal experience what I am going through, who was in the same situation and who has made it. Maybe I can also make it." Successful types of groups include mutual support groups, adolescent groups, parent groups, acculturation groups, and therapeutic groups (Berger, 1996b, 1996c).

5. *Using direct, solution-focused, and active models of treatment.* Many of the immigrants' cultures discourage sharing emotions and talking about problems with non-family members. Many immigrants expect concrete help rather than "talking therapy." They want clear advice from a professional authority, help with employment, information about available resources, directives, and "practical" guidelines, and they often fail to value opportunities to share, debate, and problem solve (Hulewat, 1996). At least in initial phases of providing mental health services to immigrants, therapeutic models that focus on concrete help, solution-focused, psycho-educational, cognitive, and behavioral approaches are more useful than traditional therapeutic approaches. For example, teaching stress management techniques and techniques for prioritizing among issues is effective because it is compatible with the strong emphasis on cognition in Chinese, Japanese, Korean, Russian, and other cultures. It also enables immigrants to regain mastery over their lives rather than feel helplessly overwhelmed by the events, thus improving their self-esteem (Berger, 1997b).

6. *Using workers from the same culture as the clients.* Recruiting the help of professionals who share the cultural background of the clients to develop and provide mental health services is of

the utmost importance. These professional compatriots are sensitive to culture-related needs and do not experience obstacles in communication that are experienced by Americans who serve refugees (Glassman & Skolnik, 1984). They can provide information about acceptable ways of addressing needs, serve as a primary helping figure and powerful role model, and advocate for clients.

7. *Providing services in the immigrants' original language.* Offering the service in the immigrants' own language (the "mother language") facilitates self-expression and communication. Providing immigrants the opportunity to receive services in a language in which they are fluent enables them to accurately describe their experience and discuss possibilities of addressing their needs with a high level of comfort. Furthermore, experiencing the limitations of the language creates a feeling of limited mastery and a sense of helplessness leading to frustration and anger. Providing services in the immigrants' language not only helps them express themselves more freely and accurately, but also conveys a message of respect for their original cultural roots and validation of those roots as part of their current identity. This reflects the ideological shift from the notion of "melting pot" to the approach of "multiculturalism." "Melting pot" represents the idea that assimilation "involves the fine-grained intermingling of diverse ethnicities and cultures into a single national 'alloy.' . . . For immigrants to assimilate, they must abandon their original cultural attributes and conform entirely to the behaviors and customs of the majority of the native born population" (Salins, 1997, p. 20). This approach assumes the superiority of American culture and calls for quick assimilation. Critics of this ideology saw it as unrealistic and harmful and suggested substituting it with "multiculturalism." Multiculturalism acknowledges the richness of diversity and seeks to maintain conditions that enable each group to retain its original cultural heritage and at the same time learn to live in the dominant culture (Handelman, 1983).

ETHICAL ISSUES IN WORKING WITH IMMIGRANTS

Providing mental health services to immigrants presents ethical dilemmas. What are the limits of respect for the culture of origin, and when does it become an obstacle to acculturation that fixates the marginality of immigrants and should not be tolerated? How can cultural norms "imported" by immigrants from their homeland be balanced with American norms? For example, when should professionals assessing immigrant families define patterns of drinking, consumption of drugs, and using physical disciplinary practices as cultural norms, and when should they view those patterns as dysfunctional and plan intervention to change them?

Ethical issues of servicing clients of a cultural background that differs from that of the majority culture have been discussed since the early 1970s (LaFromboise et al., 1996). The tendency of the helping professions to use the standards of middle-class white culture as a yardstick against which behaviors are measured has been challenged. Mental health assumptions and interventions that have been developed within the context of the mainstream culture without appropriate modifications may cause more harm than help to clients if the worker encourages clients' behaviors that are unacceptable to the clients' culture of origin.

A Case Example

Tatiana, age 14, was referred to the school guidance counselor by her 8th-grade teacher. The teacher reported that the girl, although obviously intelligent, is academically underachieving, is often absent, and, when she does attend, looks depressed and has a hard time concentrating and focusing. She also noticed that Tatiana is isolated and does not socialize with other students. She did not seem to have any friends.

Tatiana is the oldest of two children. She emigrated from the former Soviet Union 3 years prior to her referral. She lives with her mother, stepfather, 5-year-old half brother, and maternal grandparents in a tiny two-bedroom apartment in Jamaica Queens in New York City. This area is populated mostly by immigrants as well as diverse minority groups. Her stepfather, 43, was a senior engineer in a huge factory in Moscow. His command of English is limited, and he has failed to keep a stable job since the family's immigration. He had several short-term positions as a technician, far below his professional credentials and experience, and has been unemployed for lengthy periods between jobs. He is a very strict person. His aggressive behavior toward his family is often augmented by his excessive drinking of vodka, a habit that becomes more severe when he faces being fired, decides to quit his job, or is frustrated in any other way. Because of his frequent changes of employment the family moved several times, and Tatiana has attended five different schools since she came to the United states.

Her mother, 40, a pediatrician by training, works consistently as a child care worker off the books because she could not afford to devote the time and effort required to study for her medical licensing examination. She works long hours, including weekends, because the family depends on her income in addition to the father's unemployment and the grandparents' social security. They can hardly make ends meet and are often faced with financial and economic difficulties.

Tatiana was a few months old when her parents divorced and her father disappeared from her life. The family has no clue as to his whereabouts. This caused quite a few problems when they applied for immigration, since his consent was required. It is not exactly clear how they managed to settle the matter, and they have been secretive about this. Until she was 8, Tatiana's main caregiver was her grandmother while her mother worked long hours. Tatiana is very attached to her grandparents and sleeps with them in their room. When she was 8 her mother met her stepfather, who has separated from his previous wife and who has a son Tatiana's age. Her mother quickly got pregnant, and soon after Tatiana's half brother was born the parents married. The grandmother continued to be the major parental figure in the lives of the two children, and she practically raised them. When the family moved to the United States, the maternal grandparents joined reluctantly. They do not speak English and have lost their central place in the family.

Tatiana started to be seen by the school social worker, who also held several meetings with the girl and her parents as well as with the whole family, including the young brother and the grandparents. This social worker is an immigrant from the former Soviet Union. She used to be a child psychologist, and upon her immigration about 9 years ago she went back to school and earned her MSW. She held the meetings with the family in a combination of Russian and English because the children are more fluent in the latter. The individual sessions with Tatiana were in English according to the girl's preference.

The beginning was slow. Tatiana was suspicious, and her parents demanded mostly that she her improve her grades and get a part-time job. Gradually, the worker found herself intervening in many aspects of family life. She helped the grandmother join an English class for senior citizens, and Tatiana volunteered to help her with her homework. The grandfather was convinced to participate in a social club for senior citizens and to contribute from his knowledge as a professor of Russian literature. Convinced by the positive changes they observed in their daughter, the parents agreed to cooperate to a certain degree with the worker, who validated their feeling angry, concerned, and occasionally helpless and frustrated about losing their authority over their daughter. She also provided them with psycho-educational knowledge about normal adolescence and invited them to attend a mutual support group for parents of adolescents titled "Raising Adolescents in America." This group was facilitated in Tatiana's school by a worker associated with the bilingual program.

As for Tatiana herself, she gradually and cautiously "melted." She shared with the worker her ambivalence toward her parents. On the one hand, she appreciated their concern for her, and she wanted to excel and make them proud of her. On the other hand, she experienced a degree of role reversal because she had to translate for them in negotiations with their landlord and various officials, and she also felt angry about their restricting attitude and longed to have the same freedom in clothes and social life that many of her peers enjoy. She oscillated among despair, anger, depression, and frustration. She expressed disappointment with herself and her biological father who deserted her. She was furious for having to move first involuntarily from her Russian friends and then so many times in the United States: "What is the point of trying to become popular and make friends if soon HE will make us move again?" She constantly felt like the "new kid on the block" and was afraid of being rejected and made fun of. At this point the worker suggested joining a theater club, which, to her surprise, Tatiana agreed to try. It soon became apparent that she has a considerable dramatic talent. The group was working on developing a play based on their own experience, and they built it around Tatiana's story, which contributed to her feeling worthy and enhanced her self-esteem. By the end of the year, Tatiana still had fragile self-esteem and somewhat stormy relationships with her parents, but she showed considerable progress. Her absences from school decreased, she was active in the theater group on a regular basis, and she has made some social contacts.

SUMMARY AND CONCLUSIONS

Three major factors shape the mental health issues of immigrants: (1) the long, complex, and stressful process of immigration intensifies existing problems and causes new mental health issues; (2) immigration causes the loss of support systems that can help individuals and families cope with those multiplied and intensified problems; and (3) many cultures of origin discourage the use of traditional mental health services. Therefore, mental health professionals are called to develop services that address immigrants' unique mental health needs. These include developing professionals' awareness of culture-sensitive practice, providing a variety of services in the immigrant's language, avoiding unnecessary stigmatization, using case management and group work modalities, using direct, solution-focused, and active models of treatment, and providing workers from the same culture as the clients.

REFERENCES

Baptiste, D. (1990). The treatment of adolescents and their families in cultural transition: Issues and recommendations. *Contemporary Family Therapy, 12*(1), 3–22.
Baptiste, D. (1993). Immigrant families, adolescents and accul-

turation: Insights for therapists. In B. H. Settles, D. E. Hanks, & M. B. Sussman (Eds.), *Families on the move: Migration, immigration, emigration and mobility.* New York: Haworth Press.

Berger, R. (1996a). Characteristics of adolescent immigrants from the former Soviet Union. *The Jewish Social Work Forum, 32,* 42–50.

Berger, R. (1996b). *From Comsomol to group work: Myths and realities in group work with immigrants from the former Soviet Union.* New York: The Jewish Board of Family and Children Services/The Emigre Mental Health Training Program.

Berger, R. (1996c). Group work with immigrant adolescents. *Journal of Child and Adolescent Group Therapy, 6*(4), 169–179.

Berger, R. (1997a). Adolescent immigrants in search of identity: Clingers, eradicators, vacillators, and integrators. *Child and Adolescent Social Work Journal, 14*(4), 263–275.

Berger, R. (1997b). Immigrant stepfamilies. *Contemporary Family Therapy, 19*(3), 361–370.

Christensen, C. P. (1992). Training for cross-cultural social work with immigrants, refugees, and minorities: A course model. *Journal of Multi-Cultural Social Work, 2*(1), 79–97.

Coles, R. (1968). *The South goes North.* Boston: Little, Brown.

Cox, B., & Ephross, P. H. (1998). *Ethnicity and social work practice.* New York: Oxford University Press.

Drachman, D., & Shen-ryan, A. (1991). Immigrants and refugees. In A. Gitterman (Ed.), *Social work practice with vulnerable populations* (pp. 618–646). New York: Columbia University Press.

Fix, M., & Passel, J. (1994). *Immigration and immigrants: Setting the record straight.* Washington, DC: Urban Institute Press.

Furnham, A., & Bochner, S. (1986). *Culture shock: psychological reactions to unfamiliar environments.* New York: Methuen.

Garza-Guerrero, A. C. (1974). Culture shock: its mourning and the vicissitudes of identity. *Journal of the American Psychoanalytic Association, 22,* 408–429.

Glassman, U., & Skolnik, L. (1984). The role of social group work in refugee resettlement. *Social Work With Groups, 7*(1), 45–62.

Gold, S. J. (1989). Differential adjustment among a new immigrant family members. *Journal of Contemporary Ethnography, 17*(4), 408–434.

Handelman, M. (1983). The new arrivals. *New York Association for New Americans: Practice Digest, 5*(4), 3–22.

Harper, K. V., & Lantz, J. (1996). *Cross-cultural practice: Social work with diverse populations.* Chicago: Lyceum.

Hulewat, P. (1996). Resettlement: A cultural and psychological crisis. *Social Work, 41*(2), 129–135.

LaFromboise, T. D., Foster, S., & James, A. (1996). Ethics in multicultural counseling. In P. B. Pederson, J. G. Draguns, W. J. Lonner, & J. E. Trimble (Eds.). *Counseling across cultures* (pp. 47–72). Thousand Oaks, CA: Sage.

Landau, J. (1983). Therapy with families in cultural transition. In M. McGoldrick, J. K. Pearce, & J. Giordano (Eds.), *Ethnicity and family therapy* (pp. 552–578). New York: Guilford.

Landau-Stanton, J. (1985). Adolescents, families and cultural transition: A treatment model. In A. Mirkin & S. Koman (Eds.), *Handbook of adolescents and family therapy* (pp. 363–381). New York: Gardner Press.

Lantz, J., & Harper, K. (1990). Anomic depression and the migrating family. *Contemporary Family Therapy, 12,* 153–163.

Leader, E. (1991). Why adolescent group therapy? *Journal of Child and Adolescent Group Psychotherapy, 1*(2), 81–93.

Morrison, J. (1995). *DSM-IV made easy.* New York: Guilford.

Nah, K. H. (in press). Adjustment experience of new Americans: Soviet-Jewish refugees and Korean immigrants. *The Journal of Multi-Cultural Social Work.*

Salins, P. D. (1997). Assimilation, American style. *Reason, 28*(9), 20.

Stewart, E. C. P. (1986). The survival stage of intercultural communication. *Tokyo: International Christian University Bulletin, 1*(1), 109–121.

Zapf, K. M. (1991). Cross cultural transitions and wellness: Dealing with culture shock. *International Journal for the Advancement of Counselling, 14,* 105–119.

10

Palliative Care: Facilitating Decision Making About Death and Dying

*Margaret Souza, CSW, and
Eugenia L. Siegler, MD, FACP*

INTRODUCTION

TECHNOLOGICAL ADVANCES IN SCIENCE and medicine have created a hospital environment where dying is handled as a medical emergency. The dying person is subjected to multiple interventions such as resuscitation, intubation, medications to maintain blood pressure, and other invasive medical procedures. Although these procedures are designed to support and sustain life after trauma or acute medical illness, they are rarely beneficial in dying patients. These interventions are useful in acute situations and are intended for conditions in which patients are expected to return to a relatively stable medical status or can be rehabilitated to some degree of function. For dying patients, these interventions may prolong the dying process and cause physical as well as emotional pain.

The emotional impact on the family who may be unable to recognize and accept the process of dying for what it is, is also considerable. We use the term "family" throughout this chapter to include all individuals who are associated with the dying person by kinship, friendship, mutual obligations, informal caregiving arrangements, and so forth. None of these terms includes all of the relationships that we have to recognize as important to the dying person and those who survive.

Aggressive treatment usually limits the family's ability to be physically present when the patient is dying. It provides false hope that the terminal condition will be ameliorated, perhaps even reversed, enabling the dying person to return home to them. These procedures add the "miracle of medical science" to more esoteric hopes and beliefs in miracles. Family members often react to the official pronouncement of death as a traumatic recognition that a loved one is "gone" with thoughts of what they wished they had done or said. Under these conditions, the dying experience is a fight with a powerful opponent that is victorious despite heroic efforts. These battles often entail much pain, frustration, and anguish for the patient, family, and clinicians.

Although federal and state laws have promoted individual decision making through living wills, advance directives, and health care proxies, often patients and families are unaware of these documents and fail to recognize the necessity of executing them. The more vulnerable populations are less likely to possess advance directives; in a study conducted in California among those who knew of these documents, only 40% of European Americans, 17% of African Americans, and 0% of Korean Americans had advance directives (Frank et al., 1998). Although the focus of that study is on cultural values, it also reflects what is familiar and recurrent through history. As the federal government relinquishes its authority to local governments and as decreases in government spending at all levels lead to cutbacks in services, ethnic minorities are at highest risk. In the area of palliative care, providing education about health care decision making and helping patients acquire the necessary documentation is essential. With reduced funding, these tasks are often neglected or delegated to staff who lack necessary knowledge, training, and skills.

Palliative care providers recognize that dying is a process that belongs to the dying person and his or her family. Palliative care is foremost patient-centered, placing highest priority on the needs of the patient and family. By shifting treatment efforts away from cure, it provides the opportunity to enhance the care of dying persons and to understand and meet their specific needs. It also enables staff to express their concerns and respond to the dynamic of the experience in a professional but more humane manner.

This chapter will illustrate the role of the palliative care social worker in assisting dying patients and their families. The social work empowerment model enables the recipient of services to be involved in the decision-making process. We will discuss how social work professionals can participate in defining the approach that the health care team takes in understanding the time sequence of the dying process and the needs of all concerned.

Special Issues of the Hospital Site

Despite the general recognition that hospitals exist for curing acute illness, 70% of all deaths that occurred in the United States in 1995 occurred in hospitals. The hospital setting has twice as many deaths as any other place (Zuckerman & Mackinnon, 1998). In New York City, 85% of all deaths occur in the hospital, exceeding the national average.

The needs of patients who are incurable and those who are in the final stages of their lives pose a problem for health care professionals who have been trained to focus on and cure each problem. In particular, doctors and nurses seek to cure. The training that enables the health care professional to respond precisely to alleviate symptoms and promote the restoration of health may limit their view of the dying process (Muller & Koenig, 1988).

A source of discomfort for the health care staff is setting priorities when faced with competing needs of dying and curable patients. Not only does the patient who is hospitalized with an acute illness seem to have more "active" problems that require intervention, but culturally speaking, these patients are more "attractive." The societal aversion or denial of death has a firm foundation in the hospital/medical setting, where death has been the traditional enemy to be fought at all costs. Medical training reinforces these attitudes. These feelings, perhaps unconscious, inform behavior even on the professional level. The health care setting provides little opportunity for staff to process their own feelings when a patient dies (Glaser & Strauss 1980).

Professional staff often fear that being seen as "emotional" will be a disadvantage in their professional career. Physicians may maintain that emotional involvement will limit their effectiveness as doctors, believing that their role requires absolute objectivity.

Hospitals are organized to manage acute episodes of illness, to stabilize patients' medical condition, and to discharge them to a safe and appropriate environment. Emotional aspects of illness, although tacitly considered important, are not addressed. This limited view of a patient and the role of the health care provider creates a tension between managing medical problems and meeting more complex and persistent requirements of a dying patient and his or her family members. Moreover, approaching symptoms as concrete medical problems provides a certainty to a professional's actions. The procedure/order/protocol assures professionals that their actions are correct. Performing a procedure is clearer and more direct than the process of being "present" to a patient and taking the person's emotional and physical anguish into account.

Often social work staff are employed to provide assistance with discharge planning concerns. Their professional training limits their knowledge of biomedicine but provides them with the skills needed to deal with the emotional components of patients' lives. Physicians and nurses often lack the in-depth training and the confidence to deal with the emotional components of illness. Excessive patient loads often make it impossible for them to deal with the more holistic care needs of dying patients and their families.

Needs of Dying Patients and Their Families

Culture, gender, age, economics, religion, and every other facet of human existence affect our attitude toward death and dying. For hospitalized patients, the positive and negative influences of the hospital environment and lifelong human relationships have the greatest impact on the process of dying. The hospital often is a refuge for patients and families when they are unaware of what the process of dying entails or that it has begun. The hospital is the place where patients are "taken care of." In the hospital, where the focus is on cure, dying patients' needs require comfort measures. Relief of physical and psychological symptoms such as pain, nausea, constipation, and anxiety is crucial for dying patients and their families. Providers, sensing the "hopelessness" of the case, may not respond quickly to requests for palliation of symptoms. Patients, families, and staff may fail to recognize or understand palliation.

If the patient and family fail to recognize and accept the inevitable dying process, they may still demand cure or at least the maintenance of life. Patient and family may have distorted perceptions of the process or events that are taking place. Often providers will say that patients and families are "in denial" when information has not been clearly communicated to them: the focus still seems to revolve around cure, and they have not had sufficient time to process the reality of a terminal prognosis. The sense of loss and powerlessness in the face of impending death may lead to a displacement of feelings onto the caregiving staff. The lack of congruity in perceptions can result in escalating emotional responses. Staff feel and are abused and negated, while patients and families experience alienation. The "normal" avoidance of a dying patient is compounded when staff avoid a family that is seen as "problematic." This behavior adds to the frustration and helplessness that all experience as part of the dying process.

Hospital-based palliative care developed to address problems unique to dying in the acute care setting. Hospice, the primary movement in care of the dying, has existed for years as an alternative to the aggressive stance of hospital care. Because of its philosophical approach and Medicare funding constraints, it is home-based, located in a separate facility, or found in a distinct niche in the hospital setting. On the other hand, hospital-based palliative care is a broader concept, and we have applied it to the institution as a whole in order to have an impact on staff and procedures hospital-wide.

Palliative care in the hospital setting is a special challenge. Through it, providers are encouraged to ensure that decision making and health care treatment are related to the patient and family's total needs. Palliative care staff also help providers recognize that patients and their families need professional assistance to process information about death and dying. Through palliative care, experts in the medical, nursing, and psychosocial needs of dying give patients and families choices in their decision making.

A Palliative Care Program at a Community Hospital

As part of its Hospital Palliative Care Initiative (HPCI), the United Hospital Fund underwrote a research and planning grant that enabled The Brooklyn Hospital Center to determine the needs of dying patients and to develop a program to meet them. The 2-year implementation grant funded a hospital-wide palliative care program. To understand the purpose of this program, it is useful to review the definition of palliative care: "Palliative care is the active total care of patients whose disease is not responsive to curative treatment. Control of pain, of other symptoms and of psychological, social, and spiritual problems is paramount. The goal of palliative care is the achievement of best possible quality of life for patients and their families" (World Health Organization, 1990).

Brooklyn Hospital's HPCI had ongoing service, research, and educational functions. For this chapter, we will focus on the service and educational components. A full-time master's-prepared nurse managed the day-to-day operations and assessed the referrals to the program. She made recommendations to the staff about patients' ongoing needs and helped organize the services. A social worker provided counseling to patients and families about death and dying and helped them meet concrete needs. A geriatric physician oversaw the program and provided clinical input, cajoled unresponsive physicians, and advised the team about pain management, skin care, and other comfort issues.

True collaboration was essential to the work of Brooklyn Hospital's HPCI. Team members needed to be able to call upon each other for insight in their different areas of expertise. Family members often responded more readily to one team member than to others. This individual needed to be able to easily consult other members when the case presented issues that needed clarification and assistance from another discipline.

As the program evolved, physicians and other staff frequently called upon the service to provide specialized support to families and patients. They also sought that support for themselves, whether they were dealing with a patient or a family member. Discussing end-of-life issues, a task that health care professionals have traditionally avoided, was something the team was often asked to do. Using our service as an educational opportunity, we preferred to join the patient's physician or medical resident in these discussions. In this manner, modeling took place and the conversations surrounding death and dying (often termed "sensitive issues") became more commonplace. By working with us, the hospital staff learned different approaches to these discussions and were encouraged to "find their own voice."

Team members participated with hospital staff in whatever area they could to help them meet the needs of dying patients. Discussing advance directives before they are immediately necessary enables the staff to have insight into the wishes of patients surrounding their end-of-life care. It also assists families in dealing with their emotional responses. If patients make their wishes clear early in the process of a terminal illness, decision making flows more easily. Although the decision-making strategy may evolve, participants set off on a path that prepares them for impending death and provides them with a measure of control.

PSYCHOSOCIAL COMPONENTS OF CARE

The psychosocial components of palliative care encompass a variety of processes. Table 10.1 lists a number of them. The worker needs to be conscious of all the dynamics that occur and the different levels of needs among patients, families, and staff. Identifying concrete and emotional needs is essential; this enables patients and families to experience empowerment at a most vulnerable time. Preparation provides some sense of control in the face of uncertainty and change. It affords the dying person some choices and provides present and future comfort for families. The worker supports the dying process itself, assisting staff as well as patient and families. In this way, the experience of loss is anticipated and prepared for—it becomes a process, not an event.

Working with dying patients and their families requires clear goal setting, and this demands of the workers a comfort in enabling patients and families to explore and articulate their wishes in detail. The primary wish is to make the terminal diagnosis "go away." In coming to terms with that reality, however vaguely, patients and families need to express what a good death means to them. After the specifics of the goal are determined, interventions required to make it happen can begin to be put in place. The family must process their external and internal resources to achieve the goal—"What do you need to have/do to enable your loved one to die at home?" Most often the palliative care worker must cobble together a combination of family resources and outside programs (e.g., home hospice) to help the patient achieve that "good death."

As the following cases illustrate, the social worker must operate at various levels of intervention simultaneously. At times, families and patients can articulate their wishes clearly or use easily understood codes. On other occasions, they cannot achieve their goals; social workers must help them overcome their disappointment and establish alternative, acceptable goals.

TABLE 10.1. PSYCHOSOCIAL COMPONENTS OF PALLIATIVE CARE

Assisting Patient and Family
Coming to terms with dying
Empowerment
Planning for death
Emotional needs
Concrete needs
Coping with loss
Assisting Staff
Emotional needs
Educational needs

This work often needs to be done quickly, for time is limited and death is a finality.

One of the most difficult areas in dealing with the dying patient and his or her family is coming to terms with the terminality of the patient's condition. Between the physician's words that a disease is in its final stages and the individual's comprehension of that meaning is an enormous gray area. Decisions regarding how long treatment should continue, the place and manner in which a "dying patient" should spend his or her final days/weeks/months, and who should make that decision require an understanding of the patient, the options available, and the social support system. At times the patient's physical condition may preclude many choices. However, creative thinking and recognition of the process that is occurring can open up options that may not seem to be available when those involved are still focusing on "cure."

Case 1

A patient with an aggressive brain tumor wanted very much to visit her son and grandchildren out West. Since she and her husband had heard her physician say how serious her condition was, they postponed the trip until she finished an experimental and debilitating treatment. They believed that they could defeat the tumor. The husband failed to comprehend the neurosurgeon's statements to "prepare for the worst," and instead preferred to accept any hope or positive thought he could cling to.

This was the second marriage for each after very unhappy marriages. The husband was older, and both had grown children and grandchildren. What the patient and husband needed was time to process the information and verbalize their thoughts and feelings. Given time to discuss what they had heard, their goals and expectations—being asked the questions that would assist them in dealing with what was occurring—they would be able to make decisions that were in their best interest.

When he spoke with the social worker, the husband revealed how exhausting this hospitalization and surgery had been for him, something he would never admit to in his wife's presence. During her hospitalization he was always cautious to ensure that the social worker never met with her alone. Most persons, including some physicians, fear that a social worker will reveal the terminal diagnosis. In our program, the social worker has been asked by dying patients' attendings to reveal this information and obtain advance directives.

Most patients who are dying have been dealing with the terminal disease process for a long period of time. The question of when palliative care replaces active treatment is difficult to answer. In not wanting patients to "give up," physicians may be reluctant to communicate the hopelessness of a terminal condition. Patients and family who look to the physician for another cure may not want to "hear" the news. Patients, family, and staff who try hard to please one another may foster treatments and hospitalizations that are futile but which "seem" to be what the other wants.

This case illustrates the difficulty of identifying and effectively dealing with psychosocial needs. The medical treatment this patient received contributed to her remarkable recovery from two brain surgeries. The couple and both of their families did not comprehend the seriousness of her prognosis until two days before discharge after the second surgery, when the family was referred to our service. It became clear to the staff in the neurosurgery department that the couple were not dealing with or accepting—perhaps not even hearing—the terminal diagnosis. Although this family was close, the patient's children were concerned about her husband's insistence that she was going to "beat this." The staff from neurosurgery were not prepared to acknowledge her as a palliative care patient because there were still interventions that could perhaps extend her life. However, they certainly acknowledged that she had a terminal diagnosis.

This couple could have benefited from and received services from the HPCI throughout the hospitalization for aggressive intervention. The processing of a terminal diagnosis is never easy, particularly when aggressive treatment is still being pursued. Within the context of a counseling relationship, this couple would be enabled to discuss their plans, hopes, and still-unfulfilled dreams. They could have learned to accept and express the loss of their future together. They would then be able to make decisions about how they wanted to spend the rest of their time together. Lastly, they would have been able to make informed decisions about health care treatments based on a fuller understanding and acceptance of what medical science has to offer, and what benefits as well as ensuing difficulties these procedures cause.

With this information the couple could have made decisions based on the true understanding of the decline in her condition. The pain of loss at death cannot be eliminated, but knowing that time was spent as they chose assists in lessening the guilt that survivors experience (Myerhoff, 1976). Case 5 will illustrate how processing the inevitability of death empowered a couple to optimize their last month together.

Identifying Specific Concrete and Emotional Needs

Social workers in an acute medical setting are not allowed to tell patients what their prognosis is. At times in the HPCI, physicians asked the social worker to communicate a prognosis to a patient and his or her family. In general, however, most physicians (in the interest of "maintaining hope") do not want the prognosis to be clearly articulated. The balance between communicating information regarding a patient's condition and mitigating the effect it has on the patient and family is an unresolved issue in the field of biomedicine. Physicians often fear that discussing a terminal condition and advance directives may cause a patient and family to lose confidence in the physician, perhaps fearing that the physician will not do all that can be done. Compounding these concerns are the larger unresolved issues of prognosis and effect of disclosure of information on a terminal patient. As a result, patients and family may lack sufficient information to make crucial decisions.

Despite all of the aforementioned ethical and theoretical problems when discussing impending death, it has been our experience that dying patients often do not have to be told that they are dying. They simply have to be allowed to say what they are feeling and experiencing.

Case 2

A patient once clearly asked the social worker if she was dying. The worker responded by asking the patient what she thought. The patient readily responded yes and asked why the staff were telling her how well she was doing. The worker responded that, given the seriousness of her condition, she was doing well. The patient then queried how long she had to live. In response again the social worker asked what she thought; she responded, 3 to 6 months. The worker simply answered that it seemed she didn't need the social worker to tell her what she knew.

This patient was caring for her grandchildren, whose mother had already died from injection drug use. There was much she and her family needed to do prior to her death—making arrangements for custody for the children as well as helping them deal with the loss of another maternal figure in their young lives. Providing the family with the opportunity to prepare for the loss and say their farewells would help children who were not given that opportunity with their biological mother.

Case 3

Another patient indicated during interview sessions that she did not want to die. However, during one of her hospitalizations she requested assistance with getting money from the bank to pay rents—hers, her elderly mother's, and her mentally ill brother-in-law's. Alone with the responsibility for these two dependent adults, she needed to make specific arrangements for the care and finances of those dependent upon her. Not only were we able to expedite the rent payments, but we also helped her make plans for those who were unable to care for themselves. At times patients are not able to talk about the ending of their lives, but making plans for someone to replace them in the roles and functions that are ongoing in their lives indicates an awareness of and preparation for their death.

Case 4

Palliative care demands a focus on process and the ability to establish the content of the process as the client and his or her family reveals it to us. A client on our second interview sat in a chair and began by stating, "I don't want to die." The social work response is, "So what do you want?" "I want to walk to the corner and buy ice cream—it's my block, and I want to walk it!" "How about going to the corner in a wheelchair. Is that good enough?" By the end of the week the patient was home with hospice care and a wheelchair in which her daughter would take her to the corner. By enabling her to focus on what she wanted, we could move from her wish not to die, and her guilt over smoking as perhaps the cause of her terminal diagnosis, to finally making arrangements for her foster child and formulating wishes in ways that met her needs.

EMPOWERMENT

Often the return of "normalcy" (our cancer patients' terminology) prevents the patient and family from recognizing or hearing that the end is approaching. Since all previous phases of the chronic illness were treated effectively, patients and family expect that this phase, too, will be treated, even if remission is not possible. Salvage treatment options are always available, and patients and families need to decide if fighting the disease process is how they wish to spend what may in fact be their last days together.

Case 5

Another couple was referred to the service early in the program. The husband had been battling a chronic cancer for over 10 years. The patient's wife came regularly for support and concrete assistance. A long hospitalization and a very debilitated condition created tension between the wife (who stayed overnight daily and tried as much as possible to change her husband's diapers) and her husband, who seemed to her to respond to the staff but would not cooperate when she provided care. We helped her to work out the relationships with staff, to recognize that she needed their assistance and that she was entitled to ask for help when her husband needed it. Her behavior change was a great relief to the staff, who no longer saw her as distrusting and spying on them, but rather as a helper. Through discussion she was able to be more direct with her husband. She began to ask him what he meant and stopped assuming that his responses were negatively directed at her. She came to recognize his feelings of loss and anger—she was no longer his wife, and only acting in her role as his caretaker. With our encouragement, she lay next to him in his hospital bed.

After a few weeks of regular counseling, which she sought, she was able to ask more direct questions of the oncologist. She decided after discussion with her husband that what was important for both of them was to be in their home environment where he could experience the warmth of their relationship. Together we listed her needs, both concrete and emotional, and she quickly sought the assistance she needed from her informal support system. The next morning, with the treatment team gathering in the room to wish them well, say their final good-byes to the patient, and provide support, they left the hospital, electing to forego all further aggressive medical treatment. Comfort measures, the assistance of the hospice program at home, and the attention of many friends who wanted to help was the plan they chose for a "good death."

After discharge she called to tell us how things were going. For the last month of his life, her husband lived with friends, family, flowers, music, and the things of value to him surrounding him. After his death she missed him immensely. However, she lives with the knowledge that she provided him with the best last days of his life and she has no regrets.

Assisting Patients and Families in Dealing With the Dying Process

Recognizing and dealing with dying take a variety of forms. Some patients speak indirectly; others want to talk quite directly about it; others talk around it or vacillate. Most patients and families can never just discuss death; interviews usually move between hope for the future and the recognition of the reality of impending death. Most patients find a way to discuss death and what is happening without really talking about it. The key to working with these families is the ability to listen to their concerns and be ready to respond to the issues as they are tentatively introduced. A space must be created where it is safe and expected to discuss death. Having an agenda that dictates at what stage in the process of dying a patient should be and trying to get him or her to comply simply amplifies the feelings of alienation and creates miscommunication. Using the family's language and picking up on the cues they give enable the social worker to move with and in the process.

Case 6

Ms. P was interviewed after a recurrence of ovarian cancer. Since she had been successful in her first fight with cancer, she was hopeful that she would survive this episode, too. Having time to interview her enabled us to help her identify a problem in her life that required resolution. She wanted to be assured that if anything happened to her, one of her sons would care for her developmentally delayed daughter. Further discussion revealed that she wanted her youngest son to take the responsibility and that it was her wish that he would "stand up" and let her know his intent. She had never asked her son directly to take responsibility, nor had there ever been a serious conversation about her concerns. She wanted to believe that he should magically know what she wanted, but she came to a recognition that she needed to have a discussion with him. We discussed how and when the conversation would occur.

During her next hospitalization, she told the son what she wanted, and he assured her that he would be responsible for his sister "if something happened." The social worker met her son during this hospitalization; the patient spoke of her deteriorated condition, but she was never able to discuss her impending death.

During her third and last hospitalization, she remained unable to speak directly of her dying. However, her son would meet the social worker elsewhere in the hospital and begin to talk about the loss of his mother and their very close relationship. Each time she was to be discharged, something would happen that prevented her from going home. Although her family had made arrangements to provide the care she would need at home and the hospice program was going to be available, she was reluctant to be discharged. She had a conversation about her concerns. "Things didn't seem to go right," she said. Again, we spoke about her ability to ask for what she needed. We decided that we would have a discussion with the son she clearly depended upon.

During that conversation, her son responded that he thought his mother could do more for herself than she did at home. The social worker responded that although she didn't know his mother as well as he did, she felt if his mother "could do for herself she would." The patient agreed. The social worker went on to express how "when someone is ill and we don't want to deal with it we want to believe that they can do for themselves." At that moment, recognition took place. They decided to go home, and he offered to take responsibility for coordinating her home services and needs. The day before her discharge, he met with the social worker to discuss the plan. When the social worker asked him what was happening, he said that he was taking his mother "home to die." He was fully aware of and articulate about what was happening and was ready to take the responsibility with all its seriousness. A month later the social worker received a phone call from the hospice nurse asking her to speak to the son. His mother had just died. He then went on to say that she had died in his arms.

Although a death still leaves family with the sense of loss, participation in the final stages of a loved one's life can remove the guilt that so often follows death. This death, as opposed to a death in the hospital with life-sustaining equipment, enabled the family members to recognize what was occurring and make the end time of life as comfortable as it could be.

Working With Staff to Implement a Psychosocial Approach to Dying

Most hospital staff want to handle death in a way that truly meets the needs of the individual and family. With some encour-

agement and direction, they participate in ways that extend beyond the biomedical model to expedite the process. The value of
the HPCI was to encourage broader participation of staff to meet
all of the needs of the patient and family. By articulating clearly
what the patient is requesting, advocating for it, and then enlist-
ing the staff's assistance, the palliative care professionals enabled patient, family, and staff to work together to provide
holistic care.

Case 7

Ms. G had breast cancer several years ago. She was hospitalized
for extensive cancer that had metastasized (spread through her
body to other organs). She was receiving chemotherapy and
being prepared for a series of radiotherapy treatments. Well
known to the palliative care personnel, she told us one day that
she needed to go home. "I just have that feeling that I need to
be." She mentioned how she missed her grandchildren and
home itself. We planned for her discharge the next day.

Late the following afternoon the social worker happened to
be on the unit and realized that the arrangements made the day
before had not been carried out. Ambulance drivers were prepared to leave the unit, since it did not seem as if anything was
ready. Quickly, the floor staff were mobilized—the doctor writing the discharge orders and prescriptions, and the staff getting
some supplies and medication for a few days. A nurse reviewed
the medication and treatment with the patient's daughter. Lastly, the ambulance drivers, although reluctant to take her,
agreed, as the social worker told them her urgency seemed to
indicate that she wanted to leave immediately: she was going
home to die. The discharge nurse called hospice so they would
schedule an early-morning meeting. The unit staff were pleased
that evening that they were able to respond to her immediate
need. The following day the staff were even more profoundly
pleased with all the extra effort they had put in to enable her
discharge. We found out she had died at 2:00 the morning after
her discharge.

This experience taught them a valuable lesson about listening
to patients and their urgent requests. Under ordinary circum-

stances, she would have waited another day. Advocacy for the patient helps staff to focus on larger psychosocial needs. In the hospital, the biomedical needs most often take precedent. In a situation such as the one just described, staff recognized that death alone was not the problem. If she had died in the hospital without her wishes being honored, it would have been a loss for all of us. By listening carefully to the patient and family, palliative care team members were able to enlist staff support for this dying patient's decision-making ability. This process, although intended to provide assistance in a specific circumstance, has the advantage of the more long-term effect of changing the way patients' requests are heard and honored.

Case 8

More recently, a patient in the terminal stages of his advanced cancer, when asked to spend another night in the hospital so that arrangements could be made for the hospice nurse to visit on the day of his discharge, asked the worker if he would be alive another day. When she heard his request, she spoke to his partner to ensure that he was aware of the patient's condition and was prepared to take him home that day to die; she then arranged with hospice for a nurse to visit that afternoon. Before the worker could contact the ambulance company for transportation, a house officer anxious that the patient go home called the worker, seeking direction for care (in particular, advance directives). The house staff were concerned that they would otherwise be obliged to treat all of the medical problems that tests had revealed. They had come to recognize the futility of the treatments and were seeking assistance and direction to enable them to care for this patient's dying needs.

Mr. S left the hospital with a smile on his face and thumbs up as he was wheeled in the elevator at 2:15 P.M. His partner called when the hospice nurse had arrived and was relieved by her support and assistance. He telephoned again the next morning to say that Mr. S had died at 8:00 P.M. They were holding hands, and just before he died, Mr. S turned and gave him an incredible smile, then turned his head and died.

This case reflects how after 2 years with the HPCI, the hospital staff have begun to recognize the urgency and more holistic needs of dying patients and are able to seek assistance to deal with them.

Loss

Death is loss. It is often painful and frightening. No one experiences the event in a positive manner. Even when someone who has been ill for a long time or is very elderly dies, loved ones experience loss. Part of the work of the HPCI is responding to death in a real manner. So often families believe they need to be strong for the person who is dying. Be positive. Be silent. The HPCI has given them permission to grieve. Helping persons through the pain instead of avoiding it brings relief to all involved.

Staff need to feel safe in discussing how difficult it is when several deaths occur on their unit around the same time. One nurse was able to state that she went to the parking lot and sat in her car and cried during her lunch break. Others ask palliative care personnel to be there when they need us. We have found that it is not a formal weekly group session that is helpful for staff. Rather, they come individually for relief from the pain of loss. Able to express their emotions of loss and pain more openly, staff feel validated. They are able to respond to patients and their families in a more humane, holistic manner. They do not have to spend their emotional energy trying to maintain control, so they are free to spend it on the patients they care for.

"The provision of palliative care to the terminally ill is a natural extension of social work, which has traditionally provided supportive services in time of crisis" (Allison, Gripton, & Rodway, 1983). Although at the end of this century we have witnessed a diminution in the role of social work in health care, the evolving field of palliation not only provides a natural setting for social work but also needs our active contribution. Biomedicine alone does not provide an adequate model of care for palliation; it focuses on pain control and symptom relief, with less attention to psychosocial needs.

To provide a dying patient with home care and financial assistance is essential. However, the profession of social work cannot stop there. Responding to the process of dying is more difficult than providing concrete services. Patients who are dying are most vulnerable. Doubly vulnerable are populations who face discrimination. They may lack resources and knowledge. The HPCI assisted those who were unaware of their rights and at the time of their dying enabled them to understand their options and be empowered to make their own choices. Death does not need to be their final victimization.

Each death reminds us of our own vulnerability. Social workers also are culture-bound. They experience the death-denying (or perhaps more correctly death-fearing) values of the society in which they live. The social work code of ethics underscores the value of self-determination and the belief that clients know what is in their best interest. Social workers recognize that the work of practice is to assist clients in formulating their goals and actualizing them as they can. That social workers focus on the awareness of our feelings and value systems is intended to empower clients by focusing on their needs as separate and as valid and essential as our own.

Palliative care requires the expertise of medicine, nursing, and social work. It could easily become another medical discipline, focusing on pain and relief of physical symptoms. However, the field demands a holistic perspective shaped by the larger needs of life and interpersonal relationships. Each discipline must broaden its perspective by listening to the patient and family in ways that go beyond their traditional focus of training.

Although social workers in palliative care must recognize the holistic needs of terminal patients and their families, practical matters are also important. A case management model is a useful one for this type of work. It is essential to be aware of what resources exist in the local community and to be able to bring a variety of resources together to meet any particular patient and family's needs. The need for physical assistance and financial help is particularly acute in these days of managed care and cutbacks in the medical assistance program.

Another resource that is often overlooked by professional social workers is the informal family system. Although kin and friendship systems provide emotional support based on affective ties, those in need may be reluctant to ask for help. The social worker can help the patient and family process feelings of dependency and recognize the gift of letting another do the giving. Social workers must recognize the denial and fear that death often evokes. Only by developing a comfort level with the process of dying can a social worker open up a safe place for others to respond. Without this recognition, a worker can often participate in the "conspiracy of silence" that surrounds the process of dying. Providing concrete assistance is safe, but only the beginning of the journey that the worker takes with the dying and their families.

When the Hospital Palliative Care Initiative entered its second phase, it was introduced to medical staff at Grand Rounds. After the presentation the social worker was on the elevator with a senior physician. He agreed that the program would be important and valuable for patients in the hospital. As he left the elevator, however, he turned to the social worker and said, "But who wants to talk about dying?" She turned and responded, "The patients do."

REFERENCES

Allison, H., Gripton, J., & Rodway, M. (1983). Social work services as a component of palliative care with terminal cancer patients. *Social Work in Health Care, 8*(4), 29–44.
Frank, G., et al. (1998). A discourse of relationships in bioethics: Patient autonomy and end-of-life decision making among elderly Korean Americans. *Medical Anthropology Quarterly, 12*(4), 403–423.
Glaser, B., & Strauss A. (1980). *Time for dying*. New York: Aldine.
Muller, J., & Koenig, B. (1988). On the boundary of life and death: The definition of dying by medical residents. In M. Lock & D. Gordon (Eds.), *Biomedicine examined* (pp. 351–374). Boston: Kluwer Academic Publishers.
Myerhoff, B. (1976). *Number our days*. New York: Simon & Schuster.
World Health Organization. (1990). *Cancer pain and palliative care.*

Technical Report Series 804. Geneva: World Health Organization.

Zuckerman, C., & Mackinnon, A. (1998, March). *The challenge for caring for patients near the end of life*. Findings from the Hospital Palliative Care Initiative. United Hospital Fund Paper Series.

III

Call to Action:
Strengthening Communities

Introduction

Rosa Perez-Koenig, DSW, and Barry Rock, DSW

PART III, THE FINAL SECTION OF THIS BOOK, includes a variety of topics and contributions with the common theme of a call to action for change at the personal, community, organizational, and inter-organizational levels. These chapters are very much in harmony with the concept of generalist social work practice, integrating the multiple levels of intervention into a unity through general system theory and social ecology. Implications for prevention are to be found here as well.

Person-in-environment is the bedrock of contemporary social work (Germain & Gitterman, 1996). "Person" is a metaphor for all of the social systems: the individual, small groups, large groups, communities, organizations, and societies. The well-being of individuals and communities depends on the degree of their mutual interconnectedness. In professional and agency practice, mutual interconnectedness is often referred to as collaboration, collaborative practice, or interdisciplinary or inter-agency collaboration. The importance of collaborative practice with high-risk populations includes the following:

1. The more at risk the population, the greater the need for a well-functioning interdisciplinary team.
2. High-risk groups are dependent, vulnerable, sometimes abandoned or abused, as well as seriously ill—requiring a well-functioning and emotionally supportive team sharing the burden of care.
3. Multiple biopsychosocial needs require a well-organized division of labor via an interdisciplinary team.

Organizational collaboration and linkage may be understood on a continuum from communication and cooperation to merger. Netting, Kettner, and McMurty (1998, p. 178) have identified five levels of interagency interactions:

1. Communication—sharing of information.
2. Cooperation—separate programs, but all work toward common, non-conflicting goals.
3. Coordination—"Two or more separate organizations work together to plan programs and ensure that they interact smoothly and avoid conflict, waste, and unnecessary duplication of services" (p. 178).
4. Collaboration—several independent organizations sponsor a single program or service.
5. Confederation—independent organizations merge fully to create a new, single organization.

The first two chapters of Part III are on collaborative, interdisciplinary, and interagency practice. Chapter 11, by Eric Brettschneider, is on community-based interagency planning; Chapter 12, on case conferences and collaboration between lawyers and social workers, is by Mary Ann Forgey, Anne Moynihan, Virginia Strand, and Leah Hill. If we have learned anything from our experiences with managed care and the downsizing and devolving of the social welfare state, it is that both interprofessional and interagency collaboration are essential for maintaining adequate services for vulnerable populations.

The final six chapters cover a wide range of action topics, from personal spiritual renewal to global action to end poverty. They share the context of devolving and diminished resources for human services, as well as the models of generalist social work practice and the strengths perspective in pointing toward solutions.

Chapter 13, by Roslyn Chernesky and Irene Guthiel, examines aspects of organizational and policy change with a focus on agencies serving the elderly. The following chapter, by Carol Cohen, Michael Phillips, Manuel Mendez, and Rosemary Ordonez, presents a model for building a sense of community in public housing and describes the impact that welfare reform has had on that process. Elaine Congress and Yvette Sealy have contributed a timely article on social work ethics and empowerment, and John Cosgrove has written about the critical role of parish-based social services as mediators in the age of devolution. In Chapter 17, Shawn Foley tackles the growing importance of spirituality and social work, and in doing so offers a concise history of social work values throughout the 20th century. In the final chapter, Natalie Riccio shows how social indicators and the Human Poverty Index (based on the work of Marc Miringoff, as discussed in the introduction to this book) can be used at the global level to call vulnerable communities to social, political, and economic action.

Tensions have always been present in the social work profession. These tensions have been a source of conflict but also of challenge, promoting new levels of integration and synthesis between direct practice and social change, between private troubles and public issues.

REFERENCES

Germain, C., & Gitterman, A. (1996). *The life model of social work practice: Advances in theory and practice.* New York: Columbia University Press.

Netting, F., Kettner, P., & McMurty, S. (1998). *Social work macro practice* (2nd ed.). New York: Longman.

Special Preface to Part III— Getting It Together: Interagency Collaboration in an Era of Rationing in the Human Services

*Alan B. Siskind, PhD, and
Mary Pender Greene, ACSW*

INTRODUCTION

Is THERE VALUE TO COLLABORATION between providers in our increasingly competitive human service environment? Voluntary partnerships between human service providers are beneficial to both the public and to the partnering agencies. Collaboration does not require any participants to violate their essential interests, for cooperation generally permits partnering service organizations to achieve their shared goals more efficiently and effectively. The result is often organizations better adapted to a challenging and changing environment. This positive and productive view of collaboration has not, however, always prevailed in the human service community. Looking at the case of New York City, for example, we see that agencies have often operated in isolation from each other.

The habits of working and thinking in isolation have complex origins and can be linked to a number of factors. Prominent among these factors is the assumption that staff accustomed to different organizational structures and organizational practices will not be able to work effectively together. Another factor behind isolationism in the human services is an assumption that organizations founded to serve particular ethnic or religious communities might be precluded by those commitments from working with organizations that serve other constituencies. This assumption was no doubt more strongly held in the past, when the need for agencies devoted exclusively to serving a specific community was more keenly felt.

Years ago, when interagency collaboration was virtually non-existent, it was all too easy for autonomously acting agencies to develop uninformed ideas about the mission, operations, clientele, and quality of care of service providers in different communities. These misperceptions at times contributed to an atmosphere of cultural misunderstanding and even distrust, of which we still find traces to this day. To some extent this atmosphere of misunderstanding can be inadvertently perpetuated by the agendas of the federated organizations (such as the various Jewish, Catholic, Protestant, African American, Asian, Hispanic, and other associations) founded to raise money and perform advocacy functions for specific communities. Nevertheless, we are now beginning to understand that, to an unprecedented extent, the best way for religiously and culturally affiliated providers to meet the needs of the communities they were founded to serve is precisely by joining with others to create mutually beneficial partnerships that enhance the quality of life in the general community.

COLLABORATION: CHALLENGES, PRECONDITIONS, CONDITIONS, AND GOALS

We are beginning to appreciate the potential value of interagency collaboration as a strategy for invigorating human service delivery and empowering our consumers, thereby promoting greater social and economic justice for the sake of this society's most vulnerable members. We have identified several factors that must be considered for effective interagency collaboration: challenges, preconditions, conditions, and goals.

Challenges in Our New Environment

1. *Funding.* A political climate inhospitable to poor people and therefore to public support for social services for them has

shrunk the government's contribution to the funding pie. These are well addressed in the chapters by Shirley Better and Robert Hill.

2. *Managed care.* The emergence of managed care might be characterized as a mixed blessing. Barry Rock has thoroughly examined managed care in his chapter. To some extent, managed care has played a role in broadening the range of people who can access service relative to the fee-for-service insurance system. Through cost savings, it has slowed forces in a health care system beset with exploding costs that threatened to restrict services for those in need. At the same time, however, managed care's cost controls have worked to introduce their own restrictions, setting significant limits on the number of sessions (sometimes by gatekeepers unknowledgeable of the real service needs at issue) and creating stricter eligibility requirements. The cost controls introduced by managed care are forcing providers to be much more mindful of the bottom line. This inevitably affects decisions regarding practice.

3. *Efficiency and effectiveness.* Finally, providers are now more often being asked by stakeholders in the worlds of government, commercial managed care, and even foundations and philanthropy to provide data which demonstrate that dollars are being used efficiently and effectively. I do not imagine that anyone in the provider community disagrees with this goal or dissents from the belief that high standards of accountability are appropriate. Implementing the systems required to measure outcomes and cultivating buy-in among staff are time consuming, complicated, and expensive processes. Good outcome measurement will help providers immensely in their future strategic planning, but at this early stage the heightened expectations on this front represent a major environmental challenge.

Preconditions of Effective Collaboration

In order to overcome obstacles to collaboration, we must recognize and seek to cultivate the preconditions of effective collaboration. What are these preconditions?

1. *Changes in attitude.* A good starting point is a frank acknowledgment that collaborative efforts may involve fundamen-

tally changing an organization's way of working and being. Change, as all good clinicians know, is frequently painful and fraught with resistance. Changes in practice begin, in part, with changes in attitudes.

2. *Effective leadership.* To a large degree, a change in attitudes within an organization is a function of effective leadership, and this is especially the case with an issue like collaboration. If an agency's leadership does not believe in the concept of inter-agency collaboration, staff should not be expected to believe in it either. Conversely, leadership's commitment to the concept of doing business differently works to set the tone throughout the organization.

3. *Staff acceptance.* So we see that as changes in attitudes within an organization take hold and become pervasive enough to bring about a change in institutional culture, the groundwork is laid for staff buy-in. Staff buy-in is a key ingredient for any successful partnership venture. Common obstacles to buy-in are cynicism about collaboration and lingering distrust, attitudes that are as inimical to working with another agency as is short-sighted competitiveness. Once staff become more receptive to the concept of collaboration in general, commitment and buy-in to specific projects comes much more easily.

4. *Clarity about needs and goals.* Prior to proposing a collabora-tion or responding to an overture, an organization must be very clear about how it wants to position itself in the market. We need to be open to collaboration as an option because in the right circumstances it will make sense strategically. In deciding what the right circumstances are for us, we need to keep in mind that collaboration is market-driven. Going into a joint venture for reasons at odds with our overall business plans is as great an error as being closed to the whole concept of collaboration. Therefore, it is essential that each collaborating organization first achieve clarity about its needs and goals, so that once discussion begins both or all partners can more easily achieve clarity about their mutual goals and potential mutual rewards.

Conditions to Ensure Successful Collaboration

Once a collaboration is initiated, several conditions should be in place to ensure its success:

1. *A good dialogue.* Throughout the entire process a good dialogue is needed, first to build and then to maintain trust and respect.

2. *Readiness and resources.* Both partners need to be secure in their own and the other's readiness to see the project through. Concretely, this means a readiness to make an adequate commitment of resources, in terms of personnel, time, and dollars. The definition of an "adequate commitment" varies with the circumstances, but in any given collaboration it may mean being prepared to accept some added costs of collaboration. Although there are benefits that can only be achieved through partnering with other providers, it is not always or even usually the case that it is cheaper to have two parties acting together. Additionally, we may be called on to accommodate different styles and ideas to a degree, while still maintaining our basic values and mission. There may be times when we struggle to find the right balance here.

3. *Team building.* In terms of staffing structures, the key to successful collaboration lies in assembling solid teams. Teams should be composed of staff with a range of expertise and with a designated coordinator who carries the responsibility of arranging regular meetings, identifying problems, and reporting back to the CEO. The coordinator is in essence the organization's point person for that project. In collaborative ventures that involve several partners, there should be a team composed of the coordinators from those partners that meets on at least a quarterly basis. The role of this interagency team is to evaluate the process and progress of the venture, to maintain the boundaries and the focus of the work, and to recommend modifications when necessary.

4. *Leadership.* Lastly, successful collaboration requires appropriate leadership. The sort of leadership appropriate to a partnership may differ somewhat, though only somewhat, from what is appropriate in a stand-alone situation. Leadership through consensus building rather than control is sound strategy for any organization, but with interagency collaboration the task of consensus building rises even further in significance. This does not imply a tentative attitude, for an overly passive approach to leadership can be as counterproductive as an overly

aggressive one. What leaders must strive for is the proper balance between active oversight and consensus building.

Some Shared Goals

There are four goals that probably match with the strategic interests of many providers:

1. *Continuum of care.* There is a widespread consensus in our field that providers in every geographic region should strive to develop a complete continuum of care that blends the services provided by health, mental health, child welfare, juvenile justice, substance abuse, and other service organizations. Such a goal is clearly only attainable through a multiplicity of collaborations. The benefits of such a continuum for our consumers should be clear, for a gap-free continuum ensures that no one falls through the cracks. A well-coordinated continuum of care also reduces duplication of services, which is beneficial both to providers and to our funding partners. Also, depending on the way a continuum is constructed, it may create opportunities for "one-stop shopping" that are highly valued in a managed care environment.

2. *User-friendly referral networks.* In addition to establishing a comprehensive continuum of care, we must strive to develop rich and user-friendly referral networks. The shift in public philosophy from dependency to self-sufficiency makes these services especially important. As we in the provider community have begun to reassert the strengths perspective as a productive adaptation to the shift in public thinking, we need to ensure that we put in place the sort of resources which that perspective assumes will be available. It is therefore important to establish links between agencies and community groups to ensure that all consumers can quickly learn where to go to get help in meeting a particular need.

3. *Self-help.* Traditions of self-help have been recognized and documented in all ethnic groups in this country, emerging as these groups arrive in urban centers and further developing as the groups establish themselves in separate communities and sections of larger cities. Of course, brother- and sisterhoods, community associations, and churches and synagogues still

abound in African-American, Latino, Asian, Jewish, and every other cultural-ethnic group we know. The resources such organizations constitute can be catalogued and filed so that information regarding them is more broadly available through computer technology.

4. *Advocacy*. Finally, we can find numerous shared goals that fall under the general heading of advocacy concerns. While the social work field is not as ideologically homogeneous as some would contend, we share many values, interests, and beliefs about how resources can be used to meet needs effectively. Indeed, advocacy concerns is the area where we find the longest history of interagency collaboration, as well as some of our greatest successes to date. When we have joined to form coalitions that have spoken both persuasively and for many constituencies, we have had an impact on policy. There are issues today that relate to public funding of services, to certification standards, to the regulation of the managed care industry, and to many other areas of public policy as well. As the future will bring new issues and new advocacy concerns, it is critical that we cultivate the interagency systems and structures that facilitate speedy and effective responses to issues as they arise.

11

Bottom-Up Planning in a Top-Down World

Eric B. Brettschneider, MA, JD

Introduction

Policy makers have listened (or claimed to have listened) to the voices of the people long before Osborne and Gaebler (1992) wrote *Reinventing Government*. Hearings, focus groups, community forums, referenda, community boards, and school boards have long been popular devices for bottom-up planning. According to Marie Weil (1996), the social work tradition is an important part of this history: "Community practice strategies have been a critical but often under used method . . . from the inception of the profession in the settlement house and charity organization society movements[,] but these methods have received very little attention . . . in the past two decades" (p. 482).

However, community-building and empowerment efforts are more ambitious in this new era. These initiatives seek community-driven planning, more genuine collaboration between government and nongovernment stakeholders, more nonorganizational grassroots participation in governance, and a sense of welcome (full citizenship) for all levels of participants. They also encourage new connections between human services and economic development and open opportunities for faith-based coalitions. They build housing and attempt crime prevention or the reduction of infant mortality. They are based on Richman, Brown, and Venkatesh's (1996) belief that "in a community that is strengthened and feels . . . 'ownership' for the proposed changes, numerous types of reform can work" (p. 151). All these initiatives require sustaining complex collaborations in a world where power and authority remain unchanged, for better or worse.

Bottom-up planning is generally an evolutionary effort, not an alternative or adversarial challenge to elected officials, corporations, unions, or others. Community-building efforts offer a way to easily organize focus groups, obtain a local critique of demographic data, model citizen participation, and easily "dock" service integration efforts in a neighborhood. They are meant to blend in the social fabric, but not threaten it. Then why is collaboration so difficult to achieve? Why is it so hard to integrate services?

At the 1999 New York City School Board elections, it seemed that more people worked at the polls than voted. We then ask, "Who speaks for neighborhoods?" and sometimes find local demagogues or phantom elections as answers. These "artificial" bottom-up approaches breed mistrust and skepticism. However, there are examples of more natural bottom-up planning. Let me offer one example. For 10 years, the Agenda for Children Tomorrow (ACT) project has taken its cue from its 1988 study of past failed efforts to implement neighborhood-based, integrated human services and economic development. Those lessons cited the missing ingredients from such attempts: (1) up-front mayoral support; (2) involvement of key stakeholders from the onset; and (3) detailed research-based planning (Agenda for Children Tomorrow, 1990).

With an advisory committee of city commissioners, nonprofit leaders, and others, ACT set out to serve as "electricians" (making connections within neighborhoods and connecting those communities to sources of power) to 10 targeted communities. Five collaboratives were established. With neighborhood profiles (and focus groups) completed, communities (representatives from existing coalitions, churches, nonprofits, and others) gathered around those profiles as though they were fireplaces. Each was given one local planner to establish and track 10 policy- or program-development objectives. Work was accomplished by picking "low-hanging fruit" (policy- or program-development opportunities) at the margins of the power structure. The collaboratives operated by consensus and with inclusiveness as their governance principles. They did not challenge power;

rather, they collaborated with those who held power. Nevertheless, the barriers of turf protection, categorical funding imperatives, and competitiveness were formidable.

Despite challenging obstacles, two collaboratives—one in Bushwick and the other in Washington Heights—were successful in improving the transition from day care to kindergarten and first grade. Diplomacy was the key ingredient to success. Innovation was basic and often consisted of replicating existing program innovations. Hallmarks of the breakthrough were joint training for teachers from public schools and day care programs to promote compatible curricula, and improving procedures to place children appropriately as they enter first grade. The shorter registration lines for enrollment in September and more appropriate placements were two of the results that won attention from the Stella and Charles Guttman Foundation, the Danforth Foundation, and the New York City Board of Education. Change at the top was meeting change from the bottom halfway.

In recent years, ACT has been working closely with New York City's Administration for Children's Services (ACS). Under the leadership of Commissioner Nicholas Scoppetta, ACS has initiated a major push toward neighborhood-aligned child welfare services. ACS's effort, begun 8 years after the establishment of ACT's modest networks, built on existing neighborhood coalitions, as ACT had, but has since telescoped and transcended ACT's collaboratives. This reform effort leads a national movement that Doug Nelson, president of the Casey Foundation, justified by asserting that "the paramount obligation of the child welfare reformer is not to assume more responsibility for vulnerable kids and fragile families, but rather to plan fully and accountably *share* that responsibility with enough critical partners to fulfill the responsibility" (1998, p. 5).

HUMILITY

Planning itself should be approached with humility. As we begin a new millennium, it is appropriate to look back at forecasts made at the beginning of the 20th century. People believed, according to the December 30, 1900, *Brooklyn Eagle,* that "Liquid air would banish poverty from the earth, advertising would be, in the future, the breath of life in commerce; cheap and speedy transportation would decentralize populations and eliminate the horse and buggy; mail would be delivered to homes in pneumatic tubes; science would find the means to bring the dead back to life." Whereas some of these predictions are not so far from 20th-century reality, others are perfect examples of extrapolating beyond the facts. But prediction, although a necessary component of change, is a tricky enterprise. Its beauty and function lie in the balance one must maintain between a progressive, visionary role and pragmatic consideration of the facts. What are the facts?

ON FRAGMENTATION

While social reformers call for a more holistic personal style of social services, the vestiges of categorical government funding, the continuing forces of racism, and the widening gap between the poor and those who benefit from a vibrant economy create challenges to such a vision. We know that communities and agencies are divided not only by demographics, politics, funding requirements, and perceptions of conflicting roles, but also by gaps in information and new impersonal technologies of information exchange. At the same time, we know that people do not seem to talk to each other as much as they used to. Increasingly, we are overwhelmed by a mosaic of details that can seem useless because they are so unorganized. Managing the stresses of daily life may seem daunting, so planning ways to keep communities together will certainly feel overwhelming. Yet Marie Weil (1996) warns that "strong emphasis on interventions at grassroots and interorganizational levels is necessary if the [social work] profession is to remain relevant to the needs of low-income and other vulnerable populations in the changing political, social and economic context" (p. 482).

THE NEED FOR BOTTOM-UP PLANNING

Lisbeth Schorr (1988) did not have New York City in mind exclusively when she said that being flexible, comprehensive, and neighborhood-based were characteristics of programs that work. But certainly she knew that untangling New York City's complex web of services to align services to geography and to connect them would require bottom-up strategies.

President Clinton's 1995 Urban Policy Report (Cisneros, 1995) described the polarization of both economic sectors and racial groups that has occurred in urban areas. Increasingly, inner cities suffer the outmigration of business and entrapment of the working poor. This has resulted in the isolation of the urban poor from opportunities for economic growth. In a larger sphere, this polarization not only frays civic culture but also creates a drag on the nation's economy. On a local level, polarization's effect on our system of caring for kids and families has been to make the system fragile, fragmented, and difficult to negotiate. It lacks comprehensiveness and is consequently less effective.

A partial antidote is bottom-up planning. Arthur Himmelman (1994) describes two basic activities involved in the empowerment of communities: (1) "organizing a community in support of a collaborative purpose determined by that community," which (2) "results in a community's long-term ownership of its purpose, processes, and products. It also enhances a community's capacity for self-determination" (p. 29). Freeman (1996) warns that "without strong safeguards," block grant funding may move power from powerful federal officials to power-hoarding local officials and not to powerless families in each community. He recommends "mandating opportunities for communities to help make funding decisions" (p. 523). The link must be forged between a larger economic strategy and urban revitalization: to focus on a consumer-driven approach is to empower inner cities to adopt bootstrap solutions to endemic problems of poverty, violence, drug abuse, and homelessness. Empowerment is crucial to self-determination.

ON REINVENTING GOVERNMENT

Reinventing government is often confused with privatization, which represents only a single aspect of this concept. Osborne and Gaebler's (1992) *Reinventing Government: How the Entrepreneurial Spirit Is Transforming the Public Sector* has eleven chapters, and listing their titles here can help to explain why such a narrow definition fails.

1. Catalytic Government: Steering Rather Than Rowing
2. Community-Owned Government: Empowering Rather Than Serving
3. Competitive Government: Injecting Competition Into Service Delivery
4. Mission-Driven Government: Transforming Rule-Driven Organizations
5. Results-Oriented Government: Funding Outcomes, Not Inputs
6. Customer-Driven Government: Meeting the Needs of the Customer, Not the Bureaucracy
7. Enterprising Government: Earning Rather Than Spending
8. Anticipatory Government: Prevention Rather Than Cure
9. Decentralized Government: From Hierarchy to Participation and Teamwork
10. Market-Oriented Government: Leveraging Change Through the Market
11. Putting It All Together

Only by "putting it all together" is it real. Bottom-up planning must connect to changes at the top. We call this "synergy." Unfortunately, there are times where agendas are so different that they do not meet in a genuine way.

Weil (1996) writes that the challenge for social workers is to be "proactive, advocate for vulnerable populations," to "connect empowerment . . . with social and economic development," to "reshape the human services system," to "strengthen connections among public, nonprofit and for profit sectors," and to "plan . . . local service coordination and integration; through liaison with communities, . . . political and social action and building coalitions" (p. 481). Himmelman (1994) notes that the roles which government as well as private and public organizations must play are those of conveyer, catalyst, conduit, funder, advocate, community organizer, technical assistant, capacity builder, partner, and facilitator.

The desire to push for change from the bottom when the top

is resisting has led to a variety of strategies. Litigation has brought about dramatic changes. *Brown vs. Board of Education* fostered the racial integration of America's public schools. The Willowbrook Consent Decree (1975) led to the deinstitutionalization of New York's warehouses for the developmentally disabled. On the other hand, some well-placed, well-intended class actions have met the dead end of complex bureaucracies resisting change.

Saul Alinski (1971) and others have offered adversarial strategies to force policy makers to respond to the demands of communities. Yet such efforts also may resist the changes that some remedies require. Implementation of neighborhood-responsive, user-friendly personal social services requires sustained efforts at retraining and supervision for the culture of even a single social service agency to become less proactive and more empowering. The ongoing cooperation of all the stakeholders in that organization is required.

For example, some needs require differential treatment in different communities. More prenatal care, for example, may reduce infant mortality, but the community that has high infant mortality, despite available prenatal care, may require an outreach strategy.

The tensions between the real world of laws, politics, funding, and egos cannot be easily reconciled with the community planning world of visioning and one-stop shopping and a "no wrong door" access philosophy. ACT has discovered that none of these concepts and devices are magical. However, we did develop a list of Do's and Don'ts to guide the art of collaboration and bottom-up planning for service integration (see Table 11.1).

Collaboration has been called an "unnatural act between two or more nonconsenting parties." Ongoing collaboration among government, religious groups, nonprofits, businesses, unions, and communities, and among professional sectors within communities, however difficult, is a prerequisite to achieving the vision we have of services that are feasible, comprehensive, accessible, and responsive to communities.

When visiting one human services multiservice center, I spoke to social workers from two programs: one was a short-term intensive, and the other was a less intensive long-term family pres-

TABLE 11.1. Do's/Don'ts in community building (or "bottom-up planning in a top-down world")

DO'S	DON'TS
✓ Plan strategically.	✖ Insist that everything you do must come from your strategic plan.
✓ Build real neighborhoods.	✖ Build Potemkin villages.
✓ Take risks.	✖ Let a politician assume control.
✓ Empower.	✖ Justify your existence.
✓ Dump the corrupt when it's clear who they are.	✖ Compete when you could collaborate.
✓ Avoid notoriety.	✖ Rely solely on negative data.
✓ Avoid presenting coalitions with faits accomplis.	✖ Give up on any relationship building without trying three times.
✓ Let the community speak for itself when it/they are ready.	✖ Do *Night Line* to report your successes.
✓ Inventory your neighborhood assets.	✖ Boast about how much you've done.
✓ Evaluate.	✖ Leave out community boards, elected officials, and other governmental entities.
✓ Be inclusive—not only in who is invited to meetings but also in making available the language, arguments, facts, and feasible choices.	✖ Favor local boosters over caring, helpful critics.
✓ Fight for the underlying tangible program substance.	✖ Brand any organization "genuine community" based on longevity, location, or size.
✓ Be concerned about the relationship between a nonprofit and a community and how responsive and involved the organization is.	✖ Get hung up on brand names or pride of ownership.
✓ Use a consensus approach.	✖ Rely on artificial definitions of CBO.
✓ Avoid disguising top-down initiatives as bottom-up.	✖ Ignore non-geographic communities.
	✖ Let coalitions break up over "lead agency" designations or fights over funding.
	✖ Say "Wait a minute before you take that initiative."
	✖ Buy into anyone's enemies list.
	✖ Chase money for purposes that won't support your priorities.

ervation program. I asked the director of each program what complementary services each needed most. Both described the other's program. Did they refer cases to each other? "No," they both answered. Why not? The answer was deafening: "No one said we could."

Time, patience, and diplomacy can, from ACT's experience, help a coalition move through these levels of collaboration: (1) would not work together even for money; (2) would work together for money; and (3) would work together even if funding were not at stake.

This lack of permission was addressed by Richard N. Haass (1994) in *The Power to Persuade: How to Be Effective in Government, the Public Sector, or Any Unruly Organization.* He said the solution to this inertia was to exercise 20% more authority than given and to persuade those you work for, those who work with you, and those for whom you work to work together. In international affairs, it is called diplomacy.

Lessons from ACT's 10 Years in Five Communities

ACT's collaboratives have had the greatest difficulty in engaging the grass roots as equal partners. Breakthroughs, however, have occurred by engaging intermediaries such as the youth leadership group Youth Force to bring in young people and the Parks Council to recruit environmental activists. We learned that progress is built on local, not global truths. Universal or larger truths may in actuality mask information gained at the local level which, if left untapped, may impede the success of bottom-up planning. Unless the policy makers in our city halls and state office buildings and on Capitol Hill have direct access to community residents' experiences, their views can be blurred or distorted. Consider the analogy of looking at Mars through the Hubble telescope. Mars looks lifeless from our vantage point even with the best of our technology. But an actual trip to the surface has led to the discovery of possible life!

Beyond such guidelines, overarching principles apply:

- Intellectual honesty and openness are the keys to trust on the local level and with policy makers as well. On two occasions

ACT supported community withdrawal from heavily funded government projects, despite the public relations value of participation, because not to have supported withdrawal would have been a betrayal.

- Maintain modest expectations, an ambitious vision, and attainable goals (low-hanging fruit).
- Insist upon informed consent and full disclosure of the givens in each new collaborative venture. When a government agency or foundation funds a new collaborative, it requires certain targets, deliverables, or strategies. To portray such funding as an opportunity for unrestrained community planning suggests a flexibility that is usually not there. Such funding is best accepted only when it is compatible with or adaptable to the community's plan.
- Trade credit taking for results. Credit will come to the extent it is needed, but fighting for it is counterproductive.
- Do not abandon old partners for new ones. In politics it is called "maintaining your base," but when I was a child, someone who left an old friend for a new one was called a *flatleaver*. Also, existing groups like Healthy Start, Community Schools, Beacon Schools, and Empowerment Zones are natural allies, not competitors.
- Do not hesitate to take advantage of an opportunity; for example, helping write a policy maker's speech can help make a policy.
- When possible, view deficits as useful assets. A high percentage of abandoned factories can be an asset when attracting a manufacturer. Gutierrez, Alvarez, Nemon, and Lewis (1996) suggest that "building from strengths includes identifying areas of positive functioning, particularly those that have been unnoticed or unrewarded, and using them as the basis for the organizing effort" (p. 503).
- Give up saying "to hell with you." Too many long-term collaborations end in frustrations that can be overcome. ACT has described three levels of collaboration: (1) would not work together even for money; (2) would work together for money; and (3) would work together even without money. Of course, those levels sometimes coexist.
- Track tangible results. Otherwise all your process and efforts at democratizing may lose everyone's interest.
- Reach consensus whenever you can, but particularly when you hire someone who will serve to convene and coalesce the players.

The light from local coalitions can shine brightly. It can be seen by those at the top. They can use it to build a system that not only draws local efforts, but is built on them. Sometimes it helps to have an electrician who can make connections within the neighborhood and turn on the sources of power. This particular kind of electrician requires the skills of a good group worker, strategic planner, and diplomat . . . with the determination of Martin Luther King, Jr., the flexibility of Houdini, the integrity of Gandhi, and the sustained interest of John Glenn.

REFERENCES

Agenda for Children Tomorrow. (1990). *Three public policy issues in perspective: A report to the mayor.* New York: Author.

Alinski, S. (1971). *Rules for radicals.* New York: Vintage Books.

Cisneros, H. (1995). *Empowerment: A new covenant with America's cities.* Washington, DC: Clinton Administration.

Freeman, E. M. (1996). Welfare reforms and services for children and families: Setting a new practice, research and policy agenda. *Social Work, 41*(5), 521–532.

Gutierrez, L., Alvarez, A. R., Nemon, H., & Lewis, E. A. (1996). Multicultural community organizing: A strategy for change. *Social Work, 41*(5), 501–508.

Haass, R. N. (1994). *The power to persuade: How to be effective in government, the public sector, or any unruly organization.* Boston & New York: Houghton Mifflin.

Himmelman, A. (1994). Communities working collaboratively for a change. In M. Hermans (Ed.), *Resolving conflicts: Strategies for local government* (pp. 27–47). Washington, DC: International City/County Management Association.

Nelson, D. (1998). *Building neighborhood partnerships.* Speech at National Child Welfare Leadership Conference, October 5.

Osborne, D., & Gaebler, T. (1992). *Reinventing government: How the entrepreneurial spirit is transforming the public sector; From schoolhouse to statehouse, city hall to the Pentagon.* Reading, MA: Addison Wesley.

Richman, H. A., Brown, P., & Venkatesh, S. (1996). The community base for new service delivery strategies. In A. J. Kahn & S.

B. Kamerman (Eds.), *Children and their families in big cities* (pp. 151–162). New York: Columbia University School of Social Work.

Schorr, L. B. (1988). *Within our reach*. New York: Doubleday, Anchor.

Weil, M. O. (1996). Community building: Building community practice. *Social Work, 41*(5), 481–497.

Willowbrook Consent Decree. (1975). U.S. Federal Court, Southern District, Brooklyn.

12

The Professional Mandate for the Use of "Strategic Collaborations" by Lawyers and Social Workers in Child Maltreatment/Intimate Partner Violence Cases

Mary Ann Forgey, PhD, Ann Moynihan, JD, Virginia Strand, DSW, and Leah Hill, JD

INTRODUCTION

THIS CHAPTER LOOKS at the need to bring lawyers and social workers together to collaborate in cases involving both child maltreatment and intimate partner violence. Social workers and lawyers seeking to provide adequate services to families and children in such cases must overcome a two-part challenge. They must struggle with practice differences between their disciplines and with the cross fire created by the historic antipathy between the child protective and intimate partner violence service delivery systems. They must address these differences while working with the inherently complex issues presented by cases involving both child maltreatment and intimate partner violence and while working within systems that are under great pressure because of shrinking funding for both social and legal services and increasing child protective caseloads.

Lawyers and social workers cannot just depend on existing structures to provide the means by which to collaborate. Systemic collaborative structures are few and far between and—where they exist—may not be flexible enough to meet the needs of a particular case. Lawyers and social workers need to look to the norms of their own professionalism to overcome the professional and systemic differences that may be standing in the way of proper representation and assistance for their clients. Those norms suggest that the needs and rights of the partners and children in a particular family will be met only when professionals initiate collaborative approaches that are tailored to uncover and resolve the professional and systemic differences that are standing in the way of specific client goals. In this chapter, we will call such collaborative approaches "strategic collaborations."

DIFFERENCES IN THE PROFESSIONAL APPROACHES

Collaboration between lawyers and social workers is needed to overcome differing professional perspectives, training, and attitudes. A lawyer's focus on individual rights may contrast with a social worker's focus on the relationships among client, family, community, and society. A social worker's focus on psychosocial needs may contrast with the lawyer's focus on legal needs. A social worker may see collaboration as a way to share information and plan services, while a lawyer may see such collaboration as dangerous to a client caught up in adversarial legal proceedings. A lawyer's emphasis on client autonomy may contrast with a social worker's emphasis on the client's growth or stability. Parsloe (1981) notes: "If the needs of clients are to be met and their rights are to be recognized, the development of greater cooperation and shared work between lawyers and social workers is required." He continues: "Society needs a new breed of rational, sensitive individuals who can recognize and value feelings but still assess issues clearly and understand human needs without abandoning a concern for rights" (p. 183). More specific calls have been made for interdisciplinary cooperation in child protective cases based on the general need for greater efficiency and effectiveness in the child protective system (see, e.g., Johnson & Cahn, 1992; Weinstein, 1997) and on the special demands that arise in cases involving child clients (see Koh Peters, 1991). The need for collaborative, interdisciplinary approaches to meet the psychosocial and legal needs of clients experiencing intimate partner violence has also been recognized (Berry, 1994; Hamlin, 1991).

DIFFERENCES IN SYSTEMS APPROACHES

An even greater need for collaboration arises because of the different and sometimes clashing perspectives of those working within the child protective and intimate partner violence systems—systems that have developed along unconnected and markedly different tracks. Child protective services have become primarily a public child welfare function. Largely because of their mandate to protect children from maltreatment, staff in child protective services have tended to be overidentified with the child, contributing at times to a child-rescue orientation.

However, there have been oscillations along a continuum from child rescue to family preservation, with the latter reflecting a focus on preventing out-of-home placement for a child and on speedy reunification if that occurred. During those periods when there has been more of an emphasis on child rescue, conflicts between child protective workers and intimate partner violence staff have been the most virulent. This is because the child protective system often holds the non-offending parent (typically the mother) responsible for not preventing a child's maltreatment when it takes place within the family home. Women who are victims of intimate partner violence are therefore often found culpable for not protecting their children from maltreatment by their partner or not protecting them from witnessing their own abuse by their partner.

This practice has been anathema to those championing the rights of battered women, who believe that a woman who is a victim of intimate partner violence is not in a position to challenge her partner's violence or the maltreatment of her children. The service system for intimate partner violence arose during the same time frame as the child protective system, as the first shelters for battered women were opened only in 1974. The entities devoted to responding to the needs of battered women—primarily shelters, crisis hot lines, and legal advocacy efforts—had their genesis in grassroots organizations. They tended to be suspicious—or outrightly critical—of bureaucracies, especially of law enforcement and the judicial system. Services were often staffed by volunteers and paraprofessionals. They subscribed to a view of the world in which the woman (and mother) was viewed as the victim—not only of her partner's violence but also of the patriarchally organized social system. According to this worldview, women need to be empowered through the provision of services that support their independence from their abusers and through the imposition of more effective legal sanctions for batterers. Services such as batterer treatment programs or couples counseling were seen as ineffective and dangerous. Critical of what they saw as a mother-blaming orientation on the part of child protective services that stemmed from a lack of understanding of the real needs of battered women, staff in shelters were reluctant to report cases of suspected child maltreatment and hesitant to work closely with child protective services staff.

INCREASING INTERSECTION BETWEEN THE SYSTEMS

There is a growing emphasis within the child protective system on identifying intimate partner violence as a risk factor for children. Such efforts are taking place in response to the mounting evidence of the co-occurrence of child abuse and intimate partner violence (see, e.g., Straus & Smith, 1990; McCloskey, Figueredo, & Koss, 1995). Thus, for example, in a study, child protection workers in the Massachusetts Department of Social Services reported that an average of 32.48% of their cases involved child abuse and domestic violence (Edleson, 1995). Recently, child maltreatment cases have also expanded to include situations where intimate partner violence itself provides the basis for state action. This expansion is a result of increased concern based on numerous studies of the debilitating emotional and behavioral effects that witnessing parental violence has on children (Jaffe, Wolfe, & Wilson, 1990; Kolbo, Blakely, & Engleman, 1996). Such cases may take two basic forms within the child protective services system. In the first, one or both parents are seen as maltreating their children because they are permitting their children to witness intimate partner violence, thereby exposing the children to the psychological harm that is found to flow from such witnessing. In the second, the partner against whom violence is being directed—almost always the mother—is seen as "failing to protect" the children when she remains with a partner who is maltreating the children or is seen as likely to maltreat them.

This expanded response is taking place within a system that continues to be overburdened as the number of reports of child maltreatment in all categories and the number of children and families in need of care and services grows. As just one example, in the 10-year period between 1986 and 1995, New York State saw a 35% increase in child maltreatment reports (Petit & Curtis, 1997). Despite periodic reform efforts, the number of children in substitute care has remained unacceptably high, providing continuing evidence of the unmet challenge of achieving stability and permanency for children and of the systemic inability to meet the service needs of families and children.

It may be assumed that as the child protective system increasingly takes on cases involving intimate partner violence, professionals working with the children and families involved in such cases may face both the well- and long-recognized problems plaguing child protective systems generally and the particular complexities that attend cases combining child maltreatment charges and intimate partner violence. These cases often involve social workers from the intimate partner violence service delivery system and the child protection system. They begin to involve lawyers, as well, as court proceedings are initiated in criminal courts, child protective courts, and other civil forums providing civil remedies for battered partners. Thus, a woman may have multiple sets of professionals working with her. If child protective proceedings have been initiated against her, she will have a lawyer or a lawyer/social worker team representing her. She may also be required to cooperate with child protective workers and the service providers to whom they refer her. If her children are in care, she may have to work with agencies providing foster care. If she has sought help in dealing with her partner's violence against her, she may be involved with advocates and counselors from the intimate partner violence systems and may have a lawyer working with her in connection with civil protective proceedings and related custody or divorce proceedings. If criminal action has been initiated against her partner, she may have advocates and social workers working with her within the criminal court system. Similarly, her partner may have lawyers in connection with each proceeding and may or may not be involved in separate service delivery systems activated by each proceeding. Finally, the children will have advocates and social workers involved in at least the child protective proceeding and perhaps in any custody proceedings triggered by the initiation of other civil proceedings.

THE INADEQUACY OF EXISTING COLLABORATIVE STRUCTURES

The challenge for a professional working with a client involved in the intersections of the child protective system, the intimate partner violence system, and the court systems connected to them is bridging differences in professional approaches and perspectives and still carrying out one's professional role and responsibilities effectively. The need for collaboration implicit in this challenge is not being met within existing systems. Although formal collaborative structures are beginning to be seen, they are the exception rather than the rule. Furthermore, even where they are available, these structures may well not have the flexibility and purposefulness essential to designing collaborations that meet the particular needs of particular clients living within particular families under particular circumstances.

Within child protection systems, legislatures, courts, and governmental administrative agencies are beginning to attempt to create structures to facilitate collaboration between professionals. Formalized conferencing structures within child welfare have varied widely. Federal and local law have long required conferences about the continued placement of children in foster care, permitting parents, older children, and the professionals involved with them to attend and requiring the participation of independent outside observers (Adoption Assistance Act, 42 U.S.C. Section 671[16]; see, e.g., 18 NYCRR Section 430.12[c]). More and more jurisdictions are establishing Child Advocacy

Centers that work to coordinate the efforts of professionals working in the child protection system with those of the medical, prosecutorial, and police systems. The Centers coordinate work to avoid duplicative evidence collection and child interviews and to permit the development of coordinated treatment and service plans. Conferencing systems are also being designed to involve the family and community members in child protection efforts. Family Group Conferences, developed in New Zealand in the mid-1980s, were legislatively mandated there for national use in 1989 and are increasingly seen the United States (Merkel-Holguin, 1998). The model, which has been found to be effective (Pennell & Burford, 1998), is based on the idea that family and extended family members have the dispositive voice in decisions about the care and protection of children. Professionals provide information to the family at such conferences but do not offer opinions about a plan (Pennell & Burford, 1998). This, according to Lupton and Stevens, shifts the "balance of power" between families and professionals, turning the "traditional decision-making process on its head" (1998, p. 21). Professionals do provide opinions, thus playing a greater role, in Family Unity Meetings, a closely related model developed in Oregon in 1990 (Merkel-Holguin, 1998). Other states use the Family Resource Model, which also allows family members to participate in decision making but does not give families the central decision-making role (Merkel-Holguin, 1998). Finally, courts are increasingly turning to conferencing systems as alternatives to adversarial child welfare proceedings. Even in systems as large as that in New York City, Family Treatment Parts are being established in the courthouse to ensure that treatment plans and progress toward reunification of families are formulated and monitored in a collaborative and coordinated way that ensures the participation of the family, community-based treatment providers, lawyers, and the courts.

Formalized collaborative structures are less prevalent in the intimate partner violence system than in the child welfare system. This may be a result of not having a reporting requirement for partner violence like that covering violence against children. A reporting requirement that identifies children who are the subjects of indicated maltreatment reports may provide an im-

petus to create decision-making and information-sharing structures for the professionals working with such children. The
beginnings of the field of intimate partner violence, discussed
earlier, may also explain the slower development of collaborative efforts within the field of intimate partner violence. A
mostly volunteer or paraprofessional staff, suspicious of other
legal and social service organizations, was not an orientation
particularly amenable to initiating and building interdisciplinary collaboration.

As advocates of battered women have begun to recognize that
multiple interventions are needed to respond effectively to the
needs presented by the victims, collaborative relationships have
been initiated with other organizations involved in intimate
partner violence. One example of such collaborations is the Coordinated Community Action Model (CCAM), which includes
shelters, programs for batterers, the courts, and social services
as well as health care systems, educational systems, employers,
and the media (Jackson & Garvin, 1995; Pence & Paymor, 1993).
Within this model the goal has been to foster system-level coordination through the provision of training to the different
groups on the needs of battered women and the dynamics of
abuse. Specialized domestic violence courts have also begun to
develop within a limited amount of jurisdictions. In New York
City, one such court located in Brooklyn Supreme Court has victim advocates who work to ensure that the victim's legal and
social service needs are addressed, as well as domestic violence
coordinators who recommend and monitor the legal and social
service intervention plan for the perpetrator. Certain agencies
have also moved toward the provision of a range of interventive
services to victims of intimate partner violence. Such interdisciplinary agency structures have fostered collaboration among the
different disciplines responding to the diverse needs of victims
involved in intimate partner violence. Some of these agency
structures also include interdisciplinary services to both victims
and perpetrators (Wylie, 1996).

Cross-system collaboration structures between the child protective system and the intimate partner violence system are also
beginning to be developed. A survey by the National Council of
Juvenile and Family Court Judges describes programs designed

to provide mothers with shelter and supportive access to court and services. The emphasis in such programs is often on protecting and supporting mothers and children. Little attention, however, is being paid in cross-system collaborative work to the needs of fathers (Edleson, 1998). The survey also describes programs that provide system and awareness training to caseworkers and lawyers. Cross-system collaborative structures do not yet appear to be on the interdisciplinary case conferencing level where professionals involved in the child protective system, the domestic violence system, and the court system can came come together to discuss individual cases.

As *formal* collaborative structures increase within the child welfare and intimate partner service delivery systems, professionals may look to them to provide a forum in which the outcome of cases can be influenced in a way that is consistent with the needs and objectives of clients. However, such systems have limitations and may not meet all the needs of the professional working with families and children. Furthermore, existing case conferencing within or across systems may not address the particular complexity inherent in cases involving both child maltreatment and intimate partner violence. Conferencing systems that are mandated in every case may result in conferences that become exercises in form over substance. This has certainly happened with foster care reviews, which are periodically required in every case of children in foster care. The conference requirement may be ignored, potential participants are not notified of them, or when the conference is held, little may actually be achieved. Furthermore, because mandatory conferencing systems involve government actors, they must be run pursuant to general and uniform policies designed to ensure procedural fairness to parents, children, and government. Hence they may provide little choice and flexibility as to a participant list, thus deterring attendance by some potential participants who may be essential to meaningful resolution or requiring attendance by professionals who are not really needed at the conference or are ill-prepared to attend. There is also a danger that when such conferences become routinized and are the responsibility of bureaucracies to organize, a sense of urgency (imparted by parties with important interests at stake) and focus (provided by participants with specific needs) may be lost. In addition, systems run by child welfare agencies outside the courts may risk duplicating much of an expensive and time-intensive systems already in place in the courts, thus wasting and depleting limited professional resources. This may happen, for example, when key conference participants—the parents, the child welfare agency, the child, and some of the professionals involved with each—may already be appearing in court in connection with both emergency removal, fact-finding, and dispositional issues.

Lastly, family group conferencing systems, while involving family members and giving them dispositive voices in solutions, may not be best designed to deal with intimate partner violence/child maltreatment cases in which two parents are present, to whatever degree, in the lives of children and may not yet have resolved fundamental questions about the future of their relationship to one another or to the children. Such conferencing also presents problems for the rights of participants when they are conducted during any period during which criminal or child protection charges may be or have been filed against one or both parents and remain unresolved in the courts.

We envision strategic collaboration as a tool that operates outside such established collaborative structures. It bespeaks a willing participation, driven by particular objectives, with control over who is invited in the hands of the party choosing to have the collaboration. Koh Peters (1997), who has represented children in child welfare systems, has called on lawyers to consider calling and running such meetings when doing so will advance the interests of child clients. Her basic advice makes it clear that such meetings are not routinely in current use:

> On occasion, when no meeting is in the offing, the lawyer may decide to call her own meeting. Whether styled a "case conference" or something else, this meeting should usually be focused on a particular goal or agenda item. Because lawyer-called meetings are unusual and will not be something that other professionals can easily attend, the lawyer must convince others that the meeting is pressing and will be structured in a useful manner. Since the lawyer would rarely call such a meeting unless a clear and intractable problem exists, however, convincing others that the meeting will be useful should not be insurmountable. (p. 187)

Similarly, Weil (1985) stresses the social worker's responsibility to independently collaborate with other professionals as the need arises. She also raises the concern that the development of formal collaborative structures may be the result of professionals' neglecting their independent collaborative responsibility.

SOCIAL WORK PROFESSIONALISM AND INITIATING STRATEGIC COLLABORATIONS

Many professional social workers employed by voluntary agencies or in private practice find themselves involved in cases presenting issues of both child maltreatment and intimate partner violence. Their responsibilities usually include the treatment of one or several family members. These cases also involve many other professionals, including the child protective worker, the social workers treating other members of the family, and the lawyers who represent each member of the family. How does the social work professional code define the social worker's responsibility to connect with these other professionals and/or to act as a catalyst in bringing all or some of them together?

The Code of Ethics of the National Association of Social Workers (1996) gives some guidance with regard to social workers' rights and obligations in this area. Under the ethical standard of social workers' ethical responsibility to colleagues (2.01c), it states: "Social workers should cooperate with social work colleagues and with colleagues of other professions when such cooperation serves the well being of the client." The ethical standards also clearly support the professional social worker's participation in an interdisciplinary team (2.03a): "Social workers who are members of an interdisciplinary team should participate in and contribute to decisions that affect the well-being of clients by drawing on the perspectives, values, and experiences of the social work profession."

Social workers' right and responsibility to cooperate with colleagues when the client's well-being or best interests will be served is clear from the above standards. What is not clearly specified under this ethical standard are the *circumstances* under which collaboration among colleagues will enhance client well-being or interest and the *extent* to which professional social workers should take a proactive role in developing this collaboration with colleagues. The ethical principle that "social workers should challenge injustice" provides further guidance as to the circumstances under which a more proactive stance in facilitating collaboration may be warranted. Within this ethical principle it states: "Social workers *strive* to ensure access to needed information, services and resources; equality of opportunity; and meaningful participation in decision making for all people."

In cases of co-occurring child maltreatment and intimate partner violence where multiple social service and legal systems are involved, many circumstances exist in which social work collaboration with key professionals could serve the client's well-being, as well as challenge injustice. The client in these circumstances is often without adequate legal and social services or tangled in a web of fragmented services. The client is often in need of information, services, and resources that are controlled by various systems. The client is often excluded from the decision-making processes within the systems that are making crucial decisions that effect his or her well-being. The social worker is in a position to assist the client with access to needed services and to increase understanding of the client's story by other professionals who play important decision-making roles in the client's life. Given these circumstances, it can be argued that the social worker has an ethical obligation not only to participate in collaborative efforts but, more importantly, to serve as a catalyst for this collaboration.

There are also some professional attributes that will increase the likelihood that the social worker will engage in a strategic collaboration. One attribute is that the social worker must embrace a strengths-based approach to practice rather than a traditional medical model approach (Saleeby, 1997). In a strengths-based approach the social worker conducts a multidimensional assessment with the client. In this assessment process the client is viewed as the expert in the process of developing a shared understanding of the client's situation and in the development of interventive strategies based on this understanding. This type of assessment often necessitates collaboration with colleagues also involved in the multiple facets and layers of the client's life.

With this broader assessment comes an appreciation for interventions outside the client/social worker context that will assist the client in accomplishing his or her goals. In contrast, a social worker or agency that operates from a medical model or traditional approach may not readily see the appropriateness of participating in or convening a strategic collaboration. Within this type of approach the client's problem is often viewed more narrowly based on a clinical diagnosis. The client's psychological functioning becomes the major focus of the assessment and treatment process.

Another attribute that would increase the social worker's likelihood of involvement in strategic collaborations is the social worker's awareness of his or her own role limitations and an openness and respect for other disciplines and perspectives. To engage in effective collaboration with a client's lawyer, the social worker must have an understanding of the lawyer's role to zealously protect his or her client's rights and the implications of that role in the collaborative process. The social worker must be open to thinking strategically about the assessment and intervention process. This means exploring how certain issues identified in the psychosocial assessment process and addressed in the intervention plan may have an impact on the client's legal strategy. It also means a willingness to consider adjustments to the intervention plan in the light of the client's legal strategy.

In order to collaborate effectively in cases involving both the child welfare system and the intimate partner violence system, social workers also needs to be aware of their own theoretical biases with regard to intimate partner violence and child maltreatment and the theoretical biases of the systems within which they are working. This awareness is critical to ensuring that the social work assessment process is based on a full exploration of client need rather than a limited exploration that fits the theoretical perspective of the practitioner and/or delivery system within which they are working.

Lastly, to be effective conveners of strategic collaborations, social workers must place equal value on their therapeutic role as well as their case management role. Too often, as pointed out by Weil (1982), direct practitioners see case management activities as secondary to their therapeutic work. This devaluation can be partially explained by an imbalance of training in these areas. While graduate social work training for direct practitioners includes some focus on work with task groups, organizations, and communities that provides much of the knowledge base for the collaborative activities embodied in the case management role, the majority of social work education for the direct practitioner still focuses on work on the individual and—to some extent—family level.

Lawyers' Professionalism and Initiating Strategic Collaborations

Lawyers have an ethical duty to provide "competent" and "zealous" representation to clients (ABA Model Rule 1.1 and Comment 1 to Rule 1.3), and these terms are given meaning to the public by the most visible of the lawyer's roles, that of litigator in a courtroom. However, most client representation involves the far less visible roles of counseling clients and negotiating on their behalf outside the courtroom. Both of these tasks, when performed well, are collaborative in nature.

The lawyer's role calls for him or her to be agent for the client, acting for the client according to the client's instruction. Through the counseling function, a client comes to make meaningful decisions about the alternatives available. This counseling process is an inherently collaborative function as the client and lawyer work together to identify alternatives and to reach decisions regarding those alternatives. The lawyer brings legal knowledge to the table, and the client brings the context in which that legal knowledge must be applied.

There will be times when other professionals need to be brought into this counseling process. Lawyers have an ethical duty to explain a matter to a client to "the extent reasonably necessary to permit the client to make informed decisions" regarding the lawyer's representation (ABA Model Rule 1.4 [b]). This explanation may involve only legal considerations, or it may require consideration of more broad-ranging considerations. For example, in cases where the effects of decisions on other people predominate in the decision making, a lawyer's advice needs to encompass matters other than just the law if it is to be adequate (ABA Comment 2 to Model Rule 2.1). The advice may have to encompass a discussion of the "moral, economic, social and political factors that may be relevant to the client's situation" (ABA Model Rule 2.1). Where an informed client decision depends upon such considerations, the lawyer should raise them. On occasion this may call for collaboration with other professionals to ensure that the lawyer is not stepping outside his or her area of expertise:

> Matters that go beyond strictly legal questions may also be in the domain of another profession. Family matters can involve problems within the professional competence of psychiatry, clinical psychology or social work. . . . Where consultation with a professional in another field is something a competent lawyer would recommend, the lawyer should make such recommendation. (Comment 4 to ABA Model Rule 2.1)

As Janet Weinstein points out, in child maltreatment cases, "numerous psychosocial issues about the welfare of the child and the parents are presented . . . including concerns about development, relationship and self-esteem" (1997, p. 108). When such cases also involve intimate partner violence, clients must make decisions that go to the heart of their relationships with both partners and children, implicating an even broader array of social, financial, and emotional issues. They must consider not only their own evaluation of the relationships and where those relationships may be going, but, with the lawyer's assistance, must also understand and factor in the evaluations of other actors, who will include other family members and the lawyers and social workers working with them as well as the caseworkers, social workers, and lawyers representing the interests of the government in the child protective proceeding. If related criminal proceedings are pending, the client will have to understand the ramifications of decisions on the outcome of that proceeding, which may well depend on a number of psychosocial assessments by professionals advising the court or the prosecutors in that proceeding.

The lawyer also needs much of this information to advise the client properly. The normal tools available to the lawyer may not be adequate to collect the information necessary. Factual investigation, discovery mechanisms, and the retention and preparation of expert witnesses involve prolonged timetables that may be inadequate to meet the needs of clients making decisions about their safety and that of their children or facing imminent governmental action that may result in the removal of their children. Furthermore, in such cases, the tools available to the lawyer are quite blunt. For example, a formal deposition may be of only short-term use in cases where relationships are ongoing, facts unfold on a day-to-day basis, and assessments change in the light of developments. The lawyer under such circumstances needs to use tools that allow quick access to the information a client needs in order to make decisions. A strategic collaboration is such a tool. It can be undertaken quickly and when needed. It may include only those participants needed to best meet the particular need facing the client.

There are additional professional reasons for a lawyer to use strategic collaborations. They provide a way for both the lawyer and the client to explore the context of the client's life in the light of the present crisis and to do so in a "client-centered" way. Increasingly, good lawyering is viewed as lawyering informed by a broad knowledge of the context in which a client lives. In a move from "impersonal" toward "interpersonal" lawyering, there has been a shift from a lawyer's work seen exclusively in legal terms toward a recognition that "client problems are not only—and perhaps not even primarily—legal" (Stier, 1992, p. 306). This shift reinforces the idea that the client must be the decision maker in the attorney-client relationship:

> Under the traditional conception, lawyers . . . "primarily seek the best 'legal' solutions to problems without fully exploring how those solutions meet clients' nonlegal as well as legal concerns. . . . The client-centered conception . . . assumes that, because any solution to a problem involves a balancing of legal and nonlegal concerns, clients usually are better able than lawyers to choose satisfactory solutions. Moreover, the approach recognizes that clients' emotions are an inevitable and natural part of problems and must be factored into the counseling process." (Stier, 1992, p. 316, citing D. Binder, P. Bergman, & S. Price, *Lawyers as Counselors: A Client-Centered Approach*, 35 *N.Y.L.S.L. Rev.* 29 [1990]).

A client-centered, contextual approach requires that a lawyer be open to an expansive concept of relevance in the lawyer-client relationship and to the idea that a theory of a case may be changed in the light of the context of a client's life. The approach also requires an emphasis on the lawyer's self-awareness, calling for "an understanding of the lawyer's own humanity and its important involvement in every representation" (Wolfrom, 1986, p. 688; see Miller, 1994, p. 570).

Collaboration with other professionals may expand what is "relevant" for the lawyer and client. It may help the client gain perspective on his or her own interpersonal dynamics and assist the lawyer in exploring the boundaries of his or her own knowledge and biases. Working with other professionals, particularly those who focus on the psychosocial aspects of the client's life, may help the lawyer be open to not only to looking backward to determine "what happened" but to "look[ing] at the meaning of what happened" (Miller, 1994, p. 518). This may be essential if lawyer and client are to be able to look forward to the relationships among family members (see Stier, 1992, p. 517).

There are obvious obstacles to incorporating strategic collaborations into the lawyer's job. The logistics of convening and arranging collaborations are time-consuming and difficult. The time taken in organizing a collaboration, however, may resolve cases more quickly if the collaboration is successful. Another difficulty is convincing potential participants to attend. This may involve identifying for and articulating to those participants the potential benefits of collaboration with you to discuss the case. Since a benefit of a strategic collaborations may be the more efficient and appropriate settlement of cases in which each potential participant shares responsibility, the case for attendance may be crafted in the light of that responsibility.

Finally, large caseloads and inadequate reimbursement for out-of-court work in many court systems limit the regular use of strategic collaborations. Ultimately, professionalism may dictate that lawyers insist on the increased reimbursement needed to competently handle cases. In the meantime, a lawyer's work has to be guided by his or her duty to diligently and competently represent clients, and caseload size does not provide a justification for poor representation: "A lawyer's workload should be controlled so that each matter can be handled adequately" (Comment 1 to ABA Model Rule 1.3). Having undertaken representation, a "lawyer should pursue a matter on behalf of a client despite . . . personal inconvenience" (Comment 1 to Rule 1.3). In short, "a lawyer should act with commitment and dedication to the interests of the client and with zealous advocacy upon the client's behalf" (Comment 1 to Rule 1.3). If strategic collaboration provides the best tool available to the lawyer, then ethical and professional considerations may well dictate its use.

An Example of a Strategic Collaboration

As a tool in thinking through how a strategic collaboration initiated by a social worker or lawyer could result in a more effective response, we will use a case example involving both intimate partner violence and child maltreatment and the respective delivery systems set up to respond to each of these problems. In the case example we will demonstrate how the professional mandates (in both law and social work) to collaborate apply to a social worker and a lawyer involved in the case. In addition, as the strategic collaboration process is described, we will illustrate the importance of some of the professional attributes discussed earlier that can enhance the likelihood of the professional's initiating and implementing an effective strategic collaboration. The professionals have the following general background on the case:

> Mr. and Mrs. J were involved in a physical confrontation that resulted in the Mrs. J's suffering multiple bruises on her face and upper body and a cut to the left side of her head. Their 9-year-old son was in the house and could hear the confrontation. A neighbor called the police, who arrested the Mr. J and took Mrs. J, accompanied by her son, to the emergency room, where she was treated and released. A hospital intervention social worker interviewed Mrs. J, who reported a history of intimate partner violence connected to Mr. J's drinking that included several severe beatings within earshot of her son. Mr. J reportedly never hit his son, but the incidents terrified him. Mrs. J reported that she had always dropped criminal charges in the past. The hospital social

worker referred the mother to a social worker at the Women's Advocacy Center and made a report to the child protective agency based on her concern that the child's reaction to witnessing the violence raised the possibility of emotional maltreatment. The child protective agency referred the son to the Family Services Agency, where he was assigned to a social worker who specialized in treating children who had witnessed parental violence.

The child protective agency initiated court proceedings against Mrs. J for a failure to protect her son and against Mr. J for emotional maltreatment. The court issued a temporary order of protection against Mr. J requiring that he stay away from his son, and it released his son to Mrs. J. Criminal charges were filed as a result of Mr. J's arrest, and the criminal court issued an order of protection against Mr. J requiring that he avoid all contact with Mrs. J. Mr. J was referred for an assessment as part of the criminal court procedures. Recently, the lawyer and social worker, working separately with the mother, have learned that the child protective agency is seriously considering removing the child from Mrs. J because the agency has learned that Mr. J has been visiting the home while Mrs. J and her son were there, despite the two court orders prohibiting such visitation.

Under these circumstances, what would motivate the lawyer or social worker working with the mother to initiate a strategic collaboration? What might the process of strategic collaboration look like? More specifically, what professional(s) would each choose to collaborate with, in what sequence, and on what issue(s)? Clearly, prior to beginning this process each professional would need to first explore whether there are other established collaborative structures through which their purposes could be achieved. In our case example, we have assumed that adequate collaborative structures are not in place that would facilitate the professionals' getting together to deal with the possibility of imminent removal of the child.

The Mother and Her Lawyer

Upon learning that the child protective agency intends to seek removal of the child, Mrs. J and her lawyer meet to discuss how the removal may be avoided. Before this interview, they have met only once—in the courthouse when the lawyer was assigned by the court to represent Mrs. J in the child protective proceedings. At that point, they had only a short time to prepare for the court appearance and spent it briefly exploring together the history of violence between Mrs. J and her husband and the exposure of her son to that violence. Mrs. J told the lawyer of a long-term history of violence and of intermittent exposure of her son to that violence. The lawyer advised Mrs. J that the judge's usual practice in such cases was to permit the non-offending partner to keep the child and to issue an order of protection keeping the offending partner away from the child until the case could be fully investigated and presented. Mrs. J and her lawyer decided not to argue against such an order. They also decided not to raise any question of visitation of the child by Mr. J for fear that the judge might see in Mrs. J's support for paternal visitation an unwillingness to take the steps necessary to protect her child. The judge decided as the lawyer had predicted, and after the court appearance the lawyer gave Mrs. J a copy of the order of protection and explained its meaning to her. They agreed to meet the following week to discuss the case in detail.

Now, facing removal of the child because of the father's visitation, they meet for a second time. The lawyer first asks Mrs. J to talk about any contacts with her husband since the day the Family Court issued its order of protection. Mrs. J tells the lawyer that her husband has been visiting her son at the house, that she has not objected to the visits, and that she has taken no steps to contact any authority about the visits. Mrs. J explains that she is not sure how the child protective agency knows about the visits, and is concerned that if she admits to the visits she will lose her son and her husband will end up in jail. Mrs. J explains to the lawyer that she knows she was supposed to try to stop the visits but that she simply wasn't about to do so because it felt so wrong to keep Mr. J and their son apart.

At this point, the lawyer and Mrs. J are clear as to "what happened"—that is, Mr. J visited the child in violation of a court order and did so without Mrs. J.'s taking any steps to prevent or report the visitation. Some legally relevant questions are unanswered: Did his father's visits actually place Mrs. J's son at risk? Did they place Mrs. J at risk? After all, they reasoned, the visits were a new phenomenon for the family and were taking place while child protective proceedings were pending. Might these changed circumstances have acted to inhibit violence by Mr. J against Mrs. J? Certainly, no violence had actually occurred.

They recognize that the "meaning of what happened" is unclear. While Mrs. J thinks it was "wrong" for the court to keep Mr. J and their son apart, she also recognizes that it was legally wrong for her husband to violate the court order and that she was, at the very least, unwise in not taking action to prevent the visits. It appears that she has placed her custody of her son at risk so that her husband and son could visit.

Mrs. J and her lawyer begin the essential process of looking at Mrs. J's relationship with her husband and child and of deciding the weight Mrs. J wants to give to various interests in her decision making around the child protective proceeding. They identify Mrs. J's emotional interest in maintaining or severing her relationship with her husband, her financial interest in that decision, her interest in her own safety and that of her son, her interest in having sole or joint custody of her son, her interest in the outcome of the criminal court proceedings, and her interest in avoiding a finding that she was a maltreating mother. While she is clear that her relationship with her son is the most important relationship in her life, she also values her relationship with her husband and values the three-way relationship she shares with her husband and son. In the course of discussing these interests, Mrs. J reveals to the lawyer the many tensions she feels and the very mixed feelings she has toward her husband.

From the range of responses, it became clear to Mrs. J and her lawyer that Mrs. J needs to take a long and careful look at what had been happening in her home. She is facing decisions that go to the heart of her family's life and upon which her own safety and the safety of her child might depend. They decide that whatever steps they take in the legal proceeding, those steps should try to give Mrs. J some time to begin to work through her competing feelings. In the meantime, Mrs. J decides to give great weight to her short-term interest in keeping her son with her. She also places great value on not being found to be a maltreating mother. She decides that in achieving these short-term interests, she wants to do nothing that will jeopardize her long-term interest in possibly continuing her relationship with her husband and eventually reunifying the whole family. This discussion gives the client and the lawyer good reason to reach out to the social worker to whom Mrs. J has been referred. They need help in figuring out whether visits by Mr. J to his son actually pose a danger to Mrs. J and her son. They recognize that Mrs. J needs to work through a range of feelings she has about her husband if she is to be prepared to make some central decisions about the child protective proceeding and her future living arrangements. They also need a clearer understanding of why Mrs. J took the approach she did to her husband's visits if that role is going to be "explained" to the court or the other parties. They calculate that the social worker will want to support Mrs. J's desire to keep her son with her, and they want the benefit of the social worker's opinion on the wisdom of arguing for visitation in the short term.

They next consider how the child protective agency, the professionals working with the child, and, ultimately, the court will view what happened. Might they be convinced that the order of protection should be downgraded to an order permitting Mr. J back into the home or at least permitting him to visit with his son provided he refrains from harassment or assault? Would such an order be sufficient to ensure the safety of her son? Could the criminal court order be changed to permit such visits or to permit Mr. J back into the home? Does Mrs. J have any influence on the criminal proceeding? How will her actions in the criminal proceeding be viewed in the child protective proceeding? In considering these questions, Mrs. J and her lawyer identify a need to gather information, get input, and begin discussions with many others.

Mrs. J and the lawyer next decide that they will not trigger collaboration with anyone else until they have consulted with the social worker. They recognize that if the collaboration with the mother's social worker identifies ways in which Mrs. J can better understand her motivation in permitting the visits and better identify ways in which her safety and the child's safety can be better ensured, cooperation of the child's lawyer and social worker could well be more likely. They will also look to the meeting with the mother's social worker to see whether discussions with the child protective agency and the lawyers involved in the criminal proceedings would be wise.

They then engage in a detailed discussion about the information they will share with the social worker, the implications of the fact that the social worker is a mandated reporter, and the fact that information shared with the social worker may not be protected by privilege in the child protective proceeding. They weigh the risks and benefits of the collaboration and decide in its favor.

Finally, they decide that Mrs. J's participation in the collaboration with the social worker will be important if she is to make the final decisions in her case.

The Mother's Social Worker

The social worker first meets with Mrs. J following her referral from the hospital. Their initial meeting focuses on Mrs. J's immediate safety needs. Mrs. J acknowledges a history of severe abuse but states that she does not feel she or her son is in any immediate danger since the orders of protection have already been issued. The meeting is kept rather brief at Mrs. J's request. She does agree to meet with the social worker again to discuss how the social worker might be helpful to her, but she cancels this meeting. Their next meeting occurs after the child protective agency learns of Mr. J's visits to the home in violation of the protective orders and indicates an intent to remove the child from Mrs. J's custody. In this meeting, Mrs. J again states that she does not feel in immediate danger since Mr. J has not been physically violent or threatening to her since his arrest. The presenting problem, as Mrs. J sees it, is how to prevent the removal of her child. Her stated goal is to do whatever is necessary to keep her son.

Since the child protective agency's threat to remove her son seems to be based on the father's home visits in violation of one or both of the protective orders, the social worker explores with Mrs. J the individual, relationship, and environmental factors that may have had an impact on her desire or ability to maintain her own safety and her son's through orders of protection. The social worker explains to Mrs. J that the purpose of this explora-

tion is to reach a more shared understanding of Mrs. J's decision-making process with regard to the father's visits and to
jointly develop a plan that will assist Mrs. J in maintaining her
safety and that of her son.

On the individual level, the social worker explores with Mrs.
J the level of physical and psychological trauma she has experienced and how she is coping with the effects of the abuse. She
also explores with Mrs. J what she knows about abusive behavior patterns and about the effects of witnessing parental abuse
on children. On the relationship level, the social worker explores
the relationship Mrs. J has with her son, including Mrs. J's confidence in her own ability as a single parent and her ability to
deal effectively with her son's level of traumatization. In addition, the social worker explores Mrs. J's perception of the relationship between the father and son and the perceived impact of
the father's violence and the father's absence on this relationship. Also, on the relationship level, the social worker explores
with Mrs. J the dynamics of her marital relationship with a particular focus on issues of power and dependency. On the environmental level, the social worker explores with Mrs. J her
perceived level of current and past support for maintaining her
safety from both informal (family and friends) and formal systems and any obstacles she is experiencing or has experienced
from these systems. Table 12.1 depicts the mutual understanding that was developed between Mrs. J and the social worker
about these factors, how these factors may have influenced her
decision-making processes, and the interventive strategies discussed as a result of this understanding.

Based on this assessment and planned intervention strategies,
the social worker discusses with Mrs. J the need to collaborate
with other professionals involved in her situation. Collaboration
with Mrs. J's lawyer appears to be the most critical given the
impending legal proceeding to remove her child. Several issues
in the assessment process may have implications for the legal
strategies being developed to protect Mrs. J's rights. For example, Mrs. J's beginning self-awareness with regard to the effects
of the traumatization on her own emotional and cognitive reactions, as well as her current parenting difficulties with her son,
could place her in a weaker position with regard to custody. The

social worker recommends to Mrs. J that her lawyer be alerted to these issues so that the lawyer has an opportunity to address their implications and to include any planned interventive strategies to deal with these issues in the legal strategy. In the assessment, the client has also identified some financial issues whose resolution may go beyond the role and function of the social worker. Legal consultation on this issue would ensure that Mrs. J has the opportunity to explore all of her options in dealing with her financial concerns. The social worker recommends that her realistic concern about the effect of a lengthy criminal proceeding on her husband's job also be brought to her lawyer's attention. Any reluctance on Mrs. J's part to pursue the criminal proceeding must be fully understood so that her reluctance is not misconstrued by the child protective agency as a failure to protect. The possible interventive strategies involving other professionals also need to be first reviewed with Mrs. J's lawyer for their legal implications, particularly the plan to contact the child's social worker or any of the father's representatives. Based on this discussion, Mrs. J and her social worker agree to set up a joint meeting involving Mrs. J, her lawyer, and her social worker.

Results of the Collaboration Between the Lawyer, the Social Worker, and Mrs. J

As a result of their independent meetings with Mrs. J, both the social worker and the lawyer reached the conclusion that a strategic collaboration with the other was critical. All agreed that the primary purpose of such a meeting would be to work through the legal and other interventive strategies needed to avoid the removal of her son. Below is a summary of the major strategies developed as a result of the strategic collaboration between Mrs. J, her social worker, and her lawyer.

Visitation   As a result of the exploration with the social worker, Mrs. J increased her understanding of the factors that had influenced her decision making about the visits. Her lawyer was interested in her position about visitation as a result of this understanding. Mrs. J stated that she still would like some arrangement developed where her husband and son could see

TABLE 12.1. SOCIAL WORK ASSESSMENT AND INTERVENTION PLAN

	Assessment	Possible Interventive Strategies
Individual Level of Traumatization	Mrs. J has been subjected to years of abuse in which she has come to use the defenses of minimalization and denial in order to cope.	Continued individual counseling to help Mrs. J come to terms with the effects of her own traumatization through the development of more positive coping mechanisms which will place her in a stronger position to understand and deal more effectively with the effects her son's traumatization.
	Mrs. J has limited knowledge about abusive behavior patterns and the effects of witnessing parental violence on children. She expressed much relief in the fact that her son was never subjected to direct abuse.	
	Analysis—The use of denial and minimalization combined with Mrs. J's limited knowledge about violence patterns and the effects of witnessing parental violence on children contributed to her decision to allow Mr. J to visit and not fully consider the potential harm involved.	
Familial Parental Relationship	Mrs. J describes difficulties she is having controlling her son and dealing with his anger at her for not allowing him to see his father. Her son seems to blame her for all the problems. Mrs. J describes a close relationship between her husband and son.	Contact her son's social worker, who may be able to increase Mrs. J's understanding of her son's emotional and behavioral reactions to the violence and ways to deal more effectively with his anger and blame.
	Analysis—Allowing the father to visit in the home was in part an attempt to control her son's anger as well as respond to his emotional need to see his father.	Explore other visitation strategies for the father that take into consideration safety issues.

Marital Relationship	Mrs. J described feelings of extreme ambivalence about the separation and stated a desire for eventual reconciliation. She is currently feeling hopeful about her relationship with Mr. J due to his self-reported willingness to get treatment. Mrs. J states she is economically dependent on her husband. He has been giving her money since the separation but is currently in control of how and when this occurs. *Analysis*—Her ambivalence about the separation, combined with her current state of hopefulness and her day-to-day economic dependence on her husband, increased her openness to Mr. J's request for visitation.	Get more clarity from the system representatives involved with Mr. J as to what he is actually doing to address his problems so that Mrs. J is able to more objectively and realistically assess his progress in changing his abusive behavior. Explore different legal and nonlegal strategies to address her financial support needs and the current day-to-day economic dependence on her husband.
Environmental Informal Social Supports	Mrs. J disclosed many fears about being on her own after 13 years of marriage and a sense of isolation from her extended family, who are unaware of the extent of the abusive relationship. *Analysis*—This fear and isolation contributed to her openness to her husband's visitation.	Enrollment in a support group for women involved with abusive partners. Assist Mrs. J in telling trusted family members about the extent of the abuse in order to enlist their support.
Formal Social Supports	Mrs. J has concerns about her ability to survive on her part-time salary alone and fears that a drawn-out court proceeding could cost her husband his job, which is partly why she had never pursued his arrest in the past. *Analysis*—These concerns have made her less than enthusiastic about the use of legal strategies to deal with the violence.	Explore all possible legal options, keeping in mind Mrs. J's concern about how it will affect other parts of her life.

each other, but she did not want this arrangement to present any possibility of harm to herself or her son. As a result of Mrs. J's position, all agreed that an exploration into a visitation schedule outside the home would be the next step. The social worker agreed to contact the son's social worker to see if there were any concerns about this type of arrangement. The lawyer agreed to contact the child's lawyer with regard to this same issue. The social worker also thought it would be important to understand the father's status in treatment before making either of these contacts, since it could influence the position of the son's social worker and law guardian. The lawyer agreed to contact the father's defense attorney to ascertain his treatment status so that a more informed decision about the son's visitation could be made.

Orders of Protection   Mrs. J's recent behavior in not enforcing the order of protection required a discussion of how to deal with the current orders in the upcoming hearing. Her lawyer was concerned that any indication that Mrs. J did not desire an order of protection or was not able to enforce one could weaken her position in retaining custody of her son. Mrs. J responded that her increased awareness of her husband's potential to still harm her, combined with the arrangement of a safe visitation schedule between Mr. J and her son, made her more amenable to this type of legal strategy for now. Mrs. J also believed that if she didn't feel so alone and desperate in controlling her son's anger, she would be less tempted to involve her husband around these issues. The social worker discussed the planned strategies to find her more support and to connect with her son's social worker to help her deal more effectively with his reactions. While the lawyer was concerned about how vulnerable this may make her appear, the lawyer also thought the planned strategies could be used to show her determination to do all that she can to strengthen her ability to protect her son.

   While Mrs. J expressed a willingness to use an order of protection now, she was worried about the impact this strategy would have on the possibility of reconciliation with her husband in the future. In response, the lawyer proposed that after the upcoming hearing they discuss a timetable for decision making around moving toward a less restrictive order of protection if reconciliation continues to be Mrs. J's goal. The lawyer advised, however, that it would be better to avoid discussion of possible reconciliation at the upcoming hearing. The lawyer also believed it was premature at this time to mention the possibility of reconciliation to the son's social worker or to the father's lawyer. The social worker brought up the importance to this decision-making process around reconciliation of getting clarity as to exactly what Mr. J is doing in treatment. Mrs. J agreed, and the lawyer said that after the upcoming court hearing he would take initial responsibility for exploring an ongoing process for learning about Mr. J's progress.

Finances Mrs. J's need for financial support was also discussed. Available public assistance would not be adequate to keep her and her son in their home, and some type of financial arrangement with Mr. J was necessary. The lawyer thought that court proceedings to obtain support might complicate an already complicated situation, and Mrs. J agreed that she would prefer that an informal arrangement be set up. The social worker urged that the agreement clearly specify the payment amount and the timetable and felt strongly that the payment and default procedures should not involve Mrs. J's having to contact Mr. J The lawyer agreed to explore the development of this type of agreement with Mr. J's lawyer.

Child Protective Agency The decision was reached not to contact the child protective service representatives until the above strategies could be put in place. If the son's social worker and law guardian were amenable to the father's visitation with the son outside the home and to the planned strategies to strengthen the mother's ability to reinforce the order of protection, then the plan could be proposed to the child protective service representative in a meeting with all involved possibly prior to the court hearing.

CONCLUSION

Child maltreatment cases that also involve intimate partner violence are increasingly being identified within child protective service systems. Effective intervention requires the collaboration of lawyers and social workers and two distinct service delivery systems. A variety of formal structures are being developed mostly within child protective systems that are attempting to foster interdisciplinary and intersystem collaboration and deal with the systematic complexities.

Because of the limitations of these formal collaborative structures, social workers and lawyers need to act independently to foster collaboration when the need arises in individual cases. The issues generated by these cases demand more proactive responses from both lawyers and social workers. One of these responses would be the initiating of strategic collaborations to meet client needs. Social workers and lawyers responding in this manner need to understand how the strategic collaboration fits within the established collaborative structures, be clear as to their purpose and rationale in convening such a meeting, make very purposeful decisions as to whom to collaborate with and when, and take full responsibility for involving the client as a full participant in the collaborative process.

The professionalism of social workers and lawyers dictates that they improve the tools they use in working with children and families caught up in overburdened and fragmented systems. They must be constantly vigilant to the positive and negative impact of formal collaborative structures on their individual responsibility to collaborate when it will serve their clients' needs and protect their rights. Convening strategic meetings under these circumstances is a professional responsibility of both professions. Participation in established collaborative structures should never substitute for this proactive independent response.

REFERENCES

American Bar Association. (1983). *Model rules of professional conduct.* Chicago: American Bar Association's Center for Professional Responsibility.

Berry, M. (1994). A question of mission: Catholic Law School's domestic violence clinic. 38 *Howard Law Journal* 135, 150–151.

Edleson, J. L. (1995). Mothers and children: Understanding the link between woman battering and child abuse. *Synergy: The Newsletter of the Resource Center on Domestic Violence: Child Protection and Custody, 1*(3), 4.

Hamlin, E. R. (1991). Community-based spouse abuse protection and family preservation team. *Social Work, 36*(5), 402–406.

Jackson, M., & Garvin, D. (1995). Coordinated community action model. (Available from the Domestic Violence Institute of Michigan, PO Box 130107, Ann Arbor, MI 48113-0107)

Jaffe, P. G., Wolfe, D. A., & Wilson, S. K. (1990). *Children of battered women.* Newbury Park, CA: Sage.

Johnson, P., & Cahn, K. (1992). Improving child welfare practice through improvements in attorney–social worker relationships. 54 *U. Pitt. L. Rev.* 229, 156–157.

Koh Peters, J. (1991). Concrete strategies for managing ethically-based conflicts between children's lawyers and consulting social workers who serve the same client. 1 *Ky. Children's Rts. J.* 15.

Koh Peters, J. (1997). *Representing children in child protective proceedings: Ethical and practical dimensions.* Charlottesville, VA: Lexis.

Kolbo, J. R., Blakely, E. H., & Engleman, D. (1996). Children who witness domestic violence: A review of empirical literature. *Journal of Interpersonal Violence, 11*(2), 281–293.

Lupton, C., & Stevens, M. (1998). Family group conferencing: The UK experience. *Interdisciplinary Report on At-Risk Children and Families, 1*(2), 21.

McCloskey, L. A. Figueredo, A. J., & Koss, M. P. (1995). The effects of systematic family violence on children's mental health. *Child Development, 66*(5), 1239–1261.

Merkel-Holguin, L. (1998). Family group decision making: Harnessing family commitment and responsibility for the protection of children. *Interdisciplinary Report on At-Risk Children and Families, 1*(2), 1.

Miller, B. (1994). Give them back their lives: Recognizing client narrative in case theory. 93 *Mich. L. Rev.* 485.

National Association of Social Workers. (1996). *Code of ethics.* Washington, DC: NASW Press.

Parsloe, P. (1981). The interface of law and social work. *Contemporary Social Work Education, 4*(3), 183–197.

Pence, E., & Paymor, M. (1993). *Education groups for men who batter: The Deluth Model.* New York: Springer.

Pennell, J., & Burford, G. (1998). Family group decision making: Post-conference progress in resolving violence and promoting well-being. *Interdisciplinary Report on At-Risk Children and Families, 1*(4), 51–52.

Petit, M. R., & Curtis, P. A. (1997). Child abuse and neglect: A look at the states. In *1997 CWLA stat book.* Washington, DC: CWLA.

Saleeby, D. (1997). *The strengths perspective in social work practice.* New York: Longman.

Stier, S. (1992). Reframing legal skills: Relational lawyering. 42 *J. Legal Educ.* 303.

Straus, M. A., & Smith, C. (1990). Family patterns and child abuse. In M. A. Straus and R. J. Gelles (Eds.), *Physical violence in American families: Risk factors adaptations to violence in 8,145 families* (pp. 341–368). New Brunswick, NJ: Transaction.

Weil, M. (1982). Research on issues in collaboration between social workers and lawyers. *Social Service Review, 56,* 393–405.

Weil, M. (1985). Professional and educational issues in case management practice. In M. Weil & F. Carls, *Case management in human service practice: A systematic approach for mobilizing resources for clients* (pp. 357–377). San Francisco: Jossey Bass.

Weinstein, J. (1997). And never the twain shall meet: The best interests of children and the adversary system. 52 *U. Miami L. Rev.* 79.

Wolfrom, C. W. (1986). *Modern legal ethics.* St. Paul, MN: West Publishing Company.

Wylie, M. S. (1996). It's a community affair. *Family Networker, 20*(2), 58–96.

13

The Impact of a Changing Funding Environment on Agencies

Roslyn H. Chernesky, DSW, and Irene A. Gutheil, DSW

LONG BEFORE THE MACRO-LEVEL CHANGES now referred to as devolution became a critical factor threatening organizations and affecting the provision of services, the impact of turbulent and hostile environments on the functioning, survival, and effectiveness of organizations was of concern. Since the 1960s, organizational theorists and social science researchers have examined the nature of the relationship between organizations and their environments. Moreover, managers and administrators in both the profit and nonprofit sectors have found it necessary to adapt to changes in their organizations' environments and cope with shifting priorities, pressures, and demands.

As agencies try to keep pace with today's rapidly changing environment, the prospects for delivering quality services become bleaker. The political and economic forces that bring diminished governmental support for programs, privatization, and the creation of collaborative partnerships seem to lose sight of the need and demand for services to vulnerable populations who are unable to marshal internal resources or external supports required for optimal functioning and well-being. Agencies are thus challenged to find ways to continue serving clients even when funding is reduced or when mandates determining who is to be served and how dictate program operations and survival.

Experience over the past decades, and especially since the conservative Reagan era of the 1980s, has alerted agencies to the dangers of standing by and doing nothing, and has prepared them for the likelihood that changes in programs and services will accompany changes precipitated in the environment. Today, agency leadership is advised of the need for a vision, strategic management, and political skills to best adapt to this environment.

The purpose of this chapter is to review current thinking about the impact of changes in agency environments with a particular focus on strategies available to agency leadership as they contend with changes in their funding environment. A recent study that traces a cohort of administrators of agencies serving older persons and their families in a large metropolitan region over 2 years is presented to illustrate how agencies dealt with the threat of loss of funding.

INTRODUCTION

Organizations face multiple and conflicting environmental constraints, often imposed upon them, and consequently beyond their control. Changes in agency environments, whether in political, legal, technological, economic, cultural, or demographic conditions, pose both opportunities and constraints. Because these conditions are interrelated, agency environments are experienced as turbulent. A shift in one dimension has ramifications in others. Pressures coming from one area contribute to demands in other areas. Constraints coming from one area at any one time may be critical to an organization yet may pose no threat at other times (Hall, 1996).

The state of the economy in which an organization is operating is perhaps the most crucial dimension, although it is very difficult to separate economic conditions from political factors. Economic conditions affect the founding, growth and expansion, and survival or death of organizations (Hall, 1996). Prosperity fosters creation of new organizations and nurtures agency development and rapid growth. Economic affluence allows organizations to offer a wider range of programs and serve more clients. A depressed economy leads to downsizing and can precipitate organizational decline.

Agencies vary in their capacity to withstand economic and political changes. Larger and richer agencies, as well as agencies with greater service diversity, are likely to cope more easily with loss of funding since they are able to draw upon more resources to weather lean periods. Smaller agencies are more vulnerable to loss of funding and even shifts in funding, and may be ill-prepared and ill-equipped to respond appropriately or last until conditions improve.

A key determinant of agency vulnerability to environmental pressures and demands is the extent to which the agency is dependent on aspects of its environment, especially for ongoing resources and support (Hasenfeld, 1983). For example, the more dependent an organization is on government contracts, the more vulnerable it is if the contract is not renewed. In contrast, an agency with several funding streams will be less vulnerable to the loss of its federal grant if the grant is only one of many sources of financial support.

When vulnerable, organizations react in predictable ways. Confronted with turbulent environments, agencies tend to increase formalization, centralization, and bureaucratization, decrease communication, and institute a more directive or authoritarian management approach. Ironically, just when open and loose organization is needed to encourage innovation and foster support in dealing with crises, organizations tend to adopt mechanistic structures and styles that are less useful for adapting to their environments (Cameron, Kim, & Whetten, 1987).

Organizations vary in their responses to environmental changes. In general, they try to shape their environments, preserve their autonomy, increase control over their environments, and reduce the uncertainty that environments create (Hasenfeld, 1983). Each agency selects from among an array of strategies and uses them to deal with the perceived pressures. Contingency theory strongly suggests that there is no single correct or best way to respond. Organizational leadership must make strategic choices as part of a decision-making process that may not necessarily be rational and is often political. Choices are made in the context of how much environmental resources are needed in order to provide programs and services, as well as the conditions or costs placed upon accessing them (Myrtle, Wilber, & DeJong, 1997). Although the selection of strategies requires adequate and reliable information about the potential impact of the environment or the outcomes of a decision, seldom is this information available when uncertainty prevails. Moreover, decisions in response to environmental changes may not be the ones that organizations would have made under other conditions (Hall, 1996).

Regardless of the strategies that may be used, however, periods of economic hardship force organizations to tighten up, trim areas considered less vital, and essentially try to do the same with less. Invariably, agencies either reexamine their mission and priorities as they confront the need to make difficult decisions about reallocating fewer dollars among their programs or simply drift as they shift funding and cut back programs and services across the board. In either case, organizations change. There is increasing evidence that organizational change occurs as agencies attempt to survive in their environments. Not all transformation, even if triggered by environmental pressures, is problematic. In fact, innovations in functioning and service delivery can be a valuable by-product of environmental forces, especially for agencies that have become stagnant or are failing to provide the quality services for which they were established.

THEORETICAL PERSPECTIVE

To better understand the relationship between organizations and the environments that constrain them, the resource-dependence perspective is especially useful (Aldrich & Pfeffer, 1976; Pfeffer & Salancik, 1978). Resource-dependence theory is based on several assumptions:

1. Organizations cannot generate all of the resources they need or perform every activity to sustain themselves. Therefore, organizations must depend on the environment for resources, which may include funding, personnel, clients, or accreditation. The more resources an organization must garner from its environment, the more dependent it is on its environment.

2. Resource acquisition drives organizations, especially if resources are absolutely essential, scarce, or seemingly beyond reach.

3. Organizations prefer to affect their environments, thereby re-

ducing the environments' control over them and increasing their chances to thrive and survive.

4. Agency administrators routinely manage their environments as well as their organizations; the former may be even more important than the latter. When the environment is effectively managed, organizations are more able to predict or prevent changes, reduce their impact, and take measures to cushion the consequences.

5. There are alternative ways of dealing with the environment, and administrators must make choices from among a set of strategic alternatives, although the outcome of each choice is likely to be uncertain.

Thus, resource-dependence theory lays out a scenario of constant and continuous exchange between organizations and their environments. While organizations are not completely controlled by their environments, they are dependent upon them and must respond to changes in their priorities, demands, and pressures. Even in periods of relative stability, agencies must be vigilant, scanning their boundaries to be ready for threats and to avoid the unexpected environmental "jolt" (Meyer, 1982). While executive administrators are primarily responsible for acquiring and retaining the essential resources of the agency, they are equally responsible for operating effectively in the organizations' environments and for shaping their environments (Heimovics, Herman, & Jurkiewicz, 1993). Environments thus have a critical impact on organizations, and the extent of that impact can be mediated by administrators.

THE 1990s FUNDING ENVIRONMENT

The state of the economy in which organizations operate is critical to their growth or decline. As economic conditions change, periods of affluence or depression, inflation or recession, have an impact on agencies. Political conditions also affect organizations. Shifts in political climate, particularly through elections, legislation, and referenda, may constrain or support agency programs and services (Hall, 1996; Hasenfeld, 1983).

Health and social welfare organizations experienced a dramatic change in their funding environments over the past decade as a result of economic, social, and political forces. With more than a third of agency revenues coming from government (Bass, 1994), programs and services were increasingly threatened as the devolution proceeded. As part of the Contract With America (Gingrich, Armey, & the House Republicans, 1994), the shift away from federal responsibility to state and local governments for the support and provision of services led to states' having to take on an additional burden for human services. The states were not, however, given the revenues to maintain the already-existing services. The economic recession further complicated this shift. Since there was 20% less federal support, and both states and localities were unable to generate sufficient taxes to maintain services, programs were reduced (Videka-Sherman & Viggiani, 1996). The recession thus claimed the noncritical public services and their "non-essential, support positions" (Raber, 1996, p. 49.)

The fiscal climate, along with cuts in state aid and in federal spending for research contracts, created turmoil in many areas. In higher education, where universities faced large budget deficits, some academic programs and support services were eliminated, and others were consolidated. For example, it was suggested that Syracuse University combine its School of Social Work with the College of Nursing and the School of Education (Weiss, 1991). Yale University, with its first deficit in a decade and a bleak financial picture for the 1990s, planned on reducing its linguistics, sociology, and engineering departments (DePalma, 1991). Columbia University, also hit by reduced government spending, a sagging economy, and increasing demand, made $35 million in cuts and also dipped into its endowment, generally considered to be a last resort (DePalma, 1992).

In New York City, city and state contracts to social service agencies threatened services to 1 million New Yorkers—children, elderly adults, the physically disabled, the mentally ill, and the homeless population. Both older, established agencies and smaller, community-based agencies were hurt. Some senior centers, for example, had to end their transportation services or turn away elderly who arrived each day for meals. Medium-sized and large agencies scaled back staff, reassessed their priorities, asked clients to pay a little more, found ways to stretch their budgets, and where possible, dipped into their endowments (Teltsch, 1991). Even when the number of HIV/AIDS cases was rapidly increasing, far outpacing agency funding, government support was cut as the state and city faced their own budget problems (Lambert, 1990).

The growth of managed care as a cost-containing system further threatened funding and led to changes in the delivery of health, mental health, and human services (Strom-Gottfried, 1997). As Medicare payments to doctors were sharply reduced, many doctors refused Medicare patients while others dropped out of Medicare (Freudenheim, 1996). Fixed reimbursements, shorter hospital stays, and tighter rationing of highly specialized services forced hospitals to establish a vast network of neighborhood health centers in New York City—satellites, birthing centers, foot clinics, women's health, sports medicine—to serve more patients at less cost (Caravajal, 1995). These initiatives, as well as the growth of hospital mergers, are driven by the need for funding. This situation creates a much more competitive environment in the health care field.

The recession also affected private giving across the country. Downsizing at corporations, slow wage growth, and less interest in giving to health and social service agencies were among the factors that contributed to a decline in donations to the United Way in 1992, which continued through 1998 (Johnston, 1998). United Way contributions did not keep pace with the rate of inflation, leaving many agencies short of what had been a reliable source of income (Jay, 1996). Services that depended on the United Way for the bulk of their funding were forced to cut back just when soup kitchens, homeless shelters, and social service centers were experiencing record levels of demand for services (Barringer, 1992; Spayd, 1992). Many were already at bare bones, and the additional shortfall caused programs to close down, serve fewer clients, and intensify fund-raising efforts to make ends meet (Spayd, 1992). Foundation and corporate dollars could not make up for cutbacks in government funding or loss of United Way support, especially with the stepped-up requests for monies by agencies. In addition, emerging trends in foundation giving made it more difficult for agencies to obtain grants, especially for ongoing program support (Chernesky & Gutheil, 1994; Lauffer, 1997).

As recently as 1998, despite the optimistic economic forecast, instability in the funding environment continued. The Republican-controlled Congress once again cut back on domestic social programs supported by President Clinton. These included summer youth programs, tutoring for disadvantaged children, and home heating for poor households (Seelye, 1998). In New York City, the mayor refused to accept the City Council's budget, which included continuing support for social service programs that depend either largely or entirely on city money. Many of the agencies providing these services also lost money from the governor's budget (Allen, 1998).

UNANTICIPATED CONSEQUENCES

The management of organizational decline has received a great deal of attention in the literature, especially in the 1980s (Austin, 1984; Cameron, Sutton, & Whetten, 1988; Bombyk & Chernesky, 1985; Friesen & Frey, 1983; Weatherly, 1984). There has been renewed interest in this phenomenon with the economic shifts in the 1990s environment (Edwards, Lebold, & Yankey, 1998).

As agencies respond to threats or changes in their funding environment, mere survival is not adequate. Too often, the quality of services provided is jeopardized along the way. Decisions and strategic choices can have unanticipated consequences in terms of what services are provided and to whom. When agencies try to stay with their reduced budgets through cost-cutting efforts they attempt to carry on business as usual, yet the situation is not the same. Doing the same with less rarely works, unless agencies were so ill-managed and wasteful in the first place that operating with less revenue is virtually insignificant. Eventually, agencies must reckon with serving clients with fewer staff, services, and programs.

Even without laying off workers, attrition and a freeze on replacement hiring lead to rising caseloads and workloads for the remaining workers. It becomes more difficult for workers to do their jobs. Tighter budgeting leads to short supplies of materials, inability to reimburse workers for out-of-pocket expenses such as home visits, less money available for routine program operations, and spending limits placed on a range of job activities such as telephone calls and printing for what is considered to be absolutely essential. Workers with fewer qualifications or less experience are brought in to replace workers whose salaries were at the higher end. Increased use of both volunteers and student interns, when available, further affects the workforce.

The sharp contrast between what they were able to do before and can currently do is a constant reminder that the organization is under stress and declining. Workers are caught in the downward spiral as they are expected to be partners with the agency as it adjusts to the declining situation, yet their job security may be at risk, salaries frozen, compensation and perquisites eliminated, and caseloads increased. The effects of worker insecurity, anxiety, and anger during periods of organizational decline may be seen in worker attitudes, behavior, and performance (Cameron et al., 1987; Bargal, Back, & Ariav, 1992).

Workers may be asked to work with clients around payment of fees or encourage clients to use agency services that might not really be needed. They may be asked to lie to certify services, or to falsify records that claim how many clients have been served or client diagnoses, especially to meet reimbursable criteria. The end result is demoralized workers who may leave, burn out, or become dispirited and insensitive and thus reinforce the stereotype of uncaring and unresponsive bureaucrats.

To compensate for loss of funding, agencies may try to reduce the number of clients by limiting client access to services. In doing so they redefine service need, and individuals who might have been recipients of agency services earlier on find they are no longer eligible. Agencies have been found to reduce intakes, change eligibility criteria, or alter the requirements needed to document eligibility, which discourages applications (Kramer & Grossman, 1987). Greater policing of clients may also accompany declining resources to make sure that only those who truly need the service get it. Agency waiting lists become attractive to delay serving new clients with the expectation that they will eventually tire of waiting and find another agency more responsive to their needs. Similarly, when agencies choose not to schedule appointments within a reasonable time, clients become discouraged and may lose interest in continuing. More costly clients may be dropped or referred to other agencies, or simply denied the more expensive services.

Attracting new sources of funding is another key. Fees for service have become an increasingly important source of revenue for agencies in response to declining funding support (Salamon, 1992). Many agencies depend on client fees to support programs and services (Kettner & Martin, 1996). Ironically, demand for services is up from clients who can pay nothing or less than the full cost of service, and demand is down from those who can pay the full cost or even more than the break-even cost of services (McMurtry, Netting, & Kettner, 1990; Kettner & Martin, 1996). Agencies, therefore, try to attract and serve more upscale clients, and those who are unable to pay or pay the minimum may be allowed to drift away. Urban hospitals have repositioned themselves to serve more affluent clients. It is not unusual to see the closing of emergency rooms or community clinics that are not able to pay for themselves as hospitals open offices in wealthier neighborhoods where they can attract patients to expensive specialties. Shifts in funding sources frequently lead to significant changes in programs, client populations, or service technologies as agencies meet funding requirements and satisfy funders' interests.

Wernert (1994) showed how a family service agency adapted to its changing funding environment by moving into an unoccupied service niche (domain) for which there were available financial resources. The agency's usual niche was full with larger, more aggressive, and rapidly expanding organizations. However, no agencies were providing older adult services, and considerable revenue at all levels, both private and public, was awaiting any interested agency. Eager to obtain whatever foundation or government grants they can, many agencies, however, find that expansion into new service domains is not as easy as—and may actually be more costly than—they had anticipated. Moreover, the newly acquired funding cannot be used to support operations of the agency's existent programs which are experiencing cutbacks.

Purchase of service contracting is now a major means of delivering social services. The opportunity to obtain a government contract lures many agencies into formal agreements with governmental units to provide services that the public sector is obligated to serve. While contracting for services is seemingly attractive, enabling agencies to grow and extend their services, it can also be risky since it is accompanied by regulations and program requirements that can threaten an agency's mission, shift its focus from its original purpose, and affect the internal operations of the agency (Cnaan, 1995; Gibelman, 1996).

Agencies have sought new ways to generate revenues. Faced with the threat of greater competition for private funds, national voluntary health agencies successfully diversified their income sources to include membership dues, subscriptions, sales of publications and educational materials, marketing of their products, manufacturers' and dining discounts, and bank credit cards (Gibelman, 1990). Perlmutter and Adams (1990) studied the effects on agency mission, clients, and services of venturing into profit-making activities as a way to deal with declining revenue and found that the agency lost some of its autonomy.

Family service agencies provide a good example of how changes in funding patterns affect service delivery. As government funds were cut, programs without financial support were dropped, an appeal was made to clients with the ability to pay for services, and the focus shifted to services that were income producing (DiGiulio, 1983). For example, between 1980 and 1990 the greatest growth of services in family service agencies was employee assistance programs, which were income-generating services contracted with business and industry (Alperin, 1992).

STRATEGIC RESPONSES

McMurtry and his colleagues (1990) proposed a framework for categorizing strategic choices made by agencies as they adapt to economic uncertainty. They consider 3 general types of categories—protective strategies, influence strategies, and change strategies—that include close to 50 different strategies which elaborate upon earlier work (Bernard, 1983; Mordock, 1989).

First, protective strategies are intended to protect the agency's core technology, that is, the organization's raison d'être. They include strategies designed to maintain programs and services by ensuring an adequate flow of two major resources, revenue, and clients. Efforts to increase the numbers of clients served and to secure new or additional funding fall into this category. In addition, initiatives to ensure that an agency remains within its budget through cost-containment measures, reductions, or restructuring would fall into this category. This is the approach of trying to do the same with less, or trying to do less of the same (Ludwig, 1993). These strategies are generally thought of as cut-backs—across-the-board reductions in allocations to a number of programs or departments (Whetten, 1988). Although use of them does not fundamentally alter an agency's services and programs, the strategies may alter how they are delivered. Protective strategies require administrators to assess and reposition the agency and its programs to be more competitive in the context of supply and demand (Edwards, Cooke, & Reid, 1996). Today, that means efforts to become market-oriented by identifying the agency's clients-customers and determining how best to serve them.

Second, influence strategies are used to enable the agency to acquire greater control over its environment, to shape or manipulate it, in order to prevent loss of funding or to enhance the agency's position in the light of allocation or reallocation decisions. These strategies may include using board members to influence external decision makers, seeking a positive image through public relations, and broadening networking and collaborative interagency relationships (Menefee & Thompson, 1994; Schmid, 1992a). In general, influence strategies bring agencies and administrators into the political arena through lobbying and advocacy. Pelton and Baznik (1998) stress that agency administrators must be "prepared to participate and exercise leadership in public policy debate" (p. 116) and develop an overall organizational advocacy strategy. Gibelman and Kraft (1996) point out the importance of strengthening an agency's advocacy program, from testifying before elected official, to empowering clients to advocate on their own behalf, to hiring a professional lobbyist. Broadening networking, forming coalitions, and engaging in interagency collaboration are gaining attention as effective strategies to increase access to both resources and policy makers (Bailey & Koney, 1996).

Third, change strategies generally establish a new mission, vision, or direction of an agency. They involve altering an agency's service domain by broadening client groups served, expanding existing services, or moving into new program areas. They require administrators to think and act strategically to assess and plan for the future (Menefee, 1997). By reexamining their mission and priorities, agencies choose to make difficult decisions about eliminating programs or starting new ones. Change strategies expect administrators to be entrepreneurial, generating new ideas on how to deliver services and introducing and sustaining innovations (Eadie, 1998; Edwards & Austin, 1991).

McMurtry and his colleagues (1990) hypothesize that an agency's choice of strategy should be in relation not only to the availability of funding but to the demand for services. When demand is high, agencies are more likely to use strategies that protect their core services. When demand is low, agencies aim at altering their environments to expand their service domains or increase clients. Thus, agencies would need to take into account both dimensions when determining the most appropriate strategic responses.

Schmid (1992b) suggests three pairs of appropriate strategies for agencies (cooperation vs. competition, generalist vs. specialist, and rapid exploitation of resources vs. operational efficiency) and hypothesizes that an agency's choice of strategy should be in relation to the environment's level of stability, variability, heterogeneity, and certainty. Competitive strategies are likely to be used when there are scarce resources in an unstable and uncertain environment, and organizations realize that they must take actions to corner the market or at least get their fair share of the resources. Organizations operating within unstable environments in which resources are uncertain are likely to adopt the generalist strategy of offering a wide variety of services and programs to a broad range of different client populations in order to pool resources and better withstand periods in which resources are not forthcoming. Similarly, organizations in this environment would move quickly to use available resources in order to ensure their continuous flow and therefore the continuation of programs. In contrast, narrow, specialized programs, the cultivation of cooperative interagency working relationships, and focusing on demonstrating efficient use of resources are too risky for those agencies that heavily rely on the environment for their resources.

Organizational characteristics also appear to be related to choice of strategies in that some agencies are more insulated from threats and others are more able to cushion the impact. Agency structure, ideology, and availability of resources have been associated with strategies selected (Meyer, 1982; Schmid, 1992b). Organizations with greater financial resources, administrative capacity, political influence, and funding diversity seem to be at an advantage as they try to adapt to environmental pressures (Hasenfeld, 1983; Jerrel & Larson, 1984; Kramer & Grossman, 1987).

Studies of organizational survival in the face of strong threats have resulted in somewhat confusing and inconsistent findings. There seems to be no clear answer as to why some organizations successfully adapt and survive while others are unable to do so. Much more research on organizational characteristics is needed to advance knowledge in this area (Hall, 1996).

MANAGERIAL ROLES AND SKILLS

Devolution has been only the latest of a long series of transformations taking place in the social services and the delivery of them which require a reconceptualization of managerial roles and the skills needed to effectively provide quality of services (Edwards et al., 1996). The changing nature of agencies' funding environments is a challenge for social work management, whose decisions and actions (or inaction) can determine who receives services and the kind and quality of those services. Reduced federal support, smaller and tighter budgets, increasing emphasis on accountability and cost containment, a shift to a broader base of funding sources, and heightened competition for essential agency resources are all placing new demands on agency leadership. Menefee (1997) presents a grim picture of what is yet in store for social service agencies and calls for a new breed of administrators who are able to think and act strategically. Others believe that in this era of diminishing federal responsibility for providing and funding services, administrators will have to turn to total quality management and reengineering as approaches to renewing organizations (Edwards et al., 1996).

For example, agency administrators will be expected to:

- Shape and influence organizational environments as well as deal with environmental pressures and demands (Menefee & Thompson, 1994; Schmid, 1992a).
- Become entrepreneurs, generating new ideas on how to deliver services and introducing and sustaining innovations (Edwards & Austin, 1991).
- Become market-oriented, assessing and repositioning the agency and its programs to be more competitive in the context of supply and demand (Edwards et al., 1996).
- Create and maintain a positive human relations climate in which workers can be productive, satisfied, and empowered (Edwards & Austin, 1991).
- Manage smaller and flatter organizations in which fewer people supervise more workers and there are fewer middle-management positions (Ginsberg, 1995).
- Find creative ways of managing programs and services, such as redesign, continuous quality improvement, collaboration, and mergers (Menefee, 1997).

THE STUDY

Previous research, organizational theory, and the turbulent 1990s funding environment provided the context for this exploratory study. A panel study design was used to survey a cohort of agencies serving older adults and their families, located in the New York City metropolitan region, and to examine what happens to agencies when they are struggling to provide quality services while anticipating cutbacks and preparing to downsize. The research design provided an unusual opportunity to study administrators' views of how their agencies dealt with their changing funding environment over 2 years. It was anticipated that there would be significant differences in agencies' strategic responses as the funding environment changed. In addition, it

was expected that the funding environment would have a negative impact on agencies' services and programs.

Data Collection

The data for this chapter were collected through questionnaires
mailed at two points in time, in the fall of 1995 and the fall of
1996. At the first point, agencies in the New York City metropolitan area faced potentially devastating cuts. Budgeting at federal,
state, and local levels was in limbo. The extent of any cuts, their
seriousness, and where they would fall hardest had not yet been
announced, creating a climate of heightened uncertainty and anticipation. The first phase of the study was conducted to examine agency responses to funding threats and to consider the
influence of these early responses on agency services (Gutheil &
Chernesky, 1998).

One year later, in 1996, cuts that had been anticipated by the
agencies in the study had been made and for the most part were
not as extensive as expected. The cuts were, however, inequita-
bly distributed. In general, agencies with smaller budgets were
much more likely to lose their city contracts and receive fewer
and smaller government contracts. Community-based agencies
spread throughout the city were hardest hit (Meier, 1997). Given
that nearly three-quarters of all agency revenues come directly
from government grants and contracts, the loss of renewed
funding was especially difficult for agencies that had become
reliant on government support (Meier, 1997). However, agencies
serving older persons and their families, the focus of these studies, experienced more modest overall budget decreases (Meier,
1997). At the same time, greater demand for services by older
persons was becoming evident. Senior centers, for example,
were experiencing an increase in requests which may have been
triggered by the real and imagined fears surrounding cuts in
entitlements and programs (Meier, 1997). As the funding environment began to stabilize, and there no longer was the earlier
anticipation of drastic cuts, the agencies received the second
questionnaire.

During the first phase, questionnaires were first sent to 202
agencies in the New York City metropolitan area that provide

services to older persons and their families and were used as field placements for a graduate school of social work. Eighty-nine questionnaires were returned, a 44% response rate. In 1996 the questionnaires were mailed to these 89 agencies and 59 were returned, a 66% response rate. The analysis reported on here is based only on the data from the 59 agencies that completed the questionnaires in both 1995 and 1996.

The initial cover letter requested that the questionnaire be completed by the administrator most knowledgeable about the agency's services to older persons and their families. Thus, the sample included respondents from agency executive directors to social work department or program administrators, who may have had varying degrees of information about pending cuts or the ways the agency was addressing them. The second cover letter asked for the previous respondent to complete the questionnaire wherever possible. Because respondents' names were not required, it is not possible to determine the extent to which the same individuals completed both questionnaires. Given the 1-year period, it is likely that the same administrators responded.

The selection of the agency population ensured that all agencies employed at least one graduate social worker. Therefore, agencies providing similar services that did not use social workers or were not used as a field placement by this graduate school were not included in these studies. Although many of the agencies in the study served client populations other than older people and their families, administrators were asked to respond to the questions only in terms of their services to older adults. Only one question sought a comparison among services to different client populations. The loss of responding agencies from time one to time two, although not unusual in longitudinal analysis, is nevertheless of concern.

The responding agencies represented a cross section of agencies providing services to older persons and their families in the metropolitan area. Although they represented both the public and voluntary sectors, the sample was heavily voluntary. It included hospitals, nursing homes, and community agencies such as senior centers. Services ranged from primarily medical components to case management. One-third of the agencies serve only older persons and their families, whereas the majority, such as mental health agencies, serve multiple populations.

Limitations of the sample regarding the respondents and the agencies included make it difficult to generalize from the findings. However, the findings are illustrative of how one cohort of agencies dealt with the changing times. It is likely that the picture presented is not atypical.

The mailed questionnaire presented 24 strategies agencies may have used during the time when continued funding was uncertain. The list was adapted from strategies presented in the literature. They included protective, influence, and change strategies. Only the strategies, not the categories, were presented to respondents. Because agencies tend to use protective strategies in their efforts to carry on doing the same with less and thus provide essentially the same services to their clients, a wider range of protective strategies was given in the questionnaire. Strategies related to ways of processing the changing situation with staff, constituting a new category, were also included even though they had not appeared in the literature. These are referred to as processing strategies.

Respondents were asked to indicate which strategies they had used, the importance of each one, and whether they were considering using the strategy in the future. Respondents were invited to describe their agency's services and elaborate on their use of strategies. The second questionnaire presented the same strategies, again asked what the agencies were currently doing, and invited respondents to elaborate on their responses. The construction of the initial instrument and the findings of the first phase, based on all 89 responding agencies, are reported in an earlier article (Gutheil & Chernesky, 1998).

Findings

1995 The findings of the study's first phase indicated that by the fall of 1995, administrators were using a variety of strategies in anticipation of cuts and shifts in funding. Agencies serving older adults and their families were not sitting by idly waiting for changes to take place. Rather, they were taking steps to adapt and were already considering their next steps. Regardless of the type of agency or the kinds of services to older persons that were provided, steps were being taken to deal with the changing times. Although no clear pattern emerged from the data about the factors that contribute to which strategies were used, it appeared that agencies begin with more palatable, less drastic ones. However, agencies were using and expected to use more drastic strategies as part of their repertoire.

Agencies used strategies from each of the categories in their early efforts to most effectively deal with the threats in their funding base. These included a range of protective strategies to find ways that would allow agencies to continue to provide essentially the same services to the same clients, and to modify programs and/or the clients being served; change strategies to shift agencies in new or different directions; influence strategies to limit or prevent a reduction in resources; and strategies to process the changing situation with both staff and clients. Thus agencies were drawing upon strategies geared to adapting the internal functioning of the agency while attending to external factors as well.

The initial study findings supported the evidence in the literature that human service administrators handle cutbacks in ways that have an impact upon the services delivered. Moreover, the findings suggested that addressing the *threat* of funding cuts can also influence agency programs and services. As this sample of agency administrators showed, adaptation to a changing environment takes place in anticipation of cuts and shifts in funding. Even in a relatively early stage of funding uncertainty, agencies were taking steps to cushion the impact of anticipated funding cuts.

1996   By 1996, the strategies and changes introduced earlier continued to be in effect. While there were no significant differences in what the 59 respondent agencies were doing a year later, several shifts were noticeable among the 24 strategies that were offered to respondents as ways of dealing with anticipated changes. In fact, three-quarters of the strategies were reported as currently being used by more agencies than had been reported in 1995. The 1996 findings are contrasted with the 1995 findings of the same cohort of 59 agencies in Table 13.1.

TABLE 13.1. STRATEGIC RESPONSES (n = 59)

Type of Strategy	1995	1996
Protective Strategies		
Providing in-service or other training	85%	86%
Finding ways to serve more clients without adding staff or enlarging programs	81%	86%
Finding ways to provide quality service with fewer staff	78%	71%
Finding ways to help staff handle larger caseloads or more clients	75%	78%
Providing more time-limited services	63%	61%
Finding ways to provide for current clients with fewer programs or services	58%	59%
Increasing use of volunteers	53%	59%
Taking more social work interns	36%	37%
Finding ways to address fewer problems that clients bring to our agency	25%	17%
Shifting funds from other services	21%	29%
Cutting back on benefits/perquisites that were in place	17%	31%
Laying off MSW staff without replacing them	15%	20%
Taking fewer social work interns	14%	20%
Replacing MSW staff with less qualified staff	5%	15%
Change Strategies		
Locating new sources of funding	76%	85%
Adding programs or services	58%	68%
Serving a different client population	36%	46%
Closing down programs or eliminating services	29%	34%
Planning to serve or serving fewer clients	12%	10%
Power Strategies		
Spending more time and resources on activities that prevent public cutbacks or to influence funding allocation decisions.	71%	58%
Collaborating or merging programs with other service providers	59%	68%
Processing Strategies		
Communicating the reasons for changes to staff	92%	93%
Asking staff to suggest ways to deal with changes	88%	88%
Preparing staff for coming changes	86%	92%

The greatest increase in use of strategy reported between 1995 and 1996 was the agency decision to cut back on staff benefits or perquisites that were already in place. In 1996 almost one-third of the agencies reported these cutbacks, whereas in 1995 only 17% reported cutting benefits or perqs. Replacing professional social work (MSW) staff with less qualified staff (5% vs. 15%), a strategy hardly used in 1995—or even cited as an important one at that time—was one of three strategies for which there was a 10% increase in reported use. Laying off social work staff (MSW level) without replacing them was also noted, although it had already been cited as a strategy in 1995, up from 15% to 20%. Increasing the use of volunteers was also more frequently reported (53% vs. 59%). Taken together, the data, albeit not significant, indicate a shift from 1995 to 1996 in ways of adapting which was directed much more on staffing patterns than initially seen in 1995. As a result, the quality of the "same" service can be expected to change or deteriorate.

In contrast to expectations, these administrators did not report that the quality of their services to older people and their families deteriorated (Table 13.2). Over half thought the quality of services remained the same, and over a quarter thought the services improved during this period. In all, 86% of the respondents thought their services had held the line or improved. Moreover, among those agencies serving other client populations in addition to older adults, a third reported that the quality of service to older adults was better than to other populations (Table 13.3). Respondents generally accounted for this by proclaiming their agencies' mission and commitment to older adults. Because of

TABLE 13.2. QUALITY OF SERVICES, 1996 (n = 58)

Given the current constraints in the environment your agency operates in, do you think the quality of your agency's services to older persons has:

Improved	17	29%
Remained the Same	33	57%
Declined	8	14%

TABLE 13.3. COMPARING SERVICES TO OLDER PERSONS WITH
SERVICES TO OTHER POPULATIONS (n = 44)

How would you compare what your agency is doing in regard
to services to older persons with services to other populations
your agency serves?

Better Off	15	34%
About the Same	24	55%
More cut backs	5	11%

this commitment, the agencies found some way to continue providing services. Some agencies also noted that the cuts in services and programs for older adults were generally not as severe as they were for other client populations, and managed care had not yet had a serious effect on the elderly. These findings may explain why fewer administrators reported in 1996 that they were trying to find ways to provide quality services with fewer staff (78% vs. 71%). An alternate explanation of this finding is that by 1996 some agencies had already adapted to operating with fewer staff.

There were, however, indications of modifications in programs and services in 1996. For example, 10% more agencies in 1996 claimed they were serving a different client population as well as adding programs or services. One agency reported adding two new programs and a specialized geriatric inpatient unit to enhance services to the older population. Five percent more agencies reported they were closing down programs or eliminating services. One agency reported they were "going out of business serving older people," and were transferring them to nursing homes and geriatric facilities. Nine percent more agencies reported collaboration or merging programs with other service providers. A crime victims assistance and prevention program for the elderly reported it had expanded into two new neighborhoods where it could collaborate with the police precincts. At the same time, agencies were just as concerned, or slightly more concerned in 1996 as in 1995, with finding ways to serve more clients without adding staff, to help staff handle larger caseloads, and to provide for current clients with fewer services. As one agency noted, "Staff has to be more creative and willing to jump into many different roles."

In addition, in 1996 9% more administrators indicated efforts to locate new sources of funding (76% vs. 85%), and 5% more were trying to shift funds from other services (21% vs. 29%). Some agencies noted that they were successful, which may account for the maintenance of quality services. One senior center, for example, obtained two vans from a grant and would now provide field trips. Another grant enabled a senior center to provide ESL classes.

In contrast, considerably fewer administrators reported they were spending more time and resources on activities to prevent cutbacks or influence funding allocation decisions. Although almost three-quarters of the agencies reported these activities during the time of crisis, a year later, when the crisis had passed, the number reporting these activities dropped to 58%. Yet several respondents noted the absence of an "organized, clear voice in the public policy arena on services for older adults."

Strategies related to processing changes with staff were reported to be widely used in both 1995 and 1996. They were, in fact, the most widely used strategies in both years, an indication of the value agencies placed on involving staff. Because respondents did not elaborate on the ways they involved staff, it is not possible to say if staff had a voice in decision making or problem solving. In any case, staff were experiencing the changes profoundly. For example, one agency reported "there have been no raises, frozen positions, reduced outside conferences for staff, and no signed union contract." In fact, the very strategies that had been thought to be among the most drastic in 1995—laying off MSW staff without replacing them and replacing MSW staff with less qualified staff—were considerably more popular in 1996. Perhaps this should not be surprising since both were being considered in 1995, although by a small percentage of agency respondents.

DISCUSSION AND CONCLUSIONS

Adapting programs and services to changes in funding continues to be a major challenge for agencies and administrators. Although these findings are based on a small and limited study with a select cohort of agencies serving older people and their families in the New York City metropolitan region, the data present additional evidence of the relationship between agencies and their environments as well as the link between agency changes and changes in the funding environment that has been consistently reported in the literature. Agencies in this sample demonstrated that they are meeting the challenge and surviving funding threats. Administrators do not merely stand by waiting for funding cuts. They are dealing with their changing funding environments by selecting strategic responses that allow programs and services to be maintained and modified in a variety of ways. By using a number of strategies, administrators are responding on several fronts and are finding ways to continue serving clients.

Although this was not a study of executive leadership during periods of funding uncertainty, these agency administrators were making decisions and using strategies that determined how their agencies would handle the pending crisis. The findings suggest that they focused upon improving organizational efficiency, service delivery, and their capacity to garner needed resources. These are strategies that constitute downsizing. In contrast to organizational decline, downsizing is intentional, targeted on improvement, adaptation, and adjustment. Downsizing is a strategic and defensive posture taken in order to withstand or adapt to anticipated or actual changes (Freeman & Cameron, 1993). Downsizing invariably affects the size of the workforce, agency structure, and the way programs are delivered and who will be served. While these agencies used downsizing to adapt to environmental conditions, they did not appear to use these periods to reexamine their agency purpose or make fundamental changes in programs and services.

A unique aspect of this study is that it provides a picture of agencies adapting at two points in time: first, as they anticipated funding cuts in 1995; and second, after the uncertainty about impending cuts had passed and the cuts did not materialize in 1996. For this sample of agencies serving older persons, the strategic responses first used continued into the second year even though agencies were no longer being threatened by loss of funding. Agencies used the same strategies, and most strategies were being used by more agencies in 1996 than in 1995. The study therefore demonstrated that just as reduced financial support can have an impact upon the services delivered, the threat of funding cuts can also trigger strategic responses that influence agencies' programs and services. Thus it is not necessary to wait for actual funding cuts and shifts to see the impact of a changing funding environment on agencies.

It is interesting to observe that the only strategy that substantially dropped in 1996 from 1995 was "Spending more time and resources on activities that prevent public cutbacks or to influence funding allocation decisions." It is well accepted that agencies today need to engage in advocacy and that administrators need to engage in political activities given that funders' allocation of resources control agencies and service delivery (Gibelman & Kraft, 1996; Heimovics, Herman, & Coughlin, 1993). While the agencies in this study may be preoccupied with managing their services day to day, locating funds, and modifying programs, the failure to pursue advocacy efforts to prevent budget cuts and reductions in programs and services may be shortsighted, especially since pressures on agencies from social, economic, and political factors in the environment are likely to continue (Gibelman & Kraft, 1996).

It is also interesting to see that locating new sources of funding became even more important to agencies by 1996. This study did not examine how the agencies managed their funding relations and what they actually did to secure additional funding. Other studies have shown the importance of access to flexible funding, alternative funding streams, and funding reserves to cushion against sharp funding jolts (Gronbjerg, 1992). There were in fact successes among these agencies in the acquisition of new funding. Examples of foundation grants, albeit considered small by the agencies, nevertheless offered opportunities to enhance their services. Even the existence of agency endowments, although relatively rare, helped. However, there was a clear impression that additional funds did not replace those that were lost but rather were used for alternative programs or services.

This study does not capture the actual link between agency changes and changes in the funding environment. It is not possible to determine, for example, if any of the changes reported here were being considered beforehand. Nor do we know if these changes were precipitated by factors other than economic uncertainty. Agency changes can result from visionary leadership, shifts in community or client demographics and needs, or an increase in demand for services. In fact, there is a growing interest in the point of view that threats from a changing environment offer opportunities for organizational changes that might not otherwise have been possible. Similarly, some argue that organizational decline may not inhibit but instead stimulates adaptation and changes in programs and services (McKinley, 1993). More research is needed to tease out the subtleties of the agency-environment relationship and the role played by other factors. As managers in human service agencies continue to find it necessary to adapt to changes in their organizations' environments and cope with shifting priorities, pressures, and demands, the need to better understand the nature of the relationship between organizations and their environments grows.

REFERENCES

Aldrich, H. E., & Pfeffer, J. (1976). Environments of organizations. In A. Inkeles, J. Coleman, & N. Smelser (Eds.), *Annual review of sociology* (Vol. 2, pp. 79–105). Palo Alto: Annual Reviews.

Allen, M. (1998, June 22). Small programs fall victim to budget battle in city hall. *New York Times,* p. B7.

Alperin, D. E. (1992). Family service agencies: Responding to change in a conservative environment. *Families in Society, 73*(1), 32–39.

Austin, M. J. (1984). Managing cutbacks in the 1980s. *Social Work, 29*(5), 428–434.

Bailey, D., & Koney, K. M. (1996). Interorganizational community-based collaboratives: A strategic response to shape the social work agenda. *Social Work, 41*(6), 602–611.

Bargal, D., Back, A., & Ariav, P. (1992). Occupational social work and prolonged job insecurity in a declining organization. *Administration in Social Work, 16*(1), 55–67.

Barringer, F. (1992, November 20). United Way says slump and scandal are bringing sharp dip in donations. *New York Times,* p. A14.

Bass, G. D. (1994, December 13). Gingrich's "contract" would devastate charities. *Chronicle of Philanthropy,* pp. 42–43.

Bernard, S. E. (1983). *Coping with cutbacks.* Unpublished manuscript, University of Michigan.

Bombyk, M. J., & Chernesky, R. H. (1985). Conventional cutback leadership and the quality of the workplace: Is beta better? *Administration in Social Work, 9*(3), 47–56.

Cameron, K. S., Kim, M. U., & Whetten, D. A. (1987). Organizational effects of decline and turbulence. *Administrative Science Quarterly, 32,* 222–240.

Cameron, K. S., Sutton, R. I., & Whetten, D. A. (Eds.). (1988). *Readings in organizational decline: Frameworks, research, and prescriptions.* Cambridge, MA: Ballinger.

Caravajal, D. (1995, January 22). Vying for patients, hospitals think location, location. *New York Times,* pp. B1, B26.

Chernesky, R. H., & Gutheil, I. A. (1994). Foundation grantmaking in the 1980's: How three human service fields fared. *Journal of Sociology and Social Welfare, 21*(2), 153–160.

Cnaan, R. A. (1995). Purchasing of services contracting: A symbiosis of voluntary organizations, government, and clients. *Journal of Health and Human Services Administration, 18*(1), 104–128.

DePalma, A. (1991, December 4). Can Yale, with budget troubles, still be great? *New York Times,* p. B16.

DePalma, A. (1992, May 25). Short of money, Columbia U. weighs how best to change. *New York Times,* pp. A1, A25.

DiGiulio, J. F. (1983). Funding and the change process in family service agencies. *Social Casework, 64*(8), 466–472.

Eadie, D. C. (1998). Building the capacity to lead innovation. In R. L. Edwards, J. A. Yankey, & M. A. Altpeter (Eds.), *Skills for effective management of nonprofit organizations* (pp. 27–44). Washington, DC: NASW Press.

Edwards, R. L., & Austin, D. M. (1991). Managing effectively in an environment of competing values. In R. L. Edwards & J. A. Yankey (Eds.), *Skills for effective human services management* (pp. 5–22). Washington, DC: NASW Press.

Edwards, R. L., Cooke, P. W., & Reid, P. N. (1996). Social work management in an era of diminishing federal responsibility. *Social Work, 41*(5), 468–479

Edwards, R. L., Lebold, D. A., & Yankey, J. A. (1998). Managing organizational decline. In R. L. Edwards, J. A. Yankey, & M. A. Altpeter (Eds.), *Skills for effective management of nonprofit organizations* (pp. 279–300). Washington, DC: NASW Press.

Freeman, S. J., & Cameron, K. S. (1993). Organizational downsizing: A convergence and reorientation framework. *Organization Science, 4*(1), 10–29.

Freudenheim, M. (1996, February 5). Charities aiding poor fear loss of government subsidies. *New York Times*, p. B8.

Friesen, B., & Frey, G. (1983). Managing organizational decline. Emerging issues for administration. *Administration in Social Work, 7*(3/4), 33–41.

Gibelman, M. (1990). National voluntary health agencies in an era of change: Experiences and adaptations. *Administration in Social Work, 14*(3), 17–32.

Gibelman, M. (1996). Contracting for social services: Boom or bust for the voluntary sector? *Journal of Health and Human Services Administration, 19*(1), 26–41.

Gibelman, M., & Kraft, S. (1996). Advocacy as a core agency program: Planning considerations for voluntary human service agencies. *Administration in Social Work, 20*(4), 43–59.

Gingrich, N., Armey, D., & the House Republicans. (1994). *Contract With America*. Washington, DC: U.S. House of Representatives.

Ginsberg, L. (1995). Concepts of new management. In L. Ginsberg & P. R. Keys (Eds.), *New management in human services* (pp. 1–37). Washington, DC: NASW Press.

Gronbjerg, K. A. (1992). Nonprofit human service organizations: Funding strategies and patterns of adaptation. In Y. Hasenfeld (Ed.), *Human services as complex organizations* (pp. 73–97). Newbury Park, CA: Sage.

Gutheil, I., & Chernesky, R. H. (1998). The changing times and agencies serving older persons: Early responses to anticipated funding reductions. *Journal of Gerontological Social Work, 29*(4), 69–84.

Hall, R. H. (1996). *Organizations: Structures, processes, and outcomes.* Englewood Cliffs, NJ: Prentice Hall.

Hasenfeld, Y. (1983). *Human service organizations.* Englewood Cliffs, NJ: Prentice-Hall.

Heimovics, R. D., Herman, R. D., & Couglin, C. L. J. (1993). Executive leadership and resource dependence in nonprofit organizations: A frame analysis. *Public Administration Review, 53*(5), 419–427.

Heimovics, R. D., Herman, R. D., & Jurkiewicz, C. L. (1993). The political dimension of effective nonprofit executive leadership. *Nonprofit Management and Leadership, 5*(3), 233–248.

Jay, S. (1996, February 23). Charities worry as donations fade at the finish. *New York Times,* p. B2.

Jerrel, J. M., & Larson, J. K. (1984). Policy shifts and organizational adaptation: A review of current developments. *Community Mental Health Journal, 24*(4), 282–293.

Johnston, D. C. (1998, July 1). Donations rise, ending United Way slump. *New York Times,* p. B4.

Kettner, P. M., & Martin, L. L. (1996). The impact of declining resources and purchase of service contracting on private, nonprofit agencies. *Administration in Social Work, 20*(3), 21–38.

Kramer, R., & Grossman, B. (1987). Contracting for social services: Process management and resource dependencies. *Social Service Review, 61*(1), 33–55.

Lambert, B. (1990, May 6). AIDS groups feel the fiscal crisis. *New York Times,* p. B5.

Lauffer, A. (1997). *Grants, etc.* Thousand Oaks, CA: Sage.

Ludwig, D. (1993). Adapting to a declining environment: Lessons from a religious order. *Organization Science, 4*(1), 41–56.

McKinley, W. (1993). Organizational decline and adaptation: Theoretical controversies. *Organization Science, 4*(1), 1–9.

McMurtry, S. L., Netting, P. E., & Kettner, P. M. (1990). Critical inputs and strategic choice in non-profit human service organizations. *Administration in Social Work, 14*(3), 67–82.

Meier, J. (1997). *Winners and losers: Impact of budget changes on social services and on community districts in New York City, 1993–1996.* New York: Arete Corporation.

Menefee, D. (1997). Strategic administration of nonprofit human service organizations: A model for executive success in turbulent times. *Administration in Social Work, 21*(2), 1–19.

Menefee, D. T., & Thompson, J. J. (1994). Identifying and comparing competencies for social work management: A practice-driven approach. *Administration in Social Work, 18*(3), 1–26.

Meyer, A. D. (1982). Adapting to environmental jolts. *Administrative Science Quarterly, 27,* 515–537.

Mordock, J. (1989). Organizational adaptation to policy and funding shifts. *Child Welfare, 68*(4), 589–601.

Myrtle, R. C., Wilber, K. H., DeJong, F. J. (1997). Improving service delivery: Provider perspectives on building community-based systems of care. *Journal of Health and Human Services Administration, 20*(2), 197–216.

Pelton, E. D., & Baznik, R. E. (1998). Managing public policy advocacy and government relations. In R. L. Edwards, J. A. Yankey, & M. A. Altpeter (Eds.), *Skills for effective management of nonprofit organizations* (pp. 115–148). Washington, DC: NASW Press.

Perlmutter, F. D., & Adams, C. T. (1990). The voluntary sector and for-profit ventures: The transformation of American social welfare? *Administration in Social Work, 14*(1), 1–13.

Pfeffer, J., & Salancik, G. R. (1978). *The external control of organizations: A resource-dependence perspective.* New York: Harper & Row.

Raber, M. (1996). Downsizing of the nation's labor force and a needed social work response. *Administration in Social Work, 20*(1), 47–58.

Salamon, L. M. (1992). *America's nonprofit sector.* New York: The Foundation Center.

Schmid, H. (1992a). Executive leadership in human service organizations. In Y. Hasenfeld (Ed.), *Human services as complex organizations* (pp. 98–117). Newbury Park, CA: Sage.

Schmid, H. (1992b). Strategic and structural change in human service organizations: The role of the environment. *Administration in Social Work, 16*(3/4), 167–186.

Seelye, K. Q. (1998, June 24). Panel approves deep cuts in programs championed by Clinton. *New York Times,* p. A17.

Spayd, L. (1992, December 12). Pledges to area United Way drop for first time ever. *Washington Post,* pp. B1, B5.

Strom-Gottfried, K. (1997). The implications of managed care for social work education. *Journal of Social Work Education, 33*(1), 7–18.

Teltsch, K. (1991, December 29). Government's cuts to private groups threaten the charities of last resort. *New York Times*, p. A24.

Videka-Sherman, L., & Viggiani, P. (1996). The impact of federal policy changes on children: Research needs for the future. *Social Work, 41*(6), 594–600.

Weatherly, R. (1984). Approaches to cutback management. In F. D. Perlmutter (Ed.), *Human services at risk* (pp. 39–56). Lexington, MA: Lexington Books.

Weiss, L. (1991, October 2). With deficits looming, Syracuse University considers major cuts. *New York Times*, p. B3.

Wernert, S. P. (1994). A case study of adaptation in a nonprofit human service organization. *Journal of Community Practice, 1*(3), 93–112.

Whetten, D. A. (1988). The organizational growth and decline process. In K. S. Cameron, R. I. Sutton, & D. A. Whetten (Eds.), *Readings in organizational decline: Frameworks, research, and prescriptions* (pp. 27–44). Cambridge, MA: Ballinger.

14

Sustaining Strong Communities in a World of Devolution: Empowerment-Based Social Services in Housing Settings

Carol S. Cohen, DSW, Michael H. Phillips, DSW, Manuel A. Mendez, MSW, and Rosemary Ordonez, BA

INTRODUCTION

OVER 65 YEARS AGO, Mary Richmond suggested that the linkage of housing and social service should be a professional imperative in building strong communities: "Housing reform affects health, morals, economic efficiency, child-nurture, and the foundations of the family. If we are genuinely interested in these we must be interested in it" (1930, p. 325). Today, the experiences of housing developments that provide social services, such as Phipps Houses in the South Bronx, continue to bear out the wisdom of these words. Programs such as these recognize that housing is not just bricks and mortar, but also includes a sense of security and community.

Over time, the way housing and social services are integrated has changed. The inclusion of a wide range of services as an aspect of housing flourished during the late 1930s (Power, 1979) and 1960s (Bingham & Kirkpatrick, 1975), periods that saw broad social changes and upheavals. However, in times of relative social calm, society becomes more conservative, with a concomitant reduction of services.

Recent years have brought large-scale changes in the lives of residents of the South Bronx and other struggling communities in the United States, while the country as a whole has experienced relative prosperity. A growing focus on conservative political themes has brought welfare reform, coupled with cutbacks both in municipal services and in the funding of private social service agencies. While the service and funding changes have not been as dramatic as those created by the Great Depression, they have fallen disproportionately on impoverished communities. In this way, devolution may be a crisis that raises serious questions about how a viable community can be sustained in the South Bronx and other vulnerable neighborhoods.

STUDY OF HOUSING AND SOCIAL SERVICE INTEGRATION

The overall focus of this chapter is the dynamic relationship between social work practice and the sociopolitical environment in housing settings. In examining this linkage, we draw from our study of the work of Phipps Houses, the largest and oldest developer of not-for-profit housing in New York City. In undertaking this task, we are building on the 1996 analysis of two Phipps Houses sites, both in the South Bronx (Phillips & Cohen, 1997), which led to our initial development of principles to guide community-sustaining practice in housing settings (Cohen & Phillips, 1997). We returned to the same neighborhood in 1998 to explore the degree to which the principles continue to apply to social work practice and serve as guidelines for program development in other venues. Using the Phipps Houses as a case study, the question we wish to discuss in this chapter is: How has the devolution of the welfare state in the United States changed the manner in which social services need to be conceptualized and delivered in housing settings?

In 1996, two of this chapter's authors (Phillips & Cohen, 1997) traced the history of two housing developments (Mapes Court and Crotona Park West) that had been open for approximately 2 years. Through a process of interviewing staff, reading tenant service records, and interviewing a random sample of 145 tenants (approximately 50%), the study explored the tenants' sense of community and family well-being and sought to understand the impact of the array of social services integrated with the low- and moderate-income housing. Since that time, social services continue to be provided through an independent entity, Phipps Community Development Corporation (CDC). The Phipps CDC mission, to build and sustain community, focuses on three core service areas: family assistance, community organizing, and services to children and youth. Activities include advocacy, support groups. counseling, information, referral, and crisis intervention.

In 1996, 85% of tenant respondents reported a strong sense of security and stability in their housing, since many had moved frequently, spent time "doubled up" with other families, or had experienced living in shelters. Tenants overwhelmingly identified themselves as either African American (41%) or Latino (53%). Forty-three percent of the tenants received public assistance benefits, and 58% had employment income. This division, however, does not reflect the frequent shift of families back and forth from employment income to welfare benefits.

While 50% of the tenants had at least some college experience, 25% were without a high school diploma. Among the 119 families with children, 76% were headed by single women. The tenants studied had high aspirations and credited residence at Phipps Houses with fostering their motivation to achieve their dreams. Twenty-eight percent said that living in Phipps increased their commitment to education, and 17% indicated that it increased their motivation to better their lives and become more independent.

The study identified the range of Phipps CDC services and their utilization by tenants. Eighty-four percent used at least one of the services provided, or arranged for, by Phipps CDC. The most common areas of service were around rent or tenant behavior issues, employment and training, education, financial assistance, health and mental health referral, and family relationships.

Principles for Community-Building Practice in Housing Settings

The Phipps Houses/Fordham University Study in 1996 served as the basis for the identification of the following six principles for community-building practice:

1. The task of community building is constantly evolving and should be continually evaluated.
2. Housing and social work services should be integrated and provided to tenants in distressed communities.
3. Staff of social work programs in housing settings should understand and subscribe to a collective vision of the program's purpose.
4. Efforts should be made to provide services on-site.
5. Social work programs in housing settings should maintain a dual focus upon the individual family and the collective.
6. Community development activities should be extended to the surrounding community and not be limited to the building alone.

In 1998, welfare reform and other policy initiatives affecting poor people had been in place for 2 years, prompting our interest in exploring how these changes had affected the setting and whether the previously identified principles continued to apply. We met with staff and administrators of Phipps CDC from both sites to discuss changes they had seen among families in the last 2 years, as well as how the program had responded to these changes. In reviewing the principles during our return visits in 1998, we found that all of the initial six principles remained highly applicable and useful in guiding social work practice in housing settings. However, we found that the addition of the following two principles needed articulation in the light of changes brought on by the devolution of human services in the last 2 years:

7. Engagement of clients must take place in a context of needs identified within the client—those needs may be identified by tenants, workers, or management.
8. Organizations should cultivate the institutional flexibility and capacity to pursue multiple points of intervention in order to address the needs of tenants.

On further reflection, it became apparent that these new principles had been in operation during our earlier visit, but in a time of relative calm they had not been as important to community building. This experience suggests that the relative weights given to each of the principles will change over time in relation to changes in the larger social context.

This chapter will now focus on the elaboration and illustration of all eight principles in current practice. We will examine why the original six principles are still applicable and how their implementation has been modified in recent times in response to the devolution that is currently affecting poor communities. We will also provide examples of how all of the principles are implemented in practice in order to expand their application in other programs.

1. *The task of community building is constantly evolving and should be continually evaluated.* It has been recognized that social services are critical in maintaining stable and secure housing. Thus, social services should not be seen as "frills," or auxiliary activities, incidental to the main purpose of providing housing, but as a mechanism leading to the building of community, tenant self-determination, and the protection of the housing asset. This principle addresses the need for social service providers to continually assess the buildings' and the community's climate and to adjust service delivery strategies to meet new challenges. In our review we found several changes to which Phipps CDC responded.

A change that is clearly tied to devolution has been the impact of the reconstituted public assistance system and regulations. Previously, we had seen the movement of tenants in and out of the labor market, using public assistance as their safety net. We had also seen families become involved in education and then drop out, feeling that school responsibilities were too great a burden with child care and/or work responsibilities. With the new demand that persons on public assistance take jobs chosen by the city, many residents on public assistance reevaluated their situation. Many residents chose to close their public assistance cases and to seek employment on their own rather than accept the city's training opportunities, which they felt were of little or no value.

While this voluntary movement from welfare to work may at first appear to validate the cynical view that people receiving public assistance "could work if they wanted to," it is important to realize that the residents in Phipps Houses were able to attempt to find their own employment because they were not in the same restrictive situation as most other public assistance recipients. Many Phipps Houses tenants receive a Section 8 housing subsidy, enabling them to limit their rent to not more than one-third of their family's income.

All Phipps tenants, including those who were not receiving a subsidy, knew it was the management's policy to work with families to resolve rent arrears rather then moving immediately to eviction. In fact, Phipps Houses responded to tenants' increased concerns about their ability to pay their rent by developing a counseling system that emphasized contracts to resolve rent arrears rather than instituting legal avenues of collection or removal. Residents also knew that staff had always supported work efforts. Workers helped residents see the new work requirements in a positive light and to realize that getting a job was in their family's best interest in the long run. The staff also responded by making families aware of what services were still available to working parents.

It is important to realize that not all families took the option to seek their own employment. Some did go into training, and at least one was able to develop her training into a real job with a city agency. There have also been families who have not been able to adjust to the new circumstances. In the last 2 years, the staff has had to help more families seek emergency food and other necessities. While these are a minority, there is no doubt that there are families who are significantly worse off now. Even with the services that Phipps CDC staff have been able to provide, there are residents who, due to their personal functioning and the lack of flexibility of Work Experience Program regulations, are unable to meet the demands of welfare reform. Their situation promises to become even more dire in the future and will require increased worker involvement. Thus, Phipps Houses and other organizations are challenged to fulfill the tenets of distributive justice (Rawls, 1971) and create opportunities for clients least able to access services.

The issue of child care looms large when families are required to work. While the city has said it will pay for child care, this promise has turned out to be extremely difficult to fulfill. During our study, families legitimately indicated concern about the danger of crime and violence in the neighborhood, making the case for quality child care even more compelling. From the time tenants moved into the buildings, Phipps Houses has responded to this concern by providing security service at the building, and has installed enhanced intercom systems during the last 2 years. Security systems notwithstanding, residents reported in 1996 that they felt they needed to be close to home to mitigate the danger to their children. This has been a continuing concern, illustrated by one woman's recently giving up her job because her child was getting into difficulty without her supervision. Once again, this choice was only possible because she lived in Phipps Houses.

Three interesting developments have occurred in response to this concern for child care. First, some tenants responded to this need by developing their own family day care program in their apartment rather then seek employment in the community. Once again, being at Phipps was critical. Phipps CDC staff facilitated tenants' contact with licensing authorities and arranged for their training as child care providers. Second, Phipps CDC extended its collaboration with other on-site day care providers. Third, the youth center managed by Phipps CDC expanded the snack program and began serving a hot meal to all participants.

In a previous article (Cohen & Phillips, 1997), we made the point that strong communities depend to some extent upon the continued involvement of a critical mass of stable, concerned community residents. At that time, about 40% of tenants reported that they expected to have moved from the city, to their own home, or to another neighborhood within the city in the next 5 years. Two years later, with a turnover rate of approximately 25%, there was indeed evidence that some families had voluntarily moved elsewhere, some even moving out of the city. In their place, a substantial number of African immigrants have moved into the buildings, and these now comprise 11% of the population at Crotona Park West. This has led to a need for staff to work with longtime residents, who were concerned about this trend, and to overcome cultural barriers that might lead to divisions within the building.

In response to demographic changes, the on-site health center found it necessary to hire new staff who can provide services to persons speaking a different language and coming from a different culture. The center has done extensive outreach, and has enrolled 501 of the 563 Phipps families of Crotona Park West in the family medical practice. On-site services include health care to children of low-income families through New York State's initiative to improve the children's well-being.

Differences in culture have also been reflected in stricter child-rearing patterns and different perceptions of women's roles in African immigrant families. In particular, these beliefs came to the attention of Phipps CDC through reports of spousal abuse. In reaching out to African families, Phipps CDC staff noted that these families were more likely to view Phipps Houses merely as a place to live, rather than as a community to join. This perception made initial engagement more difficult, particularly when initiated following a report of family violence. Language differences have been another obstacle, though some staff have been using telephone company translation services to communicate with residents who do not speak English or Spanish. The new cultural mix in the buildings has led Phipps CDC to recognize the need to be more active in reaching out to newly arrived families in order to help them become part of the community-building enterprise.

2. *Housing and social work services should be integrated and provided to tenants in distressed communities.* Phipps Houses and similar programs have demonstrated the efficacy of integrated service delivery to families (Chaskin, Joseph, & Chipenda-Dansokho, 1997). Social services, with the support of housing management, can provide a stabilizing force needed to keep communities strong. This principle addresses how the social worker, as the pivotal person in the service delivery system, draws from a repertoire of roles and skills. In our earlier study, the social worker was identified as responding in a holistic way to both the housing and the larger community within which the client resides through the thoughtful use of self in a variety of ways. The primary roles identified in the research were workers serving as educators, mediators, and advocates. The educator function was to help tenants understand the environments in which they operated; the mediator function was to help clients establish a common purpose with people in their environment; and the advocate function was to help clients obtain those services to which they were entitled. Given the rapid changes in

services brought about by devolution, the distribution of workers' roles has shifted. Workers now need to spend far more time
educating clients on what is available and showing them how to
represent themselves in such a way as to be eligible for services.
As has been noted in relation to welfare reform, staff are active
in helping the tenants reframe the new demands so that they
can see them in terms of a newly opened window rather than a
locked gate.

While the roles of mediator and advocate remain, their relative importance have been modified within the new context of
social regression of support services that can be obtained from
the community for the tenants. As workers talked about their
experiences over the past 2 years, it became clear that the mediator function has become less useful in an environment in which
the opportunities for matching clients with services are shrinking. Workers can no longer simply facilitate a match between
clients and providers, but must take a partisan, advocacy approach on behalf of clients. There appears to be increasing resistance on the part of remaining service providers to facilitate the
application process, as evidenced by a significant increase in the
difficulties experienced by workers when they attempt to access
existing services for their clients. Workers reported that the
phones of social agencies were constantly busy. When they were
actually able to reach a worker, they detected a distinct reluctance to provide information about the service unless they had
a prior relationship. This means that staff need to spend more of
their time keeping up with the myriad changes in services and
policies so that they know what they can demand for their clients.

The advocacy function has become even more vital in an atmosphere of scarcity, where clients compete for services. Not
only is the worker's role as advocate for individual clients critical to each family's survival, but the need for workers' macro-
level advocacy to change policies has been increased. By
strengthening the community-wide advocacy function, workers
have the opportunity to join with tenants in a collaborative enterprise. This has become increasingly important in fostering a consciousness of "we" in the face of social policies that further
divide the "haves" from the "have-nots." Without this sense of

"we"-ness there will be less of a sense of security. As such, social workers' tasks go beyond the individual case to advocacy for increased services such as child care and improved educational programs.

3. *Staff of social work programs in housing settings should understand and subscribe to a collective vision of the program's purpose.* During our 1996 study, one CDC worker said, "From custodian to president, we all have a part in making it work." This reflected staff recognition that all staff were part of the same vision of building a strong community within which families could flourish. Common to all efforts was a belief in the strength of families. As such, staff do not see the provision of services as a way of making up for residents' deficits, but rather as ways of enhancing client strengths. This value stance served the staff well in the time of devolution. They were able to respond in ways that helped residents see what was positive in the demand for work while assisting tenants in obtaining available benefits. The effort in relation to welfare reform paralleled their stance regarding rent arrears, in which rent problems were seen as opportunity to help families deal with their problems in a better way.

There is a recognition that services are only as good as residents' ability to use them. While previously much of what was addressed by workers came up in the normal course of interaction with clients, this is no longer the case with clients who do not routinely interact with workers due to their work schedules. As noted, residents are less likely to be on-site during the day. Staff have responded by instituting night hours, but residents are often pressed for time when they return from work. Nonetheless, one worker "leaves the shade up" in her office so residents will know she is there and they can stop in to chat. Possibly because of Phipps social workers' previous history of helping residents, workers are still contacted for help, but now the help is not likely to be provided face-to-face. At best it is provided through phone contacts between worker and resident. Except in emergencies, an even more frequent mode of communication is the answering machine. This means that the opportunity to extensively prepare clients on a face-to-face basis for contacts with service agencies is less likely to take place. Only the name of the contact can be provided. Unfortunately, some of the educating and enabling function the social worker could provide is now diminished, even though this role is seen as critical.

Further, now the focus is less on how to help clients achieve their goals than upon helping residents fit into the highly proscribed, and often mandated, categorical service. In this new environment it is even more important that agency staff subscribe to a unified and positive message so that the resident experiences from all staff that sense of belief in the capacity of the residents.

4. *Efforts should be made to provide services on-site.* The Phipps Houses experience indicated that the best-used services are those provided in the tenants' own buildings, or as nearby as possible. This principle evolved out of a recognition that many families needed to have the security of taking risks on their own turf before they were able to effectively leave their home area and branch out. Further, it provided a sense that this was "our" program, not one imposed upon us. This sense was further reinforced by programs being developed out of identified resident needs. Thus, many Phipps CDC services were not only "community based," but also "community centered" in that they existed out of community need and operated with residents' collaboration (Ewalt, Freeman, & Poole, 1998).

With devolution it has been increasingly difficult to develop on-site services, although this continues to be a priority. Further, some on-site services have had to be closed because of the time constraints faced by residents. For example, due to the increased number of working parents, it was necessary to close the in-home, daytime program where staff and parents engaged in activities with their children. On the other hand, Phipps has extended its teen and after-school program and has launched an early-evening congregate program for children and parents to promote family literacy.

These programs have gone a long way toward helping working parents feel that their children are in a secure and supportive environment. Efforts have also been made to link residents with job training and employment opportunities in the community, continuing the tradition of enabling residents to feel that the local program is endorsed by the Phipps community. What has become clear is that on-site services provide a sense of security that enables residents to safely move beyond the security of the setting. This continues to be true, though the nature of the services being used has changed.

5. *Social work programs in housing settings should maintain a dual focus upon the individual family and the collective.* A focus on strengthening both individual resident families and building-wide communities must exist. This dual focus recognizes that even strong families deteriorate under the pressures of a chaotic environment. The residents must have the sense that they are a collective. For this reason, there is a concern that the facility be well maintained, and residents have been encouraged to report problems they see and to participate in their solution. The development of tenant councils and building meetings was a major aspect of this dual focus. Unfortunately, with the increasing numbers of residents employed, attendance at these regular meetings has declined.

It may also be possible that traditional tenant associations have a natural ebb and flow in their membership as residents' interests and concerns fluctuate. At this point, tenants appear generally satisfied with management policies, and most feel connected with others in the community. The need for a forum to air grievances and an official channel to resolve differences appears less immediate, resulting in lower attendance and interest. Ironically, it may be that fewer tenant association meetings contribute to increased dissatisfaction and renewed calls for meetings. Therefore, tenant associations have not been abandoned at Phipps Houses, but there has been a search for alternate community-building activities. The formation of the Crotona Park Conservancy is an example of a new collective that has the potential to bring tenants together (with other area residents and leaders) around the adjacent park space and quality-of-life issues of mutual concern. Special parties, as well as recognition days where tenants who have been of service to others and tenants who have obtained their GED are recognized, also continue to bring tenants together as a community.

With fewer persons at building meetings, staff working on individual problems have needed to think about how one family's problem may be reflected among the larger building community. With fewer resources, such problems have been less likely than before devolution to be responded to by new programming. The response in a time of scarcity has been to modify existing programming to meet the new need. Examples have included the hiring of translators at the health center to address the needs of the immigrant population, and the changing of social worker and rental agent schedules so they are available one night a week. Similarly, as it became clear that working residents had an increased interest in and commitment to the educational progress of their children, modifications were made to the youth program so that it had a more explicit educational focus. For example, youth center staff are working with the local principal to prepare children for the citywide achievement tests.

6. *Community development activities should be extended to the surrounding community and not be not be limited to the building alone.* Changes in social provisions (such as changes in public assistance and Section 8 funding) can make a big difference in the lives of the tenants in marginal neighborhoods. Therefore, building-based social service efforts must maintain a dual focus on individual support and advocacy for larger community changes. This requires a vision of services that recognizes their integrated nature as well as the role of staff on both the individual and community change level.

The 1996 study made clear that the interests of tenants go beyond their building. The safety of the neighborhood streets, the quality of the schools their children attend, and the availability of jobs are all larger issues that directly affect the residents' lives. As workers have helped individuals obtain employment and develop self-employment opportunities, they have always been conscious of the need to address issue of employment opportunity in the larger community. Phipps CDC has a history of providing services to non-tenants. Whether it is the fact that individuals being employed during the day leave a building empty, making it more vulnerable to theft, or the fact that the Phipps community uses more of the services Phipps can provide, there are now less services for outsiders.

Thus, devolution has increased tensions between the smaller unit and the larger unit. Just as the individual cannot stand apart from the housing community, so too the housing complex cannot stand apart from the larger community. Phipps staff recognize this and attempt to allocate some of their diminished time and resources to community work. Without such activity, they will not be able to make the contacts that will provide access for their residents.

The scarcity of devolution is a subtle destructive force thwarting attempts to create change in the larger community by pitting groups against each other for limited resources. In response, Phipps Houses has sought opportunities to engage the larger community. Some of that involves allowing residents of the city-run buildings sandwiched between the Phipps building to attend the Phipps Christmas party out of a recognition that if they are not there, some of their kids will not have any Christmas gifts. This also serves to make the block, not just the Phipps building, a community. Similarly, one-quarter of the children in the day camp program were not the children of tenants. Phipps staff has also spearheaded a community-wide clean-up day at which residents join other members of the community in cleaning up a local park. In this effort, Phipps took the lead in obtaining the necessary materials. The building community also worked together to collect food for needy families for Thanksgiving.

Devolution appears to have made such efforts less related to bringing services that all members of the community can use, and more devoted to the types of activities that help community residents interact with each other. Such activities can build a climate of trust and bring community residents closer together. Eventually, it may be possible to use that sense of togetherness for larger community change efforts.

An interesting development that shows a connection between the individual and the larger context is in the area of education. Contrary to our belief that employment requirements would lead to fewer residents' going to school, an increased number of working residents are also going to school. Residents report that they are going on with their education because they need more education to advance in the workplace. While previously they expressed this view and indicated a commitment to education, fewer acted upon this commitment. There is an increased involvement both in finishing high school and in continuing with college. It is too early to tell whether working parents will be able to meet the multiple responsibilities of education, child care, and employment.

7. *Engagement of clients must take place in a context of needs identified within the client—those needs may be identified by tenants, workers, or management.* The Phipps CDC staff have always cultivated relationships with maintenance persons, building managers, security officers, and others in order to open channels of communication about residents who were in need of service. Until devolution, this communication was based on daily face-to-face contact between these people and tenants. With the increasing number of residents who are working and the immigrant population who see the building as housing, not as a community, workers must a use range of opportunities to establish contact with families. Community-oriented activities (especially those taking place on Saturday and after the supper hour) and the intake interviews conducted when the family is accepted into the building are now major vehicles for establishing a non-problem-focused relationship with clients. In setting up community activities, workers had been able to depend upon residents to take major responsibility for planning and implementation. Increasingly, this has become the responsibility of the social service staff if the event is to happen.

In a time when more poor people are in engaged in work activities during the day, there are even fewer eyes and ears to provide security to an area. However, in cases where social services are attached to housing, more can be done to strengthen the links between persons who remain. At Phipps Houses, the security staff continues to keep workers in touch with difficulties in the building so that they can be addressed. Furthermore, the development of the teen program at Phipps included a conscious recognition that teens could be of help to other members of the community.

With devolution, the teen program provides a safe haven for an increasing number of teens, despite the fact that increasing numbers of children are now taking jobs to help their families survive. The program serves as a link between staff and parents. It increases parents' sense of security that their children are being well cared for. Since the program is on-site, residents know the staff and the program's location. Neighborhood residents use Phipps CDC staff assigned to the teen program as a conduit to keep parents informed if a child is going astray or having difficulty. In fact, the parent who had to stop work to address her child's problems was first informed of the child's troubling behavior by the youth worker. Thus, the connection between social services and housing is even more important in a time of devolution.

Another issue resulting from the increase in the number of working residents is in the area of helping families address child care needs. Increasingly, staff are asked to "watch out" for children who are in the neighborhood when parents need to work. While the on-site child care facility has a waiting list of 50 children, workers are active in helping families connect with each other to develop cooperative child care arrangements. Despite this, there is a recognition that increasing numbers of children are at home alone. It is around such emergent needs that Phipps CDC develops its contacts with residents and structures its programming.

The difficulties staff face have been in obtaining scarce resources for residents and finding a time when they can get together with residents to plan initiatives to meet their needs. This means that the intercessions with clients are now more on a crisis basis and are more focused on solving problems. The constraints on residents' time limit their opportunity to work with staff on thinking through goals and making plans to achieve them.

8. *Organizations should cultivate the institutional flexibility and capacity to pursue multiple points of intervention in order to address the needs of tenants.* In asking how Phipps Houses has been able to meet the continuing needs of its residents in this time of scarcity, we discovered this final principle. Phipps CDC has never restricted itself to address only the needs of the particular tenants in residence. It has always seen current tenants' needs in a larger, community-wide context. Recognizing the broader sphere, Phipps CDC has always worked on multiple levels. None of the programming that currently exists would be there if there had not been a clear vision supported by the capacity to write grant proposals. Further, the ability to build coalitions and

network, to lobby and advocate, and to utilize skills in working with groups has been invaluable to Phipps CDC's ability to bring to Phipps Houses the resource base it enjoys.

In developing neighborhood coalitions and in working with outside agencies, Phipps Houses has provided consultation and guidance to other agencies in programming and proposal writing. Out of this willingness to provide services to others, Phipps Houses has built up a reservoir of goodwill that can be drawn upon in this time of scarcity. The many boards on which Phipps's administrators sit are another aspect of being able to survive in a time of scarcity. Yet if this was the exclusive focus of Phipps Houses, they would not be meeting the very real needs of some of their residents for social support and counseling. It is the capacity to operate on multiple levels that has enabled Phipps to survive—they have consciously developed in staff a diversification and expertise in multiple levels of social work practice. As one service area became less important, or unfunded, they could move on and meet related needs through other services. Having a larger, systemic view, they seem able to innovate in ways that continue to meet residents' needs. This ability to operate at a variety of levels at the same time makes it possible to build and sustain a nurturing community.

Summary

In returning to Phipps Houses to investigate the impact of the devolution of services, we found that the major factor has been in the area of the work requirement in public assistance. The demand that all public assistance recipients work has had positive as well as negative impacts. The positive effects have been that the requirements have served as an impetus for many residents to take actions they had long contemplated. It is important that one realize that Phipps Houses has had a group of clients who have been encouraged over the years to plan for a different future. In that way they may be different from the average recipient. They are clearly unique in that they have lived in a supportive environment, which, in contrast to the usual landlord, is supportive of their efforts to develop their capacities. For this reason they have options and can take risks, such as setting up their own businesses, that are closed to the usual recipient. With these supports, they have obtained jobs and pursued education. The climate of the building has changed with this change. It is no longer acceptable to be sitting outside the building during the day. Residents expect that everyone will be working. Tenants support each other in job seeking by bringing to workers information about job opportunities that can be shared with others.

On the negative side, despite all the support Phipps Houses is able to provide, there are families who have not been able to adjust to the demands of work. Some are simply unable to consistently show up at work and are fired. Others cannot meet requirements due to a variety of chronic and acute individual factors. In addition, working has caused a variety of family strains. There are more money management problems that must be addressed by staff, and a emergency loan fund has been set up. The lack of available day care is a major problem, and some children are being left home alone. Furthermore, between work and family responsibilities and the addition of school for some, it is hard for families to make contact with the resources they need. These families do not work the kinds of jobs where they can take off when their child is sick or for a clinic appointment. The days of 9-to-5 social services are over. In response to residents' changing needs, Phipps Houses has modified workers' schedules to provide service on Saturdays and weekday evenings. Even with these modifications, face-to-face service contacts between workers and residents are increasingly limited, and more and more services are delivered through telephone conversations. This means that new residents will not have the reservoir of past experience with workers to draw on. Workers may only get to know families on a crisis basis.

These issues are not limited to Phipps CDC. Beyond the area of employment, staff report clear evidence of a continuing erosion in available services. Overworked staff in the social agencies that remain are increasingly unresponsive and difficult to reach. It appears that there is more red tape, and it takes longer to be accepted for services.

Despite the many problems affecting the residents, the Phipps Houses community seems to have survived. The principles for community building seem alive and well in this time of change. It is important to realize that it is the setting's continued ability to innovate, to operate on multiple levels, and to modify existing programming to address changing population needs, all within the context of a shared vision of the capacity of families to develop and grow, that has made the survival of this community effort possible. As evidenced at Phipps Houses, the eight principles can serve as guides in developing new programs, or in evaluating and adapting existing operations.

References

Bingham, R. D., & Kirkpatrick, S. A. (1975). Providing social services for the urban poor: An analysis of public housing authorities in large American cities. *Social Service Review, 49*(1), 64–78.

Chaskin, R. J., Joseph, M. L., & Chipenda-Dansokho, S. (1997). Implementing comprehensive community development: Possibilities and limitations. *Social Work, 42*(5), 435–444.

Cohen, C. S., & Phillips, M. (1997). Building community: Principles for social work practice in housing settings. *Social Work, 42*(5), 471–481.

Ewalt, P. L., Freeman, E. M., & Poole, D. L. (1988). *Community building: Renewal, well-being, and shared responsibility.* Washington, DC: NASW Press.

Phillips, M., & Cohen, C. S. (1997). *From tenant to neighbor: Community building at Phipps Houses* (Study Report). New York: Phipps Houses/Fordham University.

Power, M. E. (1979). *The pattern of emergence of social services in housing programs.* PhD dissertation, Brandeis University.

Rawls, J. (1971). *A theory of justice.* Cambridge: Harvard University Press, Belknap Press.

Richmond, M. E. (1930). How social workers can aid housing reform. In J. C. Colcord & R. Z. S. Mann (Eds.), *The long view: Papers and addresses* (pp. 320–325). New York: Russell Sage Foundation.

15

The Role of Social Work Ethics in Empowering Clients and Communities

Elaine P. Congress, DSW, and
Yvette M. Sealy, PhD

Introduction

In an era of welfare reform legislation and diminishing resources for the poor, social services agencies and providers are confronted with ethical challenges to client and community empowerment. Social work practitioners, like the clients they serve, are under assault from the changing political environment that regulates funding of social service programs. Ethical dilemmas arise from situations where client and community empowerment are threatened by adherence to policies and procedures mandated by agencies or other third parties. These policies and procedures may not be in the best interest of the client, yet they are instituted as cost-containment measures to satisfy government or private funding sources and insurance companies. As a result, clients and communities in general are placed at risk and remain underserved.

Social work ethics has been applied to social service delivery practices since the first National Association of Social Workers (NASW) Code of Ethics was adopted by the profession in 1960. This article applies social work values and ethical principles such as service, social justice, dignity and worth of the person, and the importance of human relationships to the needs of individuals and communities. These ethical principles support individual development and self-actualization of predetermined goals. Social workers strive to promote the best interest of clients in a manner that delivers competent, quality service. Yet the fiduciary relationship between client and worker often transcends the client/worker dyadic relationship and extends into the community. Communities possessing the internal resources necessary to meet the needs of their inhabitants typically reflect a higher socioeconomic status and are more independent. Communities with lower incomes and higher rates of poverty are more dependent on government subsidies for housing, education, income, and health care. Such communities have a greater need for the interventions of social service programs and advocacy. As a result, this article focuses on the role of social workers in utilizing ethical principles to assist in the empowerment process for individual clients and communities.

The authors have identified day care, education, health care, and employment as fundamental needs of individuals and communities. For each need we will examine the current system in terms of client needs, availability of resources, obstacles encountered by the client and service provider, and the ethical principles governing social work practice. Clients seeking any of the above services may be met with discriminating barriers to service in their efforts to meet particular needs due to the social injustices of economic and resource disparity that plague both inner-city and rural communities throughout this country. Using the lens of social work ethical principles, especially those of service, social justice, and human relationships, current systems will be examined in order to promote individual and community empowerment.

EMPOWERMENT DEFINITIONS

Social workers employed in schools, clinics, hospitals, mental health agencies, child welfare organization, or other community-based agencies have undoubtedly worked in the area of client empowerment. Two important questions arise in social work practice with clients and communities: "What is empowerment?" and, more specifically, "Does the NASW Code of Ethics promote empowerment?" The concept of empowerment can be applied to both the individual and the community. Although much has been written on the various methods of achieving individual and community empowerment, few authors have approached this subject from the perspective of professional ethics. Methods for achieving individual and/or community empowerment are inherently related, yet the motivations toward outcomes may vary (Lee, 1994; Cowger, 1994; Staples, 1990). The needs of the individual do not always mimic those of the community. At the same time, the community may have needs unlike those of the individual. With an appropriate needs assessment conducted by the client or members of the community with the assistance of the social worker, a plan of action can be created that prioritizes the focus of interventions on the individual and/or the community. The achievement of a successful empowerment process can result in the individual's becoming more self-reliant, able to increase personal contributions to the community, and perhaps even propelled to leaving the community in pursuit of other desired goals. The individual empowerment process should not be viewed as a vehicle for flight from urban communities; instead, it speaks to the need for individual and community empowerment interventions to be employed simultaneously for the collective good of society. Social workers must remain mindful of the importance of reciprocity when working with the individual and the community. Both the individual and the community rely on the contributions of the other to thrive and develop. If either is lacking resources, the equilibrium becomes upset and the system is placed at risk.

A plethora of definitions exists in the literature to illustrate the concept of empowerment. The term "empowerment" has been used to represent the exercising of self-determined, goal-directed, positive attributes of the individual for the purpose of meeting specific needs. Empowerment practice encourage both individuals and groups to take control of their circumstances for the betterment of a particular situation. Staples's (1990) definition of empowerment centers on the gaining or regaining of power for the individual or community. The previous position of powerlessness is shed through the empowerment process as individuals or communities exert power over their circumstances to achieve their desired goals. Empowerment returns to the individual a sense of power that has been perceived to be external and coming from the outside environment.

Although it is stated that a sense of power is returned to the individual, empowerment is not something that can be given to one person by another. Empowerment is developed internally through a two-step process. The first step is the self-defining of individual (personal) or community (collective) interests, needs, and goals. The second step involves the active pursuit of change toward identified outcomes. Both steps should be considered to have equal importance because the successful achievement of a targeted goal is contingent upon the ability of the individual or group to clearly identify the need for change, having a commitment to work for change, and a belief in their own competencies to achieve change. Individual and community empowerment efforts can result in the development of resources and opportunities necessary to have an impact on the environment and the larger social structure for all involved in the process.

The NASW Code of Ethics (1996) lists six core values of the profession. Four of these core values will be applied in this chapter to the social worker's role in the process of individual and community empowerment. An ethical principle accompanies each of the values, providing social workers with guidelines for practice. Service and social justice are the first two (and most closely related) values of the profession. The ethical principle of service states that the "social worker's primary goal is to help people in need and to address social problems." The ethical principle attached to the value of social justice charges that "social workers challenge social injustice." The social problems of people in need of services are often the result of social injustices inherent within society. These social injustices may take the form of economic disparity and limited resources for the poor and other vulnerable or oppressed groups. The ethical principle of the value of dignity and worth of the person states that "social workers respect the inherent dignity and worth of the person." Social workers are encouraged to respect diversity while working with clients to enhance their existing strengths. The ethical principle of the value of the importance of human relationships promotes the idea that "social workers recognize the central importance of human relationships." Social workers engage clients from the standpoint of "partner" in equally contributing knowledge to address clients' needs. Social workers advocate for reinforcing positive relationships among people and the systems in which they are involved.

The ethical principles of the Code of Ethics reinforce the concept of empowerment. Cowger (1994) speaks of social justice as a key element of individual and community empowerment because it calls for the equitable distribution of society's resources. Those who are unable to access society's resources may develop a powerless stance due to repeatedly failing in their efforts to achieve change. Lee (1994) describes powerlessness as comprising the following factors: "Economic insecurity, absence of experience in the political arena, absence of access to information, lack of training in critical and abstract thought, physical and emotional stress, and the aspects of a person's emotional or intellectual makeup that prevent them from actualizing possibilities that do exist" (p. 12). The incorporation of social work values and ethical principles in social work practice can help clients eliminate feelings of powerlessness and replace them with goal-driven empowerment.

The strengths perspective can be used when working with vulnerable and oppressed groups to facilitate the empowerment process. The primary purpose of the strengths perspective is to assess the strengths of the client (Saleeby, 1997). It differs from the medical model in that it does not emphasize deficits or uncover pathology within the individual. The strengths perspective incorporates the will and needs of the client with societal norms and socioeconomic factors. Although individual and community needs may vary, in this article we will focus on the availability of quality day care and education services, affordable health care, and sufficient employment (providing income above the poverty level). Under the social work value of service, the client and worker enter into an agreement to work together to explore how the client relates to others and systems within the environment. The client is helped to explore his or her understanding of the environment and the methods of relating to each system.

The strengths perspective explores the individual's drive for survival and the coping mechanisms used to balance the intrapsychic struggle between individual or community goals and societal norms. For the poor and other vulnerable groups, the desire to achieve goals is often tempered or extinguished by culturally biased societal norms created by the dominant group. Social workers and other service providers must be aware of the increasing separation between the classes due to lack of access to opportunities that allow an individual to obtain economic security and other personal goals. Excessive and continuous exposure to the endemic stressors of poverty may have long-term consequences (Myers, 1982). These stressors may not lead to clearly defined mental illness, yet most often they do contribute to low self-esteem and feelings of depression, anger, and powerlessness. The individual's reality or perception of being powerless may contribute to increased rates of alcoholism, drug abuse, mental illness, crime, child abuse, spouse battering, suicide, and homicide (Poussaint, 1983). When the client or group seeks help, the worker must remain mindful of the goals and the societal norms of the society in which the client lives.

Social workers are encouraged to help clients identify their purposes for entering into therapeutic relationships, even if treatment has been mandated. Although the worker possesses knowledge of human behavior, clients too have valuable insight into what causes them to seek help. The strengths perspective strongly suggests that the worker allow the client to direct the helping process. Through this process, clients will further develop existing strengths and become self-empowered to improve their situation. The adaptations and other behaviors clients have employed in order to cope with situations are also examined during the exchange. Social workers working out of the strengths perspective can assist clients in discussing feeling disenfranchised within the social structure.

Day Care Services for Young Children

Service in Day Care

The composition of the traditional nuclear family has undergone many transformations in the last 30 years. Between 1940 and

1989, the percentage of children 1–5 years of age living in traditional families with a breadwinner and homemaker dropped approximately 50% (Hernandez, 1998). The majority of children today are either in two-parent households where both parents work outside the home or in single-parent families (Children's Defense Fund, 1998). The economic necessity for dual-earner families, the rise in divorce rates, and out-of-wedlock births have contributed greatly to the use of day care for young children by someone other than a parent or family member (Zigler & Freedman, 1990). Child care statistics released by the Children's Defense Fund (1998) report that 65% of mothers with children under 6 years of age are in the labor force and that 78% of mothers with children 6–13 years of age are also working. The demand for two incomes or single-parent incomes has contributed to the astonishingly statistic that approximately 50% of mothers with infants under the age of 1 year are participating in the labor force (Children's Defense Fund, 1998). It is clear that the sharply increasing demands for child care will escalate as labor force participation rates for mothers continue to rise (Zigler & Freedman, 1990; Hernandez, 1998). Such a rise is already under way with the mandate that mothers receiving public assistance benefits find work independently or work for continuation of their benefits. The Personal Responsibility and Work Opportunity Reconciliation Act of 1996 included legislation that requires all adult public assistance benefit recipients who are physically able to work to obtain employment. The "welfare reform" legislation, as it is known, will be discussed in greater detail in the sections on health care and employment, yet it is mentioned here because of its effect on mothers with preschool children. Mothers with children between 3 and 6 years of age and who are receiving public assistance are being required to enroll in workfare programs designed by their individual cities or states. Mothers are temporarily exempt from mandatory workfare enrollment until their youngest child reaches 3 years of age. This requirement now challenges mothers with subsidized low incomes to establish a quality child care arrangement for the hours they are assigned to work for their public assistance benefits. Unfortunately, more emphasis has been placed on getting parents to work than on providing satisfactory child care (Schorr, 1997).

In order to understand parental options in choosing day care, we will provide a brief description of the types of day care settings. Child care settings vary in the form of services offered to the child/parent and the overall cost of care. Day care centers are those non-residence facilities that care for 13 or more children at a time. Many parents choose to engage the services of a family child care provider, where the child is supervised in the home of someone unrelated to the parents. An in-home caregiver is unrelated and hired by the parent to provide child care services in the home of the child. Relative care is the last form of day care to be listed in this section. This type of care is given by someone other than the parent and may take place in the child or the relative's home. Children's Defense Fund (1998) statistics indicate that the largest percentage (29.3%) of children are cared for in day care centers, followed by 25.2% in relative care, 23.9% with parents, 15.4% in family child care, 5.1% with in-home caregivers, and 1.0% having other arrangements. States and localities across the country have enacted regulations for the protection of children regarding child-to-staff ratios, space and facility safety, and staff training necessary for child care centers and family child care provider settings. Many states do not require such regulations with relative care or in-home caregivers. The lack of regulations for these types of care often places children at risk for physical harm and limited opportunities for developmental stimulation.

Social Justice in Day Care

In looking at different forms of child care and the average cost, are we left to draw the conclusion that comprehensive quality care is equated with higher costs? If this is the case, then are poor children relegated to marginal child care conditions? Social workers must be aware of issues of economic disparity that dictate parents' options when they place a child in day care. Ethical challenges involving access to resources frequently occur with day care placement and educational instruction in general. These challenges are often dependent on the parents' socioeconomic status. Parents with higher incomes may have additional resources to acquire day care services with specialized child development features. Parents with lower incomes may feel an overwhelming pressure and limited choices due to the high cost of day care. Most parents working a full-time schedule will also require full-day child care. The cost of such care will vary based on the type of setting, yet the average cost of care ranges from $4,000 to $10,000 per year (Children's Defense Fund, 1998). Child care that provides services to a smaller number of children and utilizes specialized learning techniques is notably more expensive and less accessible to children from low-income families. A 1996 report titled "Money and Income in the United Stated," released by the U.S. Census Bureau, indicates that approximately 50% of families with children below school age earn less that $35,000 per year, while families earning two incomes both at minimum wage will bring home close to $21,400 per year. Subtract the cost of child care from moderate to low incomes and the family may be found to be approaching or living in poverty. Governmental resources do exist to aid low-income families in meeting the cost of child care. The Child Care and Development Block Grant (CCDBG) often funds these need-based subsidies. Programs such as Head Start were designed to enhance school readiness for poor families. The criticism of CCDBG subsidies is that funding is insufficient to meet the cost of comprehensive care, thus still leaving poor children at a disadvantage (Schorr, 1997).

The Importance of Human Relationships in Day Care

The elevated percentage of mothers in the labor force raises questions regarding the impact of child care placement on the psychological development of young children. Naturally, the needs of infants differ from those of toddlers and preschoolers. Along with the development of psychomotor skills, one essential goal of infancy is the forming of secure attachments (Bowlby, 1982). In the absence of a parent, caregivers become the secondary attachment object. The infant needs nurturing reinforcement in an individual manner with consistence. Infant care is often more difficult to locate and more costly due to the small number of infants that can be cared for at one time. Maturation affords toddlers and preschoolers more independence and autonomy, thus shifting developmental goals toward peer socialization and social learning experiences (Zigler & Freedman, 1990).

Key areas of concern influencing the psychological and educational development of young children in day care are the quality of care, the cost of care, and the availability of care. The debate on the impact of day care placement on child development is a popular one, with support for both sides of the argument. However, many child care experts are in agreement as to what constitutes quality child care. The Children's Defense Fund identifies quality care as a service that provides "a safe and healthy environment, caregivers who are nurturing, knowledgeable about children's development, and a stable presence in children's lives, and a small number of children per caregiver to ensure that each child receives personal attention" (1998, p. 3). As we have seen, children of different ages have different socioemotional needs. In addition, children from lower socioeconomic backgrounds may have different child care and learning needs due to potentially compromised health and safety needs stemming from poverty. Poor children receive a lower quality of care where supervision, individualized attention, nurturing, and health and safety practices are inadequate (Hernandez, 1998). Child care facilities with limited resources were also found to have insufficient materials for stimulating the learning and development of young children. Consequently, the deprivation of appropriately stimulating materials at an early age can have long-lasting educational and professional repercussions. Impaired or delayed language development and reading skills may be the outcome of inadequate stimulation for the young child (Children's Defense Fund, 1998). Children exposed to poor-quality child care are will suffer as they enter school unready to learn (Schorr, 1997).

EDUCATION

Service in Education

Throughout history, the ability to obtain formal education has been considered an entitlement of all citizens of the United States. As a result of legislation passed during the civil rights movement, many social injustices pertaining to public education were addressed. At that time, inequality in educational materials, settings, and delivery of instruction were important factors calling for legislative change. Although cases such as *Brown vs. Board of Education* made great strides in correcting the unethical practice of providing an inferior educational environment based on race, more subtle inequalities continue to be perpetuated against children from lower-income communities within our cities.

It has been demonstrated that obtaining an education results in increased ability to secure employment in a chosen field of study and to receive satisfactory wages. Although this has proven true for a large segment of society, an alarming number of people remain unable to achieve the desired levels of employment and other personal successes. Within this group are those who for no other reason than being poor and inadequately prepared by the educational system are unable to compete in the job market. The educational deficits impairing economic stability as an adult are often the result of poverty and limited access to resources as a child.

Social Justice in Education

As technological advances develop to facilitate the expansion of learning opportunities, the educational system is still encountering children with reading and math scores below grade level. The U.S. Department of Education (1998) correlates higher dropout rates with reading difficulties not overcome by the fourth grade. Because thousands of children have difficulty achieving age-appropriate educational outcomes, in January 1997 President Clinton proposed the "Call to Action for American Education." Initiatives to enhance the learning environment, improve reading and math scores, and upgrade classroom technology are addressed in this proposal.

The modernization and construction of schools is an issue critical to the overall long-term success of the community. The modernization of existing schools and the construction of new schools are essential to providing an appropriate environment that fosters learning. In communities across the country, many children attend school in buildings that are 100 or more years old. The wear and repeated patchwork upkeep of these facilities place children in danger of physical harm. In addition, the sizable increase in the number of children entering school each year has presented many school districts with the problem of overcrowding. Children have been subjected to receiving instruction in storage areas, bathrooms, and cafeterias. Class sizes have grown to numbers ranging from 28 to 35 students. This large number contributes to lower educational achievement for students because of limited individualized attention from teachers and increased chances for disciplinary problems. The quality of educational services for children is expanding yearly with new advances in technology. Funding for computer learning centers has increased in the last 10 years to the point where nearly 65% of schools nationally are connected to the Internet (U.S. Department of Education, 1998). Federal reading programs such as America Reads are aimed at increasing the reading scores of children so that each child reads independently and on grade level by the fourth grade.

Although federal funding is being made available for programs to enrich education, are these funds being distributed equitably? Chapin (1995) highlights the fact that school districts are funded in part by local property tax funds, thus schools that exist in lower-income neighborhoods receive fewer dollars to ensure that equal educational materials and learning opportunities are available to prepare children to compete for jobs in the future. Social workers must also become political in calling for increased funding to improve the quality of education for children and adult literacy/training programs.

HEALTH CARE

Service in Health Care

Health insurance coverage remains a critical source of controversy in this country. A large segment of the population is left without any formal health insurance coverage plan to assist with the rising cost of medical expenses. These individuals are typically wedged between the very poor and the employed with modest incomes. For those with health insurance, it is typically provided as a benefit of their employment benefits package or provided by the government as a form of public insurance. The Health Security Act, proposed by the Clinton administration in 1993, was an attempt to provide national health insurance coverage for all citizens of the United States. This legislation was met with criticism from politically motivated groups and was never passed. The controversy rose out of two unresolved issues: (1) Who is eligible for health coverage? and (2) Who will pay for that health insurance coverage?

Many ethical challenges are presented to clients and social workers in the area of health care. These challenges have come to a head particularly in the light of the recent passage of welfare reform legislation and the push toward a more extensive conversion to mandatory managed care. Managed care is the coordination of health care services by an organization designed to purchase health care for its members (Mordock, 1996). The primary goals of a managed care organization are to (1) regulate the use of health care for its members eligible for the benefit and (2) reduce health care costs paid to providers of the care (Appelbaum, 1993). In an effort to control health care costs, insurers have hired managed care organizations to establish a network of service providers and set guidelines for the delivery of services. These guidelines range from fee reimbursement to the evaluation of the need for medical treatment. Managed care organizations at one time limited their involvement in client care to payors for services, but they have now expanded into the business of managing the type of treatment provided and evaluating its efficacy (Haas & Cummings, 1994). The number of people enrolled in managed care programs is steadily rising as a result of controlled privatization of health insurance coverage. As employers and the government contract with managed care organizations, the health insurance and health care options provided to people eligible for the benefit become controlled. This agreement results in a loss of autonomy in choosing health care services and service delivery for the client and provider (Munson, 1996). The social work belief in client self-determination is being opposed by the paternalistic and inflexible requisites of managed care. Despite the fact that accessible, quality health coverage is a paramount need of the poor, the implementation of mandatory managed care legislation may be a barrier to client service.

In the era of managed care and welfare reform, economic resources for human service programs are subject to scrutiny to meet specific needs according to the predetermined philosophy of those in control of the resources. Access to services and the amount of available resources are influenced by the political climate of the environment. In 1965 the federal government began to sponsor the Medicare program to pay for the cost of medical care for the aged and persons with disabilities (Bixby, 1995). During the same year, the federal government reached an agreement with the states to sponsor the Medicaid program to cover the cost of health care services to the poor. Community-based human service agencies sprang up to accommodate service needs and the financial constraints of persons with low incomes. Clients seeking services from community-based agencies frequently receive some form of government assistance, such as Temporary Assistance to Needy Families (TANF), formerly known as Aid to Families With Dependent Children (AFDC), and Medicaid. TANF benefits provide a monthly cash and food stamp allowance based on financial need and family composition. Although TANF fails to elevate recipients above the poverty level, without this benefit millions of the country's poor would be unable to meet the most basic human need for food and shelter (Schorr, 1997; Pearlmutter, 1997).

Social Justice in Health Care

Health care, like day care and education, is of particular importance to the field of social work. Increasingly, social workers are being confronted with ethical dilemmas when access to health insurance coverage is unavailable and the poor are being channeled into mandatory managed care programs. The lack of health insurance coverage and the seemingly insurmountable obstacles of mandatory managed care greatly conflict with social work's core values of social justice. The development of relationships, learning success, employment functioning, and recreation are all areas that can have a notable impact if an individual is suffering with a compromised health status. The need for preventive and corrective health care has been established to be a fundamental requirement to ensuring one's overall physical and emotional well-being. In the event of illness, the inability to obtain treatment places the individual at risk for physical and psychic death. Left untreated, a serious illness will ultimately worsen and presumably contribute to life-threatening health complications. While physical death has its focus on the body, psychic death pertains to the expiring of one's emotional fortitude. Individuals who are unable to access medical treatment due to the inability to pay for services are left with a sense of hopelessness and loss of control over their lives. The direct or indirect threat to basic survival can be a major stressor triggering systematic ramifications in all areas of a person's life.

Children and low-income adults, particularly women, make up the population being shuttled into Medicaid managed care programs (Perloff, 1996). People with low incomes who live in socioeconomically disadvantaged communities have a higher incidence of health problems due to repeated exposure to multiple stressors. Inadequate housing, poor nutrition, low birth weight babies, high infant mortality rates, tuberculosis, AIDS, and other illnesses are prevalent in poor communities (Perloff, 1996). In addition, irregular use of preventive health care services only serves to further complicate health problems of the poor. Children make up the largest group of persons without health insurance coverage. Farel and Kotch (1997) state that in 1993 approximately 15% of children in the United States were without health insurance. In 1996, 14.6% (10.3 million) of U.S. children were uninsured, up from 13.6% (9.6 million) in 1995 (Center on Budget and Policy Priorities, 1997). Children may be left without health insurance coverage if they live in a home where at least one parent works and earns an income that makes the family ineligible for TANF benefits. Although families may no longer be eligible for public assistance, federal laws permit poor children to remain on Medicaid (Center on Budget and Policy Priorities, 1997). This information is not readily made available by states, as millions of children remain uninsured. Also, many employer benefit packages have limited the extent of health care coverage, leaving children with only major medical and catastrophic coverage (Farel & Kotch, 1997). In such cases the family is considered to be underinsured because shrinking plans do not include coverage for preventive care, immunization, dental maintenance, and annual checkups ensuring proper growth and development for the child. Despite the restrictions in some insurance coverage, the number of children with private insurance rose from 46.9 million in 1995 to 47.1 million in 1996 (Center on Budget and Policy Priorities, 1997).

The Importance of Human Relationships in Health Care

Managed care efforts to contain costs and allegedly improve the efficiency of service delivery have come with a high price to client care. The confidential exchange between client and service provider has been undermined by managed care regulations. Social workers in medical and mental health care settings are confronted with the first ethical dilemma: violating client confidentiality. Service providers are now put in the position of revealing confidential information to parties who were previously thought to be outside the treatment relationship (Corcoran & Winsdale, 1994; Davidson & Davidson, 1996). In the case of mental health care, the social worker is required to provide detailed information regarding the client's presenting problems, treatment goals, and other personal issues of treatment to the insurer.

The NASW Code of Ethics (1996) declares privacy and confidentiality for clients to be an ethical standard for the profession. Since third-party reimbursement for services is a reality for the majority of clients, the Code of Ethics urges workers to receive informed consent from clients about the nature of information to be released and the consequences of such a release before disclosing information to a managed care organization. Under managed care, the relationship between client and care provider has the potential to become strained for several reasons. First, clients may minimize or fail to report symptoms to the care provider, fearing exposure of a physical or mental condition to an insurance company or employer. Second, social workers and clients must be able to build a working relationship based on trust and an agreement to work as partners to help clients improve their quality of life (NASW, 1996).

The third ethical dilemma for social workers involves adherence to treatment time limits imposed by managed care. Disparities in treatment time limits have been observed between coverage in the private and public sectors. Managed care organizations have implemented a system of inequality in terms of service choices offered to clients. Clients enrolled in Medicaid managed care experience less flexibility in choosing their own health care providers (Cuffel, Snowden, Masland, & Piccagli, 1996; Munson, 1996). The number of visits authorized for mental health services for a person with Medicaid is also monitored more closely than for a person with private insurance. Persons with private health insurance coverage are typically informed at the onset of coverage how many contacts will be approved per calendar year. Medicaid managed care clients are not afforded the same measure of security in knowing the limits of their coverage. In the case of mental health coverage, Medicaid insurance recipients are subjected to having their therapy session authorization rationed at the discretion of the managed care organization as frequently as every 5 weeks in order to monitor the progress and efficiency of the treatment. The rationing of sessions is maintained by the managed care organization to encourage service providers to complete the treatment in a predetermined amount of time regardless of the presenting problem. Opponents of time limits criticize manage care organizations for promoting "rapid service delivery of prepackaged procedures" (Munson, 1996). This process often creates a state of anxiety and frustration for the client, who is fearful of having to discontinue treatment before achieving his or her goals. Social workers are met with decreasing session time to spend with clients as the demand for documentation and the all-too-frequent need to update treatment authorization increases. This constant state of fiscal uncertainty places substantial strain on the helping process and the treatment relationship (Munson, 1996). Medicaid recipients, social workers, and human service agency administrations all become cruelly involved in the churning process that occurs when public assistance and Medicaid benefits are regularly discontinued and reinstated as recipients undergo benefit eligibility reviews (Brenner, Beallor, Mizrahi, & Kaufer, 1998).

Dignity and Worth of the Person in Health Care

An additional risk to client care occurs when a treatment modality is deemed cost effective by managed care organizations but is not in the best interest of the client. Utilization reviews conducted by managed care organizations have the primary concern of cost efficiency rather than maximizing client functioning (Newman & Bricklin, 1994; Munson, 1996). Restricted access to the best medical procedures for client care can have irreparable consequences resulting in further injury to the client. Social workers must place equal value on the lives of all people. A person's access to quality medical treatment should not be dependent on variations in health insurance coverage or the client's socioeconomic status.

A positive aspect of managed care is the focus on prevention. Clients—and especially poor clients—can now assume a more active role in pursuing their own good health. Social workers need to work to empower clients to ask questions about their health and health care and to advocate for choice among alternative treatments.

EMPLOYMENT

Service in Employment

The previous sections on day care, education, and health care can all be connected with one's employment status and income. Employment rates within a community have a significant impact on the level of individual and community empowerment that can be achieved. We will look briefly at individuals employed in private industry, those marginally attached to employment situations, and discouraged workers. The U.S. Department of Labor categorizes these three groups according to their level of employment. Employed individuals are those engaged in full- or part-time work. Marginally attached to the labor force are those persons who are available to work and have looked for work within the last 12 months. Discouraged workers are those persons who are not currently looking for work due to feeling that no work opportunities exist for them. We will also address the workfare programs for recipients of public assistance.

Social Justice in Employment

Although the U.S. Department of Labor consistently reports drops in unemployment rates, little is mentioned about the earning potential of those participating in the labor force. The Center on Budget and Price Priorities (1997) released data reporting a disparity of income growth rates among the rich and those with moderate to low incomes. It appears that although more people are actively involved in the labor force, the economic growth in dollars is being experienced by the most affluent of society. Figures for 1996 indicated that over the past year the average income for the poorest fifth of families dropped by 1.8% ($210), that for the middle fifth rose 1.5% ($630), and that for the richest 5% increased 3.1% ($6,440). The poorest households—those in the bottom fifth—received 3.7% of the national income, while the group just above them received 9.0%. The top two-fifths of households received 23.3% and 49% of the national income, respectively (Center on Budget and Price Priorities, 1997). These percentages illustrate the inherent inequality that exists in the distribution of the nation's material resources. The poverty rates for that year failed to decline, despite the increase in the number of persons participating in the labor force. Therefore, for many the incomes earned remain insufficient to meet basic living expenses.

The Personal Responsibility and Work Opportunity Reconciliation Act of 1996 is having a significant impact on the incomes of those eligible for public assistance. The title of the Act and its pet name of "welfare reform" are both deceiving at first glance. The concepts of "personal responsibility" and "work opportunity" both suggest a positive outlook for change with the likelihood of individual growth and empowerment. Most notable to this section is the mandate requiring able-bodied adult recipients of public assistance to obtain work and the 5-year time limit placed on eligibility of benefits. The welfare-to-work initiative dates back to the 1960s, when the federal government made unsuccessful attempts to provide job training for persons on public assistance. Since that time the government-funded work programs for recipients of benefits have undergone many changes in name, but few changes have been instituted to provide quality training or job placement or to create jobs. Although political references have been made to developing partnerships with the private sector to create jobs for the poor, the number of available jobs is incommensurate with the large number of persons being required to work. A practical job training and skills enhancement program must be available for those seeking employment. Instead, far too many benefit recipients are being called down to assigned sites and provided with newspaper classified ads, a business yellow pages, and the use of a telephone to independently locate work. The government alternative to this practice has been to place benefit recipients in city and state agencies to work for their monthly benefit. Workfare assignments may range from clerical work to street sanitation. For those who do obtain employment, the low wages received may keep them at the poverty level without the "public assistance safety net" of reassurance for meeting their living expenses. Thus, once again, government work programs targeting recipients of public assistance continue to fall short of addressing the larger picture promoting the actual procurement of jobs. The government and supporters of welfare reform take no responsibility for the grossly inadequate supports provided to job seekers when these persons fail to locate or maintain work. While the potential for an individual to return to public assistance is great, the new 5-year time limit for benefits will be reinforced. This time limit places children and adults alike at risk for being destitute with no alternatives for subsistence when they reach their time limit.

The Importance of Human Relationships/Dignity and Worth of the Person in Employment

The political push to overhaul the welfare system grew out of stigmatized perceptions of people receiving public assistance.

The belief that the poor are solely responsible for their circumstances remains a popular view despite the economic realities of low wages that do not yield financial stability. Persons receiving benefits are in fact eager to work, yet motivation may decline when jobs produce further stigmatization, low personal fulfillment, and meager wages. The confidentiality of benefit recipients is often violated when they enter into workfare assignments. For example, those assigned are frequently identified to supervisors and other agency staff as welfare recipients. Some recipients have reported feeling looked down upon by the employed workers, while others state that they are assigned tasks that others do not want to complete.

Social workers must continue to combat discriminating views toward the poor. The cause of out-of-control government spending is frequently projected onto society's poorest and most needy. It has been commonplace to blame the poor for their plight while continuing to reduce opportunities for their enhancement. Society has attempted to place controls on devalued groups by further segregating them or implementing obstacles to hinder their perceived deviant behavior. The concept of social role valorization can be applied to the circumstances of those who work for low wages and those participating in workfare programs. Social role valorization is defined as "the use of culturally valued means in order to enable, establish and/or maintain valued social roles for people" (Wolfenberger, 1985, p. 61). The theory further implies that persons who feel good about their social role will be open to exploring other opportunities that will further validate their positive social role and self-worth. Workfare assignments and other low-wage jobs typically do not provide individuals with the sense of accomplishment and contribution that reinforces one's social role and self-worth.

In order to empower clients and communities, we need to provide employment that is fulfilling both emotionally and financially. Curtailing welfare benefits seems in the short run to create a crisis for our clients and the communities in which they live. Yet in every crisis there is an opportunity for clients and communities to empower themselves. We as social workers can assist in this process.

EMPOWERMENT IMPLICATIONS FOR SOCIAL WORK PRACTICE

The realities of limited access and restricted opportunities to quality day care, education, health care, and employment have been demonstrated throughout this chapter. Although the obvious results of economic disparity can be witnessed in lower-income communities, the ramifications of resource inequity can be felt throughout society. It is no longer feasible to entertain the belief that the problems of the poor and other vulnerable populations will remain confined to select communities. As economic and resource disparity continue to increase between rich and poor, more low- and middle-income individuals and communities will be confronted with hardships that affect their overall well-being. Fewer people will be left untouched by circumstances of the disadvantaged as the net encompassing vulnerable and oppressed persons gets cast wider and wider into newly affected neighborhoods. An empowerment approach to social services is necessary for individual and community survival and revitalization. The core values and ethical principles of the NASW's Code of Ethics (1996) have provided social workers with a framework for addressing individual and community survival and revitalization.

We have made general distinctions between individual and community empowerment needs, yet the social work profession is grounded in the notion that the individual is integrally connected to the community and the surrounding environment. This interwoven connection must be understood and respected as social service agencies and social workers attempt to provide services. The following guidelines are provided as a method for delivering ethically sound, competent services that assist individuals and communities in meeting their identified goals and needs:

1. *Community-based social service programs must ensure that services are designed to meet the needs of the individuals and community to be served.* Social workers should conduct an in-depth needs assessment to identify client and community needs. Empowerment practices should be culturally competent and tailored to the needs of the community. This process will examine what services exist and where there are gaps.

2. *Social workers must help clients advocate for themselves within the political arena.* Once individual and community needs have been identified, social workers can assist community residents in addressing the problem of economic disparity and limited resources. Low-income communities tend to be isolated and withdrawn from the political process as their local and state elected officials go unchallenged regarding decisions made for the community. Community organization efforts should be focused on gaining increased funding for resources from the city, state, and federal governments. Social workers can assist community residents in becoming aware of the funding resources available for day care, education, health care, and job training programs.

3. *Social workers must assist individuals and communities in developing and designing internal community systems.* Using the strengths perspective, social workers work with individuals and communities to take an inventory of the assets, capabilities, and resources already present within the community. Social workers assist clients in shedding the powerless stance that attributes positive change to outside forces. By reaffirming the belief in client self-determination and empowerment, members of organized groups can motivate one another to seek equal access to society's resources. However, it is equally important that these same persons pursue a self- and community-sufficient way of life. Community residents can be helped to develop a plan to combine resources and develop strategies to meet collective needs. Residents can organize themselves to increase day care options and become involved with local school boards and parent-teacher associations. Independent of workfare mandates, adults may choose to seek educational enrichment and job training supports to increase their standing in the job market. A successful inventory of community strengths will require full participation of all elements of the community. Those involved in individual and collective empowerment efforts should include the residents, persons who work or conduct business in the community, local businesses, religious groups, civic organizations, and philanthropic funders.

Social workers may hold true to the Code of Ethics of the profession by fostering those services where the dignity and worth of individuals are reinforced, stressing human relationships in the creation and maintenance of community services, and promoting social justice by working toward creating equitable services, especially in poor diverse communities.

REFERENCES

Appelbaum, P. (1993). Legal liability and managed care. *American Psychologist, 48,* 251–257.

Bixby, A. K. (1995). Public social welfare expenditures. In *Encyclopedia of social work* (19th ed.) (1992–1997).

Bowlby, J. (1982). *Attachment and loss* (2nd ed.). New York: Basic Books.

Brenner, B., Beallor, G., Mizrahi, T., & Kaufer, S. (1998). *Social work and managed care: The impact of social risk on health care delivery and the need for social services.* Unpublished manuscript.

Center on Budget and Policy Priorities. (1997). *Poverty rates fail to decline as income growth in 1996 favors the affluent* [Online]. Available: http://www.cbpp.org/povday97.html

Chapin, R. K. (1995). Social policy development: The strengths perspective. *Social Work, 40*(2), 506–514.

Children's Defense Fund. (1998). *Questions and answers about the need for quality, affordable child dare* [Online]. Available: http://www.childrensdefense.org/ccfacts.html

Corcoran, K., & Winsdale, W. (1994). Eavesdropping on the 50-minute hour: Managed mental health care and confidentiality. *Behavioral Science and the Law, 12,* 351–365.

Cowger, C. (1994). Assessing client strengths: Clinical assessment for client empowerment. *Social Work, 39,* 262–268.

Cuffel, B., Snowden, L., Masland, M., & Piccagli, G. (1996). Managed care in public mental health system. *Community Mental Health Journal, 32*(2), 109–124.

Davidson, J., & Davidson, T. (1996). Confidentiality and managed care: Ethical and legal concerns. *Health and Social Work, 21*(3), 208–215.

Farel, A., & Kotch, J. (1997). The child from one to four: The toddler and preschool years. In J. Kotch (Ed.), *Maternal and child health: Programs, problems, and policy in public health* (pp. 115–146). Gaithersburg, MA: Aspen.

Haas, L. J., & Cummings, N. A. (1994). Managed outpatient mental health plans: Clinical, ethical, and practical guidelines for participation. In R. L. Lowman & R. J. Resnick (Eds.), *The mental health professional's guide to managed care* (pp. 137–149). Washington, DC: American Psychological Association.

Hernandez, D. J. (1998). Economic and social disadvantages of young children. In W. S. Barnett & S. S. Boocock (Eds.), *Early care and education for children in poverty: Promises, programs, and long-term results* (pp. 185–209). Albany: SUNY Press.

Lee, J. (1994). *The empowerment approach to social work practice.* New York: Columbia University Press.

Mordock, J. (1996). The road to survival revisited: Organizational adaptation to the managed care environment. *Child Welfare, 75*(3), 195–218.

Munson, C. E. (1996). Autonomy and managed care in clinical social work practice. *Smith College Studies in Social Work, 66*(3), 241–259.

Myers, H. (1982). Stress, ethnicity and social class: A model for research with black populations. In E. Jones & S. Korchin (Eds.), *Minority mental health* (pp. 118–148). New York: Praeger.

National Association of Social Workers. (1996). *Code of ethics.* Washington, DC: NASW Press.

Newman, R., & Bricklin, P. (1994). Parameters of managed mental health care: Legal, ethical, and professional guidelines. In R. L. Lowman & R. J. Resnick (Eds.), *The mental health professional's guide to managed care* (pp. 63–82). Washington, DC: American Psychological Association.

Pearlmutter, F. D. (1997). *From welfare to work: Corporate initiatives and welfare reform.* New York: Oxford University Press.

Perloff, J. (1996). Medicaid managed care and urban poor people: Implications for social work. *Health and Social Work, 21*(3), 189–195.

Poussaint, A. (1983). The mental health status of black Americans, 1983. In D. Ruiz (Ed.), *Handbook of mental health and mental disorders among black Americans* (pp. 17–52). New York: Greenwood Press.

Saleeby, D. (1997). Community development, group empowerment, and individual resilience. In D. Saleeby (Ed.), *The
strengths perspective in social work practice* (2nd ed.) (pp. 199–
216). New York: Longman.

Schorr, Lisbeth (1997). *Common purpose: Strengthening families
and neighborhoods to rebuild America.* New York: Anchor Books
Doubleday.

Staples, L. H. (1990). Powerful ideas about empowerment. *Administration in Social Work, 14*(2), 29–42.

U.S. Census Bureau. (1997). Money and income in the United
States: 1996. *Current population reports.* Washington, DC: Author.

U.S. Department of Education. (1998). *President Clinton's call to
action for American education in the 21st century: Ensuring educational excellence in 1998 and beyond.* [Online]. Available: http//
www.ed.gov/updates/presEDPlan/html

U.S. Department of Labor. (1998). *Employment situation summary.*
[Online]. Available: http//www.stats.bls.gov:80/news.rel-
ease/empsit.nws.html

Wolfenberger, W. (1985). An overview of social role valorization
and some reflections on elderly mentally retarded persons. In
M. P. Janicki & H. M. Wisniewski (Eds.), *Aging and developmental disabilities: Issues and approaches* (pp. 61–76). Baltimore:
Brookes Publishing Co.

Zigler, E. F., & Freedman, J. (1990). Psychological-developmental
implications of current patterns of early child care. In S. Cheh-
razi (Ed.), *Psychological issues in day care* (pp. 3–20). Washington, DC: American Psychiatric Press.

16

Religious Congregations as Mediators of Devolution: A Study of Parish-Based Services

John Cosgrove, PhD

Introduction

THE DEVOLUTION OF SOCIAL SERVICES is driven by the belief that communities should take more responsibility for meeting the needs of their members. Underlying this belief is the assumption that communities are capable of filling the gaps left by changes and cutbacks in services. Even if experience bears this out, there will be a period of transition during which some service needs are likely to go unrecognized and/or unmet. However, the needs are apt to be more extensive and lasting, given the likelihood of substantial and continuing reductions in public expenditures for social services and the questionable ability of communities to make up for this loss (Federal News Service, 1996).

Whatever the outcome of the process of devolution, communities will have to be prepared to identify their social needs and negotiate their resolution with authorities. At the same time, it is becoming increasingly evident that communities will also have to find, develop, and effectively use local resources to ensure that their neighbors will have the assistance, protections, and supports they need to maintain a decent, adequate standard of living.

Religious organizations have a long history of advocating for and serving the poor, dependent, and marginalized. Since the dawn of civilization, religion in its many forms has provided a framework for understanding the world and giving meaning to life. Socially, religion has most often been a force for harmony and cooperation, although at times it has been used for contrary purposes. However, all the major religions have beliefs, teachings, and practices that encourage mutual support as well as assistance for those who have problems with which they cannot cope unaided (Cnaan, Wineberg, & Boddie, 1999).

Of course, the manner and extent to which these religious values are manifest at a particular time in a society, or by groups or individuals within a society, varies. Nonetheless, the fact that these helping values are part of the socialization of most people remains a very powerful influence on attitudes and behavior. Religious organizations—churches, synagogues, mosques—also enjoy a special relationship with members through those ceremonies and rites of passage that mark key developmental milestones (e.g., birth, coming-of-age, marriage, death). In addition to involvement in these intimate moments in life, fellow congregants often have regular contact with each other and with congregation staff. These contacts can lead to close, caring relationships as well as to the ability to monitor changes in people's situations and to be accessible and able to reach out to them in times of need.

Religious values and practices regarding helping others are reinforced by the prevalence of religious beliefs and participation that have always been strong in the United States. Despite the sense of many that religion is a waning force, according to a study cited by Shorto (1997), in the United States, 96% of the population say they believe in a God versus 95% 50 years ago. The proportion of those attending weekly services is identical (41%), and other markers of religious participation remain virtually the same.

Society generally accepts as appropriate and supports the helping role of religion. Religious organizations and religious personnel are the sources that most people turn to in times of need (Goodman, 1996; Kilpatrick & Holland, 1990). In the poorest and most marginalized communities, religious congregations are often one of the few remaining viable social institutions, and ones that have traditionally advanced the welfare of their members and communities ("Faith Initiative," 1996; Allen-Meares, 1989).

CONGREGATIONS AS MEDIATORS OF DEVOLUTION

The special role of religious congregations in their communities and their relationships with those communities make it possible for congregations to act as effective mediating structures, that is, those which "stand between individuals in their private lives and the larger institutions of public life" (Berger & Neuhaus, 1977). They can help to buffer and negotiate larger, impersonal forces. With devolution, congregations have become more and more active in the exercise of these mediating functions.

They have done so by influencing the actions of the larger religious bodies of which they are a part, such as in the opposition expressed by the national leaders of many of those bodies to the 1996 welfare reform bill (Harvey, 1998). Congregations are also becoming more active and effective in education and organizing for social betterment in coalitions at the local level, bringing to these efforts their commitment to the community and helping those in need (Boyte, 1990). In addition, like "base communities" in the third world, congregations can become catalysts for the development of indigenous community leadership and organizations (Cosgrove, 1999). Cnaan (1998) found that nearly half of the more than 100 congregations he studied began and nurtured multiple programs that eventually became free-standing.

Channeling resources to existing service agencies is another way congregations have helped to buffer the effects of devolution. A 10-year study of religious support of public and private agencies in Greensboro, North Carolina, found that of 193 agencies, more received help from local congregations since devolution began in earnest, during the Reagan administration, than before. Specifically, more agencies received financial support (69%), volunteer labor (42%), and use of the facilities of congregations (47%) after the federal policies took effect (Wineberg, 1996).

However, the mediating role of congregations is perhaps best

evidenced when the congregations use their community sanction, resources, and relationships to directly help others. An
overview of a number of studies in major cities as well as a national survey found that the proportions of congregations offering some form of social service ranged from 77% to over 92%,
most dealing with basic needs (Cnaan, 1998). The same source
reports that in a six-city study, over 40% of the programs of the
congregations had been initiated in response to cutbacks in
funding from local, state, and federal sources (Cnaan, 1998).

The Urban Institute's Center on Nonprofits and Philanthropy
(1998) found that more than three-quarters of 266 congregations
responding to a survey in the Washington, DC, area offered
some type of emergency service. Forty percent of those were experiencing an increase in demand for their services, and almost
one-fifth turned people away or referred them elsewhere because the programs were already operating at full capacity.

PARISH-BASED SERVICES

Parish-based services have been a tradition in the American
Catholic Church since colonial times (Peeler, 1985). In addition,
the Catholic Church established its own social welfare institutions and services in the 19th and 20th centuries, as did other
denominations. The social service network of agencies that make
up Catholic Charities U.S.A. still provides a prodigious amount
of services, but they are also feeling the consequences of devolution. In 1982 they served 3.5 million clients, 23% of whom required assistance with basic needs such as food and shelter. By
1992, Catholic Charities was serving 12 million clients, 68% of
whom needed food and shelter (Harvey, 1997).

This period coincided with a renewed emphasis in the church
on lay involvement and a greater opening to the larger community and to other denominations. Catholic Charities began to
promote the development of what was called Parish Social Ministry (PSM), through which congregations would engage in social action and service. The term "parish" was meant to be
"*inclusive* rather than exclusive, serving *all* who are within its
geographical boundaries." "Social" meant "the parish links and

connects the church with the neighborhood." "Ministry" meant "to serve, to care, to comfort, to contribute and to utilize . . . individual gifts . . . for the benefit of the whole community" (Peeler, 1985, p. xxv).

Many congregations in other denominations are guided by similar principles, which may or may not be referred to as social ministries. What they actually do may be very different. However, even when limited to a denomination like the Catholic Church, in which consistency of belief and practice is characteristically strong, it is difficult to talk in terms of a "model" of PSM. This befits an entity that should reflect the unique qualities of the congregation that gave it life and the community it serves.

If there are forms of PSM that approach being models, one would be that of the Rockville Centre Diocese in Long Island, New York. Functioning for almost a quarter of a century, the PSM movement in the diocese is widely known for its pioneering work as well as its successful mediating efforts on multiple levels (Himes, 1986; Peeler, 1985).

PSM in the diocese consists of five interrelated components. Community Organizing helps to empower people in communities so they can have an effective voice in determining the development of their communities. The Campaign for Human Development in the diocese is part of a national endeavor by the American Catholic Church to provide funding for grassroots organizations in the development of projects to improve the quality of life in their communities. The Public Policy Education Network makes people in the diocese aware of social issues and engages them in advocacy on those issues. The Justice and Peace component of PSM unites domestic and global concerns through education and action on issues such as institutional racism, peace, human rights, the environment, and policies affecting developing nations. Parish Outreach is the provision of direct services by the parishes. Each of the five components informs and supports the others.

The establishment of a Parish Outreach program is up to the individual parish. The diocese has a central Parish Social Ministry office and staff of "developers" who encourage and guide the development of Parish Outreach. They and Catholic Charities provide training and consultation for Outreach personnel.

The usual Outreach staffing consists of a coordinator paid by the parish and volunteer or "core" staff. The coordinators come from various backgrounds. Some have had academic or professional training related to their work, a few in social work. What the coordinators do have in common is strong experience in formal or informal helping settings.

A STUDY OF PARISH OUTREACH

These Parish Outreach programs are of interest for several reasons. Most of the current research on congregation-based services has been cross-denominational. The cross-denominational aspect has been valuable in providing a sense of both the scale of the effects of devolution and the impressiveness of the response across denominations. At the same time, services that may be extremely different in their philosophy, scope, and operation have been lumped together. Furthermore, these studies have more often looked at the remarkable amount of resources that congregations have managed to put into service programs and at their impressive outcomes than at the actual workings of the programs. The findings of these studies seem to confirm both the growing involvement of congregations in the provision of social services and a manner of doing so that should diminish traditional concerns of social work and other professions about the mixing of religion and helping (Ressler, 1998).

The study, which will now be reported, reexamines these issues in the context of the operation of a particular approach to congregation-based service, in a particular denomination, in a large and differentiated area—Parish Outreach in the Rockville Centre Diocese of Long Island. The diocese encompasses the counties of Nassau and Suffolk in the state of New York. The study will identify and describe the types of needs that Parish Outreach programs in the diocese addressed, how they became involved with those in need, how the identified needs were met, and the nature of the interaction between Outreach and the formal, especially public, service system. Reflections of Outreach staff on their work will also be described.

Method

The study consisted of two phases. In the first, Parish Social Ministry and other diocesan staff were interviewed and two focus groups were conducted, one with a cross section of Parish Outreach coordinators and one with a similarly diverse group of core or volunteer staff. The interviews and focus groups were, in part, preparation for a survey of Parish Outreach programs throughout the diocese. In order to construct a survey instrument, it was necessary to know something about the universe of need to which the programs responded; the routes by which people came to their doors; the community resources with which Outreach became involved in their helping efforts; and the terminology employed by Outreach personnel in the course of their work.

The interviews with diocesan personnel provided historical background on the development of PSM as well as a grounding in the current structure and operation of Parish Outreach. The interviews also revealed a strong institutional and personal commitment to Parish Outreach. The focus groups made it possible to obtain contextual information that contributed to an understanding of how Outreach worked as well as observations and experiences that would enhance the understanding of the quantitative findings of the survey.

Those taking part in the focus groups represented ten parishes from urban, suburban, and rural communities, including those with poor, wealthy, and economically mixed neighborhoods of different ethnic composition. There were six in the coordinators group, three of whom were female religious, two laywomen (one who by the end of the year would earn an MSW degree), and one layman. There were four in the core workers or volunteer group, two laywomen and two laymen. Except as noted, there was a high degree of consistency in what emerged from the two focus groups, whose members reported on their own experiences as well as what they had learned from colleagues in other parishes.

The second phase of the research involved a survey mailed to every parish in the diocese. The survey built upon what was learned in phase one and served to document the elements of the helping process in Outreach programs across the diocese at a given point in time, the spring of 1998.

Results of Focus Groups

Initiation of Service   There was general agreement among group participants about how people arrived at Outreach. Most were said to have come because of publicity in the community about the program, word of mouth, past experience of receiving help, or through contact with someone from the congregation—clergy, lay staff, or congregant. This was consistent with the earlier citations in the literature asserting that religious organizations are one of the first places people go for help with problems with which they cannot cope. The county Departments of Social Services (DSS) appeared to be the most likely source of referral from outside the parish.

In terms of what applicants presented, contrary to expectations, relatively few people came with needs related to serious and persistent mental illness. Long Island has been home to a number of psychiatric institutions that were in the process of closing or scaling down (Nelson, 1997). However, focus group members were able to recall in detail those with whom they had worked who were mentally ill because these individuals often required additional help in making use of assistance and following through on getting services due to problems associated with their disorder. Others, especially those with dual diagnoses of substance abuse and mental illness, were memorable because they were difficult to work with.

Meeting applicants' basic needs for food, clothing, and shelter was a preoccupation for all those in the focus groups. This is consistent with the findings of other recent studies of congregation-based services (Cnaan, 1998; Printz, 1998).

Beyond need, eligibility for service was usually defined geographically in terms of residence within parish boundaries. Applicants had to be prepared to show proof of residence, and nonresidents were referred back to the parish within whose boundaries they lived. However, this policy was not rigidly adhered to if the need was emergent, if the condition or circumstances of the applicant made return difficult, or if the home parish had service limitations.

Actual membership in any parish was never a condition for receiving services. Some group members could estimate the approximate proportion of applicants who were members of the parish or who were Catholic, some could not, and one, after a puzzled pause, said, "You know I never really thought about that." The virtual irrelevance of religious affiliation was again in keeping with the other recent findings (Cnaan 1998; Printz, 1998).

Users of Services   There was considerable diversity among those who utilized Outreach services in terms of socioeconomic status, ethnicity, age, and other demographic variables. In addition to those who live chronically on the margins, there were the new and inexperienced needy, the products of corporate downsizing that seemed to be hitting Long Island particularly hard. Some had been commuters into businesses in nearby New York City, but aerospace and other local industries that had played a prominent role in the economic development of the region were also cutting back.

Accustomed to a standard of living that they could no longer afford, these newly indigent often did not know where to begin reducing their expenditures. Some continued to maintain their lifestyle by going into debt. They also had difficulty asking for help; for almost all, Outreach was the first stop in their search for solutions to their problems.

Most parishes had some legal and illegal aliens within their borders; a few had them in significant numbers. Often new arrivals to this country, they faced problems in adjusting to a new language and culture and in finding and maintaining employment. Those problems were more likely than not to be compounded by problems related to eligibility for services, and worse, the threat of deportation. The proportion of Hispanics in this category was high, and the importance of religion in Latin culture may have made them more secure and comfortable in turning to the church for help rather than to official agencies, of which they were likely to be wary.

There was general agreement that the most frequent users of

Outreach services came from a segment of the population that not only cut across the above categories but represented virtually all sectors of society—single mothers and their children. Their needs were multiple: protection from abusive partners, income, child and health care, and transportation, as well as basic needs. The parish was one of many providers from whom they were receiving services, with Outreach often attempting to assist them in coordinating those services and advocating on their behalf.

Outreach Services   Formal assessments of community need were not the rule in the Outreach programs. The development of services appeared to be the result of an experientially based sense of need (what social workers would call "practice wisdom") or because of the availability of special resources within the parish community. Nonetheless, it was more likely that services, once established, became over- rather than undersubscribed. In addition to the ubiquitous food pantries and clothing rooms, Outreach programs established home care, transportation, financial and legal counseling, parent support groups, AIDS-related services, and other services, some of which became able to function autonomously. Outreach also worked with preexisting parish services such as the St. Vincent De Paul Societies, which offer assistance with basic needs.

Sometimes neighboring parishes had agreements to service residents from outside their boundaries. This seemed to happen most often when one parish offered a service that the other did not, but there were also occasions of sharing, on a situational or ongoing basis, when one parish had relatively more resources in relation to needs than did another.

The greatest degree of variation among parishes in the provision of services had to do with food, which group members unanimously agreed was the service in greatest demand. As one group member put it, "People will pay all their other bills first, and then there is no money for food." Most parishes had pantries that were stocked with contributions from parishioners and supplemented by foodstuffs from or through tax-supported food programs. Cash or vouchers were given so that people could get food. Most parishes had special distribution programs around major holidays. Several parish Outreach programs had arrangements with local restaurants to discreetly provide meals, usually on a limited basis. The relationship with one establishment was terminated when its attempt to gain publicity for its contribution threatened to violate the confidentiality of the recipients. Some parishes prepackaged food for applicants, based on numbers to be fed, age, or special health care needs. Others allowed people to pick what they needed from the shelves. Some placed greater limits than others on when or how often people could receive food.

Service Delivery Group participants saw Outreach services as being short term and focused on clearly defined needs, even though these needs might be recurrent. Counseling around intrapsychic and interpersonal issues was handled through referral.

All Outreach programs conducted individual assessments in which applicants were helped to consider needs in addition to those that brought them to the program, including those that may have contributed to or were related to their presenting problem or which might result from it. The diocese had trained the staff to do these assessments. It was clear both from the emphasis placed on assessments by coordinators and core workers and from the details they provided that the conduct of these assessments was a consistent practice. Another practice that was universal in these otherwise diverse programs was the handling of referrals. When a service was needed and there were alternatives in the community, staff offered options from which the person requiring the service could choose.

As we have said, Outreach programs employed existing parish services for those who requested their help. In fact, Outreach was the unit of the parish that almost always coordinated the service inputs of a congregation for those in need. This was often part of a larger case management function that Outreach personnel performed for those who sought their aid. An active part of that role was the assistance given to people to help them access services, especially from DSS. This ranged from preparation for the bureaucratic prerequisites (e.g., gathering necessary documents), to physical arrangements (e.g., transportation or someone to watch the children), to preparing them emotionally (e.g., "It's going to be like the Motor Vehicles [Department] only worse"), to actually accompanying someone to apply for or appeal a denial of service.

Reflections of Outreach Workers   The focus group members made it quite clear that they saw theirs as a residual service, but one for which they believed there would always be some level of need "for those who fall through the cracks," as one Outreach worker put it. Unfortunately, they saw those cracks as widening as public services continued to be cut back. They were also upset by the way people were being treated, especially by DSS. They struggled to try to be fair in their assessment of these agencies, sympathizing with their staff over the confusion wrought by the changes and reductions in service. Nonetheless, they felt that, in addition to what they had seen themselves, "We've heard too many stories [of people being treated badly] for there not to be something wrong with the system."

For the coordinators there was another source of frustration associated with the economic strain on many people in our society. There are so many single-parent families or ones in which both parents work full time that it was difficult to find and retain volunteer staff for Outreach. The one fairly reliable source seemed to be senior citizens, although the concomitants of age imposed limits on the kind and amount of work they could do. Some elderly volunteers are further restricted by responsibilities in their own families—increasingly, care for grandchildren.

Several of the participants had gone through difficult times themselves, including being unemployed or having significant family problems and having to ask for help. However, none had had the continuous exposure to the depth and extent of human suffering that they encountered in working in Outreach. Although the focus group members varied in terms of age and class, they were all white Roman Catholics. For some, their work was a radicalizing experience, leading them to identify with people very different from themselves. The extent to which members seemed to have worked through related issues appeared to be a function of experience, with the less experienced core workers or volunteers more likely to be having difficulties dealing with people who seemed uncooperative or appeared to be trying to take advantage. Coordinators mentioned working on these issues with the volunteers. Group members placed great importance on relationship as the context for helping, and therefore they looked for things that would help them relate better to applicants. Core workers spoke several times of trying to place themselves in the position of those who had to ask for help. One found it hard to judge someone who might be manipulative when that person was hungry.

Another way of facilitating the workers' ability to relate, which was mentioned in both groups, was to "see Christ" in the face of those they helped. This was one of the ways in which faith entered into the work of Outreach staff. It was their faith that led them to and sustained them in the work. In another example of this, one worker favored spiritual retreats as a method of coping with the threat of burnout.

The informants all asserted that they in no manner imposed their beliefs on those who came to Outreach. Several said that they had prayed or would pray with someone who made such a request but would not initiate such a discussion. There were also resources in the parishes to which workers could and did refer someone when spiritual guidance was sought.

The group participants did not see the work they did as the responsibility of Outreach and other providers alone. They believed it was the obligation of everyone in the congregation and the community to help their neighbors. They have expressed this belief by actively soliciting donations of time, talent, and resources from others. This has resulted in additions to their programs as well as assistance in individual cases. Outreach personnel are also aware of the power of the societal sanction of religious organizations' helping the needy. One coordinator was fully cognizant of the influence that her association with a church could have on believers and nonbelievers alike and made no apologies for hoping that that was one reason she was able to obtain assistance for those who came to her office.

Survey

A survey of parish-based services in all 134 parishes in the diocese was conducted to determine the correspondence between the data from the focus groups and the experience of the diocese as a whole and to quantify that experience. Since most parishes had more than one person providing services, two questionnaires were sent to each parish. Ninety-six responses were received from 62 (46%) of the parishes.

Source of Referrals   Respondents were asked to answer a number of questions concerning the last person who asked them for assistance. The first question concerned how that person had ended up coming to the parish for help. As the focus groups had reported, most frequently this was through the efforts of the service staff or someone else connected with the parish (33%). Self-referrals were the next most frequent source (27%), and public agencies, almost always the DSS, accounted for 22%. The remaining 18% came from a wide variety of sources.

Types of Need   A total of 330 needs were identified, making for a mean of 3.37 per case. The survey confirmed the literature and the statements of the focus group members that food, shelter, and clothing were the greatest needs, making up 24%, 26%, and 11% of the total needs identified, respectively.
   Sixty percent of those requesting assistance had asked for help in the past, with food (35%), shelter (18%), and clothing (13%) again topping the list of the needs that were addressed. The distribution of the estimated number of times the same person was helped was skewed by four extremely high values of between 36 and 60, meaning that some people had been helped that many times (the median number of times a person received help was 7).

Meeting the Needs   The parishes themselves addressed nearly 70% of the needs. Diocesan or other formal agencies were involved in meeting 15% of the needs, and DSS in 10%. That means that DSS was involved in addressing over 30 of the needs identified. However, they also, at least initially, denied public assistance in 18 (60%) of these cases. Partial data about the nature and course of these denials were available on 15 cases. Five were not appealed. Reasons were given for three of these denials. In two, applicants were ruled ineligible because of having too much income or other resources, and the third rejection was of a medically based claim. Ten cases were appealed. One appeal, involving client noncompliance (not going for a job interview), was not successful. In five instances the appeals have been successful. Of the three successful cases on which there were data on the original reason for denial, one was of a health-related nature, one was an issue of client income, and one case had been denied for client noncompliance. The appeals of the four remaining cases were pending.

DISCUSSION

There are obviously basic human needs—especially for food, clothing, and shelter—that are not being met by the formal service system on Long Island. Parish Outreach plays an important role in meeting these basic human needs. This was attested to by the success of these programs in reaching out to, engaging, and helping those in need. Moreover, there is evidence that the recipients of the services valued them. This can be seen in the number who were self-referred, having learned of the existence and apparent helpfulness of these services by word of mouth or through their own prior experience.

Perhaps of greatest interest is the interaction between the parishes and the county Departments of Social Services. The two county DSS agencies were the third most frequent source of referrals to the parishes and were involved in addressing a number of the needs presented. However, they also denied services to applicants.

The focus groups elaborated on the process of the involvement of the parishes in the appeal of such cases and the development of their relationship with DSS. Generally, the relationship between the parish and DSS developed as follows. The local DSS office would learn of the existence of the Outreach services and would begin to refer increasing numbers of cases to the parish, sometimes after denying assistance to the applicant. Because of the number of referrals and questions about the legitimacy of the rejections by DSS, Outreach staffs acquired and studied DSS and related regulations (the diocese also provided instruction in the use of these materials) and would begin to challenge some of the referrals. Usually, the referrals become more appropriate and a better, if at times tense, relationship developed between DSS and the parish.

Thus, parish-based services can make—and, in the Rockville Centre Diocese, are making—an important contribution to filling needs that have gone unmet and which are likely to increase as the devolution of services continues. They have also been effective in holding public agencies accountable for the assistance they are mandated to provide. Whether these and other congregation-based programs will be able to continue to keep pace with the level and kinds of need that are not publicly provided for remains to be seen.

Those involved in providing help through the parishes believe that there will always be a place for what they do because of inescapable "cracks" in the formal service system. Those who fall through these cracks include people in need who are technically ineligible for currently available public benefits or those being wrongly denied assistance for which they are eligible. Those involved in the Parish Social Ministry movement seem determined, through advocacy and public education, to keep this role proportionate to community capacity. The recent decision by the diocesan Social Ministry office to systematically collect information on the service activities of Outreach in the parishes can only help to support that determination by furnishing essential and otherwise hard-to-obtain data on unmet needs to help shape social policy and programs that will be so critical to the well-being of, at least, the two counties, particularly those people who are most vulnerable.

Implications

Among the trends in contemporary religion has been the emergence of an articulate and well-organized faction that has supported the devolution of services. To a certain extent, this reflects the larger public's dissatisfaction with what are seen as the failed social programs of the past and a distrust of government and of its ability to effectively deal with social ills. However, among the supporters of devolution in the religious community are those who associate the cause of social problems with personal failings and tie the resolution of those problems to religious solutions to a degree with which our culture has traditionally been uncomfortable (Ressler, 1998). These positions have raised fears about the extent to which faith-based service initiatives are driven as much by the opportunity to evangelize as by the desire to help. These concerns have been further heightened by the increased ability of government, under the welfare reform act, to fund services under religious auspices ("charitable choice") and have resurrected old debates about separation of church and state and the proper role of each in helping (Harvey, 1997; Sirico, 1997; Harvey, 1998).

Nonetheless, the actions of many congregations—those cited in the literature as well as Long Island's Parish Outreach— indicate that adherence to religious beliefs is much more the source of motivation for most congregation-based services than their goal. They express and give witness to beliefs without imposing those beliefs or discriminating against nonbelievers. Cnaan et al. assert that "inclusion and service provision to all community residents is the practice of most church-based social service provision" (1999, p. 31). This approach is not only consistent with social work values but also bodes well for collaboration among and beyond faith communities.

Services such as the Parish Outreach and the larger Parish Social Ministry described in this chapter, along with similar programs in other areas and in other denominations, have a unique contribution to make to the future of social welfare. The broad and deep roots of the individual congregation in its community, combined with its connection to other congregations in its own and other denominations, make for a powerful network that can be and is being activated on behalf of those whom devolution may ignore or push aside. Groups such as LI-CAN (Long Island Congregations, Associations and Neighborhoods) and the Babylon Clergy Cluster, both on Long Island, are already demonstrating their capacity in this regard. Social workers have not been able to develop, and probably cannot aspire to create, as potentially powerful mechanisms as these to counter the harms devolution threatens, but the profession possesses knowledge and skills that could, in synergistic partnership with congregations, be extremely effective in direct service, program development, and advocacy.

As the social welfare system moves from what it was to what it will become, congregation-based services have the flexibility, owing to their size and relative independence, to respond more quickly to service gaps than can the larger, less wieldy formal sector. Those in the formal sector should respect and support congregations in this pivotal, stopgap role and work with them to bring about more lasting solutions to these (transitional, one hopes) problems.

Congregations can also work with agencies to prevent or limit the need for scarce services. By virtue of their regular and intimate contact with members of their faith communities as well as the numbers of nonmembers who look to them for help, congregations are in a position to identify problems in their early stages and refer them to appropriate services. In the past, such cooperation has been hampered by notions, on both sides, about antagonisms between secular and religious-based services that, as we have seen, may have little basis in fact. Not only do most congregations seem to separate evangelism from their social services, but the helping professions have substantially restored the importance of the spiritual to its rightful place in a holistic perception of human life (Ressler, 1998).

While the mediating role of congregations during any transitional period is important, the continuing need for and expansion of the private sector in social services, including that of religious congregations, appears inevitable (Weil, 1996). In addition to trying to keep expectations in this regard realistic, congregations could help reawaken an active sense of caring and interdependence about one's neighbor and community. Communities might then reclaim some of the responsibilities once ceded to social welfare institutions, responsibilities that those institutions either were prevented from carrying out or were unable to carry out. Since the latter is the prevailing public opinion, unless and until it changes, citizens will have to take a more active role in helping the needy or else see the general quality of life deteriorate. Congregations have demonstrated that they are capable of tapping into, developing, and directing the universal disposition to help that is so often the product of the inculcation of religious values or reinforced by those values. Congregation-level efforts may thus contribute to transforming fundamental ideas about helping those in need while they also serve to humanize the process of devolution.

REFERENCES

Allen-Meares, P. (1989). Adolescent sexuality and premature parenthood: Role of black church in prevention. *Journal of Social Work and Human Sexuality, 8,* 133–142.

Berger, P., & Neuhaus, R. (1977). *To empower people.* Washington, DC: American Enterprise Institute.

Boyte, H. (1990). *Commonwealth: A return to citizen politics.* New York: Free Press.

Cnaan, R. A. (1998). *Social and community involvement of religious congregations housed in historic religious properties: Findings from a six-city study.* Philadelphia: University of Pennsylvania School of Social Work Program for the Study of Organized Religion and Social Work.

Cnaan, R. A., Wineberg, R. J., & Boddie, S. C. (1999). *The newer deal: Social work and religion in partnership.* New York: Columbia University Press.

Cosgrove, J. (1999). Technology transfer in community development: The case of basic ecclesial communities. *Journal of Global Awareness, 3*(1), 4–11.

Faith initiative enhances treatment efforts. (1996, Summer). *Substance Abuse and Mental Health Services Administration (SAMHSA) News, 3,* 5–8.

Federal News Service. (1996, February 20). *Governors' welfare proposal.* Hearing of the Human Resources Subcommittee of the House of Representatives Ways and Means Committee.

Goodman, D. (1996, Summer). SAMHSA promotes dialog between faith and health communities. *Substance Abuse and Mental Health Services Administration (SAMHSA) News, 3,* 1.

Harvey, T. J. (1997, December 11). Religion can't replace opportunity. *The Chronicle of Philanthropy,* pp. 53–54.

Harvey, T. J. (1998, February 26). Solutions to poverty must be more than faith-based. *The Chronicle of Philanthropy,* pp. 50–51.

Himes, K. R. (1986). The local church as a mediating structure. *Social Thought, 12*(1), 23–30.

Kilpatrick, A. C., & Holland, T. P. (1990). Spiritual dimensions of practice. *The Clinical Supervisor, 8*, 125–140.

Nelson, S. S. (1997, February 7). State cut for mentally ill draws fire. *Newsday (Nassau Edition)*, p. A22.

Peeler, A. (1985). *Parish social ministry: A vision and resource.* Washington, DC: National Conference of Catholic Charities.

Printz, T. J. (1998, April). *Faith-based service providers in the nation's capital: Can they do more?* (Charting Civil Society Series No. 2). Washington, DC: The Urban Institute.

Ressler, L. E. (1998). When Christianity and social work conflict. In B. Hugen (Ed.), *Christianity and social work* (pp. 165–186). Botsford, CT: North American Association of Christians in Social Work.

Shorto, R. (1997, December 7). Belief by the numbers. *New York Times Magazine*, pp. 60–61.

Sirico, R. A. (1998, January 29). The poor need more than government can provide. *The Chronicle of Philanthropy*, pp. 38–40.

Urban Institute Center on Nonprofits and Philanthropy. (1998). *Services and capacity of religious congregations in the Washington, DC, metropolitan area.* Washington, DC: Urban Institute.

Weil, M. O. (1996). Community building: Building community practice. *Social Work, 41*, 481–499.

Wineberg, R. J. (1996). An investigation of religious support of public and private agencies in one community in an era of retrenchment. *Journal of Community Practice, 3*(2), 35–55.

17

Spirituality as Empowerment in Social Work Practice

Sr. Mary Sean Foley, RSM, MTS, CSW

> Dignity is the awareness of what I, as an individual, stand for, the awareness that I represent a degree of greatness, a legacy, a reality much larger than my own being. The substance of such dignity is knowledge, involvement in sacred drama, reverence, the intuition of a high purpose.
>
> Abraham Joshua Heschel

INTRODUCTION

THE 100TH ANNIVERSARY of the profession of social work in 1999 holds the magic of bringing the spirit of the past into dialogue with the reality of the present. Remembering can usher in the passion or spirit that first brought the celebrated event into being. The spirit of the past invited into dialogue in this chapter is the profound relationship between the social work profession in America and the spirituality that inspired it. This chapter shows how a spiritually sensitive social work practice can enrich the profession, empower clients, and inspire a social action that could be a liberating force in our society. The first section, on the renaissance of spirituality in the rising culture, will discuss spirituality as one of the characteristics of the postmodern era and offer a view of a possible new anthropology. From there, some distinctions between spirituality and religion will be offered. The next section will connect with the spiritual roots of the profession. The final section will speak to the implications of a spiritually sensitive social work for the development of today's professional, for social work practice itself, and for the empowerment of clients.

The professional ancestors of today's social workers were living their spirituality by loving their neighbors. In the late 19th and early 20th centuries, when the effects of rapid industrialization began to widen the gap between rich and poor, they opened their hearts, homes, minds, and political voices to bring about more humane treatment for poor people and to fight for the establishment of more just laws. They founded hospitals, orphanages, settlement houses, and numerous small neighborhood charities for the suffering poor of their day.

The reality of the present, some 100 years later, finds in that same America an economy that appears to be thriving, as well as unprecedented breakthroughs in science and technology that have revolutionized work, making it easier, safer, and more productive—while at the same time eliminating the need for millions of workers. A global market system enhanced by advances in transportation and communication has further affected employment opportunities. For example, factories are now organized practically anywhere in the world at much lower labor costs than in America. Breakthroughs in physics, chemistry, and biotechnologies have made it possible to cure in ways that seem miraculous. Yet as this dramatic technological evolution is advancing, there is a concurrent social regression. Individual human rights are threatened as government abdicates its concern for the common good to the states and to the market system—a system that increasingly controls government by its economic policies and political power (Hug & Riley, 1998). The social worker of the 21st century not only faces a widening of the gap between the rich and the poor but is also confronted with increasingly less clear strategies of intervention.

When the technological scientific worldview gained ascendance in the 19th century, social work emulated the assumptions of what Trattner (1984) called "scientific charity." It began to follow the diagnostic approaches of the medical profession in general and of psychiatry in particular. It was the adoption of this scientific paradigm that eventually led to a demise of religion or spirituality as having any deep significance in people's well-being. Things of the spirit could not bear the empirical scrutiny that characterized the scientific method. As a result, the spiritual dimension of a person as an indicator of a healthy and fully realized individual was deemphasized in social work education. In the modern age, the social worker would not find spiritual expression in any of the courses that would prepare an aspiring professional to encourage people to help themselves. The result has been that for too long, social workers and other behavioral science professionals have had to second-guess the credibility of spirituality as a powerful motivating force for personal growth and societal change.

At the same time, the accomplishments of the first 100 years of the field of social work have been heroic. Since compassion and concern for justice are expressions of spirituality, the motivation for social work is fundamentally and in essence a spiritual one (Canda, 1995). Whether named as such or not, spirituality has not been lacking in the delivery of services. The dynamic of social work activity is essentially an expression of the love of humankind. In that sense, social work is spirituality in action. It is my belief that we can cross the threshold of the second century of our profession as social workers with no better companion than a renewed consciousness of the significance of a spiritually sensitive approach, both to those who seek our help and to examining the political systems set up to secure the common good. What is suggested here is a recognition that spirituality is the mysterious essence of every human being in his or her quest for meaning and that it is that same spirituality that is also the motivating energy behind all social work and all the compassion and kindness that human persons extend to one another.

The Renaissance of Spirituality

As the profession stands on the horizon of its second century, civilization stands on the horizon of a new millennium. Looking around, in addition to a scientific and technological revolution, the rising culture is also marked by a renaissance of spiritual awareness. This renaissance is just one part of a larger paradigm shift that carries within it some profound cultural changes in human consciousness. This new paradigm, according to physicist Fritjof Capra in his book *The Turning Point,* asserts that our one-sided scientific modern culture is going through a period of rebalancing. The new paradigm of the rising culture is rooted in the protests of the social movements of the 1960s and 1970s, where many of the conventional and stereotyped images of human nature were challenged by the great number of ethnic liberation movements that revolted against prejudice and racism. These struggles were amplified by the activity of other marginalized groups—women, homosexuals, older people, single parents, the physically handicapped. Capra states that while civil rights leaders demanded that African-American citizens be included in the political process, the free speech movement demanded the same for students. As women questioned patriarchal authority, humanistic psychologists questioned the authority of physicians and therapists (Capra, 1982, pp. 416–417). The slow and steady emergence from the scientific modern paradigm is ushering in a rapid spread of the term "postmodernism."

It is important to point out that the term "postmodern" is used in a confusing variety of ways. The common element suggests that humanity can and must go beyond the modern if we are to survive. The term is used differently in literary and artistic circles, and differently again in architecture. In some circles the term is used to define the potpourri of ideas found in New Age metaphysics, which are more premodern than postmodern. It is the postmodern position of theological and philosophical circles that is of interest in discussing the emergence of spirituality in the rising culture. In these circles postmodernity seeks to transcend the limitations of the scientific worldview, but in two radically different ways. One, closely related to literary/artistic postmodernism, was inspired by French thinkers who sought to overcome modernism by an eliminative or deconstructionist philosophy—one that dismisses the elements necessary for a worldview, such as God, self, purpose, meaning, a real world, and truth as correspondence.

The postmodernism of interest in this chapter can be described as a constructive or revisionary philosophy. It seeks to build on the marvelous advances of science but refuses to allow the data of science to be the only source to contribute to the creation of a new paradigm or worldview. Going beyond the modern will involve transcending its individualism, anthropocentrism, racism, patriarchy, mechanization, economism, consumerism, nationalism, and militarism, but will not lose the unparalleled advances of the modern age (Griffin, 1988, pp. x–xi).

The prevailing beliefs of the modern age, then, affirmed only those phenomena that could be observed, measured, and counted. Only then could such phenomena be considered reliable fact. In this postmodern period we see a new appreciation of the intuitive mind and an appreciation of an emerging holistic perspective in relation to practically every aspect of life (Griffin, 1988, p. 4). This new paradigm provides support for values such as spirituality, new interdependent ways of relating to each other, nature, and the cosmos as a whole.

Along with our profession of social work, the fields of psychology, psychiatry, medicine, physics, business, and even politics are exploring or using metaphors of the spiritual. In his book *The Politics of Meaning*, Michael Lerner lays out a detailed plan for a politics of heart and spirit to replace the cynicism and divisiveness of contemporary American politics.

In their book *Timeless Healing*, Dr. Herbert Benson and Mary Stark write about the scientific exploration of the power of human persons to promote their better health and healing through their beliefs. In December 1997 the *New York Times* devoted the entire magazine section to spirituality and religion in America and cited somewhat surprising statistics: "Fifty years ago 95% of Americans believed in God and today, the number is 96%. Those who pray, 90%, remain the same today. Compared with 1947 when 43% of the population gave thanks before meals, 63% did so in 1997. Of the existing 126 medical schools in the United States, 40% are now teaching future doctors about the role of religion in health care" (Miles, 1997, p. 56).

Of the accredited graduate schools of social work in this country, 30 now offer courses in spirituality. For 25 years or more within the field of psychology, there has been a transpersonal movement that includes within its field of inquiry the dimensions of the human person that transcend or are beyond the ordinary, personal, and limited self. It seeks to include the vast realm of human potential dealing with ultimate meaning, with higher entities, with God, with love, with compassion, and with purpose (Tart, 1991, p. ix).

The inclusion of religious or spiritual problems in the *DSM-IV* marks a significant breakthrough in psychiatry. With the addition of this new category, mental health professionals may become better equipped to deal with the religious and spiritual aspects of human experience. "Surveys show that religion and spirituality play a central role in the lives of most of the population. . . . Religiosity and spirituality are linked to psychological well being, involve issues of love and relatedness, and provide a source of meaning and purpose in life" (Lukoff, Lu, & Turner, 1992, p. 680). This new consciousness of spirituality reflects a profound change in human perspective. Society has already begun to speak a new language, one that increasingly not only reveals an inclusivity in gender but also embraces and points to perceptions of all reality that are less dualistic and more holistic. It is a consciousness that attempts to heal the split between sacred and secular, between body and soul, one that encourages a deepening health and ecological awareness.

A holistic approach to life presumes that all aspects of life must be considered in the search for balance and harmony in relation to self, others, the earth, and the mystery that is often referred to as God. The approach invites a new awareness of the human within the intrinsic dynamics of the earth itself and points to a world that is taken by surprise at the stirring of a new hunger for things of the spirit. The words "holistic," "healing," and "holy" come from the Greek root "holos"—to be complete or whole.

In summary, the renaissance of spirituality can be seen as part of a new consciousness that is all around us and which has been steadily emerging during the last decades of the 20th century. It offers an image of the human as a spiritual being in relationship with self, others, creation, and the sacred. In other words, it suggests that a new anthropology or new way of looking at what it means to be human may be under way.

Spirituality and Religion

It has been said above that the popularity of spirituality in this postmodern time is expressive of a much more pervasive cul-

tural shift. This next section will examine some working definitions of spirituality and religion in order to facilitate clarity in
the discussion.

Spirituality

What is spirituality? Our sociologists remind us that spirituality
lies at the heart of culture. It shapes the beliefs, mores, and behaviors of a people and empowers them with a sense of meaning
in life. But what is it? Gerald May, psychiatrist and author of
Care of Mind, Care of Spirit, talks about the confusion around
such terms as well as "soul," "psyche," and "spirit" and the
dilemma of understanding one another's definitions before attempting to communicate. May brings out that spirit implies energy and power. He sees spirituality as the vital dynamic force
of being that brings the soul into living reality (1990, p. 7).

Canda states that most cultures do not have separate words
for "religion" and "spirituality." Spirituality is the way of
life—it is the way a people find meaning, moral guidance, and
proper relationship between themselves, all fellow beings, and
the mystery that infuses all (Canda, 1995, p. 5). "Spirituality," as
the term is used in this chapter, refers to that intrinsic and universal aspect of human being that involves the quest for a sense
of meaning and purpose. It is expressed in loving relationships
with oneself, other people, the nonhuman, and ultimate reality
(however conceived). By no means is this definition proposed as
conclusive, but merely as a clarification of the orientation from
which this chapter is proceeding.

I said earlier that spirituality is one of the characteristics of the
postmodern paradigm. It is not separate from any other aspect
of human experience, but is rather the integration of all aspects.
The use of metaphor has always served well in attempting to
articulate the mystery of ultimate meaning. The metaphor of the
human breath, for example, that which brings life, has been a
common metaphor of embodied divine spirit. It is "ruah" in
Hebrew, "pneuma" in Greek, "prana" in Sanscrit, "Chi" in Chinese, "Ki" in Japanese, "spiritus" in Latin, and "Ana" in Pali.
Pali is one of the languages of the original Buddhist scriptures.
While Buddhism and Taoism are nontheistic traditions, they are
spiritualities within our inclusive definition in that they are ex-

pressed through relationship with self, others, and the world. Buddhism, for instance, teaches that ultimate reality is universal mind, which all humans are capable of experiencing and becoming. Taoism is an ancient spiritual tradition founded by Lao-tzu in China around the sixth century b.c.e. It teaches that all of life is contained in a superior universal intelligence called the Tao which the human person can become by giving up attachment to all concepts, judgments, and desires. The mind, in surrendering to the flow of the Tao, naturally grows in compassion and comes to know within its own being the central truths of the art of living.

Religion

Most people, when asked about their spirituality, immediately think of their religion if they belong to a particular religious tradition. If they do not belong to a particular tradition, they are likely to tell you about their belief in the meaning of human life.

Religion is an institutionalized set of beliefs or doctrines and practices that express the spirituality of a particular group of people. Without an institution or a community of support and a system for carrying forward the spiritual beliefs of a people, the spiritual wisdom of the ages would have been lost. The word "religion" stems from the Latin verb "religare," meaning "to tie back" or "to bind." A particular religion, then, offers a way of relating to and uniting with the mystery that many people call God. Religion expresses one's relationship with God through the rituals and prayer experiences of the individual, the group, or the community of believers.

Since human persons cannot express or celebrate deeply held values and beliefs without metaphor, symbol, and ritual, organized religion provides these to tie the human experience to the sacred. Meaningful rituals celebrate the seasons of life: birth, childhood, coming-of-age, marriage and other forms of life companionship, and old age and death, bereavement, and remembrance. Religious rituals even provide for a harmonious division of the calendar year into seasons of mourning and joy, repentance and triumph.

Religions have their own particular theologies. Theology is

discourse about the sacred—or more simply, faith seeking understanding. It may be well to stop and remember that since the dawn of human reason, the idea of God or a supreme being has been thought by many to be incomprehensible to the limited mind of humankind. Neither individually nor collectively can we know all that we need to know, much less all that we might wonder about. A man or woman who decides to practice a religion may do so not to acknowledge the mystery of religion, but rather, first, to acknowledge the mystery in response to which religion has come into being, and second, to respond to the felt necessity—somewhat mysterious in itself—to live a moral or responsible life even when the grounds of morality cannot be known by the rational mind. The philosopher Immanuel Kant wrote 200 years ago: "Two things fill the mind with ever increasing awe, the oftener and the more steadily we reflect on them. They are the starry heavens above and the moral law within" (Miles, 1997, p. 56).

To help further distinguish between spirituality and religion, one could say that someone might adhere faithfully to the teachings and practices of a given religion and at the same time not be a spiritually mature person. The fruit of the practice of religion would lie in the way the person relates to others and all of life. On the other hand, one might have no formal religion and live life in peace and harmony with all of humankind and all of creation and be a spiritually mature individual.

The spiritual experience of relationship and unity can provide a resolution to the problem of human suffering and alienation. The spiritually mature person can realize the unity and relatedness of all things and can come to a profound desire to express compassion and justice to other people and life forms. This depth of being can be realized by any human person in any walk of life irrespective of his or her social or economic standing. It transcends formal education.

Spiritual Roots of the Social Work Profession

The primary mission of the social worker is to enhance human well-being with particular attention to the needs and empowerment of people who are vulnerable, oppressed, and living in poverty. While the 100-year-old profession of social work is a very recent event on the page of human history, its mission of enhancing human well-being is a legacy that goes back to ancestors from as far back as the beginning of recorded history. In primitive civilizations, humankind petitioned deities that were personifications of the great powers in nature. For example, the sun, the earth, and the elements were seen as mysterious and unpredictable. They were thought capable of enhancing or destroying existence, health, or security, and were worshiped as divinities that could be appealed to and who deserved expressions of gratitude. Primitive societies were not for the most part concerned with a sense of moral obligation to anyone outside their own small cultural group, and this feeling is freely shared in their religious prayers, such as the following: "Let me live, find the enemy, not be afraid of him, find him asleep, and kill many of him" (Burtt, 1982, p. 14). In the course of time, civilized societies, no longer struggling to as great a degree with the threatening forces of nature, became preoccupied with a different mystery: how to live in peace and harmony with other human beings.

The great religious traditions, such as Judaism, Christianity, Islam, and Buddhism, carry in their essential doctrines the belief in a universal moral responsibility to all persons simply because they are human. Throughout the ages we have examples of societies whose understanding of their relationship to God and neighbor compelled them to care and to perform acts of kindness. In ancient Egypt, grain was routinely stored for famines, and religious injunctions required Egyptians to give food even to strangers in times of famine. Writings buried with the dead as far back as 3500 b.c.e. noted such things as "I have not done violence to a poor man—I have not made anyone sick or weak. I gave bread to the hungry—clothed the naked and ferried him who had no boat" (Popple, Phillip, & Leighninger, 1990, p. 100).

In Jewish societies, gleanings (corners of the field and forgotten produce) were reserved for the poor. Even strangers were free to take food when they needed it. Our Jewish legacy from Deuteronomy 15 states: "If there is among you a poor man . . . in any of your towns within your land which the Lord gives you, you shall not harden your heart or shut your hand against your poor brother, but you shall open your hand to him and lend him sufficient for his need whatever it may be. . . . Take heed lest there be a base thought in your heart." The Jewish philosopher Maimonides outlined eight degrees of charity. The lowest is as follows: "Give, but with reluctance and regret. This is a gift of the hand but not of the heart." And the highest: "Lastly, the eighth and most meritorious of all is to anticipate charity by preventing poverty" (Popple et al., 1990, p. 101).

In ancient China in the first century B.C.E., granaries were established to give free grain to the poor. A common greeting in China in those days was not "Hello, how are you?" but "Have you eaten?" By the second century C.E., Christians in Jerusalem sold their possessions and gave to those in need. The legacy from Christianity holds central the cultivation in each person of virtues or strengths of faith, hope, and charity, emphasizing that the greatest of these is charity. The basis of the Christian approach to social welfare is the well-known passage from Matthew 25: "For I was hungry and You gave me food, I was thirsty and you gave me drink, I was a stranger and you welcomed me. . . . And the Righteous will ask . . . 'Lord when did we see you naked hungry, thirsty, imprisoned or sick.?' And then that beautiful mystical response: 'Amen, I say to you as long as you did it to one of these, my least brethren, you did it to me.' " For the Christian, the belief in the indwelling presence of God in humankind promotes an awesome and humble awareness. Through the centuries it invited believers to envision themselves and others as co-creators of the kingdom of God on earth.

Among the fundamental tenets of Islam in all its branches is the obligation to give charity. From the Koran we read the words: "O Ye Believers, give in alms of the good things you have earned, and of what we have brought forth from you from out of the earth."

Our professional ancestors in these earlier civilizations are varied, colorful, and inspiring. As with primitive humankind, who worshiped gods of nature out of survival needs, civilized societies tried to please their gods by right action toward other persons, but they also had developed through the experience of this effort a spiritual consciousness that true happiness or salvation consists in identifying with something that transcends self-interest and could unite the spirit of humankind with a divine Other. It was in this aspiration that the seed of social work as we know it today was sown. First people volunteered freely, then organized in response to overwhelming need, objected to the injustice they found, and finally came to the realization that helping others required skills and training.

In the mid-19th century, America saw a generous, creative, and impassioned response to grievous injustices to human beings. Among these injustices were racism, the mistreatment of prisoners, the neglect and abuse of people with mental illness, the plight of orphans and widows, the despair of homeless and poor people, and concern for children laboring in factories and sweatshops. Evolving largely from the inspiration of teachings of the Judeo-Christian religious tradition, the social work profession emerged from primarily two general movements around the middle and late 19th century: the Charity Organization Societies and the Settlement House Movement.

The hardship and destitution created by the severe depression of the 1870s gave rise to a degree of desperation by the poor unemployed. Private citizens, charitable bodies, and public authorities set up soup kitchens and breadlines and provided lodging, food, clothing, and even cash to those in need. There was little or no investigation of need or safeguards against duplicity. Many charity workers were dismayed at the excess of relief and the chaotic way in which it was distributed. They argued that the individual needs of those helped were not being met. Charity work needed to be organized along scientific lines. This gave rise to the Charity Organization Societies. These societies aimed not only at eliminating fraud and inefficiency but also at devising a constructive method of dealing with or treating poverty (Trattner, 1984, p. 92). They were patterned after the London Charity Organization Society. Social casework became the method of the time, and the diagnosis of need and the documentation that was part of this eventually gave rise to new perceptions about the causes of poverty. Society and the economy—not the individual moral failings of the poor—were seen as the primary reasons for the prevailing poverty. Social work research grew and brought forward the rise of the profession.

The American Settlement House Movement also had its roots in England, particularly Toynbee Hall in East London. Allen Davis, the historian of the movement, demonstrated that most who were inspired to begin or join the settlement movement were persons who took their religion seriously. Religious feeling was the main factor in their conversion to settlement work and social reform (Trattner, 1984, p. 164). Jane Addams, who in 1889 founded Hull House, which was to become America's first settlement house, stated that she had "an impulse to share in the life of the poor . . . to make social service express the spirit of Christ" (Trattner, 1984, p. 164). Briefly, the settlements embodied the neighborhood ideal—the desire to create an organic community among the people and institutions of a particular location. They stressed the interdependence of social groups and the state in an organically structured society. Full of optimism and zeal, the settlement house members believed that if the more fortunate members of society were to live among the less fortunate, they would understand the real problems of the poor and learn how to meet them. By 1900 there were 100 such settlements, and by 1910 there were 400 making a significant contribution to improving the nation's living conditions. Through writings, public speeches, and advocacy, the poor became less invisible in America. The settlement houses laid the ground-work for group work and community organization in social work (Trattner, 1984, pp. 155–178).

These two movements, although philosophically at odds, were born from the efforts of people whose profound belief in their teachings about love of neighbor and the dignity of human life motivated them to energetically find creative ways to respond. The two movements began to appreciate each other's strengths and began to cooperate and merge into social work by the early 20th century. The differences lay not so much in any hesitation to do something about human misery and injustice but rather in how best to go about accomplishing that goal.

Respect for human dignity, compassion, and concern for justice were the spiritual values that fired both movements. Earlier it was stated that spirituality, as it is used in this chapter, refers to that intrinsic and universal aspect of the human being that involves the quest for meaning and purpose and which is expressed in loving relationships with oneself, other people, the nonhuman, and ultimate reality (however conceived). Respect for human dignity, compassion, and concern for justice continue to be the values that are well expressed in social work's ethic of self-determination of the client, a nonjudgmental attitude, and the obligation to provide information on all sources of solutions that are available to the client. Social work has its roots in the works of individuals or groups whose efforts grew out of their beliefs in the spiritual values of love, justice, and community. These values have exerted a powerful influence on social policy affecting family and child welfare in this country. When the need for systemic remedies was realized, some social workers became political advocates and sought social justice for those who had no voice in public policy. The spirit of loving one's neighbor is deep in the psyche of humanity. It is clear that the values held within the practice of the profession of social work express an essentially spiritual consciousness, but one that must be nourished and kept alive by its acknowledgment and expression.

SOME OF THE REASONS WHY SOCIAL WORK IGNORED SPIRITUALITY

Given this brief history of the profession, what then are some of the reasons why social work ignored spirituality? Two points are noteworthy. First, as social work began to advance as a profession, particularly as it attempted to apply scientific methods to the management of giving aid to the poor, it downplayed the virtue of charity as a legitimate right of any poor person. The Charity Organization Societies' institution of an investigation of appeals for assistance became the means of separating the worthy from the unworthy poor and set out to provide the needy with moral exhortation rather than handing out relief. Friendly visitors had tried to influence and motivate the poor, believing that poverty was the result of moral weakness. These volunteer charity workers were burdened with maintaining detailed records in addition to strictly adhering to casework methods. Their experience led to the creation of training schools for charity workers, the consequent gradual demise of volunteer service, and the rise of the social work profession. Step by step, the leadership of agencies and charity organizations became the province of the professional business administrator. This business approach was no longer the inspired response of religious groups or of philanthropy to the plight of the poor (Trattner, 1984, p. 102).

The second reason is linked to the first. In the 1920s, as social work continued its struggle to strengthen its standing among the professions, it accepted readily the psychoanalytic concept that focused on the importance of childhood experiences and emotions in shaping personality and behavior. Social workers eagerly embraced psychiatry's scientific theory, since it provided them with understanding and ways of responding to behaviors they had long observed in their clients. At the same time, they also adopted psychiatry's tendency to ignore or pathologize the religious and spiritual dimensions of human experience. For example, some clinical literature has described the spiritual or mystical experience as symptomatic of ego regression, borderline psychosis, a psychotic episode, or temporal lobe dysfunction (Lukoff et al., 1992).

The professions in any of the prominent fields in the early 20th century were influenced by the premises of the scientific movement. It was this scientific paradigm that eventually led to a demise of religion or spirituality as having any deep significance in the well-being of people.

SPIRITUALITY AS EMPOWERMENT IN PROFESSIONAL SOCIAL WORK PRACTICE

What would a return to recognizing spirituality look like for social work today? Would it in any way compromise the goals of the profession? In many ways, there would be no difference at all from the way in which a majority of social workers serve their clients now. Interaction with clients always presumes a solid foundation in social work theory and practice and the commitment to embrace the primary mission of the profession—to help people in need and to address social problems. Spiritually sensitive social work is broader in that it is reflective, or it holds in consciousness the deeply held beliefs about the interdependence and essential equality of all people. This consciousness awakens a quality of response on behalf of those who are cut off from fullness of life. For the professional, the client, and the societal systems, then, there are significant implications of empowerment. Some of these will be discussed in the following paragraphs.

Interventions

With the deeper spiritual awareness of the profound relationship between mind, body, and spirit, the social work professional would always employ interventions that emphasize and encourage health practices such as good nutrition and physical fitness. Wellness enhances self-image and worth.

   Depending on the individual client, techniques of visualization, some types of meditation, and journaling activity might be selectively used in conjunction with traditional interventions. Meditation practices can be very effective in strengthening concentration and in marshaling the power of the will. With respect to visualization, journaling, or meditation, great care must be taken to avoid imposing any images or teachings that would offend the client's self-determination or the client's particular beliefs. When appropriate, a client's religious or spiritual support system might be engaged on his or her behalf. The parish community, the synagogue, or the indigenous healer might be effectively engaged as part of the client's support system. The continuing waves of immigrants to our cities and towns bring today's social workers into partnership with immigrants whose indigenous spiritualities are an integral part of their life supports. Paulino emphasizes that including spirituality and indigenous beliefs in social work education is essential to practitioners, researchers, and educators (1955, p. 106).

Professional Empowerment

Does this broadened dimension of social work practice have any implications for the professional development of the social worker? Professional social workers' awareness of their own deeply held beliefs about the meaning of life is the only basis from which they can understand and appreciate the significance of the deeply held beliefs of another. Whatever these beliefs are, they frame perceptions and feelings about the joys and sufferings life presents and offer some preparation for facing the reality of suffering and death.

Perhaps the most significant implication is the empowerment that flows from the increased sense of dignity that enriches and infuses professional identity and allows the professional to extend not only to clients but to colleagues a recognition that enhances relationship and mutual respect. A tremendous amount of energy and leadership potential in social work agencies is expended on personnel and on grievance work with staff. Real social work concerns too often flounder on in-house issues of ego and power. By contrast, the spiritually motivated professional will draw on the mission of social work, the mission of the agency or practice, and the skills of the profession to enhance truthful and courageous conversation in times of conflict.

With ongoing self-reflection on their own spiritual beliefs about self and others, professional social workers can more easily transcend the biases, prejudices, or beliefs concerning the diversity of culture, religion, gender, age, and sexual orientation. These social workers are likely to be more effective in honoring the dignity of clients, colleagues, and the values of the profession as they carry out their roles and responsibilities. Less professional burnout conserves energy for other activities—activities such as designing, proposing, networking, collaborating, and advocating more creatively for fair and effective anti-poverty programs, health care, housing, livable wages. A sense of one's spiritual identity awakens the intuitive and enriches the human mind with creative power.

SUMMARY AND CONCLUSION

In this chapter we have examined how a spiritually sensitive social work practice can enrich the profession, empower clients, and inspire social action. In conclusion, we recognize that while historical humility requires us to acknowledge that religious organizations have made many mistakes in the course of history, their spirituality unleashed a creative energy that brought about societal changes in circumstances of human destitution. Acknowledging and exploring our spirituality must be part of our profession's most treasured resource if we are to prepare well for and address the challenges of the 21st century.

In the last analysis, it is the love of neighbor and the belief in the sacred dignity of each human person that is the compelling force behind all social work and behind all the compassion and kindness that any human person can give another. Spiritually sensitive social workers will acknowledge the spiritual beliefs of their clients and recognize that these beliefs are a source of empowerment that can enable them to go beyond any psychosocial barrier to experiencing fulfillment in life.

REFERENCES

Benson, H., & Stark, M. (1996). *Timeless healing.* New York: Scribner.

Burtt, E. A. (Ed.). (1982). *The teachings of the compassionate buddha* (2nd ed.). New York: Penguin.

Canda, R. E. (1995, September). Retrieving the soul of social work. *Society for Spirituality and Social Work Newsletter*, pp. 5–8.

Capra, F. (1982). *The turning point.* New York: Simon & Schuster.

Griffin, D. (Ed.). (1988). *Spirituality and society: Postmodern visions.* New York: SUNY Publications.

Hug, J. E., & Riley, M. (1998, August). *Covenanting for a new kinship: Human rights at the heart of our mission.* Unpublished paper, Center for Concern, Washington, DC.

Lerner, M. (1996). *The politics of meaning: Restoring hope and possibility in an age of cynicism.* Reading, MA: Addison-Wesley.

Lukoff, D., Lu, F., & Turner, R. (1992). Toward a more culturally sensitive *DSM-IV. Journal of Nervous and Mental Disease, 180*(11), 673–682.

May, G. G. (1990). *Care of mind, care of spirit.* San Francisco: Harper & Row.

Miles, J. (1997, December 7). Religion makes a comeback. *New York Times Magazine*, p. 56.

Paulino, A. (1955). Spiritism, santeria, brujeria, and voodooism: A comparative view of indigenous healing systems. *Journal of Teaching in Social Work, 12*(1/2), 105–121.

Popple, D., Phillip, R., & Leighninger, L. (1990). *Social work, social welfare, and American society.* Needham Heights, MA: Allyn & Bacon.

Tart, C. T. (1991). *Transpersonal psychology.* San Francisco: Harper & Row.

Trattner, W. I. (1984). *From poor law to welfare state.* New York: Free Press.

18

Social Work (International): Economics in the Service of Social Issues—Human Development and Solution-Focused Programs

Natalie Z. Riccio, PhD

> The world social situation is . . . the most serious problem that must be tackled today, since it poses a major threat to international stability.
>
> P. Aylwin, UN General Assembly, 1990 (this led to the 1991 Economic and Social Council session to initiate and convene the 1995 World Summit for Social Development)

INTRODUCTION

THE WORLD IS WITNESSING the expansion of prosperity for some, and at the same time the expansion of deplorable, absolute poverty for others. This chapter will address social and economic concerns from an international perspective and examine issues from a macro to a micro level of attention. It will begin by looking at serious social problems as identified and studied by the United Nations and its affiliated agencies, the recent definition of human poverty and human well-being as defined in the Human Development Report, and lastly, look at solutions being applied at the local level using micro-credit methods.

BACKGROUND

We are now looking at the emerging world following the end of the cold war. The UN has initiated a series of international meetings focused on major global social, economic, and environmental problems: the Children's Summit (1991), the Earth Summit (1992), the Human Rights meeting (1993), the International Conference on Population and Development (1994), the World Summit for Social Development (1995), the Fourth Global Conference on Women (1995), and the Second UN Conference on Human Settlements (1996).

Many regard the UN as an international think tank. This is reflected in the various conference agendas (a kind of town meeting of the international community) defined collaboratively by member states, nongovernmental organizations (NGOs), and other organizations. Decisions on issues are reached through consensus. Recommendations are then made for formulating, disseminating, and adopting international standards of assessment and practice. An emphasis is placed on national sovereignty and on national action(s) implementing international goals. One of the roles of the UN is achieving peace and progress for human security and well-being through addressing questions concerning priorities for development. Until recently, the UN was considered solely a forum for sovereign states. Today, NGOs and other civil society organizations are participants in the decision-making process, contributing their knowledge, skills, and experience. Globalization has developed due to recent advances in electronic communications, international capital flows, trade liberalization, and technological achievements, increasing opportunities for communication and exchange of resources.

Attention to economic and social needs is as important as dedication to peace and security matters. With the end of the cold war, the UN needs a new organizing concept. This would include developmental approaches focused on improving the quality of life for people globally. Addressing social and economic issues gets to some of the underlying factors that contribute to instability. NGOs, governments, and the UN system have to go beyond responding to conflict situations and delivering relief services, and become involved in social service settings dealing with the underlying causes of global poverty. Progress is being made, and efforts are proceeding from relief services to establishing rehabilitation, recovery, and social development, enabling individuals on the local level to create and maintain viable institutions to improve their lives.

The UN Commission for Social Development (1993) sees "social development . . . as an approach (integrative and global) to enhance people's capacity to lead secure lives . . . with the conditions necessary for their full scale participation in society." Sustainable human development encompasses the interdependence of environmental, economic, social, cultural, and political issues and "puts people first." This is occurring increasingly in the context of globalization, in the context of scarce financial resources, and with the changing relationship between the state and civil society, by moving to a more cooperative approach to governance, resulting in global and local partnerships and a commitment to human rights.

THE 1995 WORLD SUMMIT FOR SOCIAL DEVELOPMENT

While in the past the security of the state has been more important than the security of the people, it has now been learned that real security is based upon the security of people. . . . All governments should undertake policies geared to a better distribution of wealth and income. . . . For the poorest countries, national efforts must be extended to include international efforts of solidarity. (P. N. Rasmussen, prime minister of Denmark and president of the World Summit for Social Development)

The 1995 World Summit for Social Development (WSSD) addressed a range of social problems affecting vulnerable groups and vulnerable conditions in all societies. It launched a major international effort to provide sustainable solutions to problems involving the most critical human needs. The WSSD's conclusions are based on the analysis of experts: trade unions, business people, social activists, researchers, academics, social welfare agencies, religious denominations, voluntary agencies, NGOs, the UN system, and information derived from the social field. Social tensions are identified as a major and increasing source for international tensions, affecting all our societies. More than 1.6 billion people live in absolute poverty; 40,000 children die each day from easily controllable and treatable diseases; and tens of millions of people are unemployed or underemployed. There is a need to act preventively, to acknowledge collectively that reducing social tensions is an international priority, and to place a focus on the WSSD's mission of "promoting social integration, decreasing poverty, and increasing employment." The WSSD created a political strategy for social progress, social development, and peace, based on the assumption that nations have a common interest in helping each other:

> Until this Social Summit, such social and economic issues have never been addressed by the world's leaders . . . a beginning, a start of a collaborative process on what should be done for the people(s) of the world, and for social progress . . . a commitment . . . to assess the most vulnerable groups . . . an agreement to define investment in people, and a new framework of developmental cooperation to fit the realities of the post-war era, and to defend the frontiers of global human security. (WSSD, 1995)

SOCIAL INTEGRATION AND POVERTY

A socially integrated society includes not only divergent individual and group aspirations but also shared basic values and common interests. Social integration means political, social, and economic participation by all individuals, communities, races, and ethnic groups. It is a synonym for greater social justice, equality, material well-being, and democratic freedom, manifesting itself as solidarity, interdependence, respect for cultural diversity, tolerance, and the courage to replace dysfunctional systems with equitable ones. Poverty and unemployment are major threats to social integration. They create a downward spiral, contributing to a marginalization of large portions of a population by exclusion and neglect, homelessness, high crime rates, and high mortality rates. Exclusion poses a threat, especially when the sheer numbers of marginalized minorities, including women, children, older persons, and ethnic minorities, attain critical mass. Today their numbers are increasing—for example, by 2025 the world's elderly population (60 +) will number 1.2 billion, or 14% of the projected total global population.

Historically, social work, with its origins in the local community, recognized people's participation as a requirement for sustainable human development. In these times, international interaction—an important modern-day phenomenon—contributes to the awareness of common global causes, the possibility of potential solutions, and coordinated efforts, all of which help to reduce negative effects on vulnerable groups. NGOs and people's organizations (economic and professional organizations, companies, universities, trade unions, and cultural and civic entities) are essential to democratic processes. Special programs and projects in communities help individuals empower themselves by strengthening their ability to develop organizations and attain resources and enabling them to propose policies and implement them. This includes partnership with governments and formulation of "a people's agenda" based on grassroots participation: a people-centered system based on cooperation, sharing, equity, and social justice.

Presently there is political and global acknowledgment that the eradication of poverty is the top priority, which is in contrast to previous international poverty agreements that stopped short of calling for the "eradicat[ion of] absolute poverty by a target date to be specified by each country in its national context" (Dieye & Horn, 1997, p. 66). (The World Bank has defined "absolute poverty" as when an individual survives on an income of $1.00 U.S. per day or less. Qualitatively, "extreme poverty" is defined as an absence of basic human requirements, notably safe drinking water and adequate nutrition, shelter, education, and health care.)

Social development is basic to achieving a safe, healthy, and efficient physical environment (democratic, stable, and participatory), and sound social policy is necessary to build a foundation for social development. Since politics, bargaining, competing interests, and scarce resources influence most social policy decisions, today's social policy has to be responsive to current social circumstances. A move from a service provider focus to a partnership approach to service delivery is an example, and includes the participation of recipients of services in the planning, delivery, and evaluation of those services.

The UN has an institutional framework for "promoting sustainable social development." Emanating from this framework are "existing conventions, reports, standards, guiding principles, action plans and strategies providing a foundation for an equitable, nondiscriminatory and participative social development" (WSSD, 1995). However, what is lacking is a coherent and coordinated approach to implement these mandates.

Today, international interaction, cooperation, and dialogue are part of our everyday language. One sees after World War II a more expressed desire for self-determination developing, the recognition of social and economic issues and problems transcending national boundaries, and the importance of mutual engagement and activism to advance the human condition. New models are required for social progress because hundreds of millions of the poorest, both in the North and South (the North represents the rich and industrialized world, and the South represents the poorer countries), continue on a downward slide (Moller & Rasmussen, 1995). Three-quarters of the poorest are women, who often suffer gender-based discrimination and are victims of many types of violence (domestic, financial, sexual, including genital mutilation, etc.). Increasingly, social and economic policies, programs, and practices penalizing the poor are met with inadequate attention and solutions (Dieye & Horn, 1997).

Of the 1 billion living in absolute poverty, over half are in Asia and about a quarter are found in sub-Saharan Africa. Many live in fragile environments, in rural areas, and are female. Solutions for their problems have come from high-level administration and tended to be universal, reductionistic, and standardized by centrally placed (and what are perceived as powerful) professionals. In contrast, the problems of the poor tend to be local, complex, diverse, and dynamic, constantly changing. This suggests that local communities must be included in attempts to solve their own problems.

Previously, poverty was more often defined and measured with economic indicators such as low income or income-poverty. This is only one view of poverty. It also includes such attributes as social inferiority (including being a woman), isolation, physical weakness, vulnerability, seasonal stress, powerlessness and humiliation, or social indicators. In addition, social developmental theorists are considering environmental indicators as well (UN Commission for Social Development, 1993).

EMPLOYMENT AND THE POOR

"Employment," "unemployment," and "jobs," terms originating in the urban and industrial world, are used to describe the work conditions of the rural and agricultural world and of the urban informal sectors. These concepts do not describe workers' tasks because rural and agricultural workers do different things in different places at different times of the year. Helping the poor (women, children, the elderly, men, etc.) means involving them in the analysis and action on all levels. It also involves basic social services, access to basic goods, and targeted investment policies. Investment has to be empowering and responsive to the poor's participation in their own problems, opportunities, and priorities so they gain ownership of the process. This way labor becomes more productive and the poor can improve their own well-being. Improving the well-being of the poor entails decentralization, diversity, democracy, participation, and empowerment techniques.

In both developing and developed countries, many have trouble finding productive and meaningful employment. It is clear that economic growth alone does not reduce poverty. For example, large-scale capital-intensive, energy-intensive, and environment-damaging projects of industrialization and commercialization often uproot and disenfranchise persons from their traditional habitats and their access to resources. The most important way economic growth can help is by expanding opportunities for productive and remunerative employment (International Labor Organization, 1997). Employment status includes (1) wage employed, (2) self-employed, and (3) unemployed and unemployable.

First, the wage-employed poor have regular jobs and have policies that check inflation, improve safety and other aspects of working conditions, and strengthen collective bargaining with respect to conditions of employment, wages, and medical and pension benefits. The majority of the wage-employed poor are casual workers with little job security and low wages. They have weak bargaining power, and when they are scattered in numerous farms and shops and indebted to their employers it is difficult to organize them. When they are migrant laborers, they are often taken advantage of by contractors, middlemen, and employers.

Second, the self-employed poor include peasants, artisans, petty traders, and others whose primary need is improving access to productive assets (land and human capital), production credit, environmental resources (irrigation and drainage), local public goods, and support networks of marketing outlets and supplies. Over the last two decades, in poor countries, governments have tried to provide subsidized credit to the poor, with mixed results. Credit administered through government agencies weakens incentives to invest wisely or to repay promptly. A fundamental dilemma of creditors is that outside agencies lack sufficient information concerning the borrower, and monitoring is costly. In terms of employment status, the self-employed—particularly in densely populated areas—are often underemployed during part of the year.

Third, the unemployed and unemployable poor include the physically disabled, the elderly, the ill, and women, all of whom are limited in their ability to participate in the labor force. Various policy actions include direct income transfers (welfare payments), food stamps of subsidized food distribution, low-cost shelter and housing, lunches, nutritional programs for pregnant and nursing women, basic health care (preventive care), adequate facilities for primary and secondary education, and rehabilitation programs.

A fragmented approach exists in the delivery of social services to the poor, whereas more integrated, collaborative, and partnership methods are needed. Recently, a human development perspective using indicators that define and monitor human well-being has been examined. The human development priority areas are defined as national capacity-building in basic health, basic education, water supply and sanitation, nutrition programs, and family planning services, as well as credit needs for the poor and vulnerable in order to create opportunities for self-employment and sustainable livelihood. More recent attention has focused on the development of appropriate indicators for measurement and outcome on every level (from the micro-micro to the macro-macro levels) to ascertain whether there is progress or regress, growth or decline.

SOCIAL INDICATORS AND STRENGTHENING INSTITUTIONS OF CIVIL SOCIETY

The emphasis on the quality of life and the fulfillment of life by everyone in the community can be traced back to the writings of Aristotle, Adam Smith, and Karl Marx (Sen, 1990). Today, human development specialists are calling for the inclusion of social (and other) indicators to measure the quality of life for all, especially those deprived because they are poor or because they do not have access to resources (Sen, 1993; UN Development Program, 1998). Today, some countries publish, annually or biennially, national social reports. This list includes England— "Social Trends"; France—"Donnees Sociales"; the Netherlands—"Social en Cultural Report"; and Italy—"Sintesi della vita Sociale Italian." These reports present an overview of social developments and trends, including income, health, education, poverty, housing, employment, crime, abuse, and suicide. Issues that have an impact on the human conditions are placed regularly on each nation's agenda. In the United States, no such document exists pertaining to social issues. Instead, economic indicators are used: the Gross Domestic Product, the Dow Jones Average, the Index of Leading Economic Indicators, the Consumer Price Index, and the Index of Consumer Confidence (Miringoff & Miringoff, 1994; Miringoff, 1997a; Miringoff, Miringoff, & Opdycke, 1996; Miringoff, 1995). Social indicators are reported separately from economic indicators. Social science experts agree that social and economic indicators should not be separated because they operate interdependently. In addition, although rates are reported, the changes in the rates of abuse (child, elder, domestic), crime, suicide, employment, and so forth ought to be more carefully monitored. Other indicators, such as environmental indicators, are being included for a more complete picture.

The Human Development Report: 1990 to the Present

During the 1980s, the key dimensions of development were being neglected, especially people and the environment. National and international development organizations began to create special units on women in development, NGOs, the environment, and other areas. By the 1990s the terms "human development" and "sustainable development" were being used (Ul Haq, 1995; Hijab, 1996; Griffin & Knight, 1988).

In 1990, the first annual Human Development Report (HDR), sponsored by the United Nations Development Program (UNDP) and based on the Agenda for Development, examined the impact of economic development on people. Every year since, the HDR looks at new ways to measure the quality of life of people. Instead of reporting the GNP, it looks at whether there is clean water, what children are eating, how women share in the economy, and so forth. The Human Development Index (HDI) was created and reflects the distribution of progress, measuring existing deprivations, identifying groups excluded from the mainstream, and focusing on national and/or international actions necessary to achieve higher standards of "human development and sustainable development." The HDI, a measure of national human well-being, is an annual quality-of-living index that cites social indicators such as homicides, rapes, divorces, births outside marriage, single-parent households, drug crimes, suicides, requests for asylum, numbers of prisoners, and percentage of juveniles in the prison. When the rates of these social indicators increase, so do the levels of social deterioration. The rates are increasing in economically developed countries and in countries in transition. In 1998 the Human Development Index II was created to measure human poverty in industrial countries (UN Development Program, 1998).

In 1992, the UN Conference on Environment and Development (UNCED) defined a holistic approach to development, contained in Agenda 21, an intergovernmental agreement in which nations agreed to work for sustainable development. "Sustainable development" has its roots in the Stockholm Conference on the Human Environment (1972), which focused on and promoted awareness for environmental protection to sustain livelihoods in the North and the South. In 1992, at the Earth Summit, the definition of "sustainable development" included "the interdependence of environment, economic, social, cultural and political issues." In the mid-1990s, development moved from neglected dimensions (women, the environment, and NGOs) to promoting a new development paradigm, placing people at the center, and ensuring the sustainability of development activities (from a passive view of defining areas of concern, to active, problem-solving/solution-focused strategies). UNDP refers to this as "sustainable human development" (UN Development Program, 1994).

Human development looks at three interrelated issues: investment in human capabilities; people's participation in the decision-making process; and development, which is defined as international and intergenerational equity.

The 1995 Human Development Report influenced women's human rights and measured how far countries have to go to have equal opportunity for women and men. Women continue to be 70% of the world's poor and two-thirds of the world's illiterates. In most countries, women contribute as much total labor as men, while getting back a much smaller share.

The concept of human development is used at the national level in more than half of the countries UNDP serves. For example, in Egypt a think tank on human development took place. In 1994 the Egypt Human Development Report was published, in which recommendations for sustainable human development were adopted by Egyptian governors. In Central America, UNDP was instrumental in making human development the theme of its 1991 Summit of Central American Presidents, using the data in the Human Development Report, and then allocating funds for priority social sector initiatives (UN Development Program, 1997).

In 1997, the eighth Human Development Report reported on poverty and human development, defining poverty in a human development perspective. Compiled by an independent team of international experts, it introduced a "composite multi-dimensional measure of poverty"—the Human Poverty Index (HPI), which measures the denial of basic opportunities for living a tolerable life by:

- Charting progress and setbacks in income and in human poverty across regions and time
- Examining new forces affecting the vulnerability of people in poverty—that is, violent conflict, HIV/AIDS, environmental degradation, and the ever-increasing inequities
- Examining the effect of globalization on poverty, proposing national and international policy options to monitor and ensure that globalization helps to create jobs
- Analyzing poverty from a political perspective
- Presenting six policy options to end absolute poverty in one generation:
  1. The empowerment of the poor with both social and economic assets such as land, credit, education, and training, and reproductive and other health services
  2. The promotion of gender equality and the advancement of women
  3. Pro-poor economic growth policies that mainstream poverty reduction through restructured public expenditures, livelihood generation for the rural and urban poor, and careful targeting of public and private investment
  4. Managing globalization with a greater concern for global equity. The share of the poorest 20% in global income has gone from 2.3% in 1960 to 1.1% in 1997
  5. "Good governance," or political participation by all, accountability, transparency, openness, and a strong role for NGOs and civic groups.
  6. "Special actions for special situations." Countries facing extreme poverty traps, population pressures, environmental degradation, social disintegration, and conflict deserve special measures of support (e.g., sub-Saharan Africa).
     (UN Development Program, 1997)

The 1997 Human Development Report measures human poverty (deprivation poverty) in five life attributes: illiteracy, malnutrition, early death, poor health care, and poor access to safe water. The Human Poverty Index is calculated for 78 countries. The "human poverty incidence" is about 25% in developing countries, when considered together, while income poverty affects one-third using $1.00 per day as the income poverty line. The results show that deprivation is not similar to income poverty. The correlation, as analyzed in the HPI, between the amount of income and the amount of human deprivation is not close. When using a scattergram, the plot demonstrates scattered measures, showing a lack of relationship between income poverty and human deprivation. UNDP is being helpful in 80 countries using poverty mapping, a method of examining incomes and other indicators regarding the poor.

Micro-Credit as One Solution

Micro-credit is again being used to provide credit to the needy. Micro-credit funds were utilized hundreds of years ago in different parts of the world (Hollis & Sweetman, 1996). By definition, micro-credit involves small loan programs provided for self-employment projects in order to generate income. In most cases, micro-credit programs offer a combination of services and resources, often including savings facilities, training, networking, and peer support. It is an effective anti-poverty tool, reaching about 8 million very poor people in developing countries. According to the 1997 Micro-Credit Summit held in Washington, DC: "The time has come to recognize micro-credit as a powerful tool in the struggle to end poverty and economic dependence . . . a global movement to reach 100 million of the world's poorest families, especially the women . . . with credit for self-employment and other financial and business services by 2005."

In industrialized nations, micro-credit and micro-enterprise experience and programs have grown over the last decade (Else & Clay-Thompson, 1998). Ten years ago there were fewer than ten programs in the United States, and today there are hundreds. In Europe, in 1989, France created a large-scale micro-credit program, Association pour le Droit a l'Initiative Economique. Following in France's footsteps, Belgium, Germany, and the United Kingdom are designing similar programs. In Eastern Europe a few programs have been created, among them the Village Credit Funds project in Albania and the Mikrofund in Poland.

Using different models and operating in different cultures, micro-credit programs have discovered strong repayment of loans. In developing countries, late payment and bad loan ratios are comparable to or below those of conventional banking houses. In industrialized nations, repayment rates are often lower than conventional banks. Risk levels for micro-entrepreneurs in industrialized nations are often higher because they are often engaged in start-up businesses and lack the assets that can provide an equity base.

The creditworthiness of the poor has been proved regardless of gender. Despite being prompt and reliable repayers, women have often been denied access to credit by legal and traditional barriers. Women also bring the benefits of income back to the home, where they improve the welfare of the family and benefit from the higher status and self-esteem achieved by producing and providing income.

Some micro-enterprise institutions continue to be dependent on subsidized loans, while others can continue on an unsubsidized basis. It requires several loans to enable a recent entrepreneur to stabilize and enlarge. Overall, it is a growing trend toward sustainability. The well-known record of achievement and expansion of individual programs provides evidence that micro-credit in developing countries has the potential for profit and is a successful anti-poverty tool.

Industrialized nations are developing their own micro-credit models (Dupper & Poertner, 1997; Raheim, 1996; Raheim & Alter, 1998). It seems that the economic context of micro-enterprise programs in industrialized countries differs from that of developing nations and countries in transition. In the developing world, where wage employment is scarce, self-employment constitutes 40% to 60% of the workforce, compared to 8% to 40% in industrialized countries. Usury laws, lower volumes of lending, and greater demands for training and technical assistance pose unique challenges to program operators, and accordingly preclude the possibility that the micro-enterprise field in industrialized countries will reach the scale of operations found in developing nations (Yunus, 1997).

MICRO-CREDIT MODELS: A HIGH LEVEL OF REPLICABILITY

In spite of ethnic and cultural differences, micro-credit programs are increasing. Financial resources are made available to the grassroots populations previously excluded from the formal economy. Two models will be presented to examine the basic tenets: Grameen Trust has funded start-ups in countries in Asia, Africa, and Latin America; and the Trickle-Up Program provides small loans to women and families for small business ventures.

According to Yunus (1997), creator of Grameen Trust, it is important to operate according to democratic principles—that is, he recommends that board members themselves be recruited from micro-credit organizations, women's groups, academia, and the philanthropic community. According to economists, a multiplier effect takes place when people make and spend their money locally. Making and spending money at the local level develops a stronger local economy. It alleviates the debt burden and provides a systemic source of funds, thus lessening dependence, because there is a development of local resources and a stimulation of economic growth at the base, promoting a "trickle-up effect" (Yunus, 1997; Dupper & Poertner, 1997).

Credit unions are being used in Africa, especially in villages and poor urban neighborhoods. Locals individuals are no longer waiting for governments, international financial institutions, and NGOs for financial help. Locals are reporting that self-help programs such as the credit unions are more effective because they utilize grassroots solutions. These grassroots solutions integrate traditional practices with contemporary ones, with an emphasis on education and training (Thompson, 1996). Such factors contribute to more involvement; more capable and involved boards, managers, and staff; and informed decision making. Credit unions in Africa promote regular savings and responsible credit practices, where depositors receive and borrowers pay an equitable rate and there is a pooling of savings. Commercial banks are not able to provide financial services to women, small farmers, artisans, older persons, and urban micro-entrepreneurs, so this task falls on the credit unions (Private Sector Development Fund, 1997).

U.S.-Supported Micro-Enterprise Demonstration Projects

These three federal departments have initiatives testing the efficacy of micro-enterprise:

- the U.S. Department of Health and Human Services (1994) (Office of Community Services and the Office of Refugee Resettlement). In 1987 a program was begun in New York and Vermont providing training and small business loans to public assistance recipients and other low-income people.
- the U.S. Department of Housing and Urban Development (1990) provided funds in the 1990s.
- the U.S. Department of Labor in 1987 supported several small self-employment initiatives.

SUMMARY

To reduce poverty, changes have to take place at all levels of social work practice. This includes both changes in national policies and changes in international organization in order to work toward achieving global equity. Government, NGOs, civil society, and professionals must work together to develop a new agenda for action. There is a need for coordinated planning and resource allocation for all sectors, especially utilizing business, which is a necessary partner since it is both part of the problem and part of the solution.

Putting poor people first enables them to play their part(s). Doing so first requires reversals of some professional concepts, values, methods, and behavior and attitudes. It means to do things *with* the poor, not *to* them. It is a process of inclusiveness. Today, skills, knowledge, and attitudes have to be relevant, dynamic, more globally interactive, information-rich, interdisciplinary in nature, and readily applicable to the field experience. Attitudes and behaviors of transparency, commitment, adaptability, and resourcefulness have to aid individuals in functioning effectively in their lives and in their communities.

A recognition is needed that social services, education, and health and gender issues play key roles in addressing and solving the problems of marginalization, poverty, and employment. All players need to focus on integrating development programming, targeting issues, and delivering a range of social and economic and concrete services in order to address human well-being issues. In conclusion, "a range of indicators" ought to be

defined and monitored on all levels. Indicators have to be utilized as an objective assessment tool to improve the quality of
life for everyone.

REFERENCES

Best practice in financial services to microentrepreneurs. (1994).
What Works: A Women's World Banking Newsletter, 4(2), 1–4.

Dieye, B., & Horn, A. (1997). *Report on the world social situation.*
UN Pubs. (E/1997/15/ST/ESA/252) (pp. 3–76)

Dupper, D., & Poertner, J. (1997). Public schools and the revitalization of impoverished communities: School-linked, family
resource centers. *Social Work, 42*(5), 33–40.

Else, J., & Clay-Thompson, R. (1998). *Refugee microenterprise development: Achievements and lessons learned.* Iowa City: Institute
for Social and Economic Development.

Griffin, K., & Knight, J. (1988). Human development: Case for
renewed emphasis. *Social Development Review, 10*(1), 3–20.

Hijab, N. (1996, October). *Human development.* The Ralph Bunche
Institute on the UN. The Moses Leo Gitelson Seminars.

Hollis, A., & Sweetman, A. (1996). *The evolution of a microcredit
institution: The Irish loan funds, 1720–1920.* (UT-ECIPA-ECPAP-
96-01)

International Labor Organization. (1997). *World labor report.* Geneva: Author.

Micro-Credit Summit. (1997). *Report.* Washington, DC: Author.

Miringoff, M. (1995). Toward a national standard of social
health: Need for progress in social indicators. *American Journal
of Orthopsychiatry, 65*(4), 3–10.

Miringoff, M. (1997a). Measuring our social health. *Readings: A
Journal of Reviews and Commentary in Mental Health, 7,* 8–10.

Miringoff, M. (1997b). 1997 Index of Social Health. *Fordham Institute for Innovation in Social Policy,* Fordham Graduate Center.

Miringoff, M., & Miringoff, M.-L. (1994). Context and connection
in social indicators: Enhancing what we measure. In R. Hauser
(Ed.), *Social indicators* (pp. 35–42). New York: Russell Sage
Foundation.

Miringoff, M.-L., Miringoff, M., & Opdycke, S. (1996). The growing gap between standard indicators and the nation's social health. *Challenge*, July–August, pp. 17–22.

Moller, K., & Rasmussen, E. (Eds.). (1995, March). *Partnership for new social development: UN World Summit for Social Development*. Washington, DC: Mandag Morgen.

Private Sector Development Fund. (1996). Promoting grassroots entrepreneurs. *Enterprise*, Spring (PSDF/UN-Private Sector Development Fund).

Private Sector Development Fund. (1997). *Report on the world situation: 1997*. Department for Economic and Social Information and Policy Analysis. New York: UN (E/1997/15/ST/ESA/ 252).

Raheim, S. (1996). Micro-enterprise as an approach for promoting economic development in social work: Lessons from the Self-Employment Investment Demonstration. *International Social Work, 39*(1), 69–82.

Raheim, S., & Alter, C. F. (1998). Self-employment development as a social and economic development intervention for recipients of AFDC. *Journal of Community Practice, 5*(1/2), 41–61.

Sen, A. (1990). Development as capability expansion. In K. Griffin & J. Knight (Eds.), *Human development and the international development strategy for the 1990s* (pp. 41–58). Basingstoke, England: Macmillan.

Sen, A. (1993). The economics of life and death. *Scientific American*, May, p. 18.

Thompson, D. J. (1996). Credit at the grassroots. *Africa Recovery, 10*, 1–24.

Ul Haq, M. (1995). *New imperatives of human security*. UN/New York: Division of Public Affairs, UNDP.

United Nations Commission for Social Development. (1993). *Integrative and global dimensions of social development*. (E/CN.5./ 1993/L.16)

United Nations Development Program. (1990–1998). *Human development reports, 1990–1998*. New York: Oxford University Press.

United Nations Development Program. (1995). Special Issue: Social Summit. *Social Policy and Social Progress: UN* (ST/ESA/ 244).

U.S. Department of Health and Human Services, Office of Community Services, Administration for Children and Families. (1994). *Demonstration Partnership Program: Summaries and findings, FY 1990.* Washington, DC: Government Printing Office.

U.S. Department of Housing and Urban Development. (1990). *Small business opportunities project.* Washington, DC: Government Printing Office.

World Summit for Social Development. (1995). *The Copenhagen declaration and programme for action.* Copenhagen and New York: UN Department of Public Information.

Yunus, M. (1997). Solving the debt crisis with micro-enterprise [Special issue]. *Global Exchange,* no. 30.

Micro-Credit Resources

ACCION International
120 Beacon Street
Somerville, MA 02143

Association for Enterprise Opportunity Campaign
70 East Lake Street, Suite 520
Chicago, IL 60601

Center for Policy Alternatives
1875 Connecticut Avenue NW, Suite 710
Washington, DC 20009

Grameen Foundation
1709 New York Avenue NW, Suite 101
Washington, DC 20006

Harrison Institute at Georgetown University Law Center
111 F Street NW, Suite 102
Washington, DC 20001-2095

The Microcredit Summit
440 First Street NW, Suite 460
Washington, DC 20001

The MS Foundation
120 Wall Street, 33rd Floor
New York, NY 10005-3904

RESULTS
440 First Street NW, Suite 450
Washington, DC 20001

Self-Employment Learning Project/Aspen Ins.
122 New Hampshire Avenue NW
Washington, DC 20036

Women's Environment & Development Organization
355 Lexington Avenue, Third Floor
New York, NY 10017-6603

INDEX

CONTRIBUTING AUTHORS

Roni Berger, PhD, CSW
Advanced Training Program
Jewish Board of Family and Children Services
Private Practice

Shirley Better, DSW
Professor of Social Work
California State University

Mary Boncher, MS
Clinical Coordinator, Child Sexual Abuse Treatment Service
New York Foundling

Eric B. Brettschneider, MA, JD
Director, Agenda for Children Tomorrow
Adjunct Faculty
Fordham University
Graduate School of Social Services

Ellen Brickman, PhD
Senior Researcher
Fordham University
Graduate School of Social Service

Patricia Brownell, PhD
Assistant Professor
Fordham University
Graduate School of Social Service

Roslyn H. Chernesky, DSW
Professor
Fordham University
Graduate School of Social Service

Carol S. Cohen, DSW
Assistant Professor
Director, BA Program in Social Work
Fordham University
Graduate School of Social Service

Elaine P. Congress, DSW
Professor
Director, Doctoral Program
Fordham University
Graduate School of Social Service

John Cosgrove, PhD
Associate Dean
Fordham University
Graduate School of Social Service

Sonya Dickerson, MSW
Research Assistant
New York Foundling

Sr. Mary Sean Foley, RSM, MTS, CSW
Institute of the Sisters of Mercy of the Americas
Private Practice & Consultation
Adjunct Professor
Fordham University
Graduate School of Social Service

Mary Ann Forgey, PhD
Assistant Professor
Co-Director, The Center for Family and Child Advocacy
Fordham University
Graduate School of Social Service

Mary Pender Greene, ACSW
Chief, Social Work Services
Jewish Board of Family and Children's Services

Irene A. Gutheil, DSW
Professor
Director, Ravazzin Center
Fordham University
Graduate School of Social Service

Leah Hill, JD
Clinical Professor of Law
Director, Family and Child Protection Clinic
Fordham University School of Law
Lincoln Square Legal Services

Robert H. Hill, DSW
Consultant
Director, Frederick Douglass Center
Children's Aid Society

Carol Kaplan, PhD
Associate Professor
Fordham University
Graduate School of School Service

Felix Lorenzo, CSW
Private Practice
Adjunct Faculty
New York University
Shirley M. Ehrenkranz School of Social Work

Manuel A. Mendez, MSW
Senior Executive Director/CEO
Phipps Community Development Corporation

Marilynn Moch, PhD
Adjunct Faculty
Fordham University
Graduate School of Social Service

Ann Moynihan, JD
Clinical Professor of Law
Director, Battered Women's Rights Clinic
Fordham University School of Law
Lincoln Square Legal Services

Rosemary Ordonez, BA
Director, Community Services
Phipps Community Development Corporation

Rosa Perez-Koenig, DSW
Assistant Professor
Fordham University
Graduate School of Social Service

Michael H. Phillips, DSW
Professor
Acting Associate Dean
Fordham University
Graduate School of Social Service

Mary Ann Quaranta, DSW
Dean
Fordham University
Graduate School of Social Service

Natalie Z. Riccio, PhD
Private Practice
Adjunct Faculty
Fordham University
Graduate School of Social Service

Barry Rock, DSW
Associate Professor
Director, Institute on Managed Care and Social Work
Fordham University
Graduate School of Social Service

Mel Schneiderman, PhD
Chief Psychologist
New York Foundling

Yvette M. Sealy, PhD
Clinical Faculty
Fordham University
Graduate School of Social Service

Eugenia L. Siegler, MD, FACP
Chief, Section of Geriatric Medicine
Brooklyn Hospital Center

Alan B. Siskind, PhD
Executive Vice President
Jewish Board of Family and Children Services

Margaret Souza, CSW
Principal Investigator, New York State Department of Health
Adjunct Faculty
Fordham University
Graduate School of Social Service

Virginia Strand, DSW
Professor
Director, Children First
Fordham University
Graduate School of Social Service